Money, Banking and Public Finance in Africa

Money, Banking and Public Finance in Africa

Ann Seidman

Zed Books Ltd.
London and New Jersey

Money, Banking and Public Finance in Africa was first published by Zed Books Ltd., 57 Caledonian Road, London N1 9BU, UK, and 171 First Avenue, Atlantic Highlands, New Jersey 07716, USA, in 1986.

Cover designed by Ian Hawkins
Printed and bound in Great Britain by
Biddles Ltd, Guildford and King's Lynn

British Library Cataloguing in Publication Data

Seidman, Ann
Money, banking and public finance in Africa.
1. Finance—Africa
I. Title
332'.096 HG187.5.A2

ISBN 0-86232-429-7
ISBN 0-86232-430-0 Pbk

Contents

Notes, suggested Exercises and Research, and Recommended Reading appear at the end of each chapter.

Tables

Figures

Preface

By the 1980s, as this text went to press, financial crises had engulfed many, if not most, independent sub-Saharan African countries. They were finding it increasingly difficult to mobilize the funds to finance development projects designed to spread productive employment opportunities and raise the living standards of their peoples. Most were experiencing chronic and growing budget and balance of payments deficits. Some had borrowed heavily, augmenting inflationary pressures at home and increasing dependency on international lending institutions abroad.

This text aims to provide a framework for analysing the causes underlying these mounting difficulties. In so doing, it seeks to fill two gaps in the available literature on money, banking and public finance in Africa.

First, most available materials in English relating to the issues covered in this text describe institutions and introduce data drawn from the experiences of the developed capitalist countries. Yet it is clear that the problems confronting African states, as well as the institutions and policies created to deal with them, differ qualitatively from those of the industrial capitalist countries. This text aims primarily to depict the nature and scope of the particular problems which plague banking and finance in Africa; and to outline the range of institutional structures and policies adopted by African governments in their attempts to solve them.

Second, to overcome the poverty and underdevelopment inherited from their colonial past, many African governments have declared their intention to carry out a socialist transformation. Yet most materials available in English relating to monetary and financial matters focus only on conceptual tools and theoretical models formulated for economies characterized by private ownership of the means of production. Hardly any discuss or provide evidence concerning the qualitatively different explanations and solutions proposed by socialist theories. This text seeks to outline socialist as well as capitalist theoretical approaches, to enable the reader to compare and evaluate both as potential guides for explaining and perhaps overcoming the financial crises confronted by African states.

The reader must ask two crucial questions. First, which set of theories furnishes the "best" explanation, "best" in the sense of being most consistent with the available relevant information concerning African experience in the fields of money, banking and public finance? Second, which set provides the more useful guide to solving the problems confronting African states, more "useful" in the sense of proposing effective, practical measures which an African government may adopt to help overcome the causes identified?

Because of the fundamental interrelationships between money, banking and public finance, this book—unlike most conventional western texts—encompasses all three fields in one volume. To separate them might hinder discovery of the underlying causes of the financial difficulties plaguing African states. Furthermore, socialist theory holds that, to surmount the financial crises they confront, African governments should bring under state control and co-ordinate the financial institutions in all three fields; only thus can they successfully implement comprehensive plans to restructure the national economy.

From the outset, this text rejects the simplistic notion that any theory, no matter how sound its underlying principles, can automatically provide a blueprint to surmount the complex financial crises engulfing African states. It views theories not as dogmas but as potential guides to help to explain and perhaps solve the dilemmas encountered in the complex, interrelated fields of money, banking and public finance. For this reason, it adopts a problem-solving methodology. That method, described more fully in Chapter 1, suggests identification of the nature and scope of the problems faced; and a review of alternative available theoretical explanations in the light of the objective experiences of African countries to determine which seems most consistent with the evidence. Each explanation suggests a range of possible solutions which, logically, should help to overcome the causes it identifies.

The particular historically shaped circumstances in each country will inevitably influence the particular sets of measures that decision-makers adopt. Consistent pursuit of the problem-solving methodology requires that whichever solution they choose they must constantly monitor and evaluate its consequences. This will enable them to revise their programme in view of the new difficulties that will inevitably arise.

The problem-solving methodology shapes the basic outline of this text. The first three parts briefly summarize the nature and scope of the problems independent sub-Saharan African economies confront in their attempts to accumulate and reinvest capital to attain development. Part I deals with money and banking; Part II with public finance; and Part III with the impact of international monetary issues and institutions.

The text assumes the readers are essentially familiar with the basic tools and concepts of the theories considered. On this basis, each part first outlines the explanations and solutions that the theories offer in the field of money and finance and then describes some relevant evidence drawn from African experience. The reader is left to decide which theory provides the best explanation and proposes the measures most likely to help overcome the difficulties.

The evidence indicates that, regardless of their declared ideologies, most sub-Saharan African governments—not only before, but even after independence—adopted one or another variant of capitalist monetary and financial institutions and policies. This may reflect several factors, including both the inherited characteristics of the state and international pressures. Furthermore, most African politicians and civil servants, whether they graduated from African or western universities, have had little opportunity to examine socialist financial theory and practice. So that readers—whatever their ideological perspective—may better understand the socialist alternative, Part IV outlines the evolution of socialist financial theory and practice in countries which claim to have achieved a relatively successful socialist transformation.

The reader who finds the socialist explanations most consistent with the evidence, who concludes that the socialist proposals seem most appropriate for Africa, must nevertheless treat the information presented in Part IV with caution. To acquire an adequate grasp of the full implications of socialist theory as a guide to practice elsewhere, the reader must examine the historical circumstances, the particular inherited features of the monetary and financial institutions in the public and private sectors of each particular country. Socialist theorists themselves emphasize that, for any given country, such an analysis is an essential precondition to formulating and introducing the institutional changes required to implement socialist financial plans.

In reality, no single volume could provide a thoroughgoing in-depth analysis of the manifold theoretical and practical issues confronted in the interrelated fields of money, banking and public finance. This text essentially aims to present a framework of analysis to help the reader—whether he or she is a civil servant, a trade unionist, a financier, a peasant leader or a university student—understand and address the issues raised. For this reason, at the end of each chapter, the text poses questions, suggests research projects, and lists relevant readings the reader may wish to undertake to evaluate further the alternative theories as potential guides for dealing with those issues in his or her country. The annotated bibliography may help the reader to determine which readings to pursue to study in greater depth the alternative theories as well as practical experiences of specific countries.

Finally, I would like to express many thanks to many people for reading this manuscript and making useful criticisms and comments. I particularly want to express my appreciation to the colleagues and students with whom I worked for three years at the University of Zimbabwe for their teamwork in conducting research as well as their critical discussions of the issues in classes and seminars. It would be impossible to name them all. I also learned much from Gerhart Wittich's lectures to my class on socialist monetary theory and practice, as well as from his incisive criticisms of this text. Theresa Chimombe, Rob Davies and Dan Ndlela, especially, made insightful comments. Finally, I would also like to thank Neva Makgetla and Lynn Turgeon for their encouragement as well as helpful suggestions. In the last analysis, of course, I accept full responsibility for the way I have presented the manifold issues involved.

Boston, 1985

Part I: Money and Banking

Chapter 1: The Problems of Financing Development

Introduction

In the 1980s, most independent African states confronted a deepening financial crisis. After independence, the little capital invested in productive activities had primarily financed the continued growth of a limited so-called "modern" sector, essentially an enclave geared to the export of a few raw materials. To finance essential social services and expanded economic infrastructure, most governments had borrowed heavily, both at home and abroad. A handful of people had become extremely wealthy, but the vast majority of Africans still lived in conditions of deep poverty. At the same time, extensive resources lay fallow, unutilized or underutilized.

Why? Could the newly independent African governments have pursued monetary and financial strategies that would have helped them to avoid the crises of the 1980s? This text seeks to provide the reader with the tools to evaluate the two major sets of alternative theories of money, banking and public finance that purport to explain and propose solutions to that nagging question. It also outlines the broader range of available theoretical and factual materials. The reader is urged to undertake research in his or her own country to assess the causes of its particular monetary and financial problems.

The Five Steps of the Problem-Solving Method

The text adopts a problem-solving approach to facilitate rigorous and logical testing of the available theories against evidence drawn from the African experience. That methodology consists of five interrelated steps:

1) *Define the problem to be solved.* Given theoretical perspectives shape the underlying criteria determining the problem selected for study. This text adopts the perspective that underlies most African governments' explicitly stated goals: the underlying problem in Africa is the pervasive poverty of the majority of the people.
2) *Set forth the range of explanations offered by alternative theories as to the causes of the problem.* This text primarily aims to present the two major alternative theories which purport to explain and propose solutions to the monetary and financial problems plaguing Africa. It

assumes the readers have at least an introductory knowledge of those theories' basic assumptions. The readings suggested at the end of each chapter provide more in-depth formulations of the theories discussed.

3) *Test the explanations against objective data (both quantitative and qualitative) relating to the problem; discover which explanation most consistently coincides with the available evidence*. The text summarizes some of the relevant evidence, primarily relating to Anglophone Africa. The research suggested at the end of each chapter may help the readers to gather relevant data from their own countries to test the theories further.

4) *Formulate solutions based on the theory which appears best able to explain the problem*. The text outlines the solutions offered by each major set of theories. To examine the consequences of implementing them elsewhere under comparable circumstances, the reader may wish to examine the readings reporting experiences in other countries. The circumstances prevailing in any one country are never precisely replicated in another but study of another country's experiences may suggest the possibilities as well as the pitfalls of proposed policies.

5) *Monitor the implementation of proposed solutions*. It is essential to evaluate their consequences in order to overcome difficulties which inevitably arise. The monitoring process requires repeating the four steps outlined above to examine the causes and possible cures for the new problems which arise in the course of implementing any proposed solution. The questions and research exercises suggested at the end of each chapter aim to aid readers to evaluate their own countries' experiences in attempting to implement one or another of the monetary or financial solutions offered by the alternative sets of theories.

The Underlying Financial Problem Confronting African States

The problem-solving methodology suggests the necessity, first, of more carefully defining the problem of accumulating and reinvesting capital as it affects development and the living standards of the peoples of Africa. The World Bank has asserted that a developing country, in Africa or elsewhere, should reinvest about 25 per cent of the Gross Domestic Product (GDP) every year to achieve a rate of economic growth sufficient to ensure a steady rise in per capita income for the entire population.[1] It emphasizes the crucial necessity of increasing the rate of investment. While most economists agree to this necessity, they disagree as to the nature of production relations and the distribution of income required if increased investment is to achieve development which benefits the majority of the population.

Behind the World Bank's assertion lies the mainstream argument that investment of about a quarter of GDP, under appropriate conditions of production and distribution, could lead to an annual growth rate of GDP of about 7 per cent. If the population grows by about 3 per cent each year, then per capita income would increase by about 4 per cent annually, which is quite a satisfactory rate. Over, say, a 20-year period, such a per capita growth rate could provide a steady expansion of goods and services for the population, as indicated in Figure 1.1.

Figure 1.1
Growth of GDP, Assuming a Capital Output Ratio of 3.5:1, Given the Annual Investment of 25 per cent of GDP.

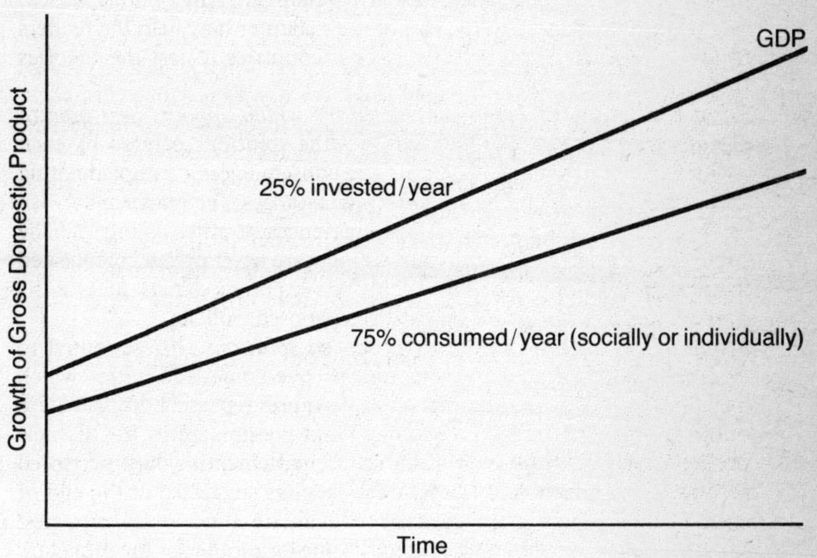

Several assumptions underlie this mainstream argument. First, it assumes a given ratio between investment of capital in infrastructure, machinery and equipment, and the consequent output of goods and services. In the typical developing country, government planners commonly assume this ratio is about 3.5:1. However, assuming everything else remained unchanged, a higher capital-output ratio, say 4:1, would lead to an overall growth rate of the GDP of only about 6 per cent, and a per capita growth rate approximating only 3 per cent. Many factors determine the capital-output ratio in a given developing economy. Two key factors are:

1) The amount of economic infrastructure—roads, electricity, water supplies, etc.,—which must be financed before investment leads to actual increases in production. If the economy must finance all these before production begins, then the capital-output ratio will be much higher than if they already exist.
2) The capital-intensity of investments made. Investment in more technologically advanced machinery and equipment may ultimately lead

to higher levels of productivity, but the initial capital expenditures tend to be much greater and the project may take much longer to begin actual production.

A second assumption affecting the per capita GDP growth rate relates to the population growth rate. A higher rate of population growth may reduce the anticipated per capita GDP growth rate. This has fostered a neo-Malthusian argument that population control is the key to development, an over-simplification that obscures basic conditions affecting production relations and distribution patterns. Nevertheless, a very high population growth rate, reflecting past social conditions of production, means a high proportion of the population aged under 15 and, in consequence, costly social burdens on the economy which must feed, clothe and educate its children. This will reduce the share of GDP available to finance the investments necessary to increase future production and future GDP per capita.

Implicit in the World Bank argument is a third assumption that investment of 25 per cent of GDP will automatically assure adequate development. Table 1.1 shows the percentage of GDP invested by several African states in the relatively prosperous 1970s. A few have achieved the recommended rate. A number have come close. But investment alone has not overcome the poverty of the mass of the population.

Table 1.1
Gross Fixed Capital Formation as a Percentage of Gross Domestic Product for Selected African States, for Selected Years.

Country	Gross capital formation as % of GDP[a]								
	1963	*1970*	*1971*	*1972*	*1973*	*1974*	*1975*	*1976*	*1977*
Botswana	22		52			27	29	26	17
Central African Republic	18	14							
Ethiopia	13	11				10	10		
Ghana	18	12			8	12			
Kenya	12[b]	20					21	20	21
Lesotho	9[b]	10		10	12	10			
Liberia	23[b]	20				17	19	22	
Malawi	9[b]	23	16	20	19				
Sierra Leone	11	14				13	13	12	
South Africa	20	25				29			26
Sudan	16	10			11	14			
Swaziland		20	20	18	14				
Tanzania	11[b]	20				19	19		17
Zambia	16	29				37	32		

[a] Defined as outlays of industries, producers of government services and non-profit services for households, minus second-hand and scrapped goods; excludes military. Given for years for which data were available after 1970.
[b] 1964.

Source: UN, *Statistical Yearbook*, 1978, Table 186, pp. 709ff.

Figure 1.2
Distribution of Income Typical of Most African Countries

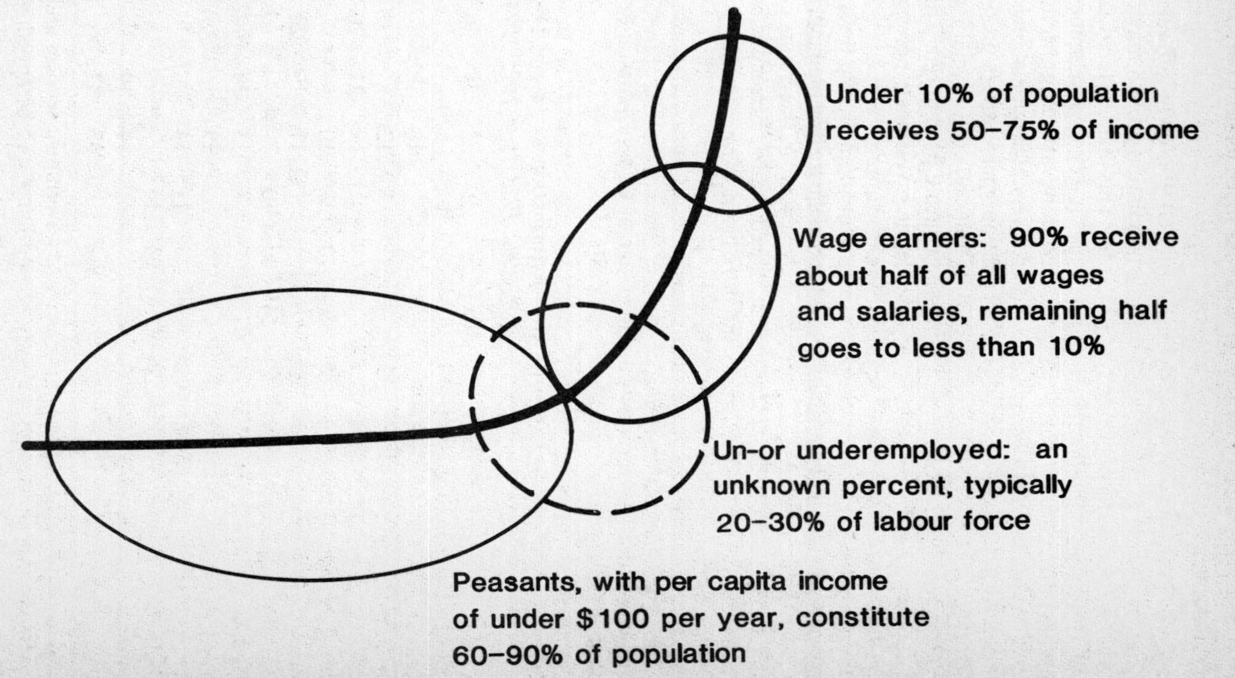

A distorted pattern of distribution of income, goods and services characterizes every African political economy. A small fraction of the population—typically less than 10 per cent—receives half to three-quarters of the national income, while the majority receives barely enough to subsist. Diagram 1.2 illustrates the typical pattern of income distribution.

A Model of Underdevelopment

The past pattern of investment—far from helping to overcome—apparently contributed to the poverty and underdevelopment characteristic of the typical African economy. This constitutes a significant aspect of the monetary and financial problem confronting African states.

A model shown in Figure 1.3 illustrates the problem. It depicts the way investment shaped trade and financial ties between the typical African economy and the developed nations of western Europe and the United States.

The model shows how the developed nations are characterized by highly sophisticated industries and complex financial centres, almost entirely and directly integrated into the world commercial system. A relatively small (shaded) area remains underutilized, incorporated only marginally into the development process. It consists of the low-paid workers, typically members of ethnic minorities and women, and especially in the 1970s and 1980s, growing numbers of unemployed. The further impoverishment of these groups persists in the developed capitalist countries despite the exponential technological growth which has created the industrial potential for the highest living standards in history.

In contrast, the colonial era only marginally incorporated less developed Third World countries, including those in Africa, into the world commercial system. Their so-called "modern" export enclaves are typically concentrated on crude agricultural and mineral products. These are exported to the developed countries for manufacture into sophisticated goods to raise living standards there. The limited reinvestment of capital in the typical African economy has failed to fulfil the mainstream prediction that it would stimulate a multiplier effect, spreading productive employment and higher living standards. On the contrary, it fostered a pervasive dualist pattern of growth which varied only due to particular historical and geographical circumstances. For example, at independence, in West Africa, Uganda and parts of Tanzania, peasant farmers, using sharecrop labour, grew cash crops: groundnuts, rubber, cocoa, cotton, coffee. A few foreign-owned mines shipped out gold, diamonds, tin, iron ore. In most of East, Central and southern Africa, European settlers employed hundreds of thousands of low-paid African labourers to carve out extensive estates. These grew export crops like tobacco, sugar and cotton, and staple foods for the hundreds of thousands more Africans—especially in southern Africa—hired by giant foreign mining complexes to dig out and ship away the region's mineral wealth.

Until World War II, these export enclaves imported almost all the manufactured goods they required, especially the machinery and equipment used by the raw materials-exporting sectors, and the luxury and semi-luxury items enjoyed by the rich few who could afford them. Colonial restrictions

Figure 1.3
Model of the Typical African Economy and its Relationships to the World Economy

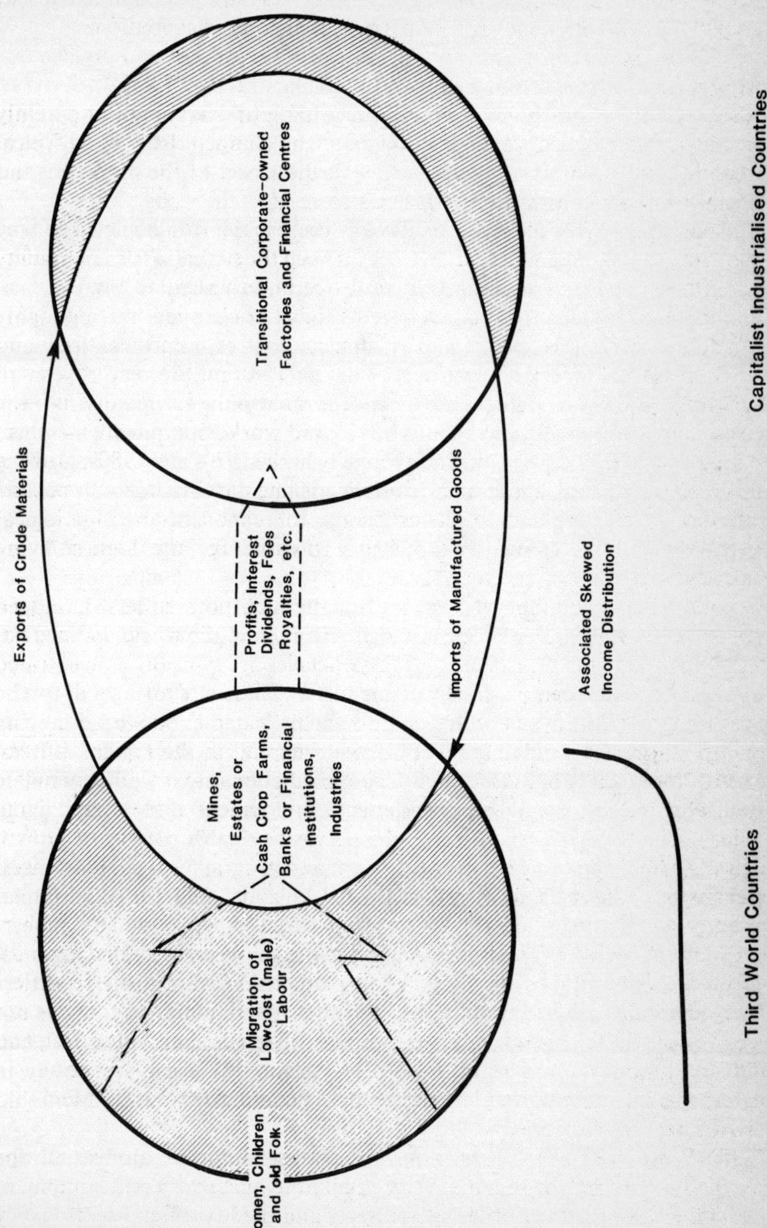

and imported manufactures had stunted or destroyed pre-existing handicraft industries.

The colonial banks typically opened branches in the less developed countries to facilitate this profitable foreign trade. They aided the colonial firms that dominated the export enclaves to repatriate a high proportion of the locally generated investable surplus in the form of profits, interest and dividends.[2] Little remained for investment in manufacturing and agricultural sectors to provide jobs and raise the living standards of the African population. Only where settler commercial farmers dominated the colonies did they influence local state and financial institutions to redirect at least part of the surplus to finance import-substitution industries to meet their needs.

Outside the narrow export enclaves, vast rural hinterlands became increasingly neglected and underdeveloped. There, peasants—mostly women, children and old men—used age-old tools (hoes, cutlasses, a few wooden, animal-drawn ploughs) to scrape a bare living out of eroded, infertile soils. The bankers, honouring profit-maximizing criteria, refused them credits to buy improved machinery or fertilizers. They argued that the very poverty of the African peasants rendered them incapable of repaying their debts. To earn the cash, first to pay taxes and later to buy a few essential manufactured goods (matches, paraffin, soap, cloth, maybe a bicycle or a radio), hundreds of thousands of young men migrated from the villages to work in the mines and on settler-owned estates in East, Central and southern Africa, men—as well as women and children—crowded into shanty towns straggling at the outskirts of mushrooming urban centres. There, they joined the growing numbers of unemployed or underemployed hoping against hope to get better-paid jobs in the steel-cement-glass office buildings and factories that symbolized the modern world.

The few decades of post-independence investment did little to alter this model's basic features. New black governments came into office, some explicitly calling for fundamental political-economic reconstruction. But, by the 1980s, regardless of their stated ideological perspectives, all confronted financial crises and growing impoverishment of the masses of their population.

Alternative Theoretical Explanations

The problem-solving methodology suggests, as a second step in analysing this problem, examination of the range of relevant theories to identify possible hypotheses which may help to explain and perhaps offer useful proposals to solve it. Most theories advanced over the years to explain and solve problems relating to money, banking and public finance fall essentially into two qualitatively different categories, here termed "mainstream" and "Marxist". The fundamental differences between these two categories relate, first, to different judgements as to the relationship between the processes of production and the use of money to facilitate the circulation of goods; and, second, to their different methods of analysing this relationship.

The "mainstream" theory embodies the main concepts and methodologies prevalent in the academic and business world of capitalist-orientated industrialized countries. The forerunners of mainstream economics long, long ago rejected the classical concept, formulated by Adam Smith and Ricardo, that money prices of particular commodities fluctuate according to the value of the labour required to produce them. Mainstream economists focus their analysis, instead, on the way forces of supply and demand in the market for particular commodities determine their money prices. Over the years, for the most part taking institutional structures as given, they have elaborated the essentially subjective concepts of marginal utility and productivity to explain how supply and demand interact with money prices in particular markets. These tend to adjust towards an equilibrium in which all factors of production are optimally allocated, each receiving their marginal product, including invested capital in the form of profit. The entrepreneur may then reinvest this profit to expand output. Given (usually assumed) adequately competitive conditions, market forces thus tend to achieve an optimal allocation of resources.

What has been termed the "Keynesian Revolution", while refocusing attention on the macro-economy and introducing important new concepts, did not upset these basic premises. As Paul Samuelson has pointed out, the pre-Keynesian Marshallian economics synthesized with the Keynesian model: in times of recession or depression, Keynesian theory proposed state intervention primarily through monetary and fiscal policies, to restore the full-employment equilibrium within which marginalist principles of economic rationality could again become relevant. Mainstream theorists have today constructed new models incorporating Keynesian concepts together with Marshallian tenets to explain not only the behaviour of individual commodity markets but also national income and production.

Mainstream economists generally treat money markets in a manner similar to those for other commodities. They construct models designed to illustrate the way interest rates, which they equate with the price of money, tend to adjust the supply of and demand for money towards an equilibrium position. They seek to utilize these models to explain and predict the consequences of various monetary and financial policies.

Today, mainstream theories underpin most of the economics taught in African universities. This text therefore only recapitulates them briefly in so far as they bear on monetary and fiscal issues. Those who wish to examine further their underlying assumptions and models may wish to peruse the relevant materials suggested at the end of this chapter.

A frequently dissenting group, the Institutionalists, pragmatically criticizes mainstream theory's failure to examine institutional constraints. Some urge greater emphasis on income equality and social welfare. But these pragmatic dissenters generally offer no consistent alternative theoretical framework or methodology, especially in the realm of monetary and financial issues. For this reason, this text has devoted little attention to this category of theorists.

A qualitatively different category of theorists, here called "Marxist"[3] after the 19th-Century political economist, Karl Marx, rejects the mainstream approach. Its adherents generally characterize as unrealistic and ahistorical the mainstream methodology which posits that market forces (typically assumed as competitive) tend towards an optimal allocation of resources. They focus their analysis, instead, on historically shaped forces and relationships of production as the fundamental source of constant social change and development.

Marxists retain the underlying premise of the classical theorists, Smith and Ricardo, that money prices develop in accordance with the labour theory of value. In contrast to their classical predecessors, however, Marxists utilize historical materialist methodology to show how the capitalist state creates and perpetuates the conditions of private capitalist ownership of the means of production within which the law of value prevails. The growing working class produces the surplus value—profits—which the capitalist class accumulates and reinvests. This private extraction of surplus value constitutes the root cause of the class struggle and the fundamentally contradictory features of national and international capitalist development. However, under capitalism the exchange of goods for money fosters the illusion that everyone receives a "fair price", or in the case of workers, a "fair wage". Thus money prices veil the process of capitalist exploitation.

This explanation leads Marxists to conclude that to overcome poverty and underdevelopment effectively, the working class, in alliance with the peasantry, must take over state power and reconstruct the national political economy to build socialism.

Other strands of socialist theory abound. But only Marxists have attempted a scientific, detailed explanation of the nature and causes of the contradictions which, they claim, are inherent in the capitalist system of money and finance. Using the historical materialist method, they have developed a theory according to which monetary and financial institutions will play an essential role in the transition to socialism.

It is impossible here to describe adequately the fundamental features of historical materialist methodology or its explanations of capitalist economic development. This text aims primarily to summarize Marxist theory as it relates to monetary and financial problems in Africa. Those interested in examining the theory in more depth may wish to read the works suggested at the end of the chapter.

By no means all the economists grouped in either category agree among themselves on every issue. For example, economists here classed as mainstream divide sharply between those who espouse Keynesian theories and those who press for stricter monetarist doctrines. Nevertheless, the leading American monetarist, Milton Friedman, reportedly once declared,[4] "We are all Keynesians now." Since both sets of theories were initially formulated in relatively more developed countries in Europe and the United States their adherents frequently disagree over aspects of their application to Third World economies.

Mainstream theorists argue over the causes and possible solutions of the problems suggested by the model of the typical African economy presented above. Some blame traditional attitudes and practices for hindering the multiplier effect which, they assume, would otherwise follow from foreign investment and expanded export-orientated production. Others object that government intervention hampers the free competitive interplay of national and international market forces required to stimulate the anticipated multiplier effect. Still others maintain, on the contrary, that state participation, alone, can contribute to redressing the inherited distorted patterns of production and income distribution which thwart the desired spread effect.

Theorists here categorized as Marxists also disagree among themselves on a number of issues. The so-called Old and New Left economists, conducting research in the intellectual centres of core capitalist nations, argue heatedly over possibilities of decentralizing decision-making and reducing the role of the state during the transition to socialism. Marxist theoreticians in socialist countries also debate the appropriate role of money and financial institutions during the actual process of building socialism. But despite these disagreements, the members of each of the major categories adopt basically similar methodologies and underlying theoretical assumptions which differ fundamentally from those of the other set.

This text outlines some of the more significant disputes within each category as well as the more fundamental disagreements between the categories as they relate to money and finance in Africa. Readers are urged to test both sets of theories by applying the problem-solving methodology to the typical problems of underdevelopment and poverty.

Summary

By the 1980s, most independent African states confronted serious financial crises. The colonial era had bequeathed them with monetary and financial institutions which proved incapable of facilitating the accumulation and reinvestment of capital require to provide increasingly productive employment opportunities and higher living standards for the majority of their populations. This text aims to utilize a problem-solving approach to provide the reader with the tools to evaluate the major sets of alternative theoretical explanations and solutions to the resulting problems which have culminated in the financial crises confronting African governments.

A simple model depicts the characteristic features of the inherited dualistic African economies and their relationships to the world commercial system. It shows how over the years the investments which did take place financed the expansion of a relatively developed "modern" export enclave. This enclave exported raw materials and imported manufactured goods. Meanwhile, the majority of the people became increasingly impoverished, barely able to scrape a living from neglected rural hinterlands.

Two major sets of qualitatively different theories, "mainstream" and "Marxist", purport to explain and propose solutions for the monetary and financial problems the model suggests. Mainstream theory centres on the way competitive market forces of supply and demand supposedly interact to determine money prices at an optimal equilibrium point which ensures adequate returns to capital to finance reinvestment. To explain the difficulties suggested by the model, some mainstream theories focus on inappropriate traditional institutions and attitudes, as well as government policies which allegedly hinder the free movement of market forces in the commodity and money markets. Others urge greater state intervention to revise production and income distribution patterns which distort the impact of market forces.

Marxist theorists, on the other hand, emphasize the need to examine the historically changing state and class relationships to the means of production which shaped monetary and financial institutions. These contribute to the distorted pattern of investment in African economies. While disagreeing on particular aspects, they generally agree that the working class, in alliance with the peasants, should take over state power and implement a process of transition to social ownership of financial institutions and, ultimately, all the means of production.

Space is not sufficient to explore in depth the arguments advanced by the theorists in the two categories. It only outlines the arguments between the major sets of theories in relation to monetary and financial issues in Africa and indicates the more significant debates within them. The recommended readings at the end of each chapter (annotated in the bibliography at the end of the book) should enable interested readers to go more deeply into these debates as well as the underlying methodologies and theoretical frameworks considered.

Notes

1. World Bank, *World Development Report 1980*, p. 9. While most economists agree a significant share of the Gross National Product must be invested, readers should remember that national income and GDP are differently defined in capitalist and socialist countries. The former include non-productive expenditure on social services, as well as military spending, in calculating the GDP. Socialist governments, in contrast, define the GDP and national income as equal only to the actual production and distribution of goods, thus arriving at a smaller figure. See Seidman, *An Economics Textbook for Africa*, Chapter 6.

2. Economists debate the meaning of the term "investable surplus". Here, it refers to the surplus over and above consumption in a given economy. In national accounts, its order of magnitude is best approximated by the Gross Operating Profits, before taxes or depreciation are deducted, since this is the surplus generated in the production process which may be reinvested in some form.

3. This category is frequently termed "Marxist-Leninist" because Lenin utilized Marxist methodology—historical materialism—to make important contributions to theoretical explanations and solutions, particularly relating to state monopoly capitalism, imperialism, uneven development affecting Third World countries, and the construction of socialism.

4. Cited in Turgeon, *The Contrasting Economics*.

Exercises and Research

1. What are the five main steps in the problem-solving methodology? Give the main reasons for each of the five steps.
2. What are the features of the main financial problems confronting African economies?
3. Why do most economists agree on the need to invest a significant share of the Gross Domestic Product?
4. What assumptions underlie the mainstream expectation that GDP will increase by 7 per cent if 25 per cent of it is invested every year? In the light of your knowledge of African economies, do you think those assumptions are valid?
5. What are the main features of the distribution of income described in Figure 1.2? Do you think they correspond with the income distribution prevailing in your country?
6. Would you agree that the model shown in Figure 1.3 is characteristic of your country's economy? In what ways does it differ? Are those differences significant?
7. Summarize the fundamental disagreements between the two categories of theories, mainstream and Marxist. Explain why these disagreements are likely to be important in considering the problems of financing development in Africa.
8. Examine government statistics relating to employment and incomes in your country to see if you can determine the pattern of income distribution.
9. Obtain the data for your economy suggested as relevant by the model shown in Figure 1.3. What is the basic pattern of ownership of productive facilities in the export enclave? What are the main exports and imports? What are the features of the labour force? Evaluate the model as a means of examining the structure of your nation's economy.

Recommended Reading

(For annotations, see bibliography at the end of the book.)

Baldwin, *Economic Development and Export Growth*
Baran, *The Political Economy of Backwardness*
Barber, *The Economy of British Central Africa*
Elyanov, *Economic Growth and the Market*
Frankel, *Capital Investment in Africa*
Lewis, *Reflections on Nigeria's Economic Growth*
Leys, *Underdevelopment in Kenya*

Marcus, *Investment and Development Possibilities*
Sandbrook, *The Politics of Basic Needs*
Szentes, *The Political Economy of Underdevelopment*
Thirwall, *Financing Economic Development*
Thomas, *Capital Accumulation and Technology Transfer*

Periodicals

The Economist Intelligence Unit, *Quarterly Economic Reviews*
Annual economic surveys and reports of governments
Government statistical reports
Income tax data published by individual governments
National plan documents of individual countries

Chapter 2: Monetary Theories and the Introduction of Money in Colonial Africa

The Role of Money in Development

A Medium of Exchange

In facilitating the exchange of commodities, money contributes to the spread of the division of labour and specialization which constitutes the foundation of increased productivity. To increase their output, people must specialize. This enables them to improve their tools and techniques for each particular productive task.

The disadvantages of lack of specialization can be seen in Africa. In some remote rural areas, peasant families work very hard to produce most of the limited range of goods they need to live on; that is they engage primarily in subsistence production. The family members know how to do all kinds of jobs; they learn many skills. But they have few tools. The division of labour remains limited, mainly drawn along sex and age lines. The women take care of children, fetch wood and water, cook and grow most of the food crops. The men clear the fields, construct houses, help with the harvest, fish and hunt. Even children and old people have their special tasks. But the levels of productivity remain very low. Such families produce most of the things they need, but they produce very little surplus. They sell very little, so they have very little money. They cannot afford to buy many of the manufactured goods that might make life more comfortable.

In more developed urban areas, on the other hand, the introduction of modern machines and equipment over the last century has raised productive capacity enormously. The more complex division of labour permits the use of more modern productive technology: each individual and group works at only a small part of a single process, but, altogether, they produce far larger quantities of goods. Giant factories specialize in producing single commodities—furniture or clothes, machines or bread. Within each factory, groups of workers run machines which perform single productive operations—making table legs, sewing on buttons, looking after temperature control or mixing dough. Individual workers are relatively unskilled, but they use advanced machinery and waste little time changing from job to job. In consequence their overall productivity is high; using machines, each worker can produce many more times more in an hour than can a peasant family in a semi-subsistence farming household.

The spread of specialization and exchange provides the key to increasing workers' productivity in industry and agriculture, thus making it possible to produce the increased amounts of goods and services needed to raise the living standards of the population. This kind of specialization, however, requires some means of exchanging the goods produced by the workers, each of whom specializes in working on only one commodity.

Money provides the medium of exchange needed to enable people to sell the goods in which they specialize and buy the things they need to live. It provides a means of comparing and measuring the value of, say, shirts in relation to food and housing. It permits the saving necessary to accumulate and reinvest capital to buy new machinery or a bigger factory building.

The Characteristics of Money

The spread of specialization and exchange requires the development of money, a special commodity capable of providing a standard of value and a medium of exchange for all other commodities. To fulfil this role, the commodity used as money must have five essential characteristics. It must be:

1) Acceptable as a means of payment to all who wish to buy and sell goods.
2) Scarce. If people could just pick up money like stones, they would never accept it in payment for goods.
3) Divisible, so that it can be used to pay for goods of very different values.
4) Transportable, that is easily carried.
5) Non-perishable, so it can be saved to pay for goods to be purchased at a later date.

The particular commodity chosen as the money commodity has changed over time in different communities. As specialization and exchange spread, most societies began to use some form of scarce metal as money. Valuable metals, like gold and silver, and, for smaller coins, less valuable metals like brass, copper and nickel, have all the necessary characteristics of money. Initially, a specific amount of metal provided the necessary standard of value, frequently measured by weight. As trade extended across continents, gold became an internationally accepted standard of value.

Historically, as trade expanded, traders needed larger amount of money to finance their growing businesses. Eventually, they found large amounts of metal currencies too heavy to carry. They gradually substituted "bank notes", a form of paper money. They deposited their metal coins with bankers. In return, the banks issued paper notes, promises to pay, to the owners of the coins. Whoever held the notes could use them to reclaim the coins whenever desired; that is, they could convert the paper money into metal currency on demand. Traders began to exchange these bank notes for goods, instead of using the coins themselves.

The continuing growth of productive forces to meet the needs of expanding trade eventually led to the industrial revolution. Emergent capitalist industrialists needed to accumulate ever larger amounts of money, capital, to finance the construction of bigger factories and better machinery, to buy larger amounts of raw materials, to hire more workers, and to transport the finished manufactures over greater and greater distances. They needed a flexible, stable form of money. Stronger and more centralized governments, as an important aspect of their role in facilitating the spread of trade, began to issue paper notes, backed by the promise to pay metal coins on demand. These notes were termed "fiduciary" notes because their value rested on people's faith that the government would convert them on demand to an equivalent amount of metal currency. Eventually, however, governments issued paper notes which could no longer be converted into equivalent amounts of metal coins. Nevertheless, because people had faith in the government's willingness to pursue appropriate policies to ensure the stability of the notes as an acceptable standard of value, they continued to use them as money.

In sum, money came to constitute an essential medium of exchange and store of value which made possible the growth of trade and investment in specialized industries on a national and even an international scale. At the same time, money itself changed and developed.

Theories of Money

Classical Theories of Value and Money Prices

The study of economics as a separate discipline evolved as early capitalism fostered specialization and exchange. Initially, economists focused on the relationship between money prices, money capital and expanded production. That is, they tried to explain, first, what determined prices, and, second, what influenced the accumulation and reinvestment of monetary capital.

In the era of the slave trade, when industry remained relatively undeveloped, mercantilists argued that European government monopolies should expand their foreign trading empires. They should buy cheap and sell dear, accumulating wealth in the form of the universally recognized money commodity, gold. As industry began to emerge in Europe, however, a new school of economists, the physiocrats, focused on agricultural production, rather than trade, as the source of wealth.

Adam Smith and Ricardo, who have since become known as the fathers of the classical school, went further to argue that labour constituted the source of value. Money prices, depending on the supply of and demand for commodities, fluctuate around the value of the labour required to produce the commodities. These classical economists did not, however, examine this proposition in much detail. They developed their argument primarily to proclaim that the wealth of nations could grow only if free trade and competition among the forces of supply and demand in the market replaced government monopolies. This, they held, would stimulate the national and international spread of specialization and exchange. Ricardo proposed that international trade should be allowed to expand the international division of labour to permit each state to specialize in producing those items in which it enjoyed a comparative advantage. Comparative advantage, he argued, would reflect the relative prices of the goods each economy produced. This, in turn, depended on the amount of labour each required to produce those goods.

Marxist Labour Theory and the Money Veil

Marx held that the labour theory of value formulated by Smith and Ricardo constituted the cornerstone of the political economy of capitalism. He examined it as a social theory which revealed the fundamental contradiction inherent in capitalism between workers and capitalists. Capitalists need capital to purchase the means of production and to pay the wages of the workers. As capitalism developed, money became transformed into capital; that is, entrepreneurs accumulated funds to purchase machinery and equipment and employ labour. Thus, money no longer merely expressed an exchange relationship, but emerged as a precondition for the extraction of surplus value by the capitalist from the working class. At the same time, money provides a veil which conceals the essential features of this process. The decisive question confronting society appears to be not producing goods for use, but the accumulation of money in the form of profit for its own sake.

Marx claimed that the classical economists, like Smith and Ricardo, who maintained that all goods sold at a money price which fluctuated around the labour time required to produce them, failed to answer the crucial question: where does profit, expropriated by capitalist entrepreneurs, come from? To provide the answer, Marx further elaborated the labour theory of value.

Labour as the Source of Value: Different kinds of goods, with different "use values", must have a common characteristic which makes them comparable. They have to share some measurable quality. Otherwise, no one would know in what proportions to exchange them. Ultimately, Marx maintained, all saleable commodities have in common only one factor: the varying amounts of labour required to produce them. A diamond, for example, is worth more than many yards of cloth, because finding and mining it requires more hours of labour than weaving a yard of cloth. Air, in contrast, is crucial for life, and so has use value; but, as no one must work to produce it, it has no economic value and so no price. On the moon, air would have to be made by human labour, and so would have a price. A product which no one wants, which has no use value, on the other hand, can have no value, no matter how much labour time its production may require.

In other words, according to Marx, the relative value of commodities can be measured by the amount of labour time required to produce them. Relatively skilled labour, which requires time in the form of training to "produce", is worth more than unskilled labour. Since a commodity can be produced in several ways, the amount of labour time each producer needs to produce it varies. From the point of view of society, the value of a commodity represents, very roughly, the dominant trend, which Marx called the "socially necessary labour time". As technology improves, the amount of labour socially necessary to produce a given commodity tends to decline; as a result, its relative value and hence its relative price tend to fall.

While the socially necessary labour time required to produce a commodity determines its value, Marx held that its money price does not necessarily equal its value at all times. For example, relatively unproductive producers receive a price equal to less than that determined by the value of the labour time they use to produce the commodity, and relatively efficient enterprises receive more. Furthermore, the price is affected by changes in demand and the degree of monopolistic power, if any, exercised by the buyers and sellers. As a result, prices tend to fluctuate around the real value.

Marx focused on the social context in which commodities are produced. He never tried to work out the value of goods in the real world by measuring the amount of labour time they embodied. Rather, he developed the labour theory of value to analyse the social relationships in capitalist society. He emphasized that under capitalism people are no longer bound together by personal relationships, as in feudalism and primitive communalism. Outside the family, they are linked by the anonymous forces of the market, which no individual can control.

Marx's theory showed how the capitalist firms, competing to maximize their share of surplus, had to invest continually in increasingly productive activity. At the same time, this process deepened the contradictions between capitalists and the growing working class.

The Production of Surplus Value: In pre-capitalist social formations, Marx held, most producers exchanged only a small part of the goods they produced. They aimed, through such exchanges, primarily to obtain other goods to fill their own personal needs. Such exchanges could be represented as:

$$C_i \rightarrow M \rightarrow C_n$$

where C_i and C_n represent different commodities with the same value, represented by the money price, M.

In capitalism, however, the entrepreneurs, the owners of the means of production, enter into exchange primarily to make a profit, not to acquire new use values. They do not care whose needs or what needs the production process fulfils, as long as they can sell their output at a profit. That is, from their point of view, they invest money in commodities to produce other commodities to be sold at a profit. The transaction could be represented as:

$$M \rightarrow C_n \ldots P \ldots C_i \rightarrow (M + p')$$

where M is the original sum; C_n are the commodities used in production; $\ldots P \ldots$ is the production process; C_i are the commodities produced; and $(M + p')$ is the money price, including the profit obtained by selling the finished commodities. The entrepreneurs aim, not to maximize the use value incorporated in the commodities, C_i, but to maximize the value they receive, incorporated in $M + p'$, that is, the original investment plus profit.

Marx pointed out that the labour theory of value, thus developed, answers the question; where does profit come from? As his analysis suggests, profit only appears to derive from trade. In fact, it is created in the course of production. The production process raised the value of the capitalists' assets from C_n to C_i. Since all value derives from human labour, *profit represents the increase in value created by the workers in the production process.* The capitalist, who participates only indirectly in production, can appropriate the increase in value, the profit, only because he owns the means of production, the equipment and raw materials the workers need to produce commodities. The workers, who own no means of production, must sell their labour power to the capitalists to earn the wages they need to live. Under capitalism, then, labour power itself has become a commodity, bought and sold on the market like any other good.

The capitalists obtained control of the means of production in the earlier stages of capitalism by a process of what Marx termed primitive accumulation. They pushed peasants off the land by force, or ruined them through measures like high taxes. Through unequal trade and enslavement of whole peoples in colonized areas, they reaped huge profits which they used to finance development of agricultural and industrial means of production. On this basis, they developed the whole system of private ownership of the means of production which enabled them to continue to hire workers and keep the profit for themselves.

Developing his analysis further, Marx divided the value of a commodity into three parts, represented as $c + v + s$; c represents "constant capital", the contribution of the means of production to the value of a commodity. It is equal to the value of raw materials plus the depreciation of the machinery and equipment needed to produce the commodity. This component merely embodies the labour time required at an earlier stage of production to produce the means of production used up in the current production process. Marx called it "dead labour" as it does not create new value in the current process of production but only passes on value created in an earlier production process.

By contrast, v and s represent the new value created in the course of production, the "living labour" incorporated in the product; v stands for "variable capital", the value of the workers' labour power used to produce the commodity. For Marx, the wage—the value of labour power—reflects the special character of human labour in its role as a commodity. Unlike the value of other commodities, the value of labour cannot be the labour time incorporated in the commodity. Rather, it is, at the most abstract level, the amount of socially necessary labour time needed to reproduce labour power: to support the worker, including his or her skills, and the family, which creates the next generation of labour power.

The wage, the money expression of the amount of socially necessary labour required to reproduce labour power, changes as capitalism develops. It depends on such factors as the prevailing levels of technology, workers' expectations, their ability to organize into trade unions and the level of education required in production. In fact the capitalists have hardly ever paid as wages the entire cost needed to reproduce the labour power consumed in the production process. In some cases, as in Africa, the workers and their families support themselves in part through small-scale farming or handicrafts. In most cases, the state pays at least part of the costs of education, health and other services.

Finally, s represents "surplus value", the amount produced by the workers in the form of commodities over and above the cost of their wages. Marx explained this concept in terms of time. If the worker labours an eight-hour day, he or she may work only, say, four hours to produce in the form of new commodities the new value required to cover the cost of the wages. The capitalist, who owns the means of production, however, owns not only the commodities incorporating the new value created in the first four hours, but those the worker produces during the entire eight hours. When the capitalist sells the commodities, therefore, he recovers not only the cost of the wages, but the surplus value. This surplus value, Marxists assert, is the source of all profit. By retaining profit—whether a lot or a little—capitalists exploit the workers: they expropriate surplus value which the workers produce and which therefore should belong to the workers.

Over time, the capitalists invest their profits in more and more complex, larger machinery and equipment, requiring the employment of more and more workers. In other words, the means of production become socialized in a special sense: more and more workers work together to operate them to produce commodities, not as individuals, but in an increasingly complex form of social organization managed by the capitalist. Thus, Marx maintained, the labour theory of value reveals the basic contradiction inherent in capitalism arising out of the continued private ownership of increasingly socialized means of production. The production process requires increasing co-operation among vast numbers of people; but the expanding means of production remain under the control of a relatively small group of capitalists who expropriate a large share of the value, the surplus value, created by the workers. The workers always struggle for higher wages, which would reduce the capitalists' profits. This is the underlying cause of the persistent class struggle inherent in capitalism. The capitalists always strive to hold down wages in order to raise their profits.

The capitalist system normally functions so as to maintain a minimum level of employment, an unemployed labour reserve. This labour reserve helps the capitalists to keep wages down and maximize profits. If the economy achieves full employment, workers might more easily push wages up, since they could not easily be replaced.

The use of money serves as a veil, which helps conceal this cause of the class struggle. It appears as though all partners to the bargain get a fair deal. The workers get money wages equal to the value of their labour. The consumers pay prices equal to the value of the commodities. The capitalist, too, obtains a profit, a fair return for investment. Behind this appearance, however, the capitalists exploit growing numbers of workers.

The Modifications of Value and Price: Marx explained, further, that, as capitalism developed, both values and prices underwent two major types of modification. First, the market functioned to equalize the rate of profit between sectors. That is, the value of each industry's commodity equalled $(c + v)(1 + p')$, where p' equals the average rate of profit in the economy. Competing capitalists, seeking to maximize profits, insisted on at least an average rate to enter production at all. But the organic composition of capital, the value of capital utilized compared to the value of labour employed, varies from industry to industry. The competitive struggle between capitalists allocates the mass of surplus value produced by all workers throughout the economy to provide a roughly equal rate of profit to all producers; this process modifies money prices to establish prices of production. Prices of production cover the costs of production of the particular commodities plus the average rate of profit. In other words, Marx asserted, at a less abstract level of analysis, the aggregate of prices of production equals the socially necessary labour time required to produce all the commodities, not separately, but for the economy as a whole.

Second, some capitalists achieve monopolistic control of the market to augment their profits by manipulating prices. Capitalist industrialization typically involves increasing the scale of production, requiring growing accumulations of capital investment. This fosters centralized control through the formation of competing conglomerates. These companies exercise monopoly pricing techniques to reap extra surplus value, either by pushing down the prices of inputs produced by smaller firms, or raising the prices to the final consumer. While the emergence of monopolistic firms did not signal the end of competition, it did enable the most powerful capitalists to acquire an additional share of the surplus value produced by smaller firms.

In short, the emergence of money as a medium of exchange and store of value facilitated the expansion of trade that led to the growth of the capitalist mode of production. As capitalism developed, money provided a veil that shrouded the cause of the associated inherent contradictions. That cause lay in the expropriation of surplus value (produced by workers) by capitalists who acquired private ownership of the increasingly socialized means of production.

Mainstream Rejection of the Labour Theory of Value

Within a few years of the publication of Marx's *Capital*, some economists began to formulate a new approach which fundamentally rejected the labour theory of value as formulated by classical economists like Smith and Ricardo and developed by Marx. They argued that supply and demand alone determined money price, without regard to any objective standard such as the value of labour embodied in commodities. This laid the foundation for the emergence and elaboration of the subjective concepts of marginal utility and marginal productivity which, to this day, underlie mainstream theories.

Supply and Demand Determine Money Prices: Mainstream economists hold that under conditions of perfect competition, the forces of supply and demand for any particular commodity interact to bring money prices towards an equilibrium point at which the producers' marginal revenues equal the marginal costs of production.

The mainstream analysis at the micro-economic level thus maintains that the relative money prices of different commodities are determined without reference to the value of labour used to produce them. Likewise, the supply and demand for various factors of production bring their "prices" to correspond to their marginal productivity: the marginal productivity of labour determines the wages labour receives. The marginal productivity of capital invested in machinery and equipment determines the profits returned to capital. And so forth.

Mainstream theorists have adapted this model to explain monopoly prices. The basic method of analysis remains the same: the monopolist, whether the sole producer of a commodity or a trade union which controls the labour supply in a particular field of employment, can push marginal returns up above the equilibrium point determined by marginal productivity.

Monetization and Development: Mainstream theorists hold that development in Third World countries, as in First World countries, requires the introduction of money to facilitate the specialization and exchange essential to increase productivity. The investment of capital from abroad provides the necessary initial stimulus. The resulting production and sale of goods creates a multiplier effect: the payment of wages to local workers gives them an incentive as well as the cash to buy new goods. The profits returned to the foreign investors provide them with an incentive to invest more. As local inhabitants accumulate and save funds, they, too, gradually begin to reinvest, replacing the foreign funds which provided the initial impetus for monetization and development.

Mainstream economists offer various explanations for the prevalent underdevelopment and poverty which persist in Third World countries despite decades of foreign investment. They focus primarily on factors alleged to hinder local saving and accumulation of capital. These include: 1) the existence of traditional institutions, like the extended family, which absorb the earnings of individuals who might otherwise save and invest them; 2) rapid population growth which requires expenditure of accumulated funds by families and nations to finance unproductive consumption by new generations, instead of saving and reinvesting available surpluses to increase productivity to raise living standards; 3) the failure to create and expand local money markets to facilitate the mobilization of accumulated savings; 4) the lack of adequately trained entrepreneurs and financial managers; 5) structural obstacles that prevent the free flow of capital to desired areas of production.

More liberal mainstream economists underscore how, especially in southern Africa, racist laws thwarted African would-be entrepreneurs from competing on an equal basis with settler capitalists. They argue that once independent governments abolish these restrictions, the free interplay of market forces should foster more appropriate development.

To stimulate market forces, once racist and other hurdles like those suggested above have gone, mainstream theorists generally advocate policies designed to attract foreign investment, especially in export production for existing markets in developed capitalist countries. Foreign investments should then introduce a positive multiplier effect, leading to the monetization of the economy and facilitating the spread of specialization and exchange to every sector. Africans, who begin work as wage earners in foreign-owned enterprises, will eventually acquire the necessary skills and appropriate capitalist motivations. They will begin to save and invest in increased production for their own profit. The market forces thus unleashed will eventually lead to increased productivity and rising living standards.

The Marxist Focus on Imperialism

Marxist theorists reject the underlying premise of mainstream theories as tautological: to say that supply and demand interact to determine money prices, while money prices determine supply and demand, is circular, and fails to explain what determines the relative money prices of particular commodities, including the workers' labour power. It ignores the one available objective standard, the relative amounts of socially necessary labour time required to produce commodities. By elaborating theories of money on this weak foundation, mainstream theorists the neoclassicists further obscure the underlying process of capitalist exploitation, the expropriation of surplus value produced by the workers.

Capitalist exploitation, Marxist theorists maintain, underpins the many contradictory features that have historically compelled the industrialized capitalist countries to penetrate the Third World, including Africa, in the era of imperialism. On the one hand, the continued accumulation and reinvestment of surplus value in the developed capitalist economies spurred technological innovation and rapidly expanded the forces of production. This fostered the socialization of the still privately owned means of production: more and more vast corporate conglomerates emerged to centralize and control the forces of production, employing hundreds, even thousands of workers, to produce more and more. The capitalists had to sell this growing output to realize their profits.

On the other hand, the capitalists' continued exploitation of the workers, through the expropriation of surplus value, systematically narrowed the market in their home countries for their expanding production. As a result, the capitalists found they could not sell all their output profitably. Periodically, they had to reduce production and lay off workers. Many went bankrupt. In other words, inherently contradictory tendencies fostered repeated crises of overproduction, which mainstream theorists have variously called "business cycles", "depressions" or "recessions".

To overcome these crises at home, the developed capitalist states embarked on imperialist expansion to open new markets, as well as to discover new sources of raw materials for their growing industries; and to enable nationally based firms to accumulate profit from the Third World. In this process, the imperialist governments, companies and banks introduced their own currencies and financial institutions. On the one hand, these facilitated the growth and spread of imperialist ventures, reserving the benefits of outright colonial rule for national firms. On the other, the resulting monetization of Third World economies served as a veil which obscured the resulting imposition of the exploitative capitalist mode of production.

Close links with banks and financial institutions helped imperial companies to accumulate and invest capital—the surplus value they had extracted over the years from the workers—to finance mines, estates and trading activities in

Africa and elsewhere in the Third World. In the typical African economy, these investments shaped export enclaves geared to the production of low-cost raw materials for their home factories. The British colonial government imposed hut and poll taxes so that Africans would have to earn cash. In West Africa, they earned money by producing and selling export crops. In East, Central and southern Africa, land alienation and discriminatory credit and marketing policies left Africans with little choice but to work for low wages on settler-owned farms and mines. The fact that African peasants and workers received cash payments for export crops or money wages for their labour, however, concealed the more significant reality: they produced far more than they received. The colonial farming, mining and trading companies, using channels established by associated banks, sent home most of the surplus value the peasants and workers produced in the form of profits, interest and dividends.

Unlike mainstream theorists, then, Marxist economists concluded that the monetization of African economies, which accompanied and facilitated foreign private investment, served to impose colonial capitalist forms of specialization and exchange. Simultaneously, monetization of the colonial economies concealed the exploitative nature of the resulting capitalist mode of production. This conclusion underpins the Marxist argument that once African states attain independence they should take over the monetary and financial institutions imposed by the colonial governments in order to restructure fundamentally the inherited political and economic system. Only then can the state control and direct money and financial institutions to help finance a more balanced, integrated economy capable of increasing productive employment and rising living standards.

The Introduction of Money in Africa

The problem-solving method suggests evaluation of available historical evidence to determine which of these sets of theories—mainstream or Marxist—best explains the development and role of money and financial institutions in Africa. This section briefly reviews the use of money in pre-colonial Africa, and the impact of the introduction of colonial monetary systems. It focuses primarily on southern Africa. As recommended in the research exercise at the end of this chapter, readers may wish to examine more fully the development of money in their own region to help them determine which set of theories appears more consistent with the available evidence.

Pre-colonial Monetary Systems

Small-scale agriculture and handicrafts, operating at relatively low levels of production, tended to predominate in pre-colonial Africa. Nevertheless, African states had developed their own money forms. In some cases, militarily strong groups captured peasants' agricultural surpluses in order to support relatively centralized states. Long-distance trade, based on a developing regional specialization of production, laid the foundations of extensive kingdoms. In West Africa, the empires of Ghana, Mali and Songhai rose out of and aimed to control the cross-Saharan trade to Europe, initially based on the exchange of gold for salt. In southern Africa, Great Zimbabwe straddled the trade routes from the gold fields in Tati (now in Botswana) down the Sabi River to the coast. Despite the destruction and looting of the great stone fortress and the town by 19th-century European treasure-seekers, the discoveries of china plateware from China and Arabic ornaments and utensils suggest that hundreds of years earlier Zimbabwean trade had extended across the Indian Ocean.

This extensive pre-colonial trade obviously required the development of a medium of exchange, some form of money. Ancient African traders used many forms of money in different times and places: cowrie shells, metal beads, gold dust, copper crosses.

The European colonizers generally destroyed these pre-existing forms of money along with the extended trading systems that had introduced them. When the Portuguese, seeking gold and new routes to Asia in the 14th and 15th centuries, travelled down along the coast of West Africa and around the Horn to what is now Mozambique, they captured the trading ports along the coast by military might. Early European traders following in their wake sometimes captured goods and slaves, sometimes—in line with mercantilist theory—buying them at low prices in exchange for their mass-produced manufactures. In some places, they deliberately undermined previous monetary systems by bringing in manufactured facsimiles, flooding the market and devaluing the local money commodities produced by African crafts workers.

The discovery of the Americas led to the need for cheap labour. This laid the foundation for the triangular slave trade, an important feature in the primitive accumulation of capital which financed industrial development in Europe. A Jamaican slave plantation owner, for example, initially established the predecessor to Barclays Bank through which he reinvested his accumulated profits in British industry. The emergence of militaristic slave-trading states in Africa disrupted pre-existing economies based on long-distance trade.

At the end of the 18th century, England sought to end slavery and introduce free trade as advocated by Adam Smith. British industrial capitalists had discovered that a free labour force, separated from the means of production and working for wages, was more efficient than slavery. Reinvesting their accumulated funds to finance the rapid growth of British industries and shipping, British companies sought, under the slogan of "free trade", to penetrate regions controlled by the monopolistic trading companies of rival nations.

Colonialism and the Introduction of New Currencies

By the late 19th century, the major European powers had begun to employ state power, backed by superior military technology, to carve out colonial empires. They aimed to impose a more secure hold on the markets and sources of raw materials required for their growing industries. This spurred the "scramble for Africa" which culminated in the Berlin Conference. The major

European powers divided the continent into over 50 colonies. Most introduced currencies and financial institutions in the colonies linked to those in their home country to facilitate their national companies' expansion of trade and investment.

Over the years, imperial companies, with the aid of colonial governments, shaped the narrow enclave development which geared the separate African colonies to the export of a few raw materials and the import of mass-produced goods. In the process, they drained away the locally generated investable surpluses in the form of profits, dividends and interest remitted through the banks to their home accounts.

The Example of Southern Africa

Despite differences in geographical and historical circumstances, the southern African experience provides a general illustration of the way in which colonial governments, in co-operation with commercial banks, imposed their own monetary systems. In the early 17th century, the Dutch set up a trading post at the Cape in South Africa as a stop on the long route to Asia. For two centuries, they gradually expanded their land holdings, importing slaves from their possessions elsewhere as well as enslaving local inhabitants of the region, to provide labour for their agriculturally based economy. To prevent the French from capturing the Cape during the Napoleonic Wars, the British took over the colonial administration. In an effort to escape the British pressures to end slavery, the descendants of the Dutch settlers, the Boers—today called Afrikaners—eventually trekked inland to the Transvaal. There, using enslaved African labour, they built their own "Republics".

The British continued to rule the Cape. They introduced their own monetary system, tied to the British pound, and encouraged British banks to set up business.

The Boer Republics also tried to establish their own monetary system in the Transvaal. Still living in predominantly agrarian subsistence economies dependent on slave labour, they did not introduce a general system of taxes. Instead, they paid officials and government debts with promissory notes based on state lands (called "good fors", since each was "good for" a given amount of state land). In effect, thus, the Republics established a paper currency backed by land, rather than gold or silver. The Republics made an attempt to establish state banks, offering foreign banks land in exchange for gold and silver. These measures reduced the available uncultivated land area. Efforts to acquire more land led to wars with neighbouring African peoples. The governments increased their debts to pay for firearms and ammunition. A few large Boer landholders grew wealthy, acquiring large numbers of cattle and African slaves.

The Boer governments borrowed from the British Cape Commercial Bank and imposed land taxes in an attempt to repay their debts. The taxes forced the poorer Boer farmers to abandon their land. The richer ones, like Paul Kruger, acquired thousands more acres.

In the 1860s, the discovery of first diamonds, then gold, made South Africa the most attractive region of the continent for investment. Enterprising British capitalists, seeking profitable areas in which to invest their accumulated surpluses, deposited funds in the British banks in the Cape, shifting them from one to another in a speculative search for high profits. These speculative activities culminated in a run on the banks in 1863-65, when 28 out of 29 Cape-based banks went bankrupt. The remaining one with strong ties to the London financial centre, emerged as the largest bank in South Africa.

The international demand for gold grew rapidly, reflecting primarily its importance as the basic internationally acceptable currency for expanding world trade. The British reopened the Tati mines in Botswana. In 1869, they began mining for gold in the Transvaal. The mines required what in those days came to vast amounts of capital to provide elevator cars on wires to lower down into the mines; and steam pumps to prevent flooding. Although the Boers claimed their Republics owned the entire region, they could not muster sufficient funds to finance the new mining development.

From the outset, the British banks provided the primary source of capital for the expanding mining business in the Transvaal. Eventually, drawing on British banks for funds, Cecil Rhode's de Beers Diamond Company consolidated the many small diamond claims into a gigantic monopolistic enterprise. This ended the competitive price cutting which threatened to bankrupt the smaller companies. To obtain labour, the British colonial authorities relaxed the ban on the sale of guns to Africans so that they would accept jobs as mine labourers to earn the necessary cash to buy them.

At the turn of the century, the British colonial officials sought to annex the Boer Republics to facilitate British investment in the mines. The British armies finally won the resulting war, but only after it had dragged on for three years.

When the war ended, the British-financed Standard Bank took over the Boers' Transvaal banks and integrated them into its own South African banking system. Meanwhile, the British administrators exercised their military superiority to subordinate the Africans throughout the region. They imposed measures to take their land and to tax them so as to coerce them to work for the expanding mining firms.

In 1910, by the Act of Union, the British and Afrikaners united to rule South Africa under a consolidated government. In 1920, the Currency and Banking Act unified all the pre-existing currencies of the country into a single one backed by gold, which remained linked to the British pound. Shortly after, another British commercial bank, Barclays, entered South Africa. It merged two smaller South African banks to form its own branch, which grew over the years to become its largest overseas affiliate.

In the late 19th and early 20th centuries, with the financial assistance of the British banks, the British South African Company extended its operations northwards in search of new regions of mineral wealth. As it went, it spread the use of the South African currency, issued through branches of the British-South African banks. Shortly after Rhodes' Pioneer Column marched into what is now Zimbabwe, Standard Bank set up branches in Bulawayo and Salisbury. The British South African Company used force to take over the best farming lands for white settlers, and extended hut and poll taxes to African males in these new areas to coerce them to work for money wages.

The British Currency Boards

While consolidating its colonial power in southern Africa the British imperial state outlawed all other forms of currency. Outside South Africa, it typically created currency boards which issued local currencies, 100 per cent backed by British pounds sterling.

The way the currency boards functioned linked each colony's currency directly to its earnings from foreign trade. When an affiliate of a colonial company exported locally produced raw materials, it deposited its foreign-exchange earnings in the account of the currency board in the British commercial banks in London. The currency board held its reserves in the form of cash, British Treasury bills, or other short-term loans in Britain itself. It issued to the colonial company's affiliate an equivalent amount of local currency by depositing it in the commercial bank's branch in the colony in the company affiliate's account. The company affiliate could then draw on that deposit to pay for local expenses, wages, purchases of materials, etc. When a colonial company wished to import manufactured goods into a colony, it had to obtain foreign exchange from the currency board through the commercial banks.

The colonial currency boards thus tied the colonial economy's money supply directly to the changes in the levels of the currency board's foreign assets, the pounds sterling or other foreign currencies which colonial company affiliates earned through exports. A fall in the colony's export earnings would lead to a fall in the currency board's holdings of sterling. This, in turn, would cause an automatic decline in the stock of money available to the colony, with attendant depressing effects on the entire colonial economy: low foreign-exchange earnings led to a low demand, cutting back on imports or reducing local production, causing a negative multiplier effect throughout the economy.

An increase in foreign earnings, on the other hand, would lead to a direct increase in the money supply, causing an expansion of domestic demand. This stimulated increased imports, or, in a few cases, a positive multiplier effect stimulating an expansion of local production.

In other words, the colonial currency boards spread the impact of the fluctuations in the value or volume of the colony's crude exports throughout its economy. When African states attained independence, therefore, whether guided by mainstream or more radical doctrines, they generally sought as soon as possible to issue their own currencies in order to begin to control their money supplies in relation to their own needs.

Summary

Economists agree that some form of money is essential to facilitate specialization and exchange and the accumulation and reinvestment of capital. Whatever the form of money used, it must have special characteristics which enable it to fulfil this role. Over time, as trade has spread, paper money, backed by governments, has replaced heavier forms of metallic money.

As trade and investment have spread the use of money, theories of money have developed. Economists have disagreed, however, about the determinants of relative money prices of different commodities. The classical economists, from Adam Smith to Karl Marx, held that labour constituted the source of value and hence, in the last analysis, determined the relative money prices of commodities. Marx went further, however, to declare that the labour theory of value revealed the way the capitalist owners of the means of production exploited the workers, a process concealed by the use of money.

Mainstream theorists then rejected the labour theory of value altogether. They argued that the interaction of supply and demand determined relative money prices of commodities on the micro-economic level. This ensured that all factors of production received the money equivalent of their marginal product.

Applied to Third World countries like those in Africa, mainstream theorists generally hold that monetization of the economy stimulated by foreign investment should create the necessary conditions for development. The causes of the failure to achieve development lie in inherent factors in the traditional sector and structural obstacles which militate against domestic accumulation and reinvestment of capital.

Marxist theorists, in contrast, hold that the imperialists introduced money and financial institutions to facilitate the competitive expansion of capitalist ventures in search of raw materials and markets. The imperial state, together with the commercial banks, created financial institutions which chained the colonial economies tightly into the orbit of capitalist imperialist exploitation.

Exercises and Research

1. Why do most economists agree that money plays a necessary role as a medium of exchange?
2. What characteristics must a commodity have to serve as money?
3. Classical theorists accepted the theory that labour determines the basis of relative money prices. But a) what key question did Marx maintain they failed to answer? b) how did Marx answer that question? c) in what way do Marxists maintain that money prices serve to conceal the underlying source of contradictions in capitalism?
4. Today, mainstream theorists reject the labour theory of value. How do they explain what determines the money prices of commodities?
5. To test these alternative theoretical explanations as they relate to Africa and your country, examine the history of the introduction of money into your country.
6. Did the European traders introduce a new currency into your country?

If so, when, why and under what circumstances?

7. How did the pattern of production and trade, introduced along with the new currency, affect the way most people lived and worked in your country?
8. In the light of the facts you have discovered, what set of theories do you think best explains the role of monetization as it has affected development in your country?

Recommended Reading

(For annotations, see bibliography at the end of the book.)

Amin, *Accumulation on a World Scale*
Aromolaran, *West African Economics Today*
Baldwin, *Economic Development and Export Growth*
Dobb, *Welfare Economics and the Economics of Socialism*
Elyanov, *Economic Growth and the Market*
Frankel, *Capital Investment in Africa*
Galbraith, *Money, Whence it Came, Where it Went*
Jucker-Fleetwood, *Money and Finance in Africa*
Kaldor, *The Scourge of Monetarism*
Koneacki, *An Economic History of Tropical Africa*
Lombard (ed.), *Economic Policy in South Africa*
Marcus, *Investment and Development Possibilities*
Marx, *Capital*
Newlyn and Rowan, *Money and Banking in British Colonial Africa*
Nkrumah, *Neo-Colonialism*
Ola and Onimode, *Economic Development of Nigeria*
Onoh, *Strategic Approaches to Crucial Policies*
Ord and Livingstone, *An Introduction to West African Economics*
Robinson (ed.), *Economic Development for Africa South of the Sahara*
Rodney, *How Europe Underdeveloped Africa*
Seidman, *An Economics Textbook for Africa*
—— *Planning for Development in SubSaharan Africa*
Szentes, *The Political Economy of Underdevelopment*
Teriba and Diejomoah (eds.), *Money, Finance and Nigerian Economic Development*
Thomas, *Capital Accumulation and Technology Transfer*
Truu (ed.), *Public Policy and the South African Economy*
Van Biljon, *State Interference in South Africa*

Chapter 3: The Banking System

Introduction

Chapter 2 showed how, from the outset, the colonial commercial banks helped to introduce and regulate colonial money supplies. In Africa, as elsewhere in the world, the banking system and associated financial institutions constitute the key features of the monetary system. By lending money, banks play a major role in determining the overall money supply. They also influence the direction of investments which, in the past, shaped the typically dualistic African economy.

This chapter discusses the general role of banks in a capitalist economy, and presents alternative theoretical explanations of the way banks function in developing countries. Chapter 4 summarizes evidence concerning two of the more sophisticated banking systems in Anglophone Africa, in Nigeria and Zimbabwe, as well as the consequences of nationalizing the banks in Tanzania.

Most people think of commercial banks primarily as convenient and safe places to deposit their money when they do not require it for daily use. They may withdraw their funds in the form of cash when they need it. This kind of deposit is called a demand deposit, for depositors can obtain their funds on demand. If they wish, they may withdraw their money from their demand deposit to pay bills in a safer and more convenient form by writing cheques. A cheque is simply a form containing the signatory's promise to pay the stated sum to the person named on it. On presentation of the cheque, together with adequate proof that the bearer is the person named on it, the bank withdraws the stated sum from the signatory's account, and either gives it to the payee in cash, or transfers it to his or her account.

If depositors are willing to leave their money in their account for a specifed period of time without withdrawing it, the bank will even pay them a stipulated rate of interest. Such a savings deposit is usually called a time deposit, since the money must remain in it for a specified time before its owner is entitled to receive the stipulated interest.

All economists agree, however, that over several centuries, the commercial banks have come to play a far more crucial role in the typical capitalist country's financial system in two respects. First, by providing credit, they critically influence the nation's total money supply. Second, directly and through associated financial institutions, they make longer-term loans and investments which fundamentally influence the overall pattern of national economic development.

This chapter outlines, first, the mainstream explanation of how the banking system creates money and influences the direction of investment in a predominantly capitalist economy; second, the Marxist explanation for the merger of banks and industry to form finance capital as a prominent feature of the imperialist stage of capitalism; and, third, the debates among and between both categories of theorists as to the role of banks in Third World countries like those in Africa.

The Mainstream Explanation of the Banking System

Providing Credit

By providing credit, commercial banks play a vital role in expanding a nation's money supply over and beyond the notes and coins issued by government.

Notes and coins issued by the appropriate authority on behalf of the government constitute a nation's initial supply of money. This is often termed M1. The authorized agent of the government determines the amount of M1 (that is notes and coins) it will issue by estimating the amount of transactions likely to require cash as a medium of exchange.

However, most payments in developed countries, as well as in the so-called "modern" sectors of developing nations, are made by cheque. Most businessmen pay their bills by cheques. They pay cash only to wage earners, most of whom spend it on the things they need to live on during the month. The workers pay cash to store-owners (in the typical African country, they spend half their wages on food); they also pay their rent and transportation costs in cash. The store-owners and landlords who receive these cash payments typically deposit them in their bank accounts. They usually use cheques drawn on their accounts to pay for bulk goods they sell to the workers.

Ordinarily, when a bank lends money to a borrower, it does not lend cash. Instead, it creates a deposit, equivalent to the amount of the loan, in the name of the borrower. The borrower may then draw on that account by cheque to pay bills as they come due. By this means, the bank actually creates new money, over and above the notes and coins issued by the government. Figure 3.1 illustrates this process.

Creating Money

When they grant credit, bankers normally assume that not all depositors will ask for cash at one time. In Figure 3.1, the bank takes A's deposit of cash and promises to honour any cheque A may wish to cash, up to the $100 deposited. But, like all bankers, the bank manager assumes A will not ask for all the money in the deposit at one time. Instead, A will usually write cheques to creditors who will in turn deposit them in their accounts in the bank. On that assumption, the bank can lend out money to other borrowers, B, C and D. The bank obtains profits from the borrowers in the form of

Figure 3.1
How a Commercial Bank Creates Money

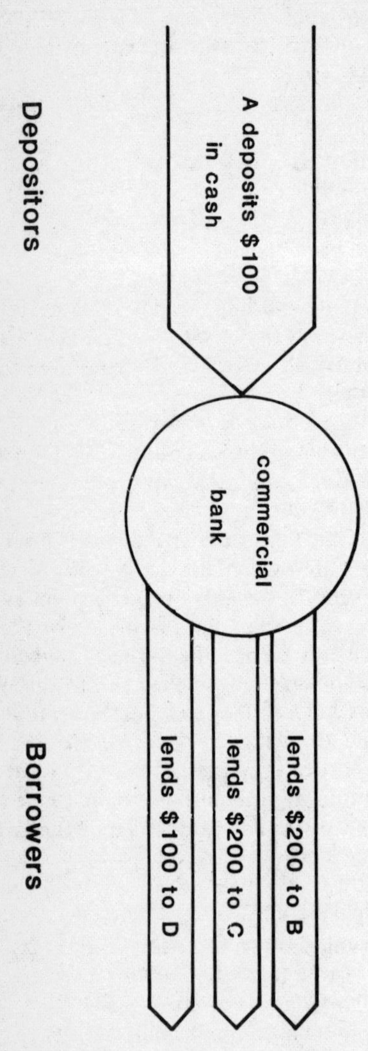

interest they pay to it for the use of the borrowed funds. Usually, the longer the borrower keeps the funds, the higher the interest rate the bank will charge.

In reality, by giving B, C and D credit, the bank creates new money. It gives each of them a deposit equal to the value of the loans it has given them. B, C and D may then write cheques, drawing on their new deposits to pay their bills. Again, most of those who receive their cheques will not ask the bank for cash. They, too, will simply deposit the cheques in their own accounts. As a result, the bank just transfers the amount of money written on the cheques from the deposits of the clients who signed them to the deposits of the clients who received them in payment for bills. The actual supply of money, however, has multiplied five times, as the bank loaned money by creating new accounts for B, C and D. The bank has, in a real sense, created new money, expanding the money supply.

The commercial banking system as a whole in any one country works much like the bank pictured in Figure 3.1. The banks establish a clearing system. Cheques drawn on one bank may be deposited in another bank. Through the clearing system, each bank cancels out cheques, drawn by other banks' clients on deposits it holds, against cheques its own clients may draw against other banks' deposits. If, at the end of a specified period, more cheques have been drawn on one bank's deposits than have been redeposited in it, the bank must transfer funds to the other banks to cover the outstanding cheques.

In other words, the banking system, by lending money and creating deposits on which borrowers may write cheques, increases the available money supply.

Short-Term Loans: "Near Money" or M2

Short-term loans are called "near-money" because they may be turned into actual cash in a short period, usually less than six months or a year. The additional supply of "near-money" created by short-term loans is sometimes called M2.

Most short-term credit in Third World countries like those in Africa consists of treasury bills or notes and bills of exchange, frequently called "short-term paper". Treasury notes represent short-term loans to the government, usually used to finance short-term budget deficits. The government guarantees to repay the notes in cash, along with interest, at the end of a fixed short period. Part II discusses treasury bills in more detail in connection with public finance.

Bills of exchange are like post-dated cheques. They are especially important for economies heavily engaged in foreign trade where delivery of goods may take several months. A creditor accepts a bill of exchange in payment for a commodity which is to be delivered in a given period, say three to six months. The creditor essentially agrees not to deposit the bill for a similar period, until the due date when the bill is said to have "matured". If the credtior needs money before the bill reaches maturity, he may discount it, that is sell it to someone for cash minus a stipulated rate of interest.

Although in most African countries, commercial banks handle bills of exchange directly through special departments created for that purpose, in some they establish affiliated accepting houses to deal with them.

An accepting house may accept or guarantee a bill of exchange to ensure that it will be paid. Typically, a commercial bank or its associated accepting house maintains agencies in trading centres throughout the world. These vouch for the credit standing of buyers who pay for goods through bills of exchange. The bank or accepting house charges a commission, its profit, for performing the function of determining the creditworthiness of particular traders, and guaranteeing the payment of the bill.

Discounting houses may be established to discount trade bills for traders once they have been accepted. They may utilize short-term loans from commercial banks to finance these transactions.

Whether a commercial bank handles short-term credits directly or through affiliated acceptance and discount houses, these credits still constitute near money, an important addition to the economy's money supply.

How Commercial Banks Influence Investments

By deciding to whom and for what purposes to lend funds, commercial banks influence the pattern of investment of capital. Once a firm makes an initial investment, buying land, buildings, machinery or equipment, it typically must borrow additional funds to keep its project going. Laws regulating the establishment of banks not infrequently restrict them primarily to granting short-term credit or very secure longer-term loans, to ensure that the commercial banks can pay cash on demand to their depositors.

Much commercial bank credit finances the working capital needs of businesses in the private sector: loans to enable firms to finance wage payments, the purchase of raw materials and spare parts for machinery and equipment, or the storage of stocks of goods until they are sold. Once the firm has sold the goods it produced with the credit, it can repay the bank, often within the year.

Not infrequently, however, firms borrow for longer periods. Commercial banks typically may make loans secured by mortgages on real property: homes, office buildings, machinery and equipment. They may provide a firm a line of credit, an agreement by the bank to extend loans to the firm up to a specified amount. In return, the firm retains an agreed portion of the line of credit (usually 10 to 15 per cent) on deposit in the bank. The bank may also provide the firm with a revolving credit, a commitment to lend up to a certain amount of funds to it. The firm pays not only the interest on the amount borrowed but a fee, normally 0.5 per cent, on the unused portion.

Firms sometimes borrow long-term funds as a substitute for investing additional equity capital. The firm may use borrowed funds to produce additional profits which, if the interest rate charged by the bank is low enough, will enable it to increase the dividends of its shareholders.

The banks' managers, seeking to maximize their profits—that is, the banks' returns in the form of interest—decide to whom and for what purposes they will lend funds. Their decisions inevitably influence the decisions of individuals or firms as to whether and how much to invest; for, without access to essential working capital or needed longer-term credits, many capital investments in plant and equipment become unviable.

Commercial banks may also indirectly influence the pattern of investments in a national economy through the activities of their affiliates. They often establish trust departments to which individuals, businesses and pension funds entrust large sums of money for investment purposes. The trust department may buy and sell shares of ownership in firms on behalf of the trustors; in reality, in so doing, it decides in what sectors and in what firms to invest the funds it holds in trust. Commercial banks may also establish affiliated merchant banks which the law usually permits to make longer-terms investments in industrial, commercial and real-estate properties. Firms seeking new funds for investment may be influenced by the criteria which these bank affiliates establish for "sound" investments.

The Establishment of Central Banks

Historical Roots: In the 19th century in what are now the industrialized countries, when, for some reason, many people all at once lost confidence and demanded cash from the banks, many banks became "bankrupt". They could not pay cash to all those who demanded it, and had to close. Their depositors simply lost their savings. Of course, the impact of bank closures seriously disturbed overall national financial stability and economic development.

As money and banking systems of capitalist countries became more complex in order to finance the expansion of trade and industry, capitalist governments co-operated with private bankers to establish systems to protect the banks and their customers. As a key feature of such co-operation, they generally established some form of central bank to provide the commercial banks with a reliable lender of last resort, that is, a bank from which commercial banks, if necessary, could borrow funds. In England, the private commercial banks, themselves, originally organized the Bank of England. It was only taken over by the British government after World War II. In the United States, the Congress established the Federal Reserve Bank whose board of directors represents government, the public and the bankers. Almost all former British colonies, as they became independent, established their own central banks, initially along the lines recommended by mainstream theorists, similar to those of developed capitalist countries.

Functions: In accordance with the basic premises of mainstream theory, the central bank in a capitalist country typically leaves the major banking functions to privately operated commercial banks and their affiliates. The central bank primarily performs two sets of functions.

As banker and financial adviser for the government, it a) issues the nation's currency and is responsible for maintenance of its value; b) helps the government to borrow funds by buying short-term bills from the treasury to cover short-term deficits (treasury notes) and helping the government to float its long-term debt, that is, arranging with banks and financial institutions for long-term loans to the government; c) handles the nation's foreign exchange reserves and gold.

Secondly, as a lender of last resort for private commercial banks, it lends

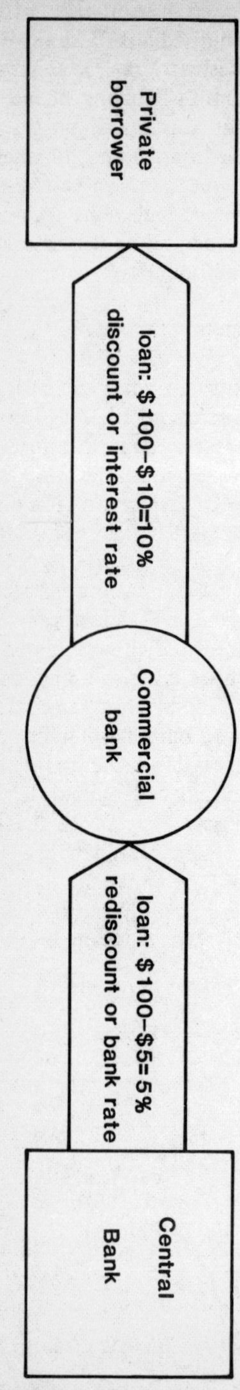

Figure 3.2
The Central Bank Controls the bank rate setting a floor under the commercial bank's interest rate

commercial banks cash to cover depositors demands. Commercial banks pay interest for loans they obtain from the central bank. This interest is often called "the bank rate". The commercial banks usually charge a higher rate of interest to those who borrow from them. The difference between the bank rate and the rate the commercial banks charge to those who borrow from them constitutes the commercial bank's profit. Sometimes, the interest rate charged by the central banks is called a "rediscount rate". The commercial banks may discount the loans they make to borrowers, that is, they may subtract an amount equivalent to the interest before giving the principal to the borrower. When the bank lends to the commercial banks to cover the loans they make to private borrowers, it may rediscount them; that is, the central bank subtracts the bank rate of interest it charges to the commercial banks before giving them the principal. In this case the difference between the discount and the rediscount rate constitutes the commercial bank's profit.

Usually, the central banks do not limit the percentage above the bank or discount rate which commercial banks may raise the rates they charge to borrowers. The commercial banks typically charge lower rates for short-term loans and higher rates for loans which the borrower will repay over a longer period. Mainstream theorists generally maintain that the difference in interest rates on long- compared to short- term loans reflects the risks and opportunity costs to the banks and the borrowers. If the bank is repaid sooner, it may sooner reinvest the funds, perhaps on more favourable terms. If the borrower has the funds for a longer period, he or she may invest them to take advantage of more profitable opportunities and therefore may be willing to pay a higher rate.

In the typical capitalist economy, the central bank may indirectly control the commercial banks' powers to lend money and alter the national money supply by using one or all of three techniques:

1) The central bank may set the cash ratio or the liquidity ratio. The cash ratio is the ratio of cash deposits—coins and notes deposited in the commercial banks—to the loans the commercial banks may make to borrowers. The liquidity ratio is the ratio of the liquid assets the commercial bank must hold to the loans it may make to borrowers. Liquid assets typically include actual cash plus short-term loans, or "near money", that the bank may quickly convert to cash on demand. The higher the cash or liquidity ratio set by the central bank, the less credit it permits the banks to create.
2) The central bank may change the bank rate (or the rediscount rate) it charges to commercial banks: if the central bank raises the bank rate, the commercial banks generally must raise the interest rate they charge to borrowers to make a profit. Since fewer borrowers can afford to borrow at higher rates, this should reduce the money supply. If the central bank lowers the interest rate, the commercial banks may lower the rates they charge. By reducing the price of money, the theory holds, more borrowers will borrow, thus increasing the money supply.
3) Open-market operations: the central bank may buy short-term paper

(loans) from commercial banks. This provides the commercial banks with additional cash as a basis for more loans, thus enabling them to increase the money supply. It may also require commercial banks to buy short-term paper, especially treasury notes,[1] to "mop up" liquidity, i.e. banks' excess holdings of cash. This reduces the commercial banks' ability to make new loans which would expand the money supply.

Central banks may also use more direct methods to control the national money supply. These direct methods include:

1) Directing commercial banks to lend to certain sectors and particular types of activities, while prohibiting them from lending to others.
2) Allocating foreign-exchange reserves according to predetermined criteria, thus limiting the commercial banks' powers to grant credit to borrowers for imports.

Most mainstream theorists, as well as commercial bankers, object to the introduction of these direct techniques. They argue that developing countries, in particular, may scare off private foreign bankers and potential investors who might otherwise facilitate the inflow of scarce capital.

In short, mainstream economists usually view banks as performing an essentially technical function of facilitating the growth of the money supply in relation to the demands of the predominantly privately owned productive sector. They generally do not examine in depth the institutional structures characteristic of the banks. Rather they describe the banks' functions and focus on the way they influence the supply of and demand for money in relation to changes in what they view as the price of money, that is the interest rate. (A graphic elaboration of these concepts may be found in the appendix at the end of this chapter.)

Regulation of Money Supplies: Mainstream theorists generally agree that the central banks should exercise the available indirect controls over the money supply to lessen the impact of business cycles. In a boom period, businessmen borrow to expand output. This increases the money supply and creates inflationary pressures, especially if—as is common in developing countries—constraints hinder the production or import of more goods. Most mainstream theorists maintain that too much money chasing too few goods causes inflation. Therefore, the central banks should take one or all of the following steps to reduce the money supply.

1) Increase the cash or liquidity ratio. This will reduce the commercial banks' ability to expand loans in relation to their cash or liquid assets.
2) Raise the interest rate (the bank or discount rate) charged to commercial banks. The commercial banks, in turn, will raise the interest rates they charge borrowers. This will increase the cost of borrowing and so fewer individuals or businesses will seek loans.
3) Sell short-term paper to the commercial banks. Assuming a fixed cash ratio, this will reduce the commercial banks' holdings of cash and reduce

their ability to make loans.

In a recession, mainstream theorists hold, the central bank should reverse some or all of these measures to stimulate increased production and employment. Consequently it should:

1) Lower the cash or liquidity ratio. This should enable commercial banks to lend more money on the basis of smaller holdings of cash and liquid assets.
2) Reduce the interest rate it charges commercial banks. They, in turn, will lower the interest rate they charge borrowers, who will borrow more to invest in expanding output.
3) Buy short-term paper in the open market. This will increase the banks' holdings of cash so they may lend more funds to borrowers seeking to increase investments.

These measures should increase bank liquidity and lower the cost of loans. They would, then, encourage borrowers to acquire more credit to expand output.

The Mainstream Debate over Monetary Policy

Over the last two decades, however, monetarist and Keynesian theoreticians and practitioners have argued—sometimes bitterly—over the appropriate role of the central bank in exercising these powers. Their arguments centre not so much on basic theoretical differences—though these exist—as on their policy implications.

The Quantity Theory of Money: Until the 1930s, mainstream theorists generally adopted a simple quantity theory of money to explain the relationship between the money supply and overall price levels. Irving Fisher summed up the quantity theory of money in a simple model:

$$MV = PT$$

where M: currency in circulation
V: velocity of currency's circulation } total money supply

P: prices of goods sold
T: transactions, or sales, of goods } total demand for money

According to the quantity theory of money, the money supply may expand or contract as a result of: 1) an increase or decrease in the amount of currency in circulation; 2) an increase or decrease in the velocity of circulation of currency; or 3) both. If the money supply expands more rapidly than the demand for it in terms of actual transactions, that is goods produced and sold, then prices will rise. If the money supply contracts while production and sales remain at the same level, prices will fall. Under competitive conditions, then, the central bank, by restricting the money supply, may restrict inflationary pressures which might otherwise lead to rising prices. If the central bank takes steps to expand the money supply, on the other hand, it may stimulate inflationary pressures, leading to rising prices.

Thus, following this early simple formulation of the quantity theory of money, mainstream theorists initially assumed that, given competitive conditions, the interaction of the supply of money with the demand for it would tend towards equilibrium, leading to the best possible allocation of all resources, including the supply of money itself. At this point, full employment would prevail. A central bank should only exercise its powers to influence the money supply to facilitate this adjustment process.

The Keynesian liquidity trap: In the Great Depression of the 1930s, however, money prices, especially for agricultural products and products of smaller manufacturing firms, tended to decline. In the major industrial capitalist nations, industries operated at less than 60% of capacity. One out of five workers in the labour force was unemployed. Central bank policies, prescribed in accord with the quantity theory of money, appeared inadequate to overcome the depression.

To explain these unanticipated problems, John Maynard Keynes wrote the General Theory of Employment, Money and Interest in which he modified the earlier quantity theory of money. He centred his explanation on the failure of entrepreneurs to invest the savings accumulated in the economy. As a result, production declined and national income failed to expand. In other words, he held that the critical cause of the depression lay in the failure of those with wealth to invest it. For some reason, a liquidity trap came into existence: People with wealth decided not to invest the funds they had accumulated. This initiated a negative multiplier effect: it restricted the expansion of the money supply, which reduced prices and discouraged further investment. This, in turn, led to a decline in consumption, a fall in national income and hence a decline in savings available for investment.

Keynes suggested that people's propensity to hold money, rather than invest it, might arise from one, or a combination, of three motives:

1) The transactions motive. Every person must spend some of his or her income on acquiring basic necessities, that is for necessary transactions. People will refrain from investing their income to the extent that they expect to spend it on consumption.
2) The precautionary motive. People may desire to keep a reserve for unforeseen contingencies such as sickness in the case of individuals, or the necessity of replacing broken or worn-out machinery in the case of a firm. The greater the risk of illness or a breakdown of machinery, the more likely people are to hold added funds in reserve as a precaution.
3) The speculative motive. People or firms may wish to hold money currently received in the expectation that it will be able to purchase more goods later, or that, if invested later, it will bring a higher interest rate. Speculation based on expectations as to future price or interest changes constitutes a third motive for holding money, rather than investing it.

Keynes did not reject the initial quantity theory of money outright. Instead, he modified it to allow for the propensity to hold money as a result of any or all of these three motives. To take this into account, he revised Fisher's equation in two ways to arrive at a new model:

$$M = kPY$$

First, he substituted the money value of national income, Y, for T. Thus he focused on the demand for money required for the transactions of the entire economy. Second, he added what had become known as the "Cambridge k" to his model to symbolize the propensity of people to hold money for any or all the reasons specified above[2] k is the inverse of velocity of money. Unless offset by changes in the quantity of money available, changes in the public's money balances—the amounts of cash held by the public (primarily businesses)—could be a major independent cause of business fluctuations. If k remained constant, the crude theory of money would hold. The monetary authority could then directly influence prices by adjusting the money supply.

But, Keynes argued, velocity is not constant. It fluctuates because of the changing propensity to hold, rather than invest, money. A decrease in k, like an increase in the production and sale of goods, T, will lead to an overall fall in prices. But k and T operate differently. An increase in T reflects improved productivity. This leads to an increase in the output and sale of real goods, contributing to rising real incomes. An increase in k, in contrast, results in a decline in investment, reducing V, the velocity of money in circulation, hence reducing the real incomes produced by the economy.

On the basis of this analysis, Keynes recommended modifying the earlier mainstream approach of relying on indirect central bank measures to influence the money supply while leaving competitive market forces to determine output and money prices. He proposed government intervention to stimulate the private sector to augment investments in one or both of two ways. First, the government itself could invest, or it could contract to purchase goods from the private sector. This would introduce a positive multiplier effect to stimulate greater production and employment. This aspect of his theory is discussed more fully in connection with public finance in Part II.

Second, Keynes elaborated the earlier arguments advanced in the context of the quantity theory of money as to the possible impact of government efforts to manipulate the money supply through the central bank. If monetary authorities, by increasing the money supply, could raise prices and increase profits, entrepreneurs might, he suggested, make new investments to take advantage of these new opportunities.

Keynes explained that the initial drop in investment might reflect a general decline in marginal revenues below marginal costs because unions have forced wages above the workers' (assumed) marginal product. Unions, he pointed out, tended to resist money wage cuts, but were less vigilant in opposing reductions in real wages resulting from inflation. A general price rise, resulting from the increased money supply, might restore the desired equilibrium by raising prices and reducing real wages.

For decades, Keynes's followers justified government monetary policies designed to encourage banks to expand the money supply in periods of recession, thus stimulating private investment and restoring near-full employment. Some argued that governments could afford to introduce a little inflation while checking unemployment. In the 1950s, A.W. Phillip claimed to have discovered a stable inverse relationship between the level of unemployment and the rate of change in money wages. During the next decade, mainstream theoreticians and practitioners transformed what became known as the "Phillips Curve" into a relationship between the level of unemployment and price inflation (see Figure 3.3) which seemed to present policy-makers with a clear-cut choice: by introducing an element of inflation, they could automatically reduce employment.

Figure 3.3
The Phillips Curve

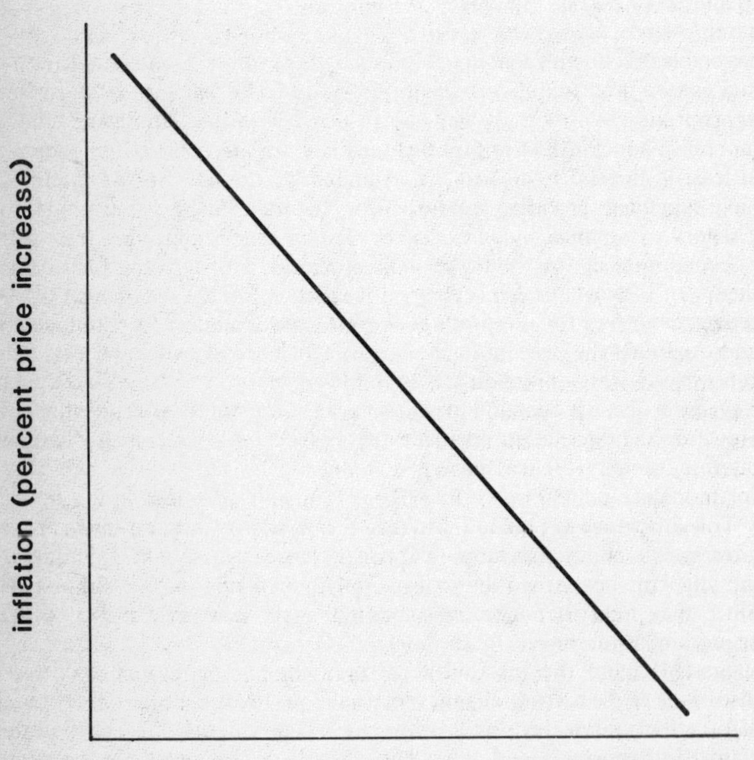

By the 1970s, however, governments of developed capitalist countries confronted an unanticipated dilemma. On the one hand, inflation appeared as a chronic feature in their economies, with prices typically rising at rates of 10 to 20 per cent annually. On the other, growing numbers of workers—10 per cent or more of the labour force, depending on the country—could not find jobs. The stable relationship on which the Phillips Curve had been assumed to rest no longer corresponded with reality.

Monetarism: The monetarists, led by Milton Friedman and the Chicago School in the United States, focused on the fact that Keynesian policies generated inflation, but failed to prevent growing unemployment. They reformulated the quantity theory of money to blend the older, pre-Keynesian version with some tenets of Keynesian doctrine.

Unlike earlier quantity theorists, the monetarists view money as more than a medium of exchange. They accept the idea that demand for money is sensitive to interest rates. Like the Keynesians, they reject the earlier quantity theorists' assumption of a constant velocity. Nevertheless, they postulate that velocity is a stable function of, among other things, nominal incomes and interest rates, and can be predicted. Thus velocity will not offset the effect on income of appropriate changes in money supply, and will not reduce the potency of monetary policy. Most important, they conclude that monetary policy can, at least in the short run and for policy purposes, affect real income. They have expanded the earlier quantity theory from a theory strictly of prices to a theory of nominal incomes.

Economists in the Keynesian tradition have also reformulated Keynes's theory of the demand for money. In particular, they have unified the three separate motives for the propensity to save into a single demand function, and expanded the concept of income to which money is related to a longer-run average which more closely approximates wealth. In essence, this neo-Keynesian demand function differs only slightly from that of the monetarists. However, the monetarists postulate a more stable demand function with lower interest elasticity. Hence they envisage a greater and more predictable impact for monetary policy.

This difference has led to significant disagreements concerning appropriate government policy measures. The monetarists deny that a Keynesian-type liquidity trap has caused the growing unemployment of the 1970s and 1980s. Since they hold that a stable and predictable demand for money exists, economic disturbances in the monetary sector do not come, as Keynes suggested, from the instability of the demand for money. Rather such disturbances stem from changes in the money supply itself. Governmental efforts to stimulate the economy by expanding the money supply, monetarists claim, lead business and labour to anticipate high inflation rates. Since businesses have come to expect that inflation, resulting from the increased money supply, will reduce their real incomes, they do not respond by expanding output and increasing employment. Instead, they simply raise their own prices. Workers, too, have become conscious of the implications of the money illusion. They no longer accept the reduction of real incomes caused by inflationary policies. Instead, they demand higher wages. In short, because of more sophisticated rational expectations, government measures to expand the money supply lead almost immediately not, as Keynesians predicted, to increased output and employment, but to further increases in wages and prices. Thus, instead of stimulating investment and alleviating unemployment, government measures to increase the money supply aggravate inflationary pressures.

Based on this refurbished version of the quantity theory of money, monetarists concluded that Keynesian prescriptions caused, rather than cured, the underlying difficulties plaguing capitalist economies in the 1970s and 1980s. They urge governments to impose effective limits on the expansion of the money supply to avoid inflationary pressures. They object to expanded government spending. Particularly when a government borrows from the banks, they assert, it aggravates inflationary pressures. Therefore, in inflationary periods, the central bank should raise the interest rate, while the government should curb its expenditures. Although this might initially increase unemployment, it will halt inflationary pressures. In the longer run, a healthier private sector will emerge, capable of making desired investments without government aid. (For discussion of the argument between Keynesians and monetarists on public debt, see Part II.)

Extension of the Debate to Third World Countries: Mainstream economists by no means always agree among themselves on the appropriate policies for dealing with the inherited banking system in the Third World. They disagree both as to the appropriate form of post-independence banking systems, and as to the kinds of monetary policies governments should seek to implement through them.

The mainstream debate concerning the appropriate form of post-independence banking system centres on the extent to which governments should take steps to influence bank lending policies, particularly towards African-owned businesses and peasant farmers. Some mainstream theorists hold that newly independent governments should set up their own central banks and leave the inherited private commercial banking system intact. They claim that small businesses and peasants usually lack viable projects or adequate security which might justify loans. African peasants, they add, seldom own title to their own land, so they cannot pledge it as security for loans.

Mainstream economists who reject these arguments while supporting retention of an essentially private commercial banking system recommend government legislation to end what they view as banks' discrimination against Africans. They often recommend that African governments pass laws requiring all banks to incorporate locally and hold fixed percentages of their assets in the country. Such laws might also require the banks to include local citizens among their shareholders and on the boards of directors of their local affiliates. The government should establish special lending agencies to assist small African business and peasants until they can stand on their own feet. Some even go so far as to argue that only government participation in ownership and on the boards of directors of local banks will ensure that they pursue lending policies favourable to the long-neglected African population.

Some mainstream theorists also criticize the indirect techniques used by central banks to regulate the money supply in predominantly capitalist developing economies. In periods of recession in developing countries, they claim, the indirect techniques prove even less effective than in the industrialized capitalist economies. Chronically high unemployment rates and poverty characterize most developing countries. Their commercial banks are frequently overliquid; that is, they usually cannot lend even as much money as the central bank would permit because private businesses cannot find adequately profitable projects in which to invest. Furthermore, recessions in developing economies usually reflect inability to export their raw materials because of world conditions. Central bank policies to stimulate borrowing cannot, by themselves, create the conditions necessary to induce private firms to invest. Such critics, while retaining an essentially mainstream framework for their analysis, often adopt Keynesian prescriptions, calling for increased direct government intervention to stimulate private investment.

Other mainstream economists may object to the central bank policies recommended by monetarists to overcome inflationary pressures. They maintain that inflation in developing countries frequently stems from causes outside the monetary system which bank policies cannot effectively counteract and may even aggravate. Structural blocks, like shortages of raw materials or skilled labour, may hinder increased production. Rising prices of imported goods, reflecting world-wide inflationary trends, will not respond to domestic interest rate increases. A high domestic interest rate may prevent small firms from borrowing to expand production and may even force them out of business. This may aggravate unemployment. At the same time, it may strengthen monopolistic firms, often affiliated to transnational corporations. These large firms may draw on internally generated funds or borrow from overseas parent firms to avoid paying the higher domestic interest rate. Their enhanced monopolistic position may enable them to boost prices still further to reap monopoly profits. Finally, governments may borrow to finance social welfare provisions for the population and infrastructure to stimulate private investment. Rising interest rates, rather than causing government to reduce its debt, may simply increase its cost to the taxpayers.

Some mainstream theorists urge more direct central bank controls, recommending for example that the central bank ration the foreign exchange which commercial banks may make available to their clients to purchase imports. Thus they sometimes seek to prevent the spending of scarce foreign currencies on luxuries for high-income groups, and favour preserving them to buy essential machinery, raw materials and consumer necessities. Others propose that the central bank issue directives requiring banks to lend money to certain kinds of firms or economic sectors.

More orthodox monetarists reject more direct government intervention as an unwarranted interference with the free play of market forces: governments, in their view, should confine their efforts to indirect methods of regulating the money supply and limit their own expenditures to prevent inflationary pressures. (Part II discusses this in more detail.)

The Banks and Finance Capital

Marxist economists view privately owned commercial banks as a crucial feature of the contradictory system built on the exploitation of workers and peasants at home and abroad. The historical evolution of banks has had two major consequences: first, in exchange for a share of surplus value in the form of interest, they helped private firms acquire the necessary funds to expand productive capacity; and, second, they merged with private industries to create the foundation of imperialist penetration of the Third World.

Interest as a Share of Surplus Value

By helping to finance capitalist production and exchange, the banks facilitate the increased socialization of the means of production, that is, the accumulation of capital in the form of increasingly complex machinery and equipment which employ growing masses of workers. At the same time, the extension of credit by the banks further obscures the developing class relationships to the means of production. The following formula illustrates the Marxist view of the role of banks in this process:

$$M - M - C_i - P \ldots C_n - (M+p) - (M+i)$$

The capitalist firm borrows money, M, from a bank to buy commodities, C_i, in the form of machinery, raw materials and labour to produce the finished goods, C_n. These incorporate surplus value produced by the workers (see Chapter 2). The firm then sells the new commodities for money, $(M+p)$, including the surplus value, which appears in the form of profit, p. The firm repays the bank the principal of the loan plus part of the surplus value, or profit, in the form of interest $(M+i)$. In other words, the bank shares with the capitalist borrowers the surplus value generated by the employment of labour. This division further tends to obscure the fact that the workers produced the total surplus value.[3]

Finance Capital and Imperialism

The emergence of banks also fostered imperialist penetration of Third World countries. Writing in the early 20th century, over 50 years after Marx first published *Capital*, Lenin asserted that as banks and financial institutions became interlocked with basic industrial firms, they formed finance capital, the financial foundation of imperialism. Imperialism, Lenin argued, did not occur simply as the result of the policies of misguided statesmen. Rather it emerged out of the fundamental contradictions of capitalism which led to the merger of banks and industries to form finance capital.

Lenin defined five essential features of the imperialist phase of capitalism. He emphasized, however, that no one should view his definition of imperialism as static. Rather, like the definition of all other phenomena, it would change as finance capital and imperialism developed and changed. The five critical features identified by Lenin as they emerged to affect development in Africa, include:

1) *Oligopolistic industries:* the development of basic iron and steel, chemicals, electrical and transport industries required vast capital investments as well as growing numbers of workers. This fostered the emergence of vertically integrated firms that controlled whole segments of industry, from the production of the raw materials to the final sale to consumers. These firms reflected the growth of increasingly large-scale factories, farms and mines, employing larger and larger numbers of workers, what Marxists call the "socialization of production". Over time, this ongoing process sharpened the underlying contradictory characteristics of capitalism (see Chapter 2) by concentrating the ownership of the increasingly socialized means of production in the hands of more closely knit private corporate units.
2) *The merger of banks with basic industries to create finance capital:* by the end of the 19th century, banks had become linked with large industrial firms through boards of directors and cross shareholdings to create finance capital. The banks provided the vast accumulations of capital required to finance industrial growth. In return, they obtained seats on the boards of directors of the industrial firms to supervise their businesses and ensure repayment of their loans.
3) *The influence of finance capital on the state:* Finance capital began in various ways to exert a major influence on the governments of the major industrial capitalist nations. Prominent members of the boards of directors of banks and industrial firms began to move back and forth between government and private corporate posts. As a result, the capitalist state typically implemented policies desired by finance capitalists' interests, particularly in questions of foreign policy. Workers and middle-class elements in the domestic economy generally know or care little about the way foreign policy issues affect them or the Third World peoples.
4) *Capitalist division of the world:* By the end of the early 20th century, finance capitalist states had divided the world among themselves, sharing out spheres of influence. The scramble for Africa culminating in the Berlin Conference, divided out the continent in a way which reflected the relative strengths of the competing national finance capitalist groupings, British, French, German and Portuguese.
5) *Redivision of the world:* Finance capitalist states could redivide the world by going to war, extending their political struggles over spheres of influence into open military conflict. Thus, on the African continent, World War I led to Germany's loss of Tanganyika, Namibia, the Cameroon and Togo, while strengthening the British position directly and through South Africa. Before World War I, when Lenin wrote "Imperialism, The Highest Stage of Capitalism", the United States had not yet become the dominant world power it is today. US finance capitalist groups came on to the world scene relatively late. They first

> penetrated Latin America and used indirect neocolonial means to squeeze out British and other rivals. During World War II, the US emerged as the dominant world creditor nation. The US government championed free trade an end to colonialism partly so as to enable US firms to break into markets like those of Africa which colonial governments had previously preserved for their own national companies.

Marxists maintain that Keynesian and monetarist monetary theories, by focusing on aggregate monetary and financial flows, obscure the underlying class relationships between the banks and the owners of the means of production. Hence they cannot adequately explain the role of banks in the growing crises of overproduction (see Chapter 2) and imperialism. Keynesian theorists essentially provided a rationale for capitalist state intervention in the era of finance capital in an effort to escape the impact of repeated and deepening economic crises. Both Keynesians and monetarists generally ignored the oligopolistic nature of finance capital. As a result, the state policies they espoused often strengthened it, as well as aggravating the inherent contradictions of capitalism which led to repeated crises and to imperialism.

Marxist Theory of Banks in the Third World

Marxists hold that in the colonial era foreign-controlled banks, closely linked to foreign-controlled industries and trading firms, provided a crucial channel for finance capitalist penetration into African and other Third World countries. Thus, banks and financial institutions, alongside basic industries and foreign and internal wholesale trade, emerged as one of the three "commanding heights" of every national economy.

Seeking to maximize profit rates, colonial banks and financial institutions helped to finance colonial firms' investments in profitable export enclave activity. This reinforced dualism and the externally dependent characteristics of typical Third World economies. The banks' lending patterns thus formed part and parcel of the historical process which continues to impoverish the majority of Africans.

After independence, the foreign-owned commercial banks continued to help transnational corporate affiliates to mobilize locally generated surplus value to finance the expansion of their control over the nation's productive resources. They advance credit to foreign companies and associated local firms to expand output of low-cost exports and import-substitution industries (using imported machinery and materials) to produce high-cost manufactured goods. Through their international financial networks, they may help their client firms to evade local taxes and exchange controls, and ship out significant shares of their profits.

The creation of a central bank to regulate privately owned commercial banks' influence over money supplies as recommended by mainstream theorists cannot overcome the unemployment and inflation characteristic of most Third World countries. These reflect the underlying contradictory consequences of imperialist penetration. The causes of unemployment lie embedded in the inherited institutional structures designed to coerce Africans into a low-cost labour force while encouraging investment in relatively capital-intensive technologies in the so-called "modern" sectors. Inflationary pressures typically reflect domestic structural blocks, including monopolistic domination, which thwart expanded production; unplanned government borrowing; and the rising prices of imports due to external factors over which African governments have no control.

A legal requirement that commercial bank affiliates permit a few wealthy African businessmen to buy shares or become members of their local boards of directors will not significantly alter the banks' role in the national economy. It might ensure that a few more Africans obtain loans, strengthening an emergent African capitalist class; but, as long as the banks seek primarily to maximize profits, their loans will go to much the same sectors as in the past, reinforcing the inherited externally dependent dualistic economy. Even government acquisition of shares or complete nationalization of the banking system cannot, by itself, significantly change this pattern. As long as the managers—whether African or foreign—follow the same banking principles as their predecessors, they will contribute little to restructuring the national economy.

Marxists conclude that the state, representing an alliance of workers, peasants and, where they exist, supportive nationalist capitalist elements, should nationalize and restructure the banks. The banks could help to implement financial plans to capture and redirect locally generated investable surpluses to finance appropriately formulated development plans. But Marxists do not pretend to have cut-and-dried formulas for this process. (This is examined more fully in Part IV.)

Summary

Most people think of banks primarily as safe repositories of savings. In reality, however, they play a far more important role. They profoundly influence the growth of the money supply and the pattern of accumulation and reinvestment of capital which shapes every nation's development.

Mainstream economists hold that private commercial banks create money by lending funds for profit—i.e., interest—to private investors to finance the necessary growth of the economy. They recommend that governments of capitalist countries co-operate with the banks to establish central banks which typically exercise indirect techniques to regulate the commercial banks' influence on the nation's money supply.

Mainstream theorists focus primarily on the way the banks influence the supply of and demand for money in relation to its price, the interest rate. They disagree, however, on the appropriate monetary policies which post-independence African governments should pursue. The stricter monetarists tend to argue that the central banks should rely primarily on indirect techniques to influence the supply of money. Others, claiming that indirect measures may aggravate the widespread problems of inflation and unemployment, recommend various forms of state intervention, up to and including government shareholdings in the banks.

In contrast to mainstream economists, Marxists view the private banking system as an integral feature of the exploitative capitalist system which aggravates the contradictions by accelerating the socialization of the means of production under the control of increasingly concentrated private ownership.

The co-operation of the banks and financial institutions with large industrial firms to form finance capital laid the foundations of imperial penetration of African and other Third World countries. Both before and after independence, the transnational commercial banks typically collaborated with transnational industrial corporations and emergent local capitalist interests—sometimes including African state capitalist governments—to mobilize and direct locally produced surplus value to finance their growing control over national productive resources.

Government efforts to utilize indirect central bank controls to regulate commercial banks cannot, Marxists assert, overcome the underlying causes of prevalent unemployment and inflation. Legal requirements that wealthy African businessmen buy shares in or become members of commercial banks' boards of directors serve to strengthen marginally an African segment of the domestic capitalist class; they do not fundamentally alter the banks' role in financing essentially externally dependent enclave patterns of growth. Marxists conclude that, to implement a planned transition to socialism, the state, representing an alliance of workers, peasants and perhaps nationalist capitalist elements, must take over and fundamentally restructure the banks.

Notes

1. Treasury notes are short-term loans to the government. See Chapter 10.

2. In the 1920s, Cambridge economists had already begun to view money not simply as a medium of exchange but in a broader context as a financial asset. They postulated that people desired to hold cash in some proportion, *k*, to their real income.

3. The relative amount of interest the bank receives as a share of profit depends initially on the relative strength of the banks versus the industrial capitalists. As more and more capital became necessary to finance large-scale industries and expanding trade, however, the largest banks merged with the largest industrial firms. (This is discussed in more detail in Chapter 5.) The rate of interest charged by the banks then becomes a matter of bookkeeping between the banks and the largest industrial capitalists.

Appendix: The Interest Rate and the Demand for Money

Mainstream theorists emphasize the role of interest, the price the banks charge for the use of money, in determining the relationship between the supply of money and the demand for it. In recent years they have elaborated a complex set of Figures (see Figures 3.1A to 3.9A) to illustrate this expected relationship. Because inflation has become such a persistent feature of capitalist economies in recent years, they now focus on the real as opposed to the nominal rate of interest, that is on the rate of interest the banks obtain minus the rate of inflation in the general price level.

Mainstream economists refer to the connection between the rate of interest and the demand for investment as the marginal efficiency of investment (MEI). This investment function is graphed in Figure 3.4.

Figure 3.4
The Investment Function

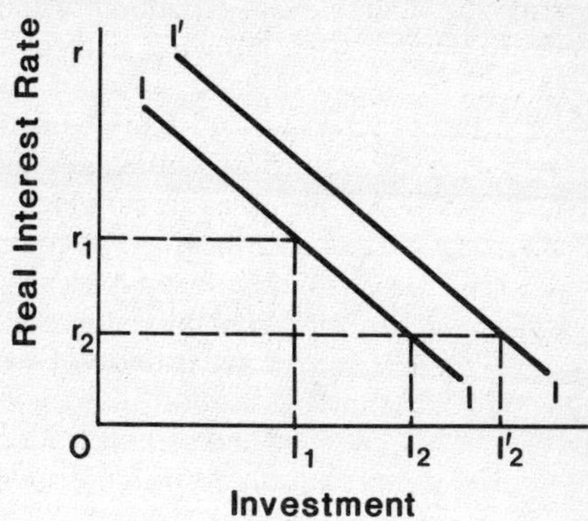

In this Figure, $I-I$ is net investment and r is the real rate of interest (that is, the stated or nominal rate minus the anticipated rate of price change). When the interest rate falls from r_1 to r_2, investment along $I-I$ will increase to I_2. If the price of capital goods falls relative to wages, or demand conditions improve, the investment schedule will shift to the right, to $I'-I'$, showing an increase in investment at each rate of interest.

Figure 3.5 shows the expected relationship between the interest rate and national income (equal to net national product), called the *IS* schedule. The *IS* curve is negatively sloped, representing the expectation that as the rate of interest declines, investment will increase. Then, in order to restore equilibrium between the supply of and demand for capital, savings must rise by an equivalent amount; that is, as income rises due to increased investment, people must save more. Conversely, a rise in the rate of interest will reduce investment, so national income will decline and people will save less.

The *IS* schedule, showing the connection between the interest rate and the equilibrium national income, derives from the relationship between the rate of interest and the amount of investment (MEI). The more the amount of investment changes as a result of a change in the rate of interest, the less steeply inclined will be the *IS* slope. This is shown in Figure 3.6.

Figure 3.5
The IS Schedule

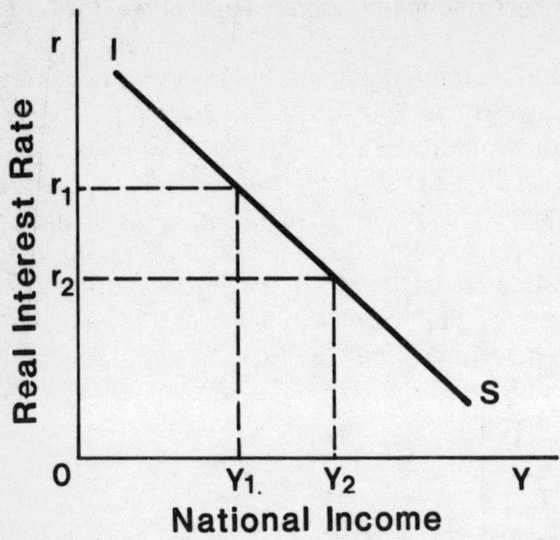

Figure 3.6
The Connection between the Interest Sensitivity of investment and the Slope of the IS Schedule

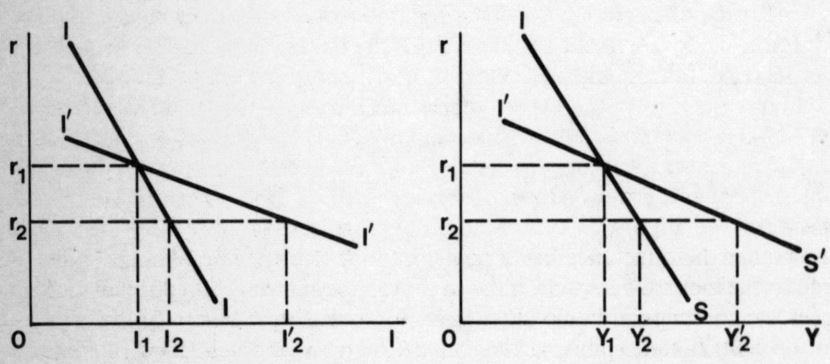

The decline in the rate of interest from r_1 to r_2 raises investment along $I-I$ by only a small amount, I_2-I_1. This means that savings need to rise by only a small amount in order to re-establish equilibrium. Therefore, national income needs to increase only a small amount to generate the needed savings, in this case by only Y_2-Y_1. On the other hand, along the less steeply inclined investment curve, $I'-I'$, investment increases by I'_2-I_2, meaning that income must rise by a larger amount, $Y'-Y'_1$, to generate the needed savings.

A shift of the investment schedule to the right, reflecting an overall increase in the demand for capital, will also shift the *IS* schedule. As Figure 3.7 shows the investment schedule has shifted from $I-I$ to $I'-I'$ by an amount, k, at each rate of interest. This means that savings must be increased by k at each rate of interest to restore equilibrium. For savings to increase, the national income must also increase as a result of the multiplier effect (m) of the increased investment. The larger the multiplier effect, the larger the effect of the change in investment, km, on the *IS* schedule. An inward shift of the investment schedule will, of course, shift the *IS* schedule inward by the multiplier, m.

Figure 3.7
The Impact of a change in the Investment Demand on the IS Schedule

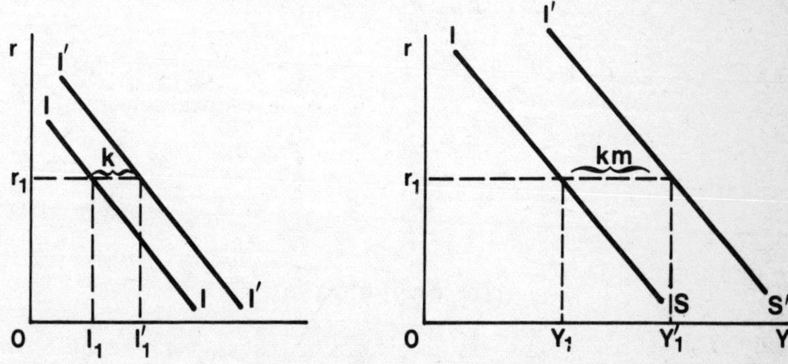

The higher the difference between the interest rate the commercial banks charge to their borrowers, and the bank or rediscount rate the central bank charges the commercial banks, the more the commercial banks will borrow from the central bank. This will reduce their excess reserves ratio, enabling them to lend more money and increase the money supply. The lower the difference between the commercial bank interest rate and the central bank rate, the more likely the commercial banks are to reduce their borrowing from the central bank, thus reducing the funds they can lend to the public and hence reducing the money supply.

Putting the supply of money and demand for money together, mainstream theorists formulate a monetary equilibrium schedule of points where the supply of money equals the demand for it. They call this the *LM* curve. Like the *IS* curve, the *LM* curve has national income on its horizontal axis and the rate of interest on its vertical axis. Unlike the *IS* curve, however, the rate of interest on the vertical axis is the nominal, not the real rate of interest, because most mainstream economists assume that monetary behaviour is influenced by the nominal rate, while the commodity market behaviour is affected by the real rate.

Figure 3.8
The Monetary Equilibrium or LM Curve

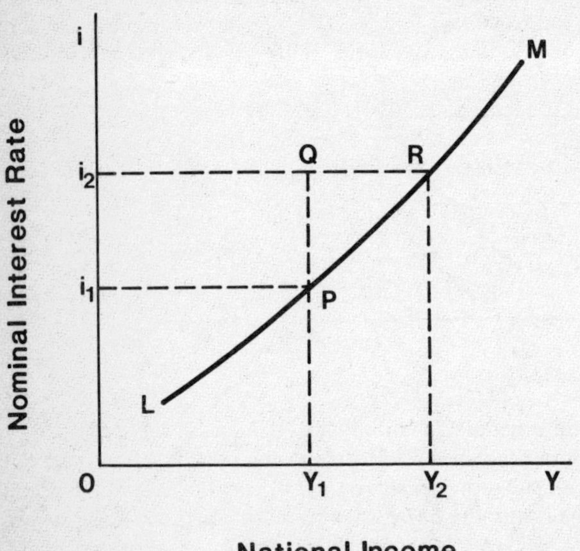

The *LM* curve has a positive slope, meaning that monetary equilibrium requires that a higher rate of interest be associated with a higher level of national income. In Figure 3.8, *P* represents the initial equilibrium point where money demand equals money supply. As a result of raising the interest rate i_1 to i_2, i.e. to point *Q*, a condition of disequilibrium emerges, in which money supply exceeds money demand has declined and money supply has increased; money supply exceeds money demand. To achieve equilibrium at i_2 money demand must increase; for this to occur, national income must grow by $Y_2 - Y_1$, achieving equilibrium at *R*. Conversely, a decline in the interest rate will increase money demand and reduce money supply, requiring a decline in national income to reduce money demand sufficiently to equal money supply.

Central bank efforts to expand the money supply, by open market operations, reducing the discount or bank rate or changing the cash or liquidity ratio, shift the *LM* curve to the right, to *L' M'*, as shown in Figure 3.9. At every possible rate of interest, i_1 or i_2 the new equilibrium point, *Q* or *R*, occurs where a greater money supply equals a greater money demand than previously.

Figure 3.9
Impact of Expanding the Money Supply on the LM Curve

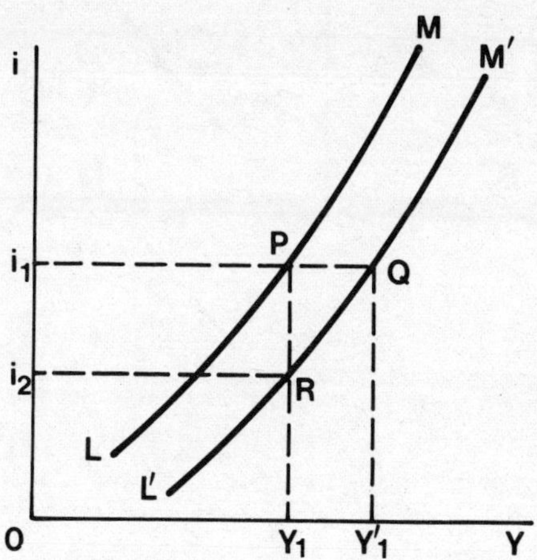

The demand schedule for money influences the *LM* schedule. The more sensitive the money demand schedule to changes of interest (the flatter the demand curve), the more sensitive the *LM* schedule is to changes in the rate of interest (the flatter the *LM* curve), as illustrated in Figure 3.10. In the left-hand diagram, $M^{D'} M^{D'}$ is more interest-sensitive, flatter, than $M^D M^D$; it changes more in response to a change in interest rate from i_1 to i_2 than does $M^D M^D$. In the right-hand diagram, *LM* derives from $M^D M^D$, and *L' M'* from $M^{D'} M^{D'}$. When the interest rate rises from i_1 to i_2, money demand along $M^{D'} M^{D'}$ declines more than along $M^D M^D$. As a result, the national income must increase more, from Y_1 to Y'_{2}', to achieve equilibrium in conjunction with the decline in money demand.

Neither the *IS* nor the *LM* schedule provides a unique equilibrium level of national income. Each provides a combination of equilibrium levels of national income and rates of interest in much the same way that demand and supply schedules for other commodities provide the combinations of quantities (demanded and supplied) at different prices. However, as noted above, the rate of interest used in deriving the *IS* schedule is the *real* rate, corrected for changes in the overall price level; whereas the rate of interest used in the *LM* schedule is the *nominal* rate, reflecting the initial assumption that

Figure 3.10
The Relationship Between Money Demand and LM

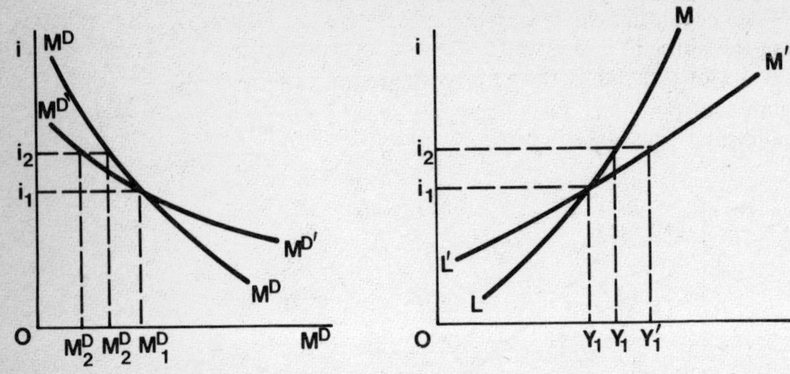

Figure 3.11
Determination of the Equilibrium Interest Rate and the Level of Net National Product when Anticipated Rate of Price Change M is Zero

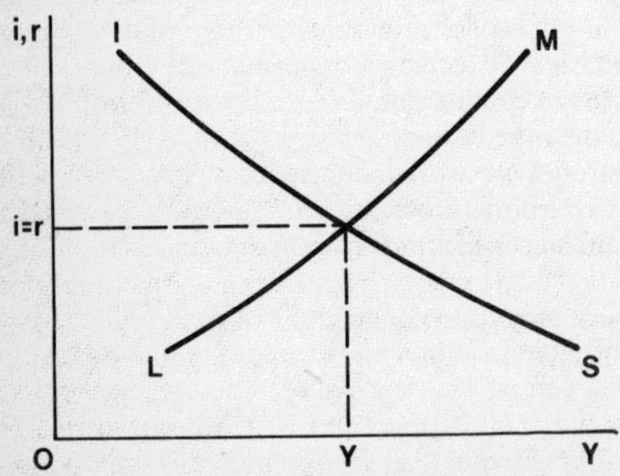

monetary behaviour responds to the nominal rate.

When people anticipate neither inflation nor deflation, the nominal and real interest rates remain the same. This results in a unique determination of the equilibrium level of the interest rate and the national income, as shown in Figure 3.11.

When people anticipate a price increase, the real interest rate, r^+ diverges from the nominal interest rate, i^+, as illustrated in Figure 3.12.

Figure 3.12
Equilibrium when inflation is anticipated ($e = e_1$)

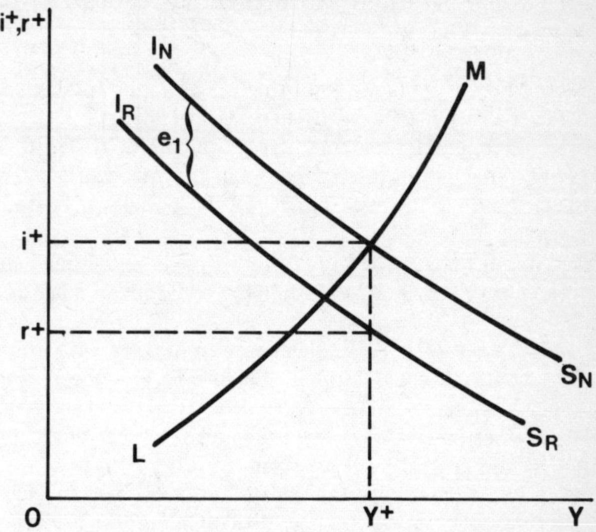

The expected rate of price change, e_1, raises the *IS* schedule from $I_R S_N$ to $I_N I_N$, expressed in terms of the nominal rate of interest. The equilibrium rate of national income is Y^+, and the equilibrium rate interest is i^+, however, is obtained by taking the equilibrium nominal rate and subtracting from it the anticipated rate of price change.

Building on this carefully constructed set of supply and demand schedules, mainstream theorists purport to explain the effects of monetary and fiscal policy on national income and, through national income, on the national product.

Exercises and Research

1. How do banks "create" money?
2. What is "near money"? How does it affect a nation's total money supply?
3. Explain how commercial banks may influence the pattern of investments in a national economy.
4. What role is a central bank supposed to play in a capitalist economy? How does it function to influence the money supply?
5. Explain the basic mainstream theory of how the rate of interest may affect the money supply in a given economy.
6. What are the nature and significance of the debate between Keynesians and monetarists? What are this debate's implications for the Third World?
7. How does the Marxist explanation of the role of banks and the banking system differ from that offered by neoclassical theory?
8. How did Lenin explain that finance capital affected Third World development? What is the role of banks in that process?
9. Examine the role of the central bank and the policies it has adopted in your country.
   a) What techniques has it used to try to influence the money supply? What effect have they had? Evaluate the consequences for development.
   b) What theory seems to guide the decision-makers who formulate monetary policy in your country? Be sure to give the reasons for your conclusion.
   c) What theory seems best to explain the consequences of the policies adopted by the central bank in your country? Why?

Recommended Reading

(For annotations, see bibliography at the end of the book.)

Abdi, *Commercial Banks and Economic Development*
Aromolaran, *West African Economics Today*
Ayida (ed.), *Reconstruction and Development in Nigeria*
Cline and associates, *World Inflation and the Developing Countries*
Curran, *Banking and the Global System*
Davis, *The Management Functions in International Banking*
DeKock, *A History of the South African Reserve Bank*
Eshag, *Fiscal and Monetary Policies and Problems*
Havrilesky and Boorman, *Current Perspectives in Banking*
Houghton, *The South African Economy*

IBRD, country studies
Kane, *Development Banking*
Kellett, *The Merchant Banking Arena*
Lenin, *Imperialism—The Highest Stage of Capitalism*
Leys, *Underdevelopment in Kenya*
Livy (ed.), *Management and People in Banking*
Llewellyn, *International Financial Integration*
Lombard (ed.), *Economic Policy in South Africa*
Marris and Somerset, *African Businessmen*
Newlyn and Rowan, *Money and Banking in British Colonial Africa*
Nkrumah, *Neo-colonialism, The Last Stage of Imperialism*
Onoh, *Strategic Approaches to Crucial Policies*
Ord and Livingstone, *An Introduction to West African Economics*
Report of a Working Party, *Who Controls Industry in Kenya*
Robinson (ed.), *Economic Development for Africa South of the Sahara*
Saylor, *The Economic System of Sierra Leone*
Seidman, *An Economics Textbook for Africa*
—— *Comparative Development Strategies in East Africa*
—— *Ghana's Development Experience, 1952-1966*
—— *Planning for Development in SubSaharan Africa*
Seidman and Makgetla, *Outposts of Monopoly Capital*
Teriba and Diejomaoh (eds), *Money, Finance and Nigerian Economic Development*
Terry, *The Desert Bankers*
Truu (ed.), *Public Policy and the South African Economy*

Periodicals

The Economist Intelligence Unit, *Quarterly Economic Reviews*
Moody's Banks and Financial Manual
Standard Charter Review
Who Owns What in Banking
Annual reports of individual commercial banks
Monthly, quarterly or annual reports of central banks of particular countries
Government statistical digests

Chapter 4: Banks in Africa: Three Case Studies

Why These Three?

To comprehend fully the role the banks play in an African economy, one must examine in detail their institutional structures. The range of theories purporting to explain the role of banks suggests the kind of information required. Gathering data on the institutional features of particular banking systems beyond the aggregated information typically published in central bank reports is, however something of a detective job. Few governments, especially in Third World countries, require and publish detailed data on the individual privately owned banks' operations. The banks themselves typically insist on confidentiality to protect their clients' interests.

Space here does not permit analysis of the full range of banking experience across Africa. This chapter will briefly outline the development of banking in three African countries: Zimbabwe, Nigeria and Tanzania. All three, as former British colonies, inherited similar banking systems. Indeed, as Table 4.1 shows, the same set of predominantly British commercial banks—Barclays, Standard and National Grindlays—dominated the financial systems of most British colonies before independence.

In Zimbabwe, during the 15 years of minority rule before independence, the foreign-owned commercial banks, together with the transnational corporations that owned a major share of the modern-sector assets, developed one of the most sophisticated financial systems in sub-Saharan Africa. Despite United Nations sanctions, they successfully helped to mobilize local savings and direct credit to facilitate investment to finance ten years of relatively high growth rates. A summary of the somewhat more detailed information available concerning the institutional structures of the banks of Zimbabwe, as well as the way they operated over the last two decades, provides useful insights into the role foreign commercial banks played in most African economies at independence.[1] In roughly the same period, Nigeria's independent government acquired shares in the commercial banks and imposed regulations to redirect credit and increase loans to African businesses. In Tanzania, the government nationalized the banks and financial institutions outright. Analysis of the changes made in these different circumstances suggests some of the problems and possibilities of the various options that African state capitalist governments may adopt.

Table 4.1
British Banks: Distribution of Branches in 1951

		Branches in the Eight Territories									
	Total branches	*Gold Coast (Ghana)*	*Nigeria*	*Kenya*	*Tanganyika (Tanzania)*	*Uganda*	*S. Rhodesia (Zimbabwe)*	*N. Rhodesia (Zambia)*	*Nyasaland (Malawi)*	*Total*	*Col (10) as percentage of col. (1)*
Bank	(1)	(2)	(3)	(4)	(5)	(6)	(7)	(8)	(9)	(10)	(11)
											%
Bank of British West Africa Ltd.[a]	41	14	18	..	..	..	..	..	..	32	78
Barclays Bank (D., C. & O.)	691	11	10	12	11	5	21	12	2	84	12
National Bank of India Ltd.[b]	46	..	..	9	4	8	..	..	..	21	46
Standard Bank of South Africa Ltd.[a]	540	..	..	10	10	5	26	12	6	69	13
Totals	*1,318*	*25*	*28*	*31*	*25*	*18*	*47*	*24*	*8*	*206*	*16*

[a] Standard Bank merged with the Bank of West Africa and moved its headquarters to London in the 1960s.
[b] National Bank of India later acquired the Ottoman Bank's assets and became National Grindlays Bank. Citycorp of the United States and Lloyd's Bank of Britain, respectively acquired 49 and 41% of the shares.

Source: *Bankers Almanac and Year Book 1951.*

The Zimbabwe Case

Historical Background

The particular historically shaped features of a country's political economy influence the structure and role of its bank and financial institutions. In the British colony of Southern Rhodesia (now Zimbabwe), a handful of settlers—about 3 per cent of the total population—usurped the reins of government before World War II. By the 1950s, some 6,000 settler farms occupied the best half of the entire national land area. Over the preceding decades of colonial rule, the minority had exercised state power to push some 700,000 African peasant families into overcrowded, infertile reserves called "Tribal Trust Lands". To earn cash, the men had little choice but to migrate to work for low wages in settler or transnational corporate farms, mines or factories.

In 1953, the settler colonial governments of Southern Rhodesia, Northern Rhodesia (now Zambia) and Nyasaland (now Malawi) formed the Federation of Rhodesia and Nyasaland, seeking a limited degree of independence from both Britain and South Africa. They anticipated that the resulting common market of over 15 million inhabitants, in a land area roughly three times the size of England, would attract foreign investment. They taxed the Northern Rhodesian mining companies to finance economic infrastructure, primarily in Southern Rhodesia. Workers migrated from impoverished Nyasaland to Southern Rhodesia, contributing to the surplus of labour that helped keep wages among the lowest in the world. To facilitate trade and the free movement of capital in accordance with mainstream prescriptions, the Federation established a central bank to expand and regulate the money supply.

The Federation proved attractive to transnational corporations. A number set up their sub-regional headquarters for their operations there in the capital, Salisbury (now Harare). The foreign-owned commercial banks expanded their activities to help finance the expanding transnational corporate investments.

The African populations of the three colonies, however, demanded an end to settler rule and the establishment of truly representative governments. In 1963, the Federation broke up. Zambia and Malawi declared independence from Britain and formed governments elected by their African populations.

The settler minority in Southern Rhodesia rejected the Africans' demands for participation in government. Instead, it made a unilateral declaration of independence (UDI) from Britain. It explicitly excluded African participation in government, and introduced laws enforcing an apartheid system much like that in South Africa.

The United Nations imposed sanctions to prohibit foreign companies or individuals from investing in or trading with the Rhodesians. South Africa and Portugal, which continued to rule neighbouring Mozambique until 1974, refused to enforce them. Throughout the 15-year UDI era, most transnational banks and financial institutions retained their links with their Rhodesian affiliates through their South African regional headquarters. Many transnational corporations, in violation of sanctions, shipped their Rhodesian exports and imports through Mozambique until the Mozambique liberation movement won independence. Then, with the assistance of the Rhodesian regime, the transnationals shifted their trade channels to South Africa.

The Rhodesian regime imposed strict exchange controls and import licensing to direct the foreign exchange earned through this illegal trade to finance the import of machinery and equipment for continued industrial growth. Locally generated surpluses[2] regularly reached 40 to 45 per cent of the growing GDP. The regime imposed legislation to thwart workers' efforts to organize. Real wages declined and the regime provided few social services for blacks. Taxes remained low. The government used the revenues primarily to finance economic infrastructure to meet the needs of transnational corporate and settler-owned industry and agriculture.

Throughout UDI, the financial structure, dominated by transnational affiliates operating through South Africa, played a major role in mobilizing locally generated investable surpluses to finance expanding investments. During

UDI the financial sector in Zimbabwe grew rapidly. The National Accounts show that the financial sector's annual contributions to GDP multiplied six times from 1963 to reach Z$109 million in 1978, growing twice as rapidly as the GDP itself. The profits of the private financial institutions multiplied twelve times over in the same period, increasing from 1.8 per cent to 6.9 per cent of the nation's gross operating profits. Probably more significant, however, the foreign banks became more closely interlinked, not only with each other but also with other financial institutions, on account of their collaboration in the face of UN sanctions to mobilize locally generated investable surpluses, primarily to finance the transnational corporate affiliates' expanding activities in the modern sector. Transnational corporations, together with local settler interests, continued to invest about 25 per cent of GDP until the mid-1970s when the mounting guerrilla war and the international recession hampered further growth. The Rhodesian regime claimed its GDP grew at 6 to 8 per cent a year until 1976. The manufacturing sector, pursuing an import-substitution strategy, essentially doubled its output. This industrial growth, mostly in Salisbury and Bulawayo, produced goods primarily for the tiny minority that controlled the government and the major means of production. Ten per cent of the capital invested financed residential housing in the burgeoning "whites-only" suburbs of the few major towns.

The investment of 25 per cent of GDP left another 15 per cent of locally generated surpluses unaccounted for. After 1975, investments declined. The net officially reported outflow of profits, interest and dividends in the five years from 1975 to 1979 totalled about US$325 million, mostly remitted to and through the transnational corporations' South African headquarters.

The Rhodesian government's exchange controls, operated through the commercial banks, prohibited transnationals from repatriating profits to countries that recognized UN sanctions. Widespread rumours suggested, however, that transnational affiliates shipped out additional investable surpluses through transfer pricing: mining and agricultural trading companies regularly sold their exports to affiliates abroad at below world prices. When their affiliates sold the produce outside the country at world prices, they reaped the difference in the form of added profits abroad. Importing firms, operating under conditions of secrecy so as to evade sanctions, often paid higher-than-world prices for imported goods to their foreign affiliates, thus shipping more unreported profits abroad.

During the 15 years of UDI, transnational corporations expanded their operations in Zimbabwe, acquiring about 70 per cent of the assets in the growing modern sector. In particular, the Anglo-American Group, the leading mining finance house in South Africa, worked closely with the commercial banks and financial institutions to expand its holdings (for its Zimbabwe holdings in 1980, see Table 4.2). It had moved its headquarters from Northern Rhodesia to Salisbury in the early days of the Federation. It reinvested part of the profits generated in the Zambian mines to buy up mines and other properties in Southern Rhodesia. During UDI, the Rhodesian regime helped Anglo-American to go on expanding its business. It permitted Anglo-American's Wankie (now Hwangwe) mine, for example, to charge prices for

Table 4.2
Partial List of Anglo-American Group's Holding in Zimbabwe 1978
(Shares held through RAL Nominees or other RAL affiliate or security nominees)

Company	*% of Shares*	*Sector of Economy*
African Distillers Ltd	4.2	Dominates wine & spirit manufacturing
Border Forests Ltd	46.7	Owns 11,391 ha of forests, gum plantations, 2 saw mills
Cairns Holdings Ltd	7.4	Holding & investment company, 39.7% of Amalgamated Motor Corp. & food companies
Clan Holding Ltd	6.7	Investment & holding
David Whitehead & Sons	3.5	Largest cotton & synthetic fibre spinner in Zimbabwe, 3 factories
Edgars Stores Ltd	3.4	Manufactures, wholesales & retails clothing nationwide
Everglo Holding	3.8	NA
Freeholds Corp.	7.2	NA
Gullivers Consolidated Ltd	6.4	One of largest civil engineering companies, in the country
Rhodesian Brick & Pottery Co.	14.8	Largest brickmaker, 2 factories
Rhodesian Cables Ltd	4.0	Manufacturers of copper, aluminium cables
Rhodesian Cement Ltd	4.3	50% of United Portland Cement, shares in other building materials companies
Rhodesian Printing & Publishing	4.6	
Rhodesian Pulp & Paper Ltd	0.9	Publishes Zimbabwe newspapers (Govt trust bought S.A. shares after independence)
Rhodesian Sugar Refineries	0.8	Owns nation's sugar refineries, sales network
Rhotread Holding Ltd	2.0	Owns 2 companies, for retreading tyres, & manufactures & retails auto parts
Rothmans of Pall Mall	4.7	Manufacturers of cigarettes, pipe tobacco
Salisbury Portland Cement Co. Ltd	1.1 1.1	owns cement factory, sells wholesale retail
T.A. Holdings Ltd	3.9	Began in tobacco, now conglomerate
Springmaster Corp. Ltd	1.3	Furniture

Company	*% of Shares*	*Sector of Economy*
Heinrich Breweries Ltd	1.9	Brewery
Radar Metals Industries Ltd	3.0	Manufactures metal nails, door frames, windows in 2 factories, wholesaler
Rho-Abextcom Investments Ltd	4.4	Industrial holding company; building materials, refrigeration, wire foundry, ceramics
Rhodesian Acceptance Ltd (RAL)	56.0	Holding company; owns RAL Merchant Bank, Sagit Group, 3% of a computer company
Rhodesian Banking Corp. Ltd (now Zimbabwean)	1.2	One of 4 commercial banks (after independence, govt bought 62% of shares)
Divide Chrome Mines Ltd	0.9	Chrome mines
Empress Nickel Co. Ltd	1.1	Empress nickel, copper mines
Falcon Mines Ltd	5.7	Owns 2 mines, 5,000 acres & 2 farms
M.T.D. (Managing) Ltd	3.7	Largest copper mine
Rhodesia Nickel Mine	86.3	Holding company; nickel mine & smelting and refining co.
Rio Tinto Zinc	1.6	Mining & industrial finance, holds 49% of Empress Nickel, other mines
Rio Trust Ltd	1.6	Investment holding company; shares in Tinto Industries, Empress Nickel & others
Shangani Mining Corp. Ltd	29.1	Shangani Nickel Mines
Wankie Colliery Co.	34	Owns one of largest coal mines in Africa

Source: Table prepared by Benson Zwizwai [University of Zimbabwe, unpublished paper, 198]

its coal that included a 12.5 per cent guaranteed profit. Under UDI conditions, Anglo-American reinvested parts of its locally generated profits and mobilized additional local investable surpluses through associated financial institutions to expand its holdings in agriculture and manufacturing as well as mining. It frequently acquired only a minority share in a company, but utilized financial leverage, its own managerial personnel, and access to technologies and markets to assert control over its entire operation.

The new Zimbabwe government inherited the financial structure that developed under these hothouse UDI conditions. In 1981, the first year after independence, estimates suggest that Zimbabwe's economy generated about

Z$1.7 billion—about 45 per cent of the Gross Domestic Product—in locally generated investable surpluses.

The Central Bank

In 1956, the Federation of Rhodesia and Nyasaland established a central bank to achieve greater control over local money supplies and increase the commercial banks' responsibility to the federated community. It issued a currency based on pounds and pence. When the Federation broke up in 1963, the new African-governed states, Zambia and Malawi, set up their own central banks and issued their own currencies, called kwacha. The Rhodesian settler regime, too, established its own central bank, the Reserve Bank, which issued its own pounds, later converted to Rhodesian dollars on a par with the South African rand.

The Reserve Bank operated as prescribed by mainstream theory. As banker to the government, it held government accounts; loaned funds, primarily in the form of treasury bills, to the government; and managed the public debt. The Reserve Bank also handled foreign-exchange reserves. After UDI, the reserves consisted of gold and foreign currencies, including some Swiss francs, but mostly South African rands. The Reserve Bank assisted the commercial banks with its foreign reserves after UDI when UN sanctions caused the banks' home countries to freeze their own reserves. The Reserve Bank relied heavily on commercial banks to administer the foreign-exchange controls imposed by the regime to conserve foreign exchange. The commercial banks provided foreign exchange to meet their clients' needs, mostly through their South African connections. The Rhodesian Reserve Bank operated in close co-operation with the South African Reserve Bank.

Throughout the UDI period, the Reserve Bank held the bank rate at a low 4.5 per cent. This spurred the rapid expansion of bank credit and investment, especially during the first ten prosperous years. Instead of adjusting the bank rate to influence the money supply, the Reserve Bank relied on buying and selling short-term paper, especially treasury bills, in the money market. It also set the minimum reserve balances which the commercial banks must hold.

The Commercial Banks

The Big Four: Four foreign-controlled commercial banks handled all of Zimbabwe's commercial banking business at independence. Three were closely interlinked with the South African-based Anglo-American Group. The fourth bank represented mainly British and some American interests.

Barclays and Standard, the oldest commercial banks in Zimbabwe, owned about two-thirds of the nation's commercial bank assets at independence. Affiliates of both were deeply entrenched in South Africa, holding between them about 60 per cent of South Africa's bank assets.

Standard, which first began operations in the South African diamond and gold business in the 19th century, operated branches in 59 countries, including nine in Africa, by the late 1970s. Its British parent had merged with the Charter Bank to become Standard Charter Bank. It had close ties with Chase Manhattan, the third largest bank in the United States. In Zimbabwe, it established a local board of directors during UDI, including a member of the Anglo-American Group, as well as other local businessmen. It established a number of subsidiaries, including Standard Merchant Bank, Standard Finance, Standard Trust, Standard Nominees and Rhodesian Insurance Brokers. It held a 12 per cent share in the Export Credit Insurance Association, as did each of the four commercial banks (see pp. 74). In 1980, at independence, Standard still held slightly over a third of all commercial bank assets in Zimbabwe.

During UDI, the Zimbabwean branch of Barclays Bank maintained ties through its South African affiliate, the British parent's largest branch anywhere outside England and the biggest bank in South Africa. The Anglo-American Group owned a major block of shares in the South African Barclays Bank. An Anglo-American Group director also sat on the local board of the Zimbabwe Barclays Bank. In Zimbabwe, Barclays had, by the mid-1970s, built up a network of some 40 branches, almost 40 fixed agencies, and 100 "stopping points" throughout the country. It had acquired a finance house, UDC. It owned the only bullion and chemical analysis equipment in the country for assaying the value of gold and minerals. At independence, Barclays held only slightly less than one-third of all commercial bank assets in Zimbabwe.

A South African bank, Nedbank, owned 62.2 per cent of the capital of Rhobank, the third largest bank in Zimbabwe. Rhobank grew rapidly during UDI, increasing its holdings from 11 to 16 per cent of all commercial bank assets in the country by 1980. Rhobank sold the remainder of its shares on the Zimbabwe Stock Exchange to "local" shareholders. These included RAL Nominees, an affiliate of the RAL merchant bank, a member of the Zimbabwe Anglo-American Group. The other local shareholders included Old Mutual Investment, associated with the Old Mutual Life Insurance Company, the South African insurance firm that conducted about half of Zimbabwe's insurance business; and several pension funds.

Under UDI, Rhobank extended its interests in several directions. It operated in the accepting and discount market through Syfrets Merchant Bank and Scottish Rhodesian Finance. It acquired four associated companies in insurance and financial business. It became involved in manufacturing through industrial holdings and financial ties.

The fourth and smallest commercial bank in Zimbabwe, National Grindlays, remained nominally British-owned. In fact, however, the US-owned Citicorp, by 1982 the largest bank in the world, had acquired a controlling 49 per cent in the 1960s. (Lloyds Bank of Britain owned 41 per cent.) National Grindlays had begun operations in East and Central Africa by taking over the Ottoman interests in 1953. By 1980, its branches reached into the Middle and Far East, East Africa and Zambia. Although it did not itself have branches in South Africa, its parent Citicorp owned branches and operated there through a representative office. In 1981, the chairman of Citibank (the US wing of Citicorp) joined the board of the Anglo-American Group's overseas investment arm, Minorca.[3] In Zimbabwe, National Grindlays primarily financed associated transnational corporate affiliates' activities.

Growth during UDI: During UDI, the commercial banks, through their South

African branch affiliates, provided a valuable financial conduit which facilitated the minority regime's efforts to evade UN sanctions. Their close ties with transnational corporate affiliates through their South African boards of directors reinforced those established on an international level and spilled over to provide financial links in Rhodesia. By shifting responsibility for implementation of foreign-exchange controls to the commercial banks, the Rhodesian Reserve Bank enabled them to help transnational corporate affiliates transfer investable surpluses out of the country despite the regime's prohibition. The fact that Barclays Bank owned the only facilities in the country for assaying the value of gold and mineral exports enhanced the possibility that mining companies might understate their value without official detection.

The commercial banks expanded rapidly during UDI. Even in the five years from 1975 to 1980, despite the intensification of the liberation war and the impact of international recession, their assets rose by almost two-thirds to Z$1 billion. They reaped high profits from their growing business. Because it sold shares on the Stock Exchange, Rhobank had to publish its profit data. This revealed that Rhobank's profits (excluding possible unpublished "hidden reserves" held by affiliated companies) multiplied seven times from 1968 to 1978.

Direction of Credit: The direction and amount of commercial bank loans influenced the pattern of national accumulation and reinvestment of capital. Table 4.3A reveals that, from 1965 to 1980, loans to private firms and individuals almost tripled. Loans to government multiplied far more rapidly, as the domestic public debt rose from less than 3 per cent to about one-third of total bank credit during UDI. This steadily increasing trend reflected the regime's growing military expenditure as the liberation struggle mounted, and its efforts to aid the private sector to escape the impact of the war and the international recession. After 1980 the independent government continued to expand its borrowing to finance its rapid expansion of social services, post-war reconstruction and continued defence expenditures (see Chapter 6).

Table 4.3B shows the concentration of commercial bank activities in the two major urban areas, reflecting and reinforcing the dualistic nature of the national economy. Throughout UDI and into the first post-independence years, the banks made over 90 per cent of their debit entries in Harare, the capital, and Bulawayo, the second largest city.

Table 4.3C shows that the commercial banks' loans to the private sector primarily financed minority-owned commercial agriculture, manufacturing and distribution. An increasing share, until 1980, went to financial institutions and real estate. The share going to commercial agriculture (represented by some 6,000 farmers) declined in the mid-70s. This reflected the impact of the war and UN sanctions on exports, and the fact that the government parastatal, the Agricultural Finance Corporation, increased loans to the commercial farmers to help tide them over the difficult period.

The mining sector borrowed relatively little from the commercial banks during UDI. This reflected, in part, the comparatively small share of their

Table 4.3
Pattern of Commercial Bank Activity in Zimbabwe

A. Commercial Bank Loans to Public and Private Sectors as % of Total

	1965	*1975*	*1980*	*1982(Nov)*
Private Enterprise	80.6	60.0	56.6	43.4
Public Sector	2.8	26.2	32.2	35.9
Private Persons	10.9	10.5	7.1	4.0
Non-residents	1.7	0.7	0.3	0.1
Unallocated and Timing Adjustments[a]	3.8	2.5	4.2	16.5
Grand total[b]	*100.0*	*100.0*	*100.0*	*100.0*
Z$ million	*98.2*	*338.9*	*388.4*	*824.2*

B. Regional Analysis of Current Account Debit Entries as % of Total

Towns	*1965*	*1975*	*1980*	*1981*
Bulawayo	14.7	17.1	12.9	14.8
Gweru	1.3	1.2	1.4	1.4
Harare	77.2	76.3	78.6	76.8
Mutare	1.8	1.3	1.3	1.4
Other	4.9	4.1	5.6	5.6
Total[b]	*100.0*	*100.0*	*100.0*	*100.0*
Z$ million	*5,721.0*	*20,471.6*	*30,493.6*	*30,493.6*

C. Commercial Bank Loans by Sector as % of Total Loans to Private Enterprise

Private Sector: Corporate & unincorporated Enterprise	*1965*	*1975*	*1980*	*1982 (Nov)*
Agricultural & Forestry	34.7	26.1	26.1	20.1
Mining & Quarrying	4.5	6.0	6.7	12.4
Manufacturing	20.8	23.3	30.7	30.5
Construction	1.3	4.0	1.5	0.7
Finance, Insurance and Real Estate	10.3	14.2	16.2	12.8
Distribution	19.8	18.2	12.8	13.8
Other	8.3	8.9	5.9	9.1
Total[b]	*100.0*	*100.0*	*100.0*	*100.0*
Z$ million	*77.2*	*203.8*	*219.8*	*357.6*

[a] Under the Bank Coding Scheme, individual banks and branches are allowed some latitude as to when their books are balanced. This category includes an adjustment which brings the total into line with the figure declared on the last day of the month.
[b] Not all totals add up to 100% because of rounding off to the nearest tenth of a percent.

Source: Central Statistical Office, *Monthly Digest of Statistics* (Harare, January 1983) pp. 61, 63.

finance which the mines require for working capital. Their major current expenditure is wages which constitute a relatively small percentage of total costs. Also, the mining companies provided much of their own finance. Those in the Anglo-American Group, for example, seldom brought outside investment funds into the company. They generally reinvested part of the profits obtained from one project to acquire control over the next. Their extensive links with the financial sector, however, ensured that when they needed additional funds they could easily obtain them.

The manufacturing sector, in contrast, needs a great deal of working capital to finance labour and materials. It consumed a growing share of bank credit in Zimbabwe unlike many other independent African countries where commerce received a far larger share. This reflected the unusual expansion of the manufacturing sector under UDI, as well as in the first post-independence year, and the transnational manufacturing affiliates' practice of using local funds to finance this expansion.

During UDI, almost a quarter of all commercial bank credit went to finance commerce. This is a somewhat lower share than in many African countries where the major role of private enterprise, apart from producing exports, is to import and distribute goods manufactured abroad. The drop in the percentage of the growing total of commercial bank credit to distribution after independence reflects primarily the sharp resurgence of demand for credit by the recovering manufacturing sector.

A considerable share of commercial bank credit financed the business of associated financial institutions. A portion of this credit also indirectly financed distribution. The commercial banks, for example, provided loans to discount and accepting houses to back their role in financing international trade.[4]

The banks provided relatively little credit to the construction business. The building societies mobilized most of the funds needed to finance the building of residential housing and commercial structures.

Financial Institutions Linked to Commercial Banks

The commercial banks, sometimes singly, sometimes in co-operation, established a number of associated financial institutions, including merchant banks, discount houses and the Export Credit Insurance Corporation. The Reserve Bank encouraged the creation of merchant banks and discount houses to foster the growth of the national money market. This enabled it to buy and sell short-term bills of exchange and treasury bills in an effort to regulate the national money supply. During UDI, merchant banks and discount houses facilitated the process of financing ongoing international trade despite UN sanctions.

Merchant Banks: The merchant banks took over the function of accepting houses in Zimbabwe (accepting or guaranteeing bills of exchange to ensure that they will be paid). In most African states, with relatively less complex financial structures, commercial banks themselves handle the acceptance and discounting of bills.

In 1956, early in the Federation era, the financial community established two merchant banks with British and South African assistance. The Philip Hill Acceptance Corporation of South Africa (a wholly-owned subsidiary of a London company) collaborated with N.M. Rothschild and British, Belgian and Italian banks to set up the Merchant Bank of Central Africa to channel funds generated in the Federation to finance international trade.

The Anglo-American Group, in co-operation with the British Lazard Brothers, established the second merchant bank, Rhodesian Acceptances Ltd., better known as RAL. The Anglo-American Group held 56 per cent of RAL through its subsidiary, Security Nominees. Standard Nominees of the Standard Bank and Rhobank affiliates both held a small percentage of the remaining shares. Pension funds and insurance companies provided the rest of the equity capital.

During UDI, the merchant banking business expanded rapidly. Syfrets Merchant Bank, in the Rhobank Group, began business in 1971. In the same year, Standard Bank set up its own merchant bank.

Merchant bank assets almost doubled during the last five years of UDI, from 1975 to 1980, reaching Z$434 million in the latter year. Despite UN sanctions, the merchant banks' international contacts enabled them to play an important role in the accepting business during UDI to finance foreign trade.

During UDI, the merchant banks also worked closely with the commercial banks and transnational corporate affiliates to mobilize domestic funds to finance the expansion of local industry. Their longer-term assets included loans and advances (about a third) and stocks and other private-sector holdings (the latter declined significantly after independence). The merchant banks acted as underwriters for securities sold on the Stock Exchange; that is, they guaranteed the sale of their corporate clients' stocks and bonds, and held the unsold stock themselves (see pp. 94-5 on the Stock Exchange).

All the commercial banks and several of the merchant banks set up trusts to manage funds entrusted to them by clients. Many of these resided in other countries and could not do business legally in Rhodesia because of UN sanctions.

Discount Houses: In 1959, during the Federation era, the commercial banking community helped expand the money market by establishing two discount houses. Discount houses discount trade bills for traders, once they have been accepted by acceptance houses. In Rhodesia, discount houses functioned as intermediaries between the Reserve Bank and the financial sector. They attracted deposits on a call basis, using the funds to purchase short-term securities. During UDI, they helped commercial banks and transnational corporate traders to "launder" bills, that is, to obscure the source of imports and the destination of exports so as to evade UN sanctions. When trade became depressed in the mid-1970s, they purchased increasing amounts of treasury bills.

A British firm, Gillett Brothers, initially co-operated with the Anglo-American Group to establish the British and Rhodesian Discount House (BARD) as a public company. Gillett retained 20 per cent of the equity and sold the rest. The Anglo-American Group acquired 30 per cent of BARD's equity. Anglo's merchant bank, RAL, initially managed it. BARD and RAL retained the same chairman and board of directors. Eventually, Gillett sold all its shares to insurance and investment companies operating in Zimbabwe. The Zimbabwe affiliates of Barclays, Standard, Grindlays and Rhobank all became shareholders, between them holding about a third of BARD's equity capital.

The four local commercial bank affiliates together also acquired about a third of the shares in the Discount Company of Rhodesia, also established in 1959. Insurance companies held a little over a third of the Discount Company's shares, and investment firms held the remainder.

Finance Houses: Each of the four commercial banks set up an associated finance house. TA Holdings, a holding company set up by wealthy local tobacco interests, joined the Merchant Bank of Central Africa to establish a fifth finance house. A group of Bulawayo businessmen set up a sixth. Only a few of the largest retailing firms in the country conducted their own hire-purchase business.

Finance houses mobilize local capital to finance local sales. They lend funds for retailers to advance to customers to purchase goods. The retailer uses the credit advanced by the finance house to finance the sale of goods to customers who lack ready cash. The customers then repay the loan over time with interest to the finance house. The interest, which tends to be high, constitutes the finance houses' profit. In Zimbabwe, this form of credit became significant in the 1970s. Early in the 1970s, despite UN sanctions, the finance houses helped local corporations to obtain machinery and credit from overseas firms by purchasing and leasing it to them at a price which included interest. The firms could thus obtain machinery without paying cash and the banks could ship the interest out of the country.

The commercial banks co-operated during UDI to establish an Export Credit Insurance Corporation. Under a 1965 Act, this provided insurance, including protection against political risk. The Export Credit Insurance Corporation interpreted the Act so as to protect companies against losses resulting from foreign governments' efforts to enforce UN sanctions by preventing the sale of Rhodesian exports or the transfer of payments back to Rhodesia.

The Post Office Savings Bank

As in most other former British colonies, the colonial government set up a Post Office Savings Bank in Southern Rhodesia. With post offices located throughout the nation, including areas where commercial banks did not establish branches, the Post Office Savings Bank provided a convenient method of collecting the small savings of many relatively low-income individuals. By the end of the 1970s, about 10,000 people had put savings in tax-free fixed accounts. These individuals generally had higher incomes and more savings than the average depositor. Although they constituted one out of six of all depositors, they held over a fourth of all Post Office Savings Bank deposits. Their fixed accounts averaged about Z$7,000. The remaining 46,000 depositors had much smaller accounts, averaging only Z$300.

Based on these deposits, the Post Office Savings Bank provided credit, primarily to the government and statutory bodies. It invested only about 5 per cent of its assets in short-term call money or in deposits. As a government bank, however, depositors could be confident that when they requested their savings in cash they would be able to obtain them.

Initial Post-independence Changes in the Banking Structure

Africanization: In the first years after independence, the new Zimbabwe government made relatively few changes in the banking structure. It focused primarily on Africanizing the central bank, reducing direct South African involvement in the commercial banks, and developing training schemes for African personnel.

The man seconded by the South African Reserve Bank to head the central bank under the previous regime remained for the first two years after independence. The government appointed as an African deputy governor a man who had for several years worked with the US Citibank in New York; in 1983, he became governor of the Reserve Bank.

Foreign Exchange Control: As one of its first post-independence measures, the Reserve Bank lifted the prohibition on remittance of profits by transnational corporations, permitting them to remit 50 per cent of current after-tax profit.[5]

The Reserve Bank initially left the inherited foreign-exchange control system intact. The commercial banks continued to make the day-to-day decisions concerning foreign exchange requests from their clients in the context of the regulations issued by the central bank. The Reserve Bank began to train a team of monitors to supervise the system more closely. (The issue of foreign exchange-controls will be discussed more fully in Chapter 14.)

Credit Control: The Reserve Bank took the steps usually advocated by mainstream theory to try to control the inflationary pressures that characterized the post-independence era. In 1979, it had raised the liquidity ratio of the commercial banks from 25 to 35 per cent. The banks remained overliquid, however, reflecting the fact that even in the brief post-independence boom they could not find enough borrowers with profitable projects to dispose of all their loanable funds. The Reserve Bank then raised the bank rate from the low 4.5 per cent that had prevailed throughout UDI. By the end of 1982, it had almost doubled the bank rate to 9.5 per cent. The commercial banks and other financial institutions raised their rates, simultaneously increasing the spread. This significantly pushed up the cost of borrowing funds throughout the economy. (Chapter 10 discusses the impact of these measures.)

Changes in the Realm of Commercial Banking: In the first post-independence years, three developments took place with respect to commercial banks. First, the new government contracted to buy the shares of the South African bank, Nedbank, in Rhobank, and changed the latter's name to Zimbank. It agreed to leave the bank's management unaltered for two years. Whether it planned to sell the rest of these shares to Zimbabwe nationals, or to acquire the remaining publicly held shares and operate the bank as a government bank remained unclear. In 1983, Zimbank Holdings, a Zimbank subsidiary (Nedbank still owned 49 per cent of it) sold its real estate holdings to a private firm in compliance with a pre-independence statute prohibiting banks from engaging in non-banking activities.

Second, the new government purchased 47 per cent of the shares of the Bank of Credit and Commerce of Zimbabwe (BCCZ), a newly created subsidiary of the Bank of Credit and Commerce, International (BCCI). With headquarters in London, BCCI owned branches in some 50 countries, including the Seychelles, Kenya, Zambia, Swaziland, Mauritius and Botswana. The directors of the Zimbabwe branch included four Pakistanis, one Indian and three Zimbabweans. Initially, BCCZ engaged mainly in trade bills and loans to government statutory bodies. It announced plans to extend credit to peasants and small African businesses in the neglected rural areas, but as long as it used the same lending criteria as the other commercial banks, this seemed unlikely.

Third, several transnational banks established representative offices in the country. Typically, such offices operate on a retail level through existing bank structures. They provide international contacts which enable local banks to help transnational corporate clients to borrow money abroad. For example, the US-based Citibank opened a representative office in 1982, although it also owned 49 per cent of the London parent of Grindlays, apparently wanting to broaden its contacts with other banks in Zimbabwe, possibly because it had cemented close relations with Anglo-American's overseas investment arm, Minorca. Two other foreign banks opened representative offices. One, the Bank of Boston, one of the 20 largest banks in the United States, had earlier established financial ties in South Africa. The second, the Banque Internationale pour l'Afrique Occidentale, had long been a leading French commercial bank operating in former French colonies. This trend appeared to reflect the transnational commercial banks' growing interest in extending loans to the more prosperous African states, as well as establishing Zimbabwe as a possible additional regional subcentre, outside their longer-standing South African base, to strengthen their position in independent Africa.

In sum, independent Zimbabwe inherited a relatively sophisticated banking system dominated by foreign banks with regional headquarters in South Africa. Under UDI, the banks had played a major role in mobilizing local funds to finance expanding transnational corporate affiliates as well as local businesses. In the process, they had become closely interlinked with each other, as well as increasingly intertwined with the South African mining finance house, Anglo-American. In the first years of independence, the Zimbabwe government left the inherited financial structure largely intact, though it acquired shares in the third largest bank and helped establish a fifth one. It focused primarily on Africanizing the existing structures. Other transnational banks opened representative offices, apparently viewing Zimbabwe as a potential base for expanding their role in independent southern African states.

The Nigerian Banking System[6]

With a much larger economy than Zimbabwe, Nigeria's state capitalist government adopted a similar approach to its banking system but has developed it further in a much longer post-independence period. During the first two decades after independence, African private and state participation significantly increased in the commercial banking sector. The federal and state governments also created development banks.

With a population estimated at over 80 million, Nigeria enjoyed a major economic boost as a result of the exploitation of its rich oil wells and rising world oil prices in the 1970s. GDP nearly doubled in the second half of that decade to reach about ₦30 billion (US$47 billion). In this prospering environment, the banking and financial structure evolved rapidly.

The Spread of Banking

Commercial banking in Nigeria began in the 19th century when the Bank of British West Africa, now the First Bank of Nigeria (linked with Standard Banks), opened its doors in 1894. The colonial government left the commercial banks to operate almost without regulation: instability and the failure of smaller banks characterized the system, especially in the 1950s.

In 1959, just prior to independence, the British established the Central Bank of Nigeria with the typical features recommended by mainstream theory. After independence, as the Nigerian economy expanded and the federal government created new states, the central bank established a network of branches, currency centres and clearing houses throughout the country.

The Commercial Banks: In the 1970s, after the civil war, as the Nigerian economy mushroomed under the impact of its newly developed oil wealth, the commercial banks expanded rapidly.

As Table 4.4. shows, total assets of commercial banks and the value of bank deposits rose significantly as a proportion of the rapidly increasing GDP. After 1978, bank credit rose from less than 67 per cent to over 80 per cent of the money supply, nearing the 90 per cent typical of advanced capitalist countries. The commercial banks still provided the bulk of available savings outlets in the Nigerian economy, but to a decreasing extent, indicating that other financial institutions had begun to play a more significant role. The use of cheques, however, remained relatively low, as indicated by the relationship of demand deposits to the money supply.

The increased use of bank facilities reflected the spread of banking as well as the impact of the oil boom. The number of banks increased from 14 to 20, while the number of banking officers almost tripled to reach 740. This reduced the number of inhabitants served by each bank office from 242,000 to 115,000. Nevertheless, these averages conceal an uneven distribution of banking offices among the states, reflecting the typically uneven development of the Nigerian economy. About a fifth of the nation's banking offices remained concentrated in Lagos state, although it comprised only 0.15 per cent of the national land area.

Table 4.4
Development of Commercial Banking in Nigeria: Selected Relative Indicators, 1970 and 1979 (in Percentages)

Indicator	*1970*	*1979*
Banking Ratio (BA/GNP)	22.29	39.14
Bank Deposits to GNP (TD/GNP)	12.11	24.37
Rate of Credit Creation (LA/M)	55.65	82.23
Credit Deposit Ratio (LA/TD)	56.14	65.99
Demand Deposit-Money Supply Ratio (DD/M)	45.77	58.14
National Savings Rate (S/M)	54.13	74.01
Saving Deposits to National Savings (SD/S)	98.51	89.81

BA/GNP = Commercial bank assets as percentage of Gross National Product
TD/GNP = Total deposits (including government demand deposits at commercial banks) as percentage of Gross National Product
LA/M = Loans and advances of banks as a percentage of money supply (including currency outside banks, all demand deposits, and domestic deposits with central bank)
LA/ID = Loans and advances of banks as a percentage of total deposits at banks
DD/M = Total demand deposits as percentage of money supply
S/M = Savings and time deposits as percentage of money supply
SD/S = Savings deposits as 4 per cent of national savings

Source: Calculated from Central Bank of Nigeria, *Economic and Financial Review*, December 1972 and December 1979; in Okafor, *Transnational Banks in the Nigerian Economy*

Nigerianization

Legal Restrictions on Foreign Banks: In 1970, after the civil war, the government imposed regulations to accelerate Nigerianization of the financial system along with the rest of the economy. In its efforts to increase national, though not necessarily state, control over the banks, the Nigerian government imposed legal restrictions on foreign banks. In 1968, it required all banks, including transnational corporate banks, to incorporate in the country. A decade later, in 1977, the Nigerian Enterprises Promotion Act stipulated minimum indigenous participation in different business categories, requiring that 60 per cent of the banks' shares be held by Nigerian interests.

By 1980, 20 commercial banks were operating in Nigeria. Private Nigerian interests, including several co-operative societies[7] and local state interests, owned eleven of them. The federal government, together with various transnational corporate banking and domestic private interests, owned the remaining nine, called "joint banks". Before the 1977 law, the transnational commercial banks controlled over half the joint banks' equity, as Table 4.5 indicates. After the 1977 law, the government acquired a controlling interest in the joint banks. The foreign partners did not reduce their equity; they created and sold additional shares to the Nigerian government and private shareholders.

Table 4.5
Top Three Joint Banks in Nigeria: Assets, Compared to All Commercial Banks in 1979 and Distribution of Ownership, Management and Directors, 1972, 1975, 1980.

Bank	Assets, 1979		Ownership (%)						Nigerian Participation in Management % of Managers, % of Directors			
			Federal Govt		Foreign		Private Nigerian					
	mil.	% of total	1975	1980	1975	1980	1975	1980	1972	1980	1972	1980
All Commercial Banks	11,238.6	100.0										
3 Major Joint Banks	4,383.4	39.01										
First Bank (Nig)	1,653.0	14.71	36.08	44.8	51.03[a]	17.2[a]	12.89	38.0	10.0	NA[d]	33.3	60.0
Union Bank (Nig)	1,445.2	12.86	40.00	51.67	51.67[b]	20.00[b]	8.33	28.35	16.7	87.1[d]	33.3	78.6
United Bank for Africa	1,285.2	11.44	37.09	48.89	51.8[c]	40.00[c]	11.11	11.11	12.5	63.2[d]	41.7	60.0
3 Major Indigenous Banks (Combined)	1,774.09	15.78										

[a] Standard Bank Ltd, London
[b] Barclays Bank International Ltd
[c] The foreign partner included (% ownership):

	1975	1980
Banque Nationale de Paris Internationale	6.60	5.20
Banque Nationale de Paris Ltd	32.50	25.50
Bankers of Trust Company	5.70	4.50
Banca Nazionale del Lavoro	3.10	2.40
Monte dei Poschi de Siena	3.10	2.40

[d] The chief executive was Nigerian in 1980.

Source: Extracted from Okafor, *Transnational Banks in the Nigerian Economy*, Tables 7, 18, 19.

A Quota Allocation Board, dealing with all companies, determined the number and calibre of expatriate personnel the banks could employ. In practice it limited them to top managerial and technical/professional positions. By 1980, Nigerians held all the top executive and 60 to 90 per cent of the top managerial posts in the three largest joint banks; and constituted 60 to 80 per cent of the members of their Nigerian boards of directors.

The Biggest Three: Despite the increase in the total number of banks to 20 by 1980, six—three joint and three indigenous—controlled over half the bank assets (see Table 4.5) and about three-quarters of the deposits and branches. Two joint banks, the First Bank and the Union Bank of Nigeria, in which Standard and Barclays, respectively, still retained about a fifth of the equity, continued to dominate the commercial banking scene in the country. Between them, they controlled over a third of all branches, a third of the deposits, and over a quarter of the assets of the 20 banks. Nigerian experts in the banking field maintained that this reflected the conviction of the biggest clients, mostly transnational corporate affiliates, that the joint banks, with their international banking connections, provided better services.

Central Bank Policies

Objectives: The Central Bank relied primarily on regulations to aid the government to achieve its short- and long-term goals. In the late 1970s, its stated short-term objectives centred on stimulating domestic output and employment, and stabilizing price levels; mobilizing domestic savings and correcting the balance of payments position; and mopping up excess liquidity to restrain commercial and merchant bank credit to the private sector. Though less easily identified, the longer-term goals apparently included increasing per capita incomes; Nigerianization of economic activity; diversification of the economy; more equitable distribution of income; and regionally balanced development. Further research is needed to determine the long- and short-term impact of the measures described below.

Interest Rates: The Central Bank made little effort to control the money supply through manipulation of the interest rate. It kept the rediscount rate relatively low, raising it only from 4.5 per cent in 1970-74 to 6 per cent in 1980. The treasury bill rate remained between 2.5 per cent in 1975 and 5 per cent in 1980. The Central Bank raised the savings deposit rates only slightly from 3 per cent in 1970-74 to 5 per cent in 1980; and 6 to 12-month time deposit rates from 3.5 to 6.25 per cent (over a 12-month time deposit rates were consistently 0.5 per cent higher). The increased volume of deposits during the period thus appeared to result more from the expansion of discretionary incomes than changes in the interest rates.

The Central Bank set minimum and maximum interest rates for bank loans. The minimum rose only slightly from 7 to 7.5 per cent over the decade, while the maximum fell from 12 to 9 per cent in 1975, and rose again to 11.5 per cent in 1980. The rapid expansion of credit by over a third during the boom peak of 1976-77 apparently reflected increased demand rather than interest rate changes, as in Zimbabwe. The joint banks tended to restrict their credit expansion significantly more than did the banking system as a whole.

Cash and Liquidity Ratios: The Central Bank relied primarily on aggregate credit ceilings and cash and liquid assets reserve ratios to control the money supply. It kept the liquidity ratio at 25 per cent, but varied the basket of qualified liquid assets. Between 1972 and 1974, for instance, it permitted the banks to include government stock of within three years of maturity. In 1977, it excluded stabilization securities,[8] advance deposits for letters of credit, and cash holdings.

The Central Bank manipulated the cash reserve ratio relatively frequently. In the mid-1970s, when the banking system suffered excess liquidity, the Central Bank deliberately set high cash ratios, and then progressively lowered them to offset the adverse effects of the credit squeeze. It applied different ratios to different categories of banks. These ranged from 12.5 per cent for the larger banks to 5 per cent for smaller banks in 1976; and dropped to 5 per cent for the larger and 2 per cent for the smaller ones in 1980.

Credit Ceilings: Unlike the Zimbabwe Reserve Bank, the Nigerian Central Bank set quantitative and qualitative guidelines for credit expansion. It fixed quantitative credit ceilings, expressed as a maximum annual percentage increase in the level of credit. In the early 1970s, it set the ceilings as low as 8.4 per cent; in the mid-1970s, it set no ceiling at all; and in the late 1970s, it reintroduced ceilings of 30 to 40 per cent. In 1979-80, the Central Bank applied a two-tier ceiling, lower for larger banks (30 per cent); higher for smaller banks (40 per cent).

Direction of Credit: Prior to 1977, the Central Bank tried to stimulate a wider geographical spread of banking by tying approval of new urban branches to a definite commitment by applicants to open new rural branches. In 1977, after this strategy failed, the Central Bank required that each joint bank should, by 1983, open a specified number of rural branches.

The Central Bank also sought to control the sectoral distribution of credit which, in Nigeria as elsewhere in Africa, had traditionally flowed primarily to trade. Before the Central Bank introduced sectoral allocations, the banks advanced two-thirds of all loans to finance general commerce. The Central Bank first specified permissible percentage increases in credit to various sectors, setting a minimum for such preferred sectors as industry at 45 per cent; and a maximum of 10 per cent for less preferred sectors like commerce. During the 1970s, the required minimum for productive sectors rose to 56 per cent, while that for the less preferred general commerce went up to 32 per cent in 1975 and fell again to 17 per cent by 1980. By and large, at least up to 1980, especially when co-operative bank data are included, the joint banks—even after government acquisition of control in 1977—responded less favourably than the banking system as whole to these directions. From 1979, the Central Bank required commercial banks which did not attain the credit targets for housing and agriculture to deposit with it funds equal to the shortfall; it neither paid interest for these deposits nor counted them among the banks' liquid assets.

The Central Bank took concrete steps to remedy the widespread complaint that commercial banks discriminated against Nigerian borrowers. It introduced regulations requiring the banks to allocate a gradually increasing percentage of total credit, rising from 35 to 70 per cent by 1980, to Nigerian businesses (defined as businesses in which Nigerians held 51 per cent or more of the equity). In 1979, the Central Bank required the commercial banks to reserve 10 per cent of the 70 per cent of total credit set aside for Nigerian business for wholly Nigerian-owned small enterprises with an annual turnover of less than ₦500,000. In 1980, the Central Bank raised this proportion to 16 per cent, although the total share of credit allocated to indigenous business remained at 70 per cent.

Under the Nigerian Exchange Control Act, as in Zimbabwe, the commercial bank branches acted as agents handling foreign payments by all firms, including repatriation of profits, dividends, interest and capital. This represented an important source of income for the banks.

Regulation of Bank Profit

The Nigerian government regulated the banks' use of their profits. They were subject to the general exchange control restrictions on profit remittances. The Banking Act, in addition, restricted the banks' payment of dividends to their shareholders until all preproduction and other preliminary capitalized expenses were written off and until adequate provisions had been made for bad and doubtful debts. The Central Bank also required each bank to transfer to a reserve fund 25 per cent of its net annual profits, or 12.5 per cent where the reserve exceeded the bank's paid-up capital.

The government's income policy, starting in 1976-77, imposed maximum limits on bank dividend payments, initially to 30 per cent of profits, rising, by 1980, to 60 per cent of after-tax profit or 25 per cent of paid-up capital, whichever was higher.

Other Banking Institutions

Nigerian law limited commercial bank activities in the non-banking financial field. The Banking Act prohibited any commercial bank from engaging in wholesale or retail business; owning subsidiary companies which did not carry on banking business; engaging in real-estate business; or granting any single person any form of credit exceeding one-third of the bank's paid-up capital and reserves. The banks, over the years, nevertheless expanded their activities, acting as agents for distribution of new securities and serving as registrar for public companies. Further research might reveal other kinds of links—for example through boards of directors—between the commercial banks and other financial institutions.

Six merchant banks operated in Nigeria in 1981, primarily in the financial centres of Lagos, Kaduna and Port Harcourt. These provided the usual services of merchant banks elsewhere: wholesale "customer made" banking; medium-term financing, including loan syndication; new issue business, underwriting and marketing new securities issues; investment promotion services; and equipment leasing. More research is required as to possible relationships between these merchant banks and transnational commercial banking interests, as well as the developing Nigerian commercial banking community.

The federal government owned a majority of shares in the four national development banks in Nigeria in 1981. Each tended to specialize in a particular sector, the Nigerian Industrial Development Bank provided financing and supportive services to manufacturing, mining and tourism. Its initial capital of ₦9 million in 1965 had multiplied many times over to reach ₦273 million in 1980. The Nigerian Bank for Commerce and Industry, established in 1973, financed enterprises in virtually every sector of the economy, and carried out wholesale banking for its clients. The Nigerian Agriculture and Co-operative Bank extended loans to agricultural and agro-allied activities, either directly or through on-lending institutions like state agricultural development corporations or co-operative societies. The Federal Mortgage Bank provided long-term credit facilities for owner-occupied residential buildings and commercial estates.

Individual states or groups of state governments had established development finance banks to finance and provide promotional services to deserving enterprises. These tended to serve enterprises in a broader range of economic sectors than the development banks, but confined their operation to the regions or states which sponsored them.

In short, Nigerian state authorities sought to Africanize the commercial banks and use the full range of regulations recommended by the more liberal mainstream theorists to foster their contribution to national development. The national and local governments intervened directly in development banks. More research is needed, however, to assess the full consequences of these measures.

Nationalization in Tanzania[9]

Historical Background

Tanzania's colonial history bequeathed it a relatively underdeveloped economy. The British took over Tanganyika from the Germans after World War I and incorporated it into the East African Common Market dominated by the Kenyan European settlers. They turned over the Tanganyikan sisal and coffee estates, which provided the main exports, to a new set of expatriate owners, and encouraged the peasants to grow more coffee and a little cotton.

After World War II, technological advances enabled the developed countries to produce synthetic substitutes for sisal, undermining the profitability of Tanganyika's main export. Shortly before independence, a World Bank study recommended that Tanganyika expand coffee, cotton and other agricultural exports; it warned that Tanganyika could hardly hope to compete with Kenya's more developed settler-orientated industrial sector.

Tanganyika's inherited banking sector reflected the country's underdeveloped state. The colonial government left the overall regulation of the regional money supply to the East African Currency Board. As Table 4.6 indicates, the three biggest banks, Barclays, National and Grindlays, and Standard Bank, which operated in Tanganyika through from the Common Market headquarters in Kenya, controlled the regional banking business. They focused primarily on financing export-import trade and estate agriculture. They held the major share of their reserves and paid-up capital in their home offices in the United Kingdom.

Table 4.6
Banks Operating in East Africa

Name	*Nationality*	*Number of offices in East Africa*
Barclays, DCO	British	119
National & Grindlays	British	70
Standard Bank	British	65
Bank of India	Indian	5
Ottoman Bank	Turkish	8
Bank of Baroda	Indian	10
Commercial Bank of Africa	Tanzanian	3
Nederl Handel Maatschappij	Dutch	4
Habib Bank (Overseas)	Pakistani	1
Uganda Credit & Savings Bank	Ugandan	10
Co-operative Bank of Tanganyika	Tanzanian	5
Jetha Lila — Bankers	Indian (private)	1
National Bank of Pakistan	Pakistan	1

In 1963 Kenya had approximately 161 bank offices, Tanzania 76 and Uganda 65. These were mainly located in trading centres. Bank deposits approximately doubled between 1950 and 1963.

After independence, the Tanzanian government[10] initially pursued the World Bank team's advice. It encouraged peasants to multiply their production of export crops, diversifying to grow tobacco and tea as well as coffee and cotton. It planned for increased foreign investment. It left the inherited banking system intact. It only established a central bank, the Bank of Tanzania, in 1966. From 1963 to 1968, despite the government's efforts to create an attractive investment climate, the net inflow of non-monetary sector capital totalled only 131.4 million shillings, about a third of the outflow of income payments abroad. At the same time, deteriorating terms of trade curbed the country's foreign-exchange earnings despite the increased resources devoted to expanding agricultural exports.

Nationalization of the Banks

In 1967, following the Arusha Declaration announcing that it aimed to embark on a socialist path, the Tanzanian government nationalized the commercial banks. Simultaneously, it increased its control of export-import trade, and took 51 per cent of the shares of the largest manufacturing firms and agricultural estates. The authorities expected the new national banking system to make a serious and determined effort to mobilize domestic savings from both rural and urban areas by expanding banking facilities and offering attractive rates of return on financial savings. The government also purchased 51 per cent of the shares in the larger firms operating in the truncated industrial sector and acquired the major importing houses.

The Role of the Bank of Tanzania: The Bank of Tanzania, the government-controlled central bank set up only seven months prior to the nationalization of the entire banking system, continued to function primarily as banker to the government and bank of last resort, along lines advocated by mainstream theory. It could impose reserve requirements on banks by type of deposit; regulate deposit rates of banks and specified financial institutions; rediscount advances against commercial paper and government securities; employ open market operations; and exert direct control over credit. It also handled the nation's foreign-exchange reserves.

The bank sought to promote conditions in which the supplies of credit and foreign exchange matched planned demand, ensuring adequate allocation of credit by sector. Official pronouncements indicated that its managers considered their primary responsibility to be the maintenance of monetary stability.

During its first four years the Bank of Tanzania provided only a small amount of credit to the government, actually reducing this as a share of government's annual revenues from 12 to 5 per cent. Its share of government's development expenditures dropped from about a fifth in 1966 to less than 2 per cent in 1970. The bank enjoyed a large inflow of foreign exchange as Tanzania enjoyed a temporary improvement in its terms of trade and received additional development assistance funds.

In the 1970s, however, Tanzania's efforts to restructure its economy encountered worsening terms of trade and drought. In the mid-1970s, the Ugandan dictator, Idi Amin, invaded the country, engaging it in a protracted, expensive war. The government began to borrow increasingly heavily from the central bank. By 1975-76, it was borrowing an equivalent of 44 per cent of its ordinary revenues. This seriously aggravated inflationary pressures.

Throughout this period, the central bank retained relatively low interest rates, ranging from 4.27 per cent for 35-day treasury notes in 1975-79 to 7.5 per cent for 90 to 180-day non-agricultural loans in 1979. In the mid-1970s, it resisted rates which would have increased government's debt servicing burden. Nevertheless, it failed to introduce significant shifts towards more direct socialist controls to enforce effective financial planning. This reflected, in part, the failure of the government to introduce and implement long-term plans to restructure the national economy.

Restructuring the Commercial Banking System: Following nationalization, the transnational corporate commercial banks immediately withdrew 52 bank managers and senior executives from Tanzanian banks. They demanded extremely high compensation, about 15 times the amount finally settled through arbitration, and blocked their branch balances in England, although these far exceeded their net head-office investments in Tanzania.

The new banking system drew on local manpower and recruits from friendly countries, mainly Denmark and the Netherlands. A three-member management committee under the Ministry of Finance met almost daily to reorganize it so as to implement the government's proposed new financial strategy. They combined the assets of all the commercial banks to create the National Bank of Commerce (NBC) under a board of directors appointed by the Minister of Finance.

The NBC closed down the least efficient branches in the urban centres and set up new branches and agency units to reach out more widely into the rural areas. Table 4.7 illustrates the gradual spread of branches into more remote regions.

Table 4.7
National Bank of Commerce Branch Expansion Programme in Tanzania 1970-79

Table as of 30 June	*1970*	*1971*	*1972*	*1973*	*1974*	*1975*	*1976*	*1977*	*1978*	*1979*
Cities and towns:										
Large branches	31	31	33	33	34	35	39	40	40	40
Agencies	83	90	99	111	137	129	152	150	84	85
Small/Medium towns:										
Large branches	4	5	6	14	23	28	32	35	38	41
Agencies	6	13	22	37	80	85	135	139	85	82
Minor rural settlements:										
Large branches	-	-	-	4	8	12	16	18	21	23
Agencies	-	-	-	1	3	22	30	33	37	43
Total Branches	*35*	*36*	*39*	*51*	*65*	*75*	*87*	*93*	*99*	*104*
Total Agencies	*89*	*103*	*121*	*149*	*220*	*236*	*317*	*319*	*204*	*210*

Source: *NBC Annual Report and Accounts* for the years 1970 to 1979.

A debate ensued as to appropriate criteria for the new bank's loans. Its board of directors resolved that:

> A national banking system would be carried on, not with a view to make huge profits, but as an essential service to the people at large which service would, while being completely self-supporting and offering reasonable surplus on the turnover, be run with the idea of service first and surplus next.[11]

The bank established three principles for loans, related to a) the purpose; b) the creditworthiness of the borrower; and c) the security provided to ensure repayment. Bank officials apparently interpreted these on a rather *ad hoc* basis, however, since the government failed to formulate an overall national financial plan. The bank's managing director observed,

> Parastatals did not find it easy to borrow from the NBC merely because they and we are both publicly owned. The nationalisation of banks is no licence for the reckless granting of credit to any particular sector of the economy, be it to Ujamaa Villages, private traders or parastatal organisation.[12]

In the mid-1970s, the bank began to provide assistance to help priority government projects to become viable.

The NBC did successfully mobilize domestic savings and expand credit. From 1968 to 1979, the banking system's total deposits, 90 per cent from non-government sectors, increased nearly ninefold. Loans and advances to the productive sectors multiplied just over sixfold, primarily in the form of relatively short-term credits. The bank's purchases of government securities, on the other hand, multiplied over 60 times totalling almost a fifth of its loans.

The bank sought to shift the inherited pattern of credit allocation by providing preferential treatment to certain sectors of the economy. It charged concessionary rates of interest (0.5 to 1.5 per cent below normal rates) to multipurpose co-operatives and Ujamaa villages; marketing co-operatives; District Development Corporations; and firms manufacturing goods for export. It charged higher than normal rates for personal consumption (1 to 2.5 per cent above normal) and to foreign-controlled companies. It also limited foreign firms' borrowing to a maximum of 50 per cent of paid-up capital, compared to 75 per cent for local firms.

During the 1970s, as the public, parastatal and co-operative sectors expanded, the bank's credit to the private sector declined from over half to a fifth of the total. From 1970 to 1975, its loans to mining and manufacturing increased sevenfold from less than a fifth to more than a quarter of its total expanding credit allocations. Most of this went to the final rather than intermediate manufacturing industries. Hardly any went to capital goods production, reflecting the government's failure to formulate and implement a long-term industrial strategy. In agriculture, most of the bank's credit financed the estate sector, now largely state-owned. A relatively small share (less than 5 per cent) went to the Ujamaa villages, partly because they had access to funds from the Rural Development Bank.

Apparently, however, the NBC could not exercise overall control over credit allocations, as socialist banks typically do. Parastatal organizations and other pre-1967 agencies continued to extend credit outside its jurisdiction. Other specialized banks, too, operated outside and sometimes in competition with it. This hindered the bank from exercising the monitoring role which most socialist bankers consider critical. As one authority observed,[13]

> Nationalisation of the banks, insurance business and other means of production as the first step in implementing the government's declared policy of socialism, has not, however, led to a redefinition of the functions of the financial institutions which were taken into the government sector in the pre-1967 "gradualist" period. No attempt has been made to formally integrate the monetary institutions or to ensure that their policies and practices are harmoniously co-ordinated. There is still a great deal of autonomy within individual institutions and so far no systematic overhaul of their policies and practices has been carried out.

He added, particularly in relation to the role of the banks as possible monitoring institutions,

> Given the lack of central control over the various types of public or socialist organisations—parastatals, co-operatives, workers organisations, ujamaa villages, and local councils—most of which suffer from acute skilled manpower problems, the (commercial) bank has argued strongly in favour of abolishing the more obvious forms of inter-enterprise lending where these are clearly designed to avoid bank scrutiny, and also for a tight control over the ploughing back of profits.

Specialized Banks

The government established specialized banks to handle long-term investment loans and rural credit.

The Tanzania Investment Bank (TIB): Established in 1970, the Tanzania Investment Bank aimed to provide long- medium-term finance for economic development of manufacturing industries and large-scale corporate agriculture. External sources provided almost two-thirds of the TIB's funds. The government itself provided about a fifth, and most of the remainder the bank obtained from domestic loans.

During 1970 to 1980, the TIB loaned only about 45 per cent of its 3,459 million shillings in assets on a long-term basis. About two-thirds of these loans went to manufacturing, about 10 per cent to engineering, and the remainder to miscellaneous activities. Surprisingly, the TIB retained over half its assets in liquid form, three-quarters of these as treasury bills. In other words, under the impact of the drought, international recession and the war with Uganda, the government apparently drew heavily on the TIB as an additional source of current finance. This hindered the bank from playing its intended role of expanding productive activity.

The Tanzania Rural Development Bank (TRDB): In 1971, the government established the Tanzania Rural Development Bank to provide a more dynamic credit mechanism for promoting rural development by making medium- and long-term loans, providing technical assistance, and facilitating the purchase of agricultural inputs.

The TRDB focused on "technically and economically viable" projects, rather than demanding collateral for loans. To ensure repayment it required potential borrowers to provide a history of technical success in the use of inputs to improve yields. It provided about half of its loans for agricultural production, over half to small farmers through Ujamaa villages. It also funded district development corporations, regional transport companies, national institutions and crop authorities. As of 1975, it loaned about two-thirds of its credit on a short-term basis. As more peasants formed Ujamaa villages in the latter 1970s, their share of TRDB credit reached 55 per cent of its 1979 total of about 200 million shillings.

The TRDB loaned about two-thirds of its funds in the five regions which produced most of the nation's export crops. Over two-thirds went to finance inputs for tobacco production. This reflected, in part, the fact that much of its funds came from the World Bank which initially required that they be devoted to export crops so as to ensure repayment.

Summary

Most former British colonies in Africa, at independence, inherited the same set of predominantly British-owned commercial banks. The experiences of two countries, Zimbabwe and Nigeria, illustrate the consequences of policies typifying those advocated by variants of mainstream theory. Tanzania's nationalization of the banks without planned restructuring of the national economy achieved little more success.

During UDI in Zimbabwe, despite United Nations sanctions, the foreign-owned banks worked closely with the transnational corporations and locally owned settler businesses. The banks and financial institutions contributed significantly to the mobilization of locally generated investable surpluses to finance a relatively high rate of growth in the narrow modern sector, primarily to meet the needs of the high-income minority. The simultaneous impoverishment of the African population, however, spurred many to join the liberation struggle which ultimately led to independence. After independence, the new government did little to alter the basic structure of the banks, severing only the most obvious direct links with South Africa's banks.

Over the 20 years after independence, the Nigerian government introduced several measures to modify its inherited banking system. It strengthened the Central Bank's role in the exercise of direct as well as indirect techniques proposed by some mainstream theorists. It first required the transnational parent commercial banks to incorporate their Nigerian affiliates locally, and then to sell shares to them as well as the few wealthy Nigerians who could afford them. The prosperity enjoyed by the Nigerian economy in the 1970s should, however, be attributed to its new-found oil wealth rather than to its success in achieving a fundamentally altered pattern of investment directed to more balanced integrated development. By the early 1980s, as the world market for oil deterioriated, Nigeria, like its less prosperous neighbours, confronted serious financial difficulties.

After 1967, Tanzania nationalized its banking system in the context of its declared aim of building socialism. The partially restructured banking system successfully mobilized significant amounts of locally generated savings and expanded credit. The government failed, however, to formulate and implement long-term plans to restructure and increasingly socialize the national economy. Without clear guidelines, the specialized banks and parastatals occasionally even pursued conflicting policies. The nationalized banking system alone could do relatively little to create a more balanced, integrated economy. As the economy deteriorated in the latter 1970s, the government's heavy borrowing from the central bank to finance current account deficits inevitably aggravated inflationary pressures. By the early 1980s, Tanzania, too, confronted a serious economic crisis.

Notes

1. This section summarizes the evidence gathered by Zimbabwe students shortly after Zimbabwe achieved independence. Each student collected information about a bank or financial institution along the lines suggested for research projects at the end of the next chapter. Hopefuly, presenting their findings here will encourage others to conduct similar research on the banks and financial institutions of their own countries.

2. Here defined as gross operating profits. This includes depreciation funds which are also available for investment, either to replace old machinery, equipment, etc., or to finance new projects.

3. Based in the Bahamas, Minorca apparently used much of the profits the Anglo-American Group managed to ship out of Zimbabwe and Zambia to become the second largest investor in the United States in the early 1980s (see Inness, *Anglo-American Group*).

4. In Zimbabwe, these function as separate merchant banks.

5. The new measure enabled the companies to invest previously blocked funds in six-year government bonds with low rates of interest which could be remitted; after six years they could also remit the principal.

6. Data relating to the Nigerian financial system are from Okafor, *Transnational Banks in the Nigerian Economy*. (Enugu: Faculty of Business Administration, University of Nigeria, unpublished paper, mimeo. 1982.)

7. Co-operative banks operated according to the same principles as non-cooperative banks.

8. Non-negotiable securities, with 4 per cent interest issued by the Central Bank to mop up liquidity and control credit expansion.

9. Much of the material for this section is drawn from Chimombe "The Role of Banks and Financial Institutions".

10. Its name change reflected Tanganyika's post-independence merger with Zanzibar, an island off the coast whose economy was geared primarily to the production of cloves.

11. Nsekela, "The 1971/72 NBC Credit Policy". *The Standard*, 22 June 1971.

12. Ibid.

13. Loxley, in Cliffe and Saul, *Socialism in Tanzania*, Vol. 2, p. 108.

Exercises and Research

1. Which theory described in Chapter 3 offers the best guide to explaining the development and role of the banks in the three countries discussed? Identify as many specific features of the banking systems and the way they function in each country as you can to support your answer.
2. Study the banking system in your country to determine how it works and evaluate its consequences for the pattern of accumulation and reinvestment of capital in the economy.
   a) Examine the laws setting up the commercial and other private banks in your country to determine the scope of their activities as permitted by government.

b) Do the commercial banks tend to provide more long- or short-term credit? To what sectors do they lend? What geographical areas receive most of their loans? Do they suffer ''excess liquidity''? Can you explain the reasons for the particular pattern of loans.
c) Identify the individual banks operating in your country, and find out how they work: i) Are they locally incorporated? Who owns the shares? Who sits on the boards of other companies or financial institutions? Do they hold positions in government? ii) Do the banks hold other kinds of assets? What proportion of their total holdings does each asset constitute?
d) What is the banks' role in handling foreign-exchange controls? How effective are they?

Recommended Reading

(For annotations, see bibliography at the end of the book)

Aromolaran, *West African Economics Today*
Ayida (ed.), *Reconstruction and Development in Nigeria*
IBRD country studies
Newlyn and Rowan, *Money and Banking in British Colonial Africa*
Ord and Livingstone, *An Introduction to West African Economics*
Report of a Working Party, *Who Controls Industry in Kenya*
Teriba and Diejomaoh, (eds), *Money, Finance and Nigerian Economic Development*

Periodicals

Moody's Banks and Financial Manual
Standard Charter Review
Who Owns Whom in Banking
Central Bank Annual reports of commercial banks
Government Registrar's reports on commercial banks

Chapter 5: Other Financial Institutions

The Need for Long-Term Investment

Modern enterprise requires investment of long-term capital to finance the purchase of buildings and increasingly complex and expensive machinery and equipment. Commercial banks and the financial institutions directly associated with them, with the exception of merchant banks, generally provide loans primarily to cover the costs of the production and distribution cycle; to hire labour, buy spare parts, equipment and materials, and store and transport goods to the final consumers. In the typical capitalist economy, several other financial institutions have emerged, usually closely associated with the commercial banks, to facilitate the mobilization of locally generated savings for longer-term investments. These include stock exchanges, and insurance, pension and building funds.

The relatively sophisticated financial structures of Nigeria and Zimbabwe include most of these kinds of institutions. In both countries stock exchanges enable wealthy inhabitants to buy stock in local companies, including locally incorporated affiliates of foreign firms. By 1980 a large number of privately owned insurance companies—over 70 in Nigeria and over 60 in Zimbabwe—offered insurance policies to cover a wide range of risks, from fire and theft to life insurance. The less developed Tanzanian economy, in contrast, inherited only a few of these financial institutions, which it gradually nationalized after independence.

This chapter briefly summarizes the alternative theoretical explanations as to the role of these other financial institutions in mobilizing local savings for investment. Relatively little detailed information has been published about these kinds of financial institutions in African countries. The Zimbabwe evidence[1] is summarized here to suggest the kinds of data researchers may look for in their own countries to assess the role of these institutions, as well as the theories to explain them. This chapter also describes aspects of Nigeria's other financial institutions and outlines Tanzania's approach to incorporating these kinds of institutions into its public sector.

Mainstream versus Marxist Perspectives

Mainstream theorists generally view the emergence of a stock exchange, a market for long-term investment capital, as an indication of a relatively high level of economic development. The corporate form came into being in the capitalist world in the 19th century. Every capitalist state passed laws to permit many individuals to combine their savings into one corporation under a central management by purchasing shares of ownership. The corporate form provided the individual shareholders with limited liability: if, for any reason, a corporation went bankrupt, the individual shareholder was legally required to pay its creditors only the amount he or she had invested in its shares. Since individuals could sell, as well as buy, shares of corporations, wealthy people could safely afford to invest their savings and withdraw them at need. This enabled corporate managers to amass the large amounts of capital needed to finance increasingly costly technological advances, especially in basic industries like steel, chemicals and transport. At the same time, corporate boards of directors and managers could exercise effective centralized control over the growing corporate units.

Mainstream theorists hold that the presence of a stock exchange in a nation facilitates the accumulation and reinvestment of local savings to finance corporate growth. The stock exchange, or stock market, functions as a capital market in which people may buy and sell capital stock or bonds like any other commodity. Competition between buyers and sellers on the stock market determines the relative prices the purchasers must pay for specific securities.

Over the years, mainstream economists have concluded that for a stock market to remain effectively competitive companies must provide full information about the securities they wish to sell on the stock exchange. In the Great Depression, many investors, especially when speculative companies in which they had invested failed, lost all their savings. Governments in developed capitalist countries like the United States, therefore, require corporations to publish a great deal of information to protect potential investors from being misguided by false corporate advertising. United States laws requires "full and fair" disclosure of facts concerning the nature and history of each corporation's business; the capital structure; a description of all registered securities; the salaries and security holdings of all officers and directors; details of underwriting arrangements; the estimated proceeds of securities sales and the proposed uses; detailed financial information including a summary of earnings, certified balance sheets, and supporting information. The Securities and Exchange Commission, appointed to enforce the US Act, comprises an extensive bureaucracy with hundreds of employees stationed in branches throughout the nation to verify the corporations' submissions of the required information.

Mainstream theorists view other financial institutions, like insurance, pension and building funds, as serving more than their stated functions: insurance of risk; pension benefits for the sick and elderly and their families; mortgage financing for housing. They also provide channels for mobilizing local savings to invest in corporations, thus helping to finance large-scale modern industrial growth. Some have even argued that pension funds, by channelling workers' savings into shares of ownership in giant companies, have introduced a type of "pension fund socialism".

Marxist theorists generally consider these financial institutions as features of the capitalist process of accumulating and reinvesting surplus value expropriated from the working class to expand private capitalist ownership of the means of production. Other institutionalist theorists, as well as Marxists, criticize the way the corporate form and the purchase and sale of shares on the stock market permit corporate boards of directors and managers, owning only a minority of shares, to control vast corporate empires. Most shareholders remain too distant and divided from the business to participate effectively in company decision-making. Furthermore, one company can effectively exercise control over several others by controlling a minority of the shares, along with their managements and their boards of directors. The emergence of interlinked groups of companies increases the oligopolistic characteristics typical of capitalist economies. The growth of privately held insurance companies, pension funds and building societies provides an added means by which closely knit finance capitalist groups can capture the savings of middle-income individuals and even workers to expand their control over whole sectors of the national economy. Bound together by interlocking directorships and shareholdings, these financial institutions contribute to the monopolistic features of finance capital identified by Lenin.

The Stock Exchange

Among all the independent sub-Saharan African countries, only Zimbabwe Nigeria and Kenya possess stock exchanges. These provide local markets for buying and selling shares in locally registered private companies.

The longer history of the Zimbabwe Stock Exchange reflects both the pre-independence emergence of a wealthy settler minority and its close ties with the much larger South African economy. The Zimbabwe Exchange first opened in Bulawayo in 1946 with a duplicate floor in Salisbury (now Harare) in 1951. From the outset, it associated itself with the Johannesburg Stock Exchange, helping to mobilize savings generated in then Southern Rhodesia for South African firms. During the period of the Unilateral Declaration of Independence (UDI), UN sanctions hindered the entry of new funds into the country, and exchange controls limited the outflow of locally generated capital. The Stock Exchange became predominantly a venue for new issues. Locally incorporated transnational affiliates sold new shares on the Exchange to obtain local savings.

Transnational corporate subsidiaries in Zimbabwe, as elsewhere in the Third World, often prefer to utilize locally generated savings instead of bringing in new capital from outside. In addition to borrowing funds from the local banking system, they arrange with local stockbroking firms to sell shares and bonds on the local stock exchange. This enables them to utilize local savings instead of investing their own capital from abroad. Although all corporations operating in Zimbabwe must register (at independence in 1980, 4,974 companies had registered), only 60 or so, mostly large transnational corporate affiliates, had put their shares up for sale on the Stock Exchange.

Under the Zimbabwe law setting up the Stock Exchange, a committee comprising two members appointed by the Minister of Finance and five to seven elected by Exchange members, operates the Exchange. The Exchange committee determines which stock issues may be sold on the Exchange, publishes necessary information about securities listed, and decides who may be members of the Exchange. Stockbrokers, acting under requirements set by the committee, act as agents to buy and sell securities on behalf of their clients. As elsewhere in Africa, the Zimbabwean Companies Act, though 213 pages long, requires very little information from the companies.[2]

In reality, only a few wealthy individuals can afford to buy and sell securities on the Exchange. In 1979 in Zimbabwe, out of a population of almost eight million, only about 4,500 individuals had incomes over Z$18,000, enough to accumulate sufficient savings to buy stock. The primary buyers and sellers of shares on the Zimbabwe Exchange were not individuals, but institutions like insurance companies, pension funds, building societies and the unit trusts of the commercial banks.

By the time Zimbabwe attained independence in 1980, only three of the ten listed stockbrokers remained active; one of these went out of business two years later. To continue in business, the Stock Exchange proposed a more active role for merchant banks and discount houses in the stockbroking field.

The Nigerian Stock Exchange, with its main trading floor in Lagos and subsidiary floors in Kaduna and Port Harcourt, only grew significantly as a capital market during the oil boom of the 1970s. Until 1972, federal government bonds had dominated trade. After that, industrial securities (equity shares and bonds) rose in importance in terms both of market capitalization and the frequency and value of transactions. By 1980, some 154 securities were quoted on the Stock Exchange, including 53 government stocks, 89 equity securities, and 12 industrial bonds and preference shares. The quoted companies included six financial institutions, 49 manufacturing firms, 25 commercial firms, and nine service firms.

Nigerian investors apparently bought securities to hold rather than to trade. This limited the intensity and frequency of their dealings on the Exchange. Nevertheless, the value of total transactions expanded rapidly from ₦11.8 million in 1976 to ₦189.8 million in 1978. With the Nigerian Enterprises Promotion Acts of 1972 and 1977, and the government's efforts to promote Nigerian participation in foreign-owned businesses, increasing numbers of foreign firms used the Stock Exchange to draw on locally accumulated investable surpluses by selling shares to nationals.

Insurance Companies

Private insurance companies play an important role in accumulating and reinvesting capital in Zimbabwe, as in most other capitalist countries. Holders of insurance policies must pay insurance companies fixed monthly amounts, called premiums. These provide a pool of funds out of which the insurance companies pay the policy holders for their claims in the event of loss due to the various insured risks, including accidents, fire and death. Until such time as they must pay the claims of the policy holders, the insurance firms typically invest these funds to obtain added profits. Since insurance company contracts with their policy holders constitute long-term obligations which may be fairly accurately forecast, insurance companies in Zimbabwe, as elsewhere, generally invest their accumulated funds in the capital market.

At independence, the Zimbabwe law setting the conditions under which local and foreign insurance companies could operate required foreign companies to register and permitted local companies to incorporate. Foreign companies controlled over 90 per cent of the 62 direct insurers operating in the country. A third of these were South African, another third were British, and the rest included Italian, US, Swiss and New Zealand firms. Sixteen of the 17 insurance brokers—companies that sold insurance for insurance firms—were locally registered. Barclays Bank was the other. All eight reinsurance firms were registered in South Africa.

Zimbabwean insurance companies annually paid claims to cover insured losses of policy holders equal to only a third or less of the premiums the policy holders paid in. This left the insurance companies with large amounts of locally generated savings. By 1980, insurance firms had accumulated assets totalling almost Z$700 million from their premium income, in addition to the profits from their investments.

The government, through the Treasury, had reached a gentlemen's agreement with the insurance companies on the minimum amount of funds they had to invest in government securities. After independence, the government raised this minimum from 35 to 50 per cent of the insurance firms' assets. Zimbabwe government securities provided tax-free interest which the insurance companies could remit to their foreign parent companies. The insurance companies also invested in long-term loans, including mortgages, and bought shares in private companies. Insurance firms with the closest ties to transnationals provided the latter with a source of domestic funds.

Although the presence of many insurance companies gave the appearance of competition in Zimbabwe, in reality the business had become highly concentrated. At independence, the top ten companies, all foreign-owned, held 85 per cent of the assets of all insurance businesses in the country. One, Old Mutual of South Africa, handled almost half the total. Through their boards of directors, furthermore, the top ten insurance firms were extensively linked with the nation's major transnational corporations and banking interests. Old Mutual interlocked with the Nedbank group, as well as with three Anglo-American Group affiliates. The others among the top ten likewise shared directorships with major industrial and financial interests, three of them with the Anglo-American Group. Thus the top ten foreign firms exercised an important influence over the pattern of investment of hundreds of millions of dollarsworth of domestically generated investable surplus. Interlocking directorships tended to put these funds at the disposal of major transnational corporate affiliates.

In Zimbabwe, as elsewhere in Africa and the Third World, foreign-owned insurance companies could ship domestically generated savings out of the country in several ways. First, they could remit their after-tax profits to their parent companies. Local law permitted insurance companies which invested in government securities to remit the full interest repayments tax-free. During UDI, since South Africa refused to recognize UN sanctions, Rhodesian law permitted many to send their after-tax profits home to their South African affiliates.

Second, the insurance companies reinsured their insurance policies, especially those on non-life business, with their parent companies outside the country. That is, they paid reinsurance premiums to their parent firms abroad. The rationale behind reinsurance is that, if a disaster, like a serious flood affecting a whole region, should occur, a local insurance firm could draw on its parent's international pool of funds to finance the full payments required to cover the losses of the affected policy holders. Presumbably, life insurance companies need relatively less reinsurance than non-life companies because the normal death rate may be relatively accurately predicted, whereas non-life insurance firms are more likely to be affected by unpredictable disasters.

Recent studies (for example Murray, *Multinationals beyond the Market*) have shown that non-life insurance commonly provides a channel through which transnational affiliates transfer locally accumulated funds abroad to avoid taxes and foreign exchange controls. A locally incorporated transnational affiliate registered in Zimbabwe, for example, could buy a great deal of non-life insurance and pay high premiums to a "captive" insurance company established by its parent and controlled through the latter's board of directors. The captive insurance company in Zimbabwe could pay its parent company reinsurance premiums well above those actuarily necessary. Zimbabwe's exchange control regulations permitted the commercial banks to more or less automatically give insurance firms the foreign exchange to pay reinsurance premiums to foreign affiliates. Thus, the captive company in Zimbabwe would send its parent a significant share of the transnational affiliate's profits generated in Zimbabwe.

In 1980, all non-life insurance companies in Zimbabwe paid their affiliates abroad a total of Z$25 million in reinsurance premiums. They paid out in reinsurance claims to Zimbabwean claimants only about a quarter of that amount. In other words, these insurers might have sent as foreign exchange to cover their reinsurance premiums to their foreign affiliates anywhere from Z$19 to Z$25 million. In addition, the eight reinsurance companies concentrating primarily on financing international trade in Zimbabwe paid for reinsurance to their South African parent companies Z$7 million, or about 60 per cent of their premium income. Assuming they remitted these reinsurance premiums, too, the amount of foreign exchange Zimbabwe lost through reinsurance premiums in 1980 alone may have totalled as much as Z$30 million.

The close links between the largest insurance firms and major transnational corporate affiliates reinforced the possibility that the latter used reinsurance premiums to transfer locally generated investable surpluses out of Zimbabwe. In 1980, the Anglo-American Group reported that insurance income provided almost 10 per cent of the funds it invested in South Africa.

A third method by which local insurance firms could ship investable surpluses out of Zimbabwe was through the payment of management fees to their foreign parent firms. In 1980 alone, Zimbabwe-based insurance firms shipped almost Z$7 million out of the country as management fees. The amounts shipped annually had risen almost 30 per cent since 1977. Although the Zimbabwe Insurance Company Registrar repeatedly noted this outflow, the Insurance Act apparently did not empower him to stop it.

Pension Funds

In Zimbabwe, pension funds provided another channel for mobilizing locally generated savings for investment. Private pension schemes in Zimbabwe, as elsewhere, required both employers and employees to contribute regularly to pension funds, providing a form of group savings. The managers of these funds then paid benefits to employees on retirement, or to their dependants in cases of accident, illness or death. The pension scheme managers invested the accumulated funds until they had to pay out the scheduled benefits.[3]

By 1978, the 1,334 pension funds in Zimbabwe had accumulated Z$628 million, the savings of some 390,000 wage and salary earners, about 40 per cent of all wage earners in the paid labour force. Pension fund contributions were tax deductible, but these deductions benefited only salaried workers with incomes high enough to pay income tax. Private and parastatal managers controlled these funds, often in close co-operation with other financial institutions, particularly insurance companies. Insurance firms managed pension schemes involving about two-thirds of all pension fund members. Because they typically managed funds for relatively small private employers, however, they held only about 45 per cent of all pension fund assets.

At independence in Zimbabwe, most pension fund benefits went primarily to the higher-income wage and salary earners (mostly white) for three reasons. First, the funds typically paid benefits according to the premiums paid in, so the higher-income salaried workers usually received higher benefits. Second, the pension law specifically excluded married women and casual workers. Third, other lower-wage workers failed to receive benefits because they did not remain in the same job the required minimum number of years.[4]

The pension fund managers, with hardly any government supervision, made the decisions as to how the bulk of the pension funds should be invested. Like other insurance firms, the pension fund managers reached a gentlemen's agreement to buy a minimum percentage of government securities, 35 per cent in 1981, to be raised to 50 per cent in 1983.

The fund managers also invested about a quarter of the funds in property and mortgage loans. The four leading self-managed funds—those of the railway, electricity, local government, and mine workers—were among the top ten shareholders of a number of major transnational corporate affiliates.

At independence, the Zimbabwean self-administered pension funds invested significant amounts of Zimbabwe workers' savings outside the national economy.[5] In 1978 alone, these schemes invested Z$8.8 million abroad, bringing their total reported investments outside the country to Z$29 million. This exceeded the total estimated amount of new capital investment in Zimbabwe in the first year after independence. In 1980, the Railway Pension Fund, the only one for which information was available, reported that it invested another Z$3.5 million outside the country. This increased its total external investments to Z$24.6 million. If all pension funds had increased their investment by the same proportion, external pension fund investments abroad would have totalled almost Z$45 million. Government regulations apparently did not restrict this outflow.

Building Societies

Three privately owned building societies constitute a third set of financial institutions; these mobilize locally generated funds for residential housing and office buildings in Zimbabwe. Building societies pay low fixed rates of interest to encourage members of the public to deposit their savings in various savings, share and fixed-deposit accounts. Although the interest on these deposits may be taxed, unlike the interest on Post Office savings accounts or government securities, fairly large numbers of people save with building societies hoping thus eventually to obtain mortgage funds to buy their own homes.

In Zimbabwe, the three building societies that survived UDI (several had merged with the assistance of major insurance firms) had accumulated about Z$615 million in assets by mid-1981.

Building societies' profits accrue from the difference between the rates of interest paid to depositors and these charged for mortgages. In Zimbabwe in 1981, they paid depositors 4.5 per cent interest. The mortgage rates they charged borrowers varied depending on the type of property, from 12.5 per cent for a housing loan to Z$12,000 to 14.75 per cent for commercial and industrial properties. The demand for mortgages usually exceeded the supply.

The three Zimbabwe building societies invested about two-thirds of their funds in mortgages under conditions regulated by law. Until just before independence, nearly 100 per cent of their mortgages financed minority-owned residential and commercial properties in major urban centres. Africans living in government-built townships could not buy their own homes. Even after independence, only a tiny percentage of Africans could afford to buy houses in the former all-white suburbs. The building societies did agree to lend funds to municipal governments for low-cost housing, but they loaned them only about 20 per cent of their available funds for this purpose.

The government required the societies to hold about a fifth of their assets in liquid form, a ready source of short-term funds for banks and discount houses. Government securities held by the societies—another fifth of their assets—had to mature in less than six years.

The board members of all three building societies sat on the boards of directors of insurance companies, other financial institutions and transnational corporate affiliates. The largest interlocked with several Anglo-American affiliates and the South African Old Mutual Insurance firm. One of the other two also interlocked with Anglo-American affiliates as well as several other companies.

Three of the largest insurance firms in Zimbabwe each provided the major source of investment for the initial establishment of each of the building societies. In return for their investments, the building societies provided the insurance companies with a ready market for insurance: no home-buyer could obtain a mortgage bond without insuring with the company nominated by the building society. The big insurance firms and the societies claimed that these ties reduced costs and led to better service, although the smaller non-tied insurance companies complained that the system reduced competition. From a national perspective, the close ties between several of the largest insurance firms and the building societies constituted a further centralization of capital.

Tanzania's Other Financial Institutions

In Tanzania, reflecting its relative underdevelopment, the other kinds of financial institutions that developed prior to independence mainly operated from their regional headquarters in Kenya. There, the settler community set up a stock exchange. Transnational insurance companies generally operated in Tanzania from their Nairobi offices and invested their surpluses in Kenya or shipped them to their overseas parent companies. Reinsurance drained additional funds out of the East African economy. At independence, therefore, the Tanzania government initiated steps to develop insurance, pension and housing schemes more appropriate to national needs.

Insurance

Shortly after independence, the government and various insurance and reinsurance companies with business interests in Tanzania established a National Insurance Company. After 1967, the National Insurance Corporation received the sole right to transact all forms of insurance business. Its capital reserves and life and general insurance funds provided its assets. These rose by 328.4 million shillings from 1972 to 1978. The number of life policies increased sixteenfold. The National Insurance Company invested over half of its funds in government securities, and another third in short-term bank deposits. Clearly, it facilitated the flow of savings to the government.

In 1964, the government set up a National Provident Fund as the principal social security scheme to which employees were required to contribute 5 per cent and employers 10 per cent of monthly wages. This provided an annually increasing sum which by 1978 reached 250 million shillings. The fund invested primarily in government securities.

The Tanzania Housing Bank

In 1972, the government established the Tanzania Housing Bank (THB) to replace the private building societies, mobilizing local savings and external resources for housing construction. The THB provided savings deposit accounts on which it paid interest. Its total assets rose from 102 million shillings in 1973 to 450 million shillings in 1977. Public deposits provided half to two-thirds of these. Internal loans provided a growing amount, reaching 25 per cent in 1977. Government and external funds provided a decreasing share as deposits and internal loans increased, each providing only 10 per cent in 1977.

From 1975 to 1977, about a quarter of THB funds went on low-cost housing and almost two-thirds on medium-cost housing. The remainder—less than a fifth—the THB invested in commercial loans.

Summary

Several kinds of privately held financial institutions emerged to mobilize longer-term investment funds for private enterprise in more developed African countries. These generally include a stock exchange, insurance firms, pension funds and building societies.

Mainstream theorists regard stock exchanges in developing countries as a capital market in which people may invest their savings, buying and selling shares of corporate stock, thus providing funds for the growth of private companies. They see other financial institutions, like those handling insurance, pensions and building funds as useful channels for mobilizing local savings for needed investment, as well as performing important specified functions.

Marxists theorists assert that these privately held financial institutions provide a means through which closely knit transnational corporate financial groups capture additional surplus value produced by the domestic working class to finance their increasingly concentrated control over the modern sectors of the national economy.

The available detailed evidence relating to Zimbabwe shows that these kinds of financial institutions grew especially rapidly during the 15-year UDI period prior to independence. The Stock Exchange, which had a longer history than that in Nigeria, was initially established in close co-operation with the South African Exchange. During UDI, it provided a market through which mainly institutional buyers like insurance firms and pension funds invested locally generated savings in the stock of locally incorporated transnational corporate affiliates.

Although more than 60, almost all foreign-owned, insurance firms operated in Zimbabwe, one, Old Mutual of South Africa, handled almost half of the country's insurance business. The top ten—all linked with the commercial banks and transnational corporate affiliates—held 85 per cent of the total insurance assets. These companies not only controlled the investment of hundreds of millions of dollars of local savings; they also shipped significant amounts out of the country in the form of profits, reinsurance and management fees.

The pension funds in Zimbabwe, over the years, accumulated several hundreds of millions of dollars worth of workers' savings. Their managers, half of them the larger insurance firms, made the decisions as to how to invest these funds. The leading pension firms invested large amounts of capital to become the biggest local shareholders of major transnational corporate affiliates. Several invested capital outside the Zimbabwean economy.

The three Zimbabwean building societies, each closely affiliated with one of the top ten insurance firms, invested most of their accumulated funds to finance minority-owned housing and commercial properties in the major urban centres.

Before independence, Tanzania's non-banking financial institutions largely operated out of their regional headquarters in Kenya. So that the investable surplus which they mobilized should be used to serve the interests of their clients and the national economy, the government either gradually nationalized these institutions or established new ones in the public sector.

Notes

1. Gathered by Zimbabwe University economics students.

2. A Southern Africa Development Coordination Conference (SADCC) Regional Workshop of lawyers and economists on how to deal with transnational corporations, meeting at the University of Zimbabwe in June 1982, proposed that SADCC member states should pass laws requiring that transnational corporate affiliates doing business in their countries should file with the governments the same information required elsewhere in the world. This would result in much more information becoming available to SADCC member states.

3. In most developed capitalist countries, the state has taken over the management of some or all of such funds as part of a national social security scheme.

4. In 1980, the Anglo-American Group's Hwangwe Colliery workers struck against the compulsory deduction of pension fund contributions from their wages for which they received little or no pension benefits.

5. These investments abroad did not include the remission abroad of pensions, guaranteed by the Lancaster House Constitution, to pensioners who left the country on retirement.

Exercises and Research

1. Contrast the mainstream and the Marxist theories relating to financial institutions which help to mobilize long-term investment funds in an essentially capitalist Third World economy.
2. What is the role of a stock exchange in a capitalist economy?
3. Compare the status of insurance, pension funds and housing finance in Zimbabwe and Tanzania. What conclusions do you draw as to their impact on long term investment funds in the two countries?
4. Conduct research to learn the details of the operation of one of the following types of financial institutions in your country: the stock exchange; an insurance company; pension fund or social security scheme; building society or other system of financing housing.
   a) How does the institution function? Does it have a board of directors and if so who sits on it? Does it have links with other private financial institutions or the government?
   b) What sections of the population benefit from the activities of the

institution? Provide data and explain why some sections benefit and others do not (if that is the case).

c) What kinds of investments are made by or through the institution? Who makes these decisions? Evaluate the impact of these decisions on the pattern of economic development in your country.

Recommended Reading

(For annotations, see bibliography at the end of the book.)

Boddy, *The Building Societies*
Drury, *Finance Houses*
Houghton, *The South African Economy*
IBRD country studies
Newlyn and Rowan, *Money and Banking in British Colonial Africa*
Report of a Working Party, *Who Controls Industry in Kenya*

Periodicals

Annual reports of individual financial institutions or their parent companies
Government Registrar's reports on particular types of financial institutions
Stock Exchange reports

Part II: Public Finance

Introduction

A pattern is visible in the life of socialist regimes. Grasping the levers of state power generates euphoria. Now at last they can raise wages, subsidize food prices, launch schemes, increase social services, build schools and hospitals, etc., etc. At the same time large fragments of the private sector can be taken over and made to serve public interest, not private profit.

There is of course very good justification for such measures. Objectively, no doubt, they are all essential. Moreover, they are accepted by the working classes and the left-wing intelligentsia that have helped the government to power. To refrain from carrying them out may cost important political support, especially in the trade unions. But a terrible price has to be paid. Typically inflation gathers pace, and the economic situation deteriorates, leading eventually to political crisis, a complete reversal of policy, and often of the social gains.

A socialist government is naturally much plotted against. There are always high-ranking officers and foreign government officials only too willing to engineer the downfall for a government of this hue, if need be by violence. They are to "blame" for what happens, of course, but—and this is something that has to be faced—a government which loses control of the economy plays into their hands and sets itself up for a coup.

Those socialist governments which have survived the traumas of birth and childishness have grown up to be extremely careful about their financial health, guarding their foreign exchange reserves with scrupulous care and imposing balanced budgets not merely in their own accounts but throughout the range of public institutions.

Dudley Seers, "The Tendency to Financial Irresponsibility of Socialist Governments and its Political Consequences", IDS Discussion Paper, 161, June 1981.

Chapter 6: The Dilemma of Public Finance

On independence, every African state sought to increase spending on education, health and welfare to meet the aspirations of the broad mass of the population. Many government leaders proclaimed these as socialist measures, although they did little to restructure the inherited, essentially capitalist, political-economic productive structures. They raised tax revenues, too, but not as rapidly as social expenditures. As a result, most African states borrowed heavily, both domestically and abroad.

This chapter provides data to delineate the nature and scope of the resulting dilemma confronting new African governments. Chapter 7 discusses some of the basic theoretical explanations and debates. The remaining chapters in Part II present some of the available evidence relating to African governments' efforts to finance their growing expenditure in the face of the worsening international situation.

Rising Expenditures

At independence, the peoples of the new African states demanded better job opportunities and higher living standards, more and better education, improved health and housing facilities: essential symbols of the freedom for which they had supported national liberation. If only to retain legitimacy in the eyes of their citizens, the new nationalist governments had to make visible efforts to fulfil these basic needs. And, as Figure 6.1 shows, most tried.

Capital Constructon Projects

The independent governments spent heavily on new capital construction: schools, roads, bridges and ports. As Table 6.1 shows, these consumed a major share—from 10% to 40%—of government funds, depending on the particular circumstances of the individual countries. Only on-site investigation can reveal the particular features of each government's capital spending. Nevertheless, certain characteristics stand out.

Poor countries, such as Mali and Upper Volta, had relatively little surplus which they could spend on capital development. In more fortunate countries, such as Botswana, the governments spent heavily to finance roads and other

Figure 6.1
Percentage Increase in Total Government Expenditures in Selected African States, Showing Major Items as a Percent of Totals, 1972 and 1980

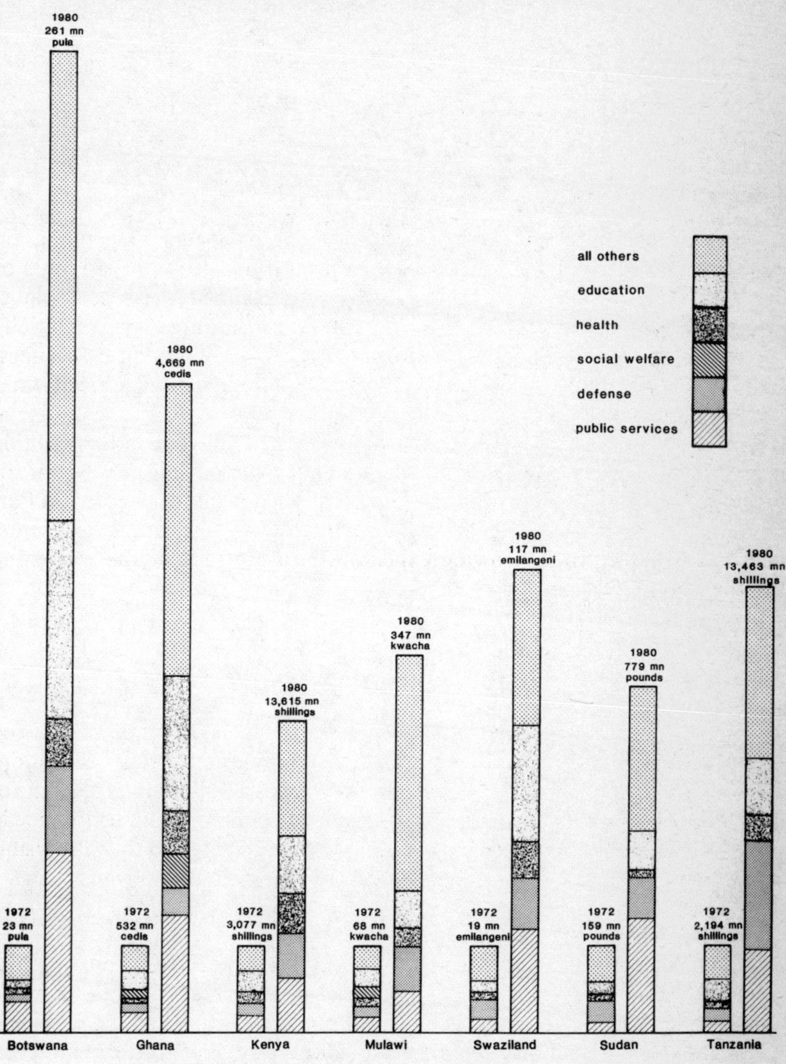

Source: Calculated from IMF, Government Finance Statistics Yearbook, 1982, Country Tables.

essential infrastructure to facilitate the opening of new mines and other productive activities. These, in turn, provided revenues which enabled the

Table 6.1
Capital Expenditures of Selected African States as a Percent of Total Expenditures (including lending minus repayments) 1974-1982

Country	*1974*	*1977*	*1980*	*1981*	*1982*
Africa (average)	17.82	23.63	17.95	19.75	...
Botswana	36.49	30.78	27.5	26.45	25.15
Burundi	...	...	...	45.29	...
Burkina Faso	12.53	17.01	12.65	16.71	12.65
Cameroon	...	34.47	32.77	41.26	42.44
Ethiopia (A)	11.31	17.14	...	...	...
Gambia (A)	24.47	34.49	...	...	...
Ghana	16.74	34.82	10.27	17.41	9.55
Ivory Coast	...	...	25.79	...	...
Kenya (A)	20.01	22.17	21.62	21.58	14.51
Liberia (A)	16.08	30.79	32.3	31.58	19.14
Malawi (A)	35.62	39.39	46.4	32.75	28.24
Mali	...	8.19	8	...	...
Mauritius (A)	14.07	21.6	18.74	18.91	...
Morocco (B)	23.4	49.17	30.96	32.74	33.66
Niger	...	35.88	46.89	...	...
Nigeria	...	34.1	...	...	...
Rwanda	17.06	33.53	34.43	...	...
Senegal	...	...	6.97	12.73	12.99
Seychelles (A)	30.86	21.17	...	...	...
Sierra Leone	16.43	19.94	20.32	22.16	22.62
Somalia	19.06	19.6	...	...	...
South Africa (B)	11.18	12.73	11.64	11.92	...
Sudan (A)	23.43	42.3	22.58	...	23.04
Swaziland (A)	31.09	29.72	30.02	29.36	...
Tanzania	27.38	29.3	...	...	...
Togo	...	34.56	...	27.08	28.81
Tunisia (A)	27.61	33.74	26.83	30.81	27.1
Uganda	...	16.83	14.06	16.46	20.02
Zaire (A)	37.06	21.54	19.13	29.42	21.45
Zambia	19.26	15.1	9.06	10.59	12.15
Zimbabwe	...	8.81	5.25	4.91	8.63

Notes: Letters A, B, following country name indicate percent of general government tax revenue accounted for by central government, as follows: A = 95% and over; B = 90-99%.

Source: International Monetary Fund, Government Finance Statistical Yearbook, 1982, 1984 (here only provide information for states where available).

governments to build new schools, hospitals, and other forms of social infrastructure, long neglected under colonial rule. By the end of the 1970s, however, even these governments found their current expenditures beginning to increase more rapidly than capital spending as they began to finance the personnel to run them. Formerly relatively well-off countries, such as Zambia and Zaire, hard hit by falling prices of their exports, cut capital spending sharply; growing shares of their government budgets were devoted to administering, staffing and maintaining existing projects.

Current Expenditures

Everywhere in Africa, after independence, current educational expenditures multiplied, frequently exceeding a fifth of the government budget. Improved health measures, both preventative and curative, designed to raise life expectancy, accounted for increased government spending. Social welfare measures, pensions, social security and low cost housing added to the burden.

All the governments had to employ additional personnel to operate their newly constructed capital projects. This led to rapidly rising current expenditures.

The costs of administration also rose. This reflected governments' employment of increased numbers of workers at all levels, as well as rising costs of wages and materials.

For a wide variety of reasons, some states spent heavily to expand their military establishment. In Southern Africa, new independent states such as Botswana and Zambia, that had never before had an army, now began to build up their military forces to protect themselves against South Africa. Countries such as Zimbabwe and Mozambique confronted the task of reorganizing armies—both those inherited from the previous regimes, and the freedom fighters who had won liberation—to strengthen their defences against possible incursions from the south. In West Africa, the civil war that rent Nigeria created a large military force which, because of persistent widespread unemployment, the government could not easily demobilize. In the mid-1970s, Tanzania expanded its army to repel an invasion by, and ultimately to overthrow the Ugandan dictatorship of Idi Amin. In several countries, coups installed military governments which quickly raised the armed forces' pay and provided them with additional benefits.

Figure 6.1 shows the impact of all these and other factors in multiplying current government spending in selected African countries in the 1970s.

Inflationary Pressures

In almost every African country, rising domestic prices pushed up the cost of all government expenditures. By the late 1970s and early 1980s, inflationary pressures further distorted income distribution patterns and threatened economic stability. Table 6.2 reveals the impact of inflation on several countries' price levels. In Ghana, runaway inflation pushed prices up at rates exceeding several hundred per cent a year, disrupting normal production and trade patterns. Many other countries suffered annual rates of inflation of 20 per cent or more.

Table 6.2
Price Indices of Selected African Countries (1975 = 100)

	1975	*1976*	*1977*	*1978*	*1979*	*1980*	*1981*	*1982*
Botswana	100.0	111.8	126.5	137.9	154.0	175.3	203.7	222.7
Ghana	100.0	156.1	337.8	584.8	903.0	1,355.5	2,934.3	3,404.4
Kenya	100.0	111.4	128.0	149.6	161.6	183.9	205.6	235.1[a]
Lesotho	100.0	111.4	130.0	140.8	163.3	188.9	217.0	233.1
Malawi	100.0	104.3	108.7	118.0	131.3	155.4	170.2	179.4
Nigeria	100.0	124.3	188.3	176.0	195.6	217.9	263.2	–
Sierra Leone	100.0	117.2	130.8	140.8	170.7	189.6	233.8	257.5[a]
South Africa	100.0	111.2	123.6	136.2	154.1	175.3	201.9	228.6
Sudan	100.0	105.7	118.7	142.3	186.1	233.3	–	–
Swaziland	100.0	104.7	126.5	136.1	155.6	188.2	–	–
Tanzania	100.0	106.9	119.2	132.8	151.1	196.8	247.3	–
Zambia	100.0	118.8	142.3	165.6	181.1	202.9	231.3	258.9
Zimbabwe	100.0	109.6	119.0	129.7	147.7	157.8	176.8	193.5

[a] First quarter 1982

Source: IMF, *International Financial Statistics*, December 1982, country tables.

Table 6.3
Overall Government Deficit/Surplus as Percentage of Total Expenditures (Including Lending Minus Repayments) of African States

	1974	*1975*	*1976*	*1978*	*1979*	*1980*	*1981*	*1982*
Africa (average)	– 14.94	– 20.31	– 25.80	– 24.35	– 23.08	– 19.27	....	....
Botswana	– 7.92	1.41	– 19.65	– 3.81	– 4.12	9.64	– 42	....
Burkina Faso	16.07	– 9.08	– 5.52	15.91	4.82	– 13.65	....	....
Burundi	– 1.50	– 15.83	– 2.73	– 7.44	....	....	....	....
Cameroon	....	– 12.49	– 12.63	– 2.22	2.33	16.63	3.24	....
Chad	– 13.21	– 10.48	– 12.31	....	....	....	....	....
Congo (C)	....	....	....	....	....	....	– 10.50	....
Djibouti	....	....	....	....	....	9.14	14.87	....
Ethiopia (A)	– 5.75	– 21.90	– 27.55	– 17.50	– 25.09	....	....	....
Gabon	– 14.77	– 18.09	– 45.55	....	....	....	....	....
Gambia	– 9.38	– 15.87	– 12.28	– 29.08	– 25.86	....	....	....
Ghana	– 25.15	– 33.07	– 45.79	– 47.43	– 57.65	– 40.91	– 38.00	....
Ivory Coast	....	....	....	....	....	– 26.48	– 31.06	....
Kenya	– 13.71	– 20.29	– 24.30	– 17.21	– 14.80	– 22.99	– 16.48	....
Liberia	6.18	2.64	– 8.89	– 11.77	– 22.13	– 38.63	– 28.16	– 30.98
Malawi	– 28.52	– 32.55	– 26.04	– 24.79	– 29.06	– 24.29	– 32.28	....
Mali	....	....	....	– 48	– 10.86	– 19.63	– 6.31	....
Mauritania	....	– 6.51	– 16.14	– 15.19	– 8.19	– 13.16	....	....
Mauritius (A)	– 30.47	– 20.46	– 16.39	– 28.02	– 37.08	– 38.35	– 33.10	– 38.42
Morocco	– 13.73	– 25.96	– 42.91	– 38.27	– 30.20	– 27.65	– 29.10	....
Niger	....	....	– 15.21	– 12.26	– 20.03	– 16.21	– 24.58	....
Nigeria	40.76	– 23.25	– 25.55	– 24.27	....	....	....	....
Rwanda	– 17.77	– 12.67	– 15.36	– 10.55	– 12.33	– 11.50	....	....
Senegal	....	– 2.77	....	– 14.89	1.54	– 3.81	....	....
Seychelles (A)	– 87	– 72	– 2.39	12.23	– 12.78	....	....	....
Sierra Leone	– 18.56	– 38.22	36.14	– 30.38	– 25.22	– 27.53	– 40.97	– 33.60
Somalia	– 9.24	– 10.44	– 14.59	– 29.82	– 34.11	....	....	....
South Africa (B)	– 18.34	– 19.27	– 23.22	– 21.32	– 18.88	– 15.27	....	....
Sudan (A)	– 4.79	– 22.42	– 16.47	– 32.44	– 27.32	– 19.89	– 16.33	....
Swaziland (A)	3.72	33.04	– 13.43	– 9.54	– 27.52	2.97	21.37	....
Tanzania	– 22.40	– 30.86	– 25.79	– 20.70	– 25.83	– 40.39	....	....
Togo	....	....	....	– 45.48	– 50.95	– 20.40	– 6.04	....
Tunisia (A)	– 3.56	– 4.64	– 10.09	– 16.74	– 14.14	– 12.34	– 7.95	....
Uganda	....	....	....	....	....	....	....	....
Zaire (A)	– 35.54	– 30.58	– 41.77	– 35.15	– 39.55	– 18.36	....	....
Zambia	11.00	– 42.44	– 36.88	– 32.94	– 36.07	– 28.00	– 41.78	....
Zimbabwe	....	– 18.38	– 10.62	– 26.72	– 25.71	– 34.14	– 20.9	– 13.27

See note for Table 6.1.

Source: IMF, *Government Finance Statistical Yearbook*. 1982.

Table 6.4
Mounting Domestic and Foreign Debts of African Countries as percentage of government expenditures (including lending minus repayment)

A. Domestic debts

Country	*1974*	*1977*	*1980*	*1981*	*1982*
AFRICA:	92.38	102.68	98.38	92.43	...
Botswana	...	12.79	4.84	0.4	0.14
Ethiopia (A)	31.14	55.12	...	...	...
Gambia	14.16	13.72	...	...	...
Ghana	163.59	143.9	160.17	148.34	180.23
Ivory Coast	...	...	9.07	...	...
Kenya (A)	60.19	55.34	48.86	...	...
Liberia	...	17.46	30.42	42.8	43.86
Malawi	...	53.87	...	...	...
Mali	...	...	34.25	32.49	37.66
Mauritius (A)	81.22	81.12	108.24	106.76	121.09
Morocco	32.31	29.57	41.31	37.53	38.17
Rwanda	9.57	8.77	5.99	...	...
Senegal	...	...	...	25.71	...
Seychelles (A)	6.87	9.61	...	...	...
Sierra Leone	39.52	81.4	105.48	121.33	...
South Africa	130.86	142.46	123.61	115.31	...
Sudan	62.01	...	...	...	...
Swaziland (A)	26.9	11.42	...	...	...
Tunisia	32.52	29.23	25.47	24.9	21.31
Uganda	...	...	175.19	169.35	103.78
Zaire (A)	37.51	89.49	62.65	64.51	78.84
Zambia	58.88	144.46	...	...	...
Zimbabwe	...	110.37	112.79	105.52	78.83

B. Foreign Debts

Country	*1974*	*1977*	*1980*	*1981*	*1982*
AFRICA:	32.89	40.44	46.36	49.16	...
Botswana	...	84.67	32.59	39.173	48.87
Ethiopia (A)	53.85	52.63	...	...	...
Gambia (A)	56.99	36.91	...	...	...
Ghana	33.85	...	65.25	44.94	42.07
Ivory Coast	...	...	81.44	...	...
Kenya (A)	63.79	59.42	...	...	...
Liberia	125.98	104.67	150.29	150.45	137.35
Malawi	174.7	147.35	102.06	107.98	171.77
Mali	...	...	...	...	...
Mauritius	31.42	19.82	52.84	65.9	96.27
Morocco (B)	44.22	57.25	83.34	90.59	114.92
Rwanda	...	53.92	101.91	...	...
Senegal	...	...	...	174.38	...
Seychelles	6.32	5.23	...	...	...
Sierra Leone	62.79	89.27	109.55	111.1	...
South Africa	8.14	6.88	3.7	4.67	...
Sudan	68.08	...	...	...	...
Tunisia	73.66	71.26	72.93	76.59	75.14
Zaire (A)	41.83	84	152.35	170.05	...
Zambia	...	70.17	...	...	...
Zimbabwe	...	14.47	34.93	39.76	40.51

Notes: Letters A, B, following country name indicate percent of general government revenue accounted for by central government, as follows: A = 95% and over, B = 90-99.9%.
Source: International Monetary Fund, Government Finance Statistics Yearbook, 1982 and 1984, country tables. (Here include only countries for which information is reported.)

Lagging Revenues and Mounting Debts

The new African states attempted to improve their inherited tax structures and raise revenues to finance their mounting costs. Few succeeded completely. Even Nigeria, despite its newly discovered oil wealth, confronted serious budget deficits by the mid-1970s. By the early 1980s, almost all found themselves deeply embroiled in debt. The costs of debt repayment mounted. In Ghana, the repayment of debt became one of the largest budget items, exceeding education. But, as Table 6.5 shows, other countries, too, were spending a significant percentage of their revenues just to finance their past debts.

Table 6.5
Rising Interest Payments of African States as a percentage of government expenditures (including lending minus repayments), 1974-1982

Country	*1974*	*1977*	*1980*	*1981*	*1982*
AFRICA:	4.34	5.16	6.69	7.47	...
Botswana	1.82	3.12	1.68	1.69	2.71
Burkina Faso	...	3.81	2.69	2.72	2.06
Cameroon	...	1.55	0.6	1.01	...
Ethiopia	2.32	3.19	...	...	...
Gambia	0.24	0.8		...	...
Ghana	8.67	7.93	15.25	12.79	20.3
Ivory Coast	...	...	7.18	...	...
Kenya (A)	5.6	6.21	6.57	7.57	11.43
Liberia (A)	3.91	2.38	8.8	5.9	9.8
Malawi (A)	6.37	6.37	9.1	13.6	15.1
Mali	...	0.7	0.84	...	...
Mauritius (A)	4.7	4.5	11.96	13.71	17.46
Morocco (B)	2.9	3.81	7.12	9.43	8.88
Niger	...	6.32	5.45	...	...
Rwanda	1.73	0.67	2.07	...	...
Senegal	...	...	5.22	2.95	7.72
Sierra Leone	3.11	6.06	...	...	...
South Africa (B)	4.91	5.74	7.02	8.16	...
Sudan (A)	3.7	4.95	6.03	...	...
Swaziland (A)	1.97	0.42	0.27	1.61	5.79
Tanzania	3.98	4.5	...	...	...
Togo	...	0.93	...	8.54	7.73
Tunisia (A)	3.91	2.71	4.1	4.49	5.15
Zaire (A)	3.57	8.36	7.79	8.89	11.68
Zambia	6.1	9.1	7.55	7.75	6.72
Zimbabwe	...	5.75	6.54	8.18	8.3

Notes: See bottom of Table 6.1

Source: International Monetary Fund, Government Financial Statistical Yearbook, 1982, 1984 (here including only countries for which information is available).

Exercises and Research

1. Compare the reasons given by your government for increasing current and capital expenditures with those given by other African governments.
2. Evaluate the effect of inflation on public spending in African states and in your country.
3. Are domestic and foreign debt and interest payments in your country, as a percentage of total government spending, greater or less than in most other African states? Explain why.
4. Examine the extent of the problem of public finance as it affects your country.
   a) Prepare a table of your government's expenditures over the last five years. What percentage are capital expenditures, as opposed to current expenditures? Estimate the percentage of expenditures that may be considered direct investments in the productive sectors.
   b) Estimate the effect of inflation in increasing your government's expenditures in each of the last five years.
   c) Prepare a table of the main sources of government revenues in your country over the last five years and show the government's deficit or surplus on the current account both in terms of your national currency and as a percentage of total expenditures.
   d) Prepare a table showing your government's domestic and foreign debt over the last five years, in terms of your national currency and as a percentage of total expenditures. Include data showing the cost of the interest payments on that debt as a percent of government expenditures.

Recommended Reading

(For annotations, see bibliography at the end of the book)

Elliott (ed.), *Constraints on the Economic Development of Zambia*
Eshag, *Fiscal and Monetary Policies and Problems*
Hicks, *Development Finance*
Ilugbuh, *Nigeria's Experience in Domestic Financing of Development*
IBRD country studies
IBRD Surveys of African Economies
Jackson (ed.), *Economic Development in Africa (1962)*
Koneacki, *An Economic History of Tropical Africa*
Lewis, *Reflections on Nigeria's Economic Growth*
Morton, *Aid and Dependence*
Odenigwe (ed.), *A New System of Local Government*
Sandbrook, *The Politics of Basic Needs*

Saylor, *The Economic System of Sierra Leone*
Seidman, *Comparative Development Strategies in East Africa*
—— *Ghana's Development Experience, 1952-1966*
Teriba and Diejomaoh (eds), *Money, Finance and Nigerian Economic Development*
Uppal and Salkever (eds), *African Problems in Economic Development*
Wetham and Currie, *Readings in Applied Economics of Africa*

Periodicals

The Economist Intelligence Unit, *Quarterly Economic Reviews*
IMF, *Government Statistics*
Government budget estimates
Government plan documents
Government statistical digests
Ministers of Finance, annual budget speeches

Chapter 7: Theories of Public Finance

Mainstream economists and Marxists explain the problems of public finance in qualitatively different ways. These reflect not only their fundamentally different theoretical views on money and finance but also their qualitatively different perceptions of the role of the state in the development process. Mainstream theorists essentially perceive the state as an administrative body which maintains law and order so that private enterprise can accumulate and reinvest capital to expand production, thus meeting the basic needs of the population. Marxists, in contrast, hold that despite significant contradictory features and, except for brief periods of revolutionary change, the state tends to represent the dominant economic class. This chapter discusses the alternative explanations which these theories suggest for the problems of public finance plaguing the newly independent countries of Africa.

The Mainstream Approach

Mainstream theorists have focused primarily on the public finance problems arising in the changing conditions of industrialized capitalist countries. They basically assume that the government should facilitate endeavours by private enterprises to maximize their profits, so that, under the impetus of the competitive market forces, they will reinvest to expand the productive sectors. The resulting growth in productivity and output will spread higher living standards throughout the economy. The government should intervene in this process as little as possible. Instead, it should confine its efforts to taxing the private sector and, if necessary, borrowing money from it, to create the necessary socio-economic environment to enable private enterprise to achieve these goals.

Changing Concepts of State Spending

Mainstream theorists generally agree that the state should collect revenues from the private sector to finance the essential administration, social and economic infrastructure, and military and police forces for defence and maintenance of law and order. In different countries and at different times in the same country, however, the concept of the kinds of infrastructure governments should finance varies. To this day, for example, railways in the United States remain predominantly privately owned. At the outset, the government subsidized them through provision of vast areas of free land to railway builders. In recent years, it has provided them with massive loans to enable them to continue to operate profitably. In countries like England, France and Germany, on the other hand, the governments own the railways outright and operate them as a public service.

In the area of social services, too, mainstream concepts of the role of state finance have changed. In the 19th century, students in most developed countries had to pay to go to school, at least beyond the primary level. Today, governments of developed capitalist countries usually also pay for secondary and, sometimes, university education. Until World War II, in most developed capitalist countries people paid for their own health care. Today, the state has assumed a major share of this function in most developed capitalist countries except the United States.

Over the years, the typical capitalist government created institutional structures—ministries or departments—to provide those services it regarded as essential for the successful expansion of the private sector and for general social welfare. The state budget allocates finance for the projects proposed by these ministries or departments.

Balanced Budgets vs. Deficit Spending

Since the private sector produces the bulk of the nation's wealth, the government must tax it to finance departmental or ministerial expenditure. Most mainstream theorists initially assumed that governments should balance their budgets; that is, their revenue from taxes should always cover their expenditure. During the Great Depression of the 1930s, however, Keynesians began to argue that government efforts to balance the budget aggravate cyclical upswings and downswings of the economy. In a boom, increased incomes in the private sector automatically increase tax revenues so governments can spend more. Given the already full employment of resources, the subsequent positive multiplier effects contribute to inflationary pressures. In a recession, falling incomes in the private sector reduce tax revenues. Governments then cut expenditures to balance the budget. This leads to negative multiplier effects, aggravating the problems of unemployment and declining demand, and further reducing investment.

Keynesians proposed that governments exercise fiscal powers as well as monetary policies, through the central bank, to cushion the impact of business cycles. In a recession, the government should borrow from the private sector to finance increased expenditure. This should stimulate a multiplier effect, leading to increased private investment and employment. In a boom, the government could use part of the increased tax revenues it obtains from the private sector to pay off the debt, thus balancing the budget over the cycle. In a recession, a government might expand expenditure in several ways:

1) It might increase its own expenditure, constructing roads, schools, housing and other kinds of social and economic infrastructure. It might

contract such projects to private construction firms. It might provide additional funds to the military. Keynes himself said that although housing and similar projects might be more desirable, military expenditures are politically more acceptable. He suggested, however, that no matter what government did to expand demand—even if it buried money in bottles and let private enterprises dig it up for a profit—it could help to stimulate the desired multiplier effects.[1]

2) To reduce the costs of inputs or hold down prices of outputs, the government might subsidize private enterprise indirectly through tax deductions, or directly through grants or low-cost loans.

3) The state itself might create state corporations, sometimes called parastatals, to take over failing enterprises or to launch new projects which private entrepreneurs might not initially consider profitable. Mainstream theorists generally hold that state corporations, whether fully financed by government or held jointly with private investors, should operate outside the bureaucratic structures of government. Government may appoint members to the board of directors, but each state corporation should seek to maximize its own profits, functioning as much as possible like a private enterprise. Thus it would avoid becoming enmeshed in the red tape associated with the civil service, achieving maximum efficiency in response to market forces. However, once a project actually becomes fully profitable and can survive without government support, many mainstream theorists recommend that the state should restore it entirely to the private sector. Figure 7.1 illustrates the use of fiscal and monetary policies to offset business cycles.

Figure 7.1
Co-ordinated Fiscal and Monetary Policies to Offset the Business Cycle

Government Policy	*Phase of Business Cycle*	
	Recession	Boom
Fiscal Policy:	Lower taxes, borrow money to increase spending.	Collect higher taxes, repay debts, perhaps reduce spending.
Monetary Policy:	Reserve bank reduces cash/liquidity ratio; lower bank rate; buys securities in open market.	Reserve bank raises interest rate; increases liquidity/cash ratio; sells securities in open market.

Tax Policies

Following Keynes's path-breaking analysis, mainstream economists engaged in two sets of debates on public finance, the first on appropriate tax policies, the second on the accumulation of public debt.

Mainstream theorists frequently disagree over the appropriate structure of taxes. Sometimes using older concepts, sometimes formulating newer ones, they argue over three basic issues:

Progressive vs. Regressive Taxes: Mainstream theorists generally term taxes which fall more heavily on higher-income than lower-income groups "progressive", and those falling more heavily on lower-income groups "regressive". Some maintain progressive taxes free the purchasing power of larger, lower-income consumer groups, who must spend most of their income on consumption goods. This provides the demand enabling private enterprise to sell its output. Concerned with the issues of demand, they have been called "demand-side" economists.

Taxes and Incentives: While most mainstream theorists agree that taxes can influence private investment and consumption behaviour by providing appropriate incentives, they disagree on what is appropriate. Some, usually monetarists, claim that low taxation on high-income groups and business profits provides incentives to save and invest. Particular tax deductions may encourage specific kinds of investments. Thus, these kinds of tax incentives aim to stimulate production, an essential goal of what has become known as "supply-side" economics.

Taxes as Income Transfers: Other mainstream economists, concerned with the welfare of lower-income groups, recommend progressive taxes to finance government programmes to improve social welfare. Commonly called "welfare" economists, they view such taxes as a justifiable transfer of wealth from the rich to the poor to provide more equitable income distribution.

Supply-side economists tend to support taxes which fall more heavily on lower-income groups and are used to finance government programmes to stimulate capital formation. Such programmes may include low-interest long-term loans and/or outright subsidies to private enterprise. Welfare economists, however, often criticize such programmes for transferring income from the poor majority to the wealthy few, thus aggravating income inequalities.

Public Debt

The second set of debates on public finance set off by the Keynesian "revolution" relates to the public debt. During World War II, the major capitalist countries accumulated enormous military debts which they found difficult if not impossible to repay. After the war, they continued to borrow funds to meet rising expenditures. However, most Keynesians argued that the existence of such debts caused no serious problems. A government could easily roll it over; that is, contract new debts to pay off the old. Moreover, the government could manage the debt as a powerful anti-cyclical lever. It could use increased tax revenues to pay off the debt in times of boom, while reducing taxes and increasing the debt in recessions.

Monetarists objected. The very existence of large government debts, they asserted, introduced inflationary pressures. After World War II they used a modified quantity theory of money to argue that increasing the amount of money in circulation without necessarily increasing production would inevitably push prices up. Nevertheless, in the post-war era, the major capitalist governments, using variants of Keynesian doctrine to buttress their policies, continued to expand their debts. The US government spent billions of dollars on the Korean and Vietnam wars, as well as on social welfare programmes. They financed current account deficits by borrowing.

By the 1970s, the developed capitalist countries confronted contradictory tendencies not anticipated by Keynesian theorists. Unemployment began to mount alongside growing inflation. Keynesian techniques designed to combat unemployment seemed to aggravate inflation. Measures advocated to curb inflation caused further increases in unemployment.

Monetarists, led by the American Nobel Prize-winning economist, Milton Friedman, called for reductions in government debts, as well as increased interest rates and other central bank measures to reduce the money supply and defuse inflationary pressures. They advocated sharp cuts in government spending. To provide private enterprise with incentives to expand investment, they urged lower taxes on business profits and the higher-income groups. They claimed that, despite initial setbacks and growing unemployment, these policies would eventually lead to sound economic recovery.

By the early 1980s, unemployment in most of the developed capitalist countries had reached 10 per cent or more of the labour force. Major industries operated at two-thirds of capacity or less. The theoretical debate raged: policies recommended by monetarists to reduce inflation, Keynesian theorists argued, caused rising unemployment; policies urged by Keynesians to reduce unemployment, the monetarists insisted, spurred inflation.

The Debate Transferred to Africa

Economists trained in the mainstream tradition transferred these debates to Africa and the Third World. Colonial governments in Africa had generally pursued monetarist policies of balanced budgets. They collected taxes primarily to finance economic infrastructure, and to stimulate colonial companies and farmers to invest in productive sectors.

After World War II, finding theoretical justification in Keynesian doctrine, several colonial administrators established development corporations to initiate new types of productive activity through projects which the private sector found unprofitable. Nevertheless, they generally still sought to balance their budgets.

At independence, African governments had little choice but to multiply expenditures, even if they had to borrow to do it. Their populations demanded more schools and hospitals as well as new roads, electricity and water supplies to serve the needs of the African inhabitants in neglected rural areas. As in the developed capitalist countries the colonial governments had created departments to deal with roads and railways, posts and telecommunications, agriculture, the police and military, health and education. Typically, post-independence African governments transformed these, with marginal alterations, into ministries. In accordance with mainstream theoretical premises, these functioned primarily as a framework for private enterprise.

These ministries often vied with each other, rapidly expanding capital and current expenditures, and increasing government budget deficits.

Some mainstream economists, concerned about lagging tax revenues and mounting public debts, sought to determine whether developing countries could increase their tax capacity. They tried to use regression analysis to determine the relationship between taxes, national income and the structure of the economy.[2]

But most economists readily admit that in developing countries lack of accurate data renders the validity and utility of this kind of effort to measure tax capacity questionable. Furthermore, some add that the government's own role and administrative ability—neither of which can be judged quantitatively—influence tax capacity. Many economists emphasize that the lack of adequate data and trained personnel aggravate the difficulties of collecting taxes. Widespread illiteracy and the fact that many people live in semi-subsistence sectors with very low cash incomes also hinder effective tax collection.

When expanded tax revenue failed to keep pace with expenditure, many economists drew on Keynesian theory to justify government borrowing. They claimed that government expenditures stimulated a positive multiplier effect in the private sector, helping to combat widespread unemployment and poverty. The growth of public debt gave the African governments more leverage to exercise fiscal policy to stimulate development. Some added that a little inflation tended to augment profits, thus enticing more private investment.

The theoretical debates that rent academic and government circles in the developed capitalist countries spread to African states: how to explain mounting under-employment and unemployment while inflation pushed prices up? Popular pressure for more jobs led some government leaders and academics to continue to opt for investment in infrastructure and even the establishment of state corporations to attract private investment.

Monetarist theorists called for governments to retrench: to hold down business taxes to stimulate private investment, if necessary raising taxes on lower- and middle-income groups; to cut expenditure; and to reduce borrowing to halt inflationary pressures.

Marxists

A Different Theory of the State

Marxist political economists draw on the historical materialist theory of the state and imperialism to explain the problems of public finance. That theory suggests that in industrialized countries, over time, the capitalist state developed as a result of and to foster the reproduction and expansion of private ownership of the means of production. The state primarily represents the interests of the capitalist class, though varying factors, especially the level and character of class struggle in a particular country, introduce contradictory elements. The capitalist state imposes taxes to finance administration and infrastructure so as to maintain an orderly context for profitable investment. It employs police and military to protect and expand the area of capitalist reproduction. The police maintain internal "law and order", restricting the efforts of the workers to organize and strike for wage increases. In the imperialist era, the military forces of competing capitalist states seek to protect and expand capitalist interests beyond national boundaries as they did in the scramble for Africa, in both world wars, and in the subsequent "brush fire" wars in Korea and Vietnam.

Economically, military expansion provides a gigantic, although temporary, Keynesian-type boost to a capitalist economy. The capitalist state finances non-productive expenditures to stockpile weapons which may or may not ultimately be destroyed by outright war. The multiplier effect may stimulate expansion of other industries. At the same time, however, military expenditure aggravates the underlying contradictions inherent in the capitalist economy. On the one hand, it fosters technological advance and concentration in increasingly capital-intensive military-related industries. As these multiply their output, they require ever-growing material resources and markets. At the same time, they become increasingly concentrated and centralized, achieving oligopolistic control over basic sectors of the national economy; this enables them to push up prices to maximize profits. On the other hand, the continuing expansion of capital investment raises the amount of capital invested compared to the amount of labour employed.[3] Since labour is the only source of surplus value, this pushes down the average rate of profit, which is calculated as the return on the total amount of capital invested. Simultaneously, the ongoing extraction of surplus value by the capitalist owners of the means of production continually narrows the market. These interrelated phenomena aggravate the objective conditions, giving rise to repeated crises of overproduction. As a consequence these crises became more frequent and disruptive in the 1970s and 1980s, culminating in a re-emergence of the general crisis of capitalism.

These growing contradictions forced governments of industrialized capitalist countries to intervene more directly in the political economy, greatly increasing their expenditures, to: 1) regulate and expand the national reproductive process; 2) deal with the political and economic demands of the growing working class; and 3) participate more effectively in the international arms race. This gave rise to the essential features of state monopoly capitalism as they evolved in the post-World War II era.

The Class Struggle and the Welfare State

The growth of national class struggles within the developed capitalist countries, as well as the conflicts between competing groups of capitalists within and among them, have led to contradictory state policies. The debates between Keynesians and monetarists reflect these contradictions and conflicting interests.

The Marxist analysis of the ramifications of these contradictory features is too complex to discuss fully here. In broad outline, however, Marxists generally agree that the expansion of social welfare policies in developed capitalist countries, especially during and after the Great Depression of the

1930s, reflected two fundamental characteristics of the imperialist stage of capitalism. First, the growth in numbers and class consciousness of the workers forced the state to ameliorate the most brutal aspects of capitalist exploitation. However, some Marxists argue that social welfare measures, like those introduced under President Roosevelt's New Deal in the United States and by the Labour Party in England, merely constituted part of a demagogic ploy to legitimate capitalism and prevent more fundamental social change. Others assert that the workers' successful political action led to the election of government representatives who carried on the struggle for workers' rights within and through the structures of the state itself.

Secondly, imperialist expansion reaped superprofits for the capitalist combines which dominated political economies of the industrialized, as well as the colonized, countries. Without too severely reducing the overall profits of private enterprise, therefore, the capitalist governments could tax these superprofits to finance expanded social welfare measures to meet the workers' demands. Britain, from the 1870s to the 1950s, benefited from an inflow of profits from its empire that offset its continual balance of trade deficits. Once the empire collapsed after World War II, however, the British government found it increasingly difficult to finance the welfare state within the framework of capitalism. Saddled with outdated technologies protected by imperial preference, its economy stagnated. For several decades after the war, the British government expanded its public debt to cover its rising expenses. Inflationary pressures mounted while real production lagged.

After World War II, the United States, enjoying almost half the world's resources and a continuing inflow of profits from its Third World holdings, likewise financed the growth of a welfare state benefiting most segments of the population.[4] In the 1970s, as the US hegemony weakened and crises of overproduction deepened, both the federal and state governments, regardless of their political persuasion, began to reduce social welfare spending. Military expenditures, however, still financed by growing debt, continued to rise. The resulting expanding money supply and stagnating real production contributed to conditions in which increased oligopolistic control of production led to mounting inflationary pressures.

Monetarism and the Crises of Capitalism

Marxists view the monetarist policies of the early 1980s—Thatcherism in England and Reagonomics in the United States—as the capitalist class's response to these inevitable contradictory phenomena. To balance the budget the developed capitalist state seeks to throw the burden of the crises on the workers by cutting social welfare spending and raising taxes on lower-income groups. At the international level, it supports policies—including military measures—facilitating the national firms' intensified exploitation of Third World peoples.

As part of this pattern, transnational corporations invest in expanding manufacturing capacity in regional sub-centres like South Africa, as well as Brazil, Taiwan and South Korea, aggressively oppressive states which restrict or outlaw unions, hold down taxes and social welfare expenditures, and expand their military forces to repress emergent liberation struggles. Thus the transnationals transfer productive capacity to such regional sub-centres where they employ the oppressed, impoverished workers to produce superprofits. This strategy further serves to undermine the wages and working conditions which the workers in the transnationals' own homelands have won over the years.

The "Silent Class Struggle" over Public Finance in Africa

In the independent African countries, the role of the state reflects an ongoing struggle between transnational corporate affiliates, local capitalist and petty-bourgeois classes, including the peasants, and workers. Colonial rule had structured the state to foster an alliance between transnational corporate capital and a majority of local capitalist interests. It had imposed taxes primarily to finance economic infrastructure designed to facilitate the growth of the export-orientated modern sector and coerce Africans into the low-paid labour force. In countries like the then Rhodesia and Kenya, as well as South Africa, settler capitalists had used racist arguments to justify their use of state power to finance segregated social infrastructure—schools, hospitals, recreation areas—for themselves.

When the national liberation movements won state power, a "silent class struggle" ensued over the role of the state. Ongoing conflicts over the appropriate taxing and fiscal policies reflect this struggle.

Marxists generally view the tax capacity of developing countries in a different light from mainstream economists. They focus on the surpluses currently or potentially generated domestically as a crucial source of capital for reinvestment to restructure and raise productivity in all sectors of an increasingly self-reliant national economy.[5] They hold that low business taxes, tax deductions and the elimination of foreign-exchange controls, advocated by many mainstream theorists to attract private, usually foreign, investment, are counterproductive because they permit foreign firms to ship out a major share of the locally generated surplus value, leaving the people more impoverished.

Many Marxists maintain that, regardless of their stated ideologies, most new African governments are run by African petty-bourgeois elements, who often use their control of the state to acquire big farms or enter speculative trade or real estate. They seek more funds to finance their own enterprises as well as to legitimate their rule with the workers and peasants by raising social welfare expenditures. Unwilling to shoulder increased tax burdens themselves, these elements sometimes seek to exert greater control over and extract more revenues from the transnational corporations which dominate the economy. Transnational corporate managers, on the other hand, make every effort to persuade petty-bourgeois officeholders to exercise state power in their favour. They sell them shares in local affiliates and offer them prestige and wealth as directors of local boards of directors. They bring them in on profitable deals. Not infrequently they offer outright bribes to obtain favourable government decisions in matters affecting them.

The general crisis of capitalism of the late 1970s and early 1980s—the culmination of the contradictory features described above—worsened the terms of trade and reduced the export earnings on which the newly independent African states relied. Their tax revenues inevitably declined. Unable or unwilling to tax high-income groups or corporate incomes more heavily, African governments had to borrow extensively to finance current expenditures. Their mounting domestic debts—especially given oligopolistic control in key sectors of the national economy—fuelled inflationary pressures. Their external debts tied them ever more tightly into the international capitalist financial system.

The African states' adoption of monetarist solutions only aggravated their problems. As long as they fail to build more integrated, balanced economies, less dependent on uncertain capitalist world markets and transnational corporate investments and control, they cannot hope to finance even the basic needs of their populations. Moreover, their use of monetarist measures which impose the burden of the crises on the workers and peasants inevitably intensifies the national class struggle.

Most Marxists hold that only a dedicated and well-organized vanguard party can rebuild the inherited state machinery to represent the interests of the workers and peasants. This requires institutionalizing new channels to mobilize these classes, informing them publicly of the issues and enabling them to participate in the crucial decisions which shape the government's role. That colonialism denied the workers and peasants the basic elements of education in most of Africa makes this task doubly difficult. Yet most Marxists believe that the failure of the new rulers to build a vanguard party and overcome these difficulties constitutes a crucial factor explaining their inability to exercise state power to reconstruct the national economy to meet the people's needs. (Part IV of this text more fully outlines Marxist theory and practice relating to finance during the transition to socialism.)

Summary

Mainstream and Marxist theorists seek to explain the problems of public finance in Africa from qualitatively different perspectives. Mainstream economists generally view the state as spending tax revenues primarily to create a framework within which private enterprise can function smoothly and invest in increased production to meet the needs of society. Initially, they assumed state should balance the budget, ensuring that tax revenues collected covered required expenditures. Following the Great Depression of the 1930s, Keynesians argued that the state should utilize fiscal, as well as monetary, policies to offset business cycles. This led to debates on appropriate tax measures and debt policies. "Demand-side" economists usually call for progressive taxes which fall more heavily on higher-income groups. "Supply-side" economists more typically advocate low business taxes and incentives to encourage business investment. "Welfare" economists tend to recommend taxes on high-income groups to transfer income to finance improvements in the conditions of the poor.

On the issue of public debt, Keynesians generally maintain that governments should borrow to combat recessions, managing the resulting debt to counter further cyclical fluctuations. Monetarists object that government borrowing causes inflation without necessarily increasing production. In the 1970s, the onset of "stagflation"—unemployment accompanied by inflation—strengthened the monetarists' call for government austerity.

Mainstream theorists transferred this debate to the Third World including African countries. Their efforts to assess tax capacity encountered data collection difficulties compounded by weak administrative capacity. When tax revenues lagged, new governments initially borrowed heavily to finance neglected social and economic infrastructure, seeking to attract increased private investment. Keynesian economists still tend to justify expanded government debt, arguing that a little inflation may help to stimulate investment. Monetarists, while advocating low taxes on high-income groups and corporations to attract private investment, call for sharply reduced government spending and borrowing to halt inflationary pressures.

Marxist economists reject as unrealistic both the Keynesians' and the monetarists' view of public finance. Despite contradictions reflecting the history and level of class struggle in particular cases, developed countries' governmental financial policies respond primarily to the concerns of growing monopoly capitalist interests. The government must collect taxes to provide the necessary administration and social and economic infrastructure to facilitate capitalist accumulation and reinvestment; and finance the police and military to maintain and expand the areas of capitalist reproduction. Military production has provided temporary Keynesian-type boosts to capitalist economies; but simultaneously, it has deepened their inherent contradictions. The mounting demands of the working classes, furthermore, lead to contradictory state policies. Marxists hold that the debates between the Keynesians and monetarists tend to reflect these kinds of conflicting interests and contradictions.

The capitalist welfare state, most Marxists agree, arose in response to the growing demands of the workers. The government taxed the superprofits obtained through imperialist exploitation of Third World countries to finance various welfare programmes. In the 1970s, however, as overproduction, unemployment and inflation spread throughout the capitalist world, more and more developed capitalist states imposed monetarist policies, sharply cutting back social services and placing the burden of the crisis on the lower-income groups.

The emerging African national state experience an ongoing struggle, shaped by almost a century of colonial rule, between transnational corporate affiliates, local capitalists and petty-bourgeois elements, and the peasants and workers. The continuing argument over fiscal policies reflects this ongoing "silent class struggle".

Marxists focus attention on the surplus value currently or potentially produced in developing countries. They hold that the low taxes on business profits advocated by most mainstream economists simply permit foreign firms to ship investable surpluses out of the national economy. They note that petty-bourgeois nationalist elements, seeking to use state power to legitimate their government while enriching themselves, sometimes come into conflict with transnational corporate interests. Transnationals, however, frequently seek to co-opt these elements by offering them directorships and shares of equity in local corporate affiliates—and even outright bribes.

In the 1970s and 1980s, African states' efforts to escape the impact of the general crisis of capitalism by adopting monetarist policies, Marxists assert, inevitably worsen the conditions of the African majority. Only a dedicated vanguard party, representing the workers and peasants, can rebuild the state machinery and implement financial and fiscal policies designed to lay the foundation for an increasingly balanced, integrated and socialized national economy.

Notes

1. J.M. Keynes, *General Theory of Employment*, New York, Harcourt, Brace & Co., 1935, p. 129.
2. Mikesell and Zinser, "The Nature of the Savings Function in Developing Countries: A Survey of the Theoretical and Empirical Literature," *Journal of Economic Literature*, Vol. 11, March 1973, pp. 12-15.
3. Marxists term the relative amount of capital invested (c), compared to the amount of labour employed (variable capital, *v*), the "organic composition of capital".
4. Even in the prosperous 1960s, official reports said one out of six Americans, a high proportion of them blacks, lived below the official poverty level.
5. Baran, *The Political Economy of Backwardness*, points out that reducing the conspicuous consumption of the wealthy few, and directing investment to more appropriate productive sectors, would augment the actual amount of surplus generated.

Exercises and Research

1. To what extent have mainstream concepts on appropriate government expenditures changed over the last century?
2. Compare Keynesian and monetarist theories concerning governments' efforts to balance their budgets. How would Keynesians propose that governments use their fiscal and monetary policies to counterbalance business cycles?
3. What is the nature of the mainstream debate over taxes in terms of their progressivity, their role as incentives, and their effect in transferring income?
4. How do monetarists criticize the Keynesian theory concerning government debt?
6. Contrast the Marxist theory of the capitalist state to that implicit in the mainstream theory of public finance.
7. Examine the debate among Marxists over the way imperialism and the class struggle affect the welfare state under capitalism. How do Marxists tend to explain the rise of monetarism in developed capitalist countries?
8. How do Marxists suggest that the class struggle affects government fiscal policies in most African states?
9. Evaluate your government's fiscal policies to determine what theory or theories seem to have influenced their formulation.

Recommended Readings

(For annotations, see bibliography at the end of the book.)

Baldwin, *Economic Development and Export Growth*
Clower *et al.*, *Growth without Development*
Cox-George, *Finance and Development in West Africa*
Falkena, *The South African State and Its Entrepreneurs*
Ghai (ed.), *Economic Independence in Africa*
Hartman, *Enterprise and Politics in South Africa*
Houghton, *The South African Economy*
IBRD country studies
Issawi, *Egypt in Review*
Jackson (ed.), *Economic Development in Africa*
Kaldor, *The Scourge of Monetarism*
Lenin, *State and Revolution*
Lewis, *Reflections on Nigeria's Economic Growth*
Llewellyn, *International Financial Integration*
Lombard (ed.), *Economic Policy in South Africa*
Morton, *Aid and Dependence*

Nnoli, *Path to Nigerian Development*
Norval, *A Quarter of a Century of Industrial Progress in South Africa*
Ola and Onimode, *Economic Development in Nigeria*
Sandbrook, *The Politics of Basic Needs*
Sarant, *Zero-base Budgeting in the Public Sector*
Saylor, *The Economic System of Sierra Leone*
Seidman, *Comparative Development Strategies in East Africa*
—— *An Economics Textbook for Africa*
—— *Ghana's Development Experience, 1952-1966*
—— *Planning for Development in SubSaharan Africa*
Uppal and Salkever (eds), *African Problems in Economic Development*

Chapter 8: Tax Policies

Upon independence, most African governments sought to alter their tax structures to increase tax revenues. Some also tried to achieve a more equitable distribution of the tax burden. This chapter first considers, briefly, the issue of tax capacity of sub-Saharan African countries. Then it outlines the major tax patterns as they have evolved since independence. Finally, it discusses the possibilities and obstacles involved in introducing land taxes.

Table 8.1
Central Government Tax Revenues of Selected African States, as Percentage of Gross Domestic Product, 1982.

Country	*Currency*	*Tax Revenue (mn.)*	*Tax as % of GDP*
Botswana	Pula	217.9	29.6%
Ghana	Cedi	4180.9	...
Kenya	Shilling	13486	19.8%
Lesotho	Maloit	46.63[a]	19.3%
Malawi	Kwacha	207.67	16.5%
Nigeria	Naira	5155.9[b]	15.3%
Sierra Leone	Leone	175.3	11.0%
South Africa	Rand	14122[c]	20.2%
Sudan	Pounds	673.3	10.8%
Swaziland	Emalangeni	120.82[c]	21.8%
Tanzania	Shilling	8151[c]	17.9%
Zambia	Kwacha	776.2	21.8%
Zimbabwe	Dollar	1364.5	27.2%

Notes: (a) 1977 data; (b) Latest data for tax revenue = 1978; (c) 1981 data.

Sources: Tax data from International Monetary Fund, Government Finance Statistics Yearbook, 1982 and 1984, country tables; Gross Domestic Product data from International Monetary Fund, International Financial Statistics, December, 1984.

Tax Capacity

As noted in Chapter 7, IMF economists formulated a regression equation for evaluating the tax capacity of developing countries. Difficulties of obtaining adequate data, however, hinder its use. Table 8.1, therefore, simply indicates the relationship between tax revenues and GDP, in selected African countries. It reveals that their average tax revenues constitute a significantly smaller share of GDP than in developed capitalist countries, where taxes typically total a quarter to a third.

The relatively low ratio of tax revenue to GDP in independent Africa reflects in part the prevailing low per capita incomes. A low-income population cannot pay high taxes without reducing consumption of necessities. Various combinations of factors, however, may cause the differences between the ratios in particular countries. These include: very low per capita incomes (e.g. Lesotho); concentration of incomes in the modern sector combined with fairly high tax rates (e.g. Botswana, diamond mines); low effective tax rates despite very high rates of profit (e.g. South Africa).

In the 1970s, Ghana appeared to be a special case: instead of taxing urban cash incomes, the government relied on export taxes on cocoa. This discouraged cultivation of cocoa and stimulated smuggling through neighbouring countries, leaving tax revenues chronically too low to meet expenditures.

In Zimbabwe, throughout UDI and in the first year of independence, tax measures introduced in line with mainstream theory left hundreds of millions of dollars worth of domestically generated surpluses untaxed, even though they were not invested (see Table 8.2). By 1982, however, the government had

Table 8.2
The Disposal of Investable Surpluses in Zimbabwe, 1975, 1978, 1982

	1975		*1978*		*1982*	
	($mn)	*(%)*	*($mn)*	*(%)*	*($mn)*	*(%)*
Domestic Product[a]	1,917	100	2,231	100	4465	100
Gross Operating Profits[b]	833	44	867	39	1478	33
Capital Formation[c]	467	25	330	15	950	21
Net reported outflow of profits, dividends, interest & other remittances[d]	79	4	35	2	218	5
Direct taxes levied on companies[e]	138	7	125	6	364	8
Remaining investable surplus[f]	187	9	377	16	−54	−1

Notes to Table 8.2 overleaf.

Notes to Table 8.2: (a) Gross Domestic Product (GDP) at factor cost paid by resident producers to resident and non-resident factors of production for all goods and services within national boundaries. The GDP may have been reduced by transfer payments (see note 4 below).
(b) Gross Operating Profit (GOP) is factor income (after payment of wages and salaries) attributable to factors of production employed by but not necessarily owned by the establishment. Part is distributed to owners of the factors of production in the form of investment income (interest, dividends, distributed profits) and to other final recipients in the form of transfer income (direct taxes, pensions, bursaries, etc.). Estimates of depreciation of capital goods are not available. One could argue that the significant investable surpluses returned to the less than 10% of all wage and salary earners who earn about half the nation's wage bill constitute additional surpluses—perhaps as much as $800 million in 1982. Transfer payments would reduce the reported GOP (see note 4 below).
(c) Gross fixed capital formation is made up of all purchases, lease-hire acquisitions and own-account production of fixed assets, less sales of similar fixed assets, whether for new capital formation or to replace depreciated capital. About a tenth of gross fixed capital formation represented residential housing in 1978, most of it for the high income minority. By 1981, this had dropped to about 7%. Almost 45% was invested in buildings or civil engineering work, however, much of it financed by long term loans and government expenditures with little direct contribution to increased future productivity.
(d) Net investment income paid abroad, as officially reported. Unreported transfer payments—ie transfers through transnational corporate affiliates charging high prices for imports from or low prices for exports to their parent companies abroad—totalled an estimated additional $250-300 million in 1982. These would also have reduced the officially-reported GDP and GOP.
(e) Companies, public and private, pay about 60 percent of Zimbabwe's direct taxes. Taxes on the investable surpluses returned to self-employed individuals constitute a negligible additional percent of GDP.
(f) Unused investable surpluses remained in the hands of companies or individuals in Zimbabwe after taxes, capital formation and outflow of incomes until independence. By 1982, as the Zimbabwe government allowed increased remittances of funds abroad, these reported available investable surpluses had disappeared despite the growing GDP, and the country had to borrow abroad to offset the minus figure.

Source: Calculated from: Central Statistical Office, National Accounts of Zimbabwe, 1980; The Monthly Digest of Statistics, Feb., 1984; and Zimbabwe Income Tax Statistics, 1981 and 1983 (Harare: Government Printer)

increased its tax revenues, while permitting the companies to remit more investment income to their parent company abroad, so that no investable surplus remained unused within the country.

Governments may impose innumerable varieties and variations of taxes, far too many to survey fully in this text. Examining selected African countries, this chapter briefly reviews the status of company and individual income taxes; sales, excise and customs duties; export taxes; and the possibility of introducing agricultural taxes.

Direct vs. Indirect Taxes

Taxes generally fall into one of two major categories. The first, direct taxes, are imposed directly on incomes earned by individuals or companies. The second, indirect taxes, falling primarily on the sale of goods, must be either absorbed by the seller or passed on to the buyer.

At the beginning of the 1980s, direct taxes on incomes and profits generally provided between 15 and 45 per cent of African countries' revenues. Most African governments rely more heavily on indirect than direct taxes for several reasons:

1) Indirect taxes are usually easier to collect from non-wage earners than direct taxes. Most people, no matter how they obtain their incomes, buy goods. The sellers of the goods collect the taxes on their purchases and turn them over to the government.
2) Indirect taxes provide a broader tax net, reaching a large number of people who are not wage earners. In the typical African country, these constitute three-quarters or more of the population. Even in Zimbabwe, with the largest industrial sector per capita in independent sub-Saharan Africa, individual income tax payers at independence constituted less than 3 per cent of the adult population, since most African wage earners received less than the taxable minimum.
3) Governments may employ indirect taxes to influence the pattern of consumption. They may set high taxes on luxuries and commodities like cigarettes and alcohol considered injurious to health, to reduce consumption as well as to increase government revenues.

Direct Taxes

The two primary direct taxes are those imposed on the incomes of companies and wealthy individuals. These incomes constitute the main investable surpluses generated within a nation.

The Company Tax: In some African countries, as Table 8.3 indicates, taxes on corporate incomes provides a larger—in some cases much larger—share of income tax revenue than any other tax. This reflects the fact that private, usually foreign, firms dominate the modern sectors of most African states. In Nigeria, for example, during the 1970s oil boom, oil companies provided over three-quarters of the nation's tax revenues. In South Africa, where the low wages of Africans under apartheid help to ensure high company profits, company taxes also provide a large share of revenue. In other countries, given the corporations' typically dominant role in the economy, their contribution to total revenues appears surprisingly low.

Table 8.3
Corporate Income Taxes in Selected States, in millions of national currency unit and as percent of total tax revenue, 1972 and 1982

		1972		*1982*	
Country	*Natl. currency*	*Natl. currency (mn.)*	*Tax revenue (%)*	*Natl. currency (mn.)*	*Tax revenue (%)*
Ghana	Cedi	40.6	10.9	575.70	13.7
Kenya	Shillings	901.0	42.2	1548.00[a]	29.2[a]
Malawi	Kwacha	7.6	21.1	45.17	21.7
Nigeria	Niara	452.5[b]	49.3[b]	3542.90[b]	68.7[b]
Sierra Leone	Leones	25.9[c]	30.4[c]	21.80[c]	12.4[c]
South Africa	Rand	977.0	34.1	4772.00	33.8
Sudan	Pound	10.6	8.4	83.30	12.3
Swaziland	Emalangeni	3.0	19.2	18.00[d]	15.0[d]
Tanzania	Shillings	NA	NA	16.47	20.2
Zambia	Kwacha	NA	NA	132.70	17.0

Notes: (a) The latest available data is for 1977; (b) Oil companies paid 85% of Nigeria's 1972 corporate tax, and 65% of its 1978 corporate tax (the data here used); (c) The iron mining company tax revenue declined in absolute as well as relative terms from an earlier 6.1 million Leones to 2.4 million Leones in 1972, and provided no revenue in 1982; (d) 1981 data.
NA — not available.

Source: International Monetary Fund, Government Finance Statistics Yearbook, 1982 and 1984, Country tables.

Companies typically pay income tax on the net profits which remain after they have paid all operating costs. As Table 8.4 shows, most African governments set the company tax at a flat rate, typically between 35 and 51 per cent of net profits. Governments could impose a more progressive tax, graduated to tax a higher proportion of higher corporate profits. Tax collectors, however, find such taxes more difficult to calculate and administer. In the mid-1970s, Nigeria, for example, taxed profits at 40 per cent up to ₦10,000 and 45 per cent on profits beyond that amount. By 1980, however, it had reinstated a flat 45 per cent tax rate.

Companies typically pay an effective tax rate somewhat lower than the nominal rate stipulated, by taking advantage of various deductions permitted by the law. Some of these are noted in Table 8.4. Popular parlance has dubbed these "tax loopholes" because they frequently permit company managers to allocate funds, which might otherwise be taxed as net profits, to expenditure categories on which the government sets lower taxes or none at all. Governments may seek to use deductions to influence taxpayer behaviour.

The more complicated the deductions, however, the more difficult and expensive it may be to administer them. Sometimes, too, they lead to unintended consequences.

Many governments provide allowances for capital expenditure on farm improvements, industrial buildings, railway lines and machinery. In effect, such deductions, which aim to stimulate investment, constitute subsidies for those expenditures. In Zimbabwe, for example, until 1982, the government permitted entrepreneurs to deduct 100 per cent of new investments from profits before paying the company tax. Thus a commercial farmer who purchased a new tobacco barn could deduct 100 per cent of the purchase price from his profits. In 1982, the government reduced the permissible deduction to 30 per cent of capital expenditures, except when the investment was made in rural areas in which case it was still 100 per cent deductible. Thus the commercial farmer could still deduct 100 per cent for his new barn, but the owner of a factory in a city could only deduct 30 per cent of the cost of a new machine.

Some tax experts point out that deductions for investment in machinery and equipment encourage companies to invest in capital-intensive production techniques. They recommend, instead, that governments permit tax deductions when companies provide additional employment or use local instead of imported raw materials.

Governments frequently allow depletion allowances for mining companies. This allowance purports to compensate the mining company for the declining value of the mine as the ore is extracted. If the company initially invested $100,000 in the mine, and expected to remove all the ore over a ten-year period, a depletion allowance might enable it to deduct $10,000 from its profits each year before paying taxes. If, in fact, more ore remains after the ten-year period, some tax laws permit the company to go on deducting the allowance from the profits generated by its continued operations even though previous deductions had enabled it to recover fully its initial investment.

Many tax laws permit companies to deduct interest paid on loans from their profits before tax. In effect, such laws subsidize borrowing. For example, a company, which would ordinarily pay a 45% tax on its net profit would have to pay $4500 on a $10,000 net profit. Now suppose it pays $5,000 in interest on a loan from a bank or from another affiliated corporation. It then pays tax only on the remaining $5000, that is $2250.

Corporate groups may take advantage of such provisions in the law to reduce their overall tax liability, for example, when a company borrows from its own affiliate. It benefits from the deductions on its repayments, while the affiliate pays a lower rate of tax on interest payments than on operating profits.

Table 8-4 Corporate Tax provisions in selected African States and the United Kingdom

Country	*Corporate*	*Tax on Branch Income*	INCOME DETERMINATION *Inventory valuation*	*Capital gains*
Botswana	35%	35%	Valued at cost less reasonable loss thru damage, etc.	35% on net capital gains.
Kenya	local inc = 45%; mining cos. = 27.5% for 1st 5 yrs, then 45%; resident insurance cos. = 40%.	52.5%	At lower of cost or market.	Corporate rate; losses may be carried forward against future gains.
Malawi	50% on income from within; plus 5% on dividends distributable abroad.	50%	At lower cost or net realizable value.	Taxable if considered to be trading.
Nigeria	45%	illegal to establish branches (some exceptions)	FIFO usually followed.	Gains taxed at 20% for all forms of assets.
South Africa	Normal: 42%, surcharge = 5%, total = 46.2%; gold, oil cos. pay on formula; diamond cos. = 51.75%.	Same as on co. profits; no tax withheld on transfers of profits to head office.	Lower of cost or market value; may use LIFO with permission.	No tax.
Zambia	45%; (25% on farm income).	Same as corp. tax, but no withholding tax on profits to head office.	Lower of cost or net realizable value.	No tax.
Zimbabwe	45% + 15% surcharge = 51.75%.	15% of 56% of taxable income + corp. tax.	Lower of cost or market value; FIFO not permitted.	30% on sales of immovable property, marketable securities.
United Kingdom	52%	Same as for corps.	Lower of cost or market value; LIFO not permitted; special deduction for effect of inflation.	30% of gain.

Intercompany dividends	*Foreign income*	*Stock dividends*	*Depreciation allowances*	*Depletion allowances*
Taxed only when resident private co. receives dividend from a resident co.	No tax on income to resident cos. except from South mines, prospecting	10% on straight line for 10 yrs.	10-25% capital allowances on fixed assets other than land and bldgs., 25% on new industrial bldgs in 1st yr. of use, 2.5% for other industrial and commercial bldgs.	
Domestic co. may exclude dividends from domestic corps. or subsidiaries where own 12.5% or more equity.	Taxed at branch income rate unless Kenya has treaty with parent country providing otherwise.	Domestic corps. can distribute common stock dividends tax free.	Heavy machinery = 37.5%; other vehicles = 25%; ind'l bldgs, hotels, = 12.5%, ships = 40%.	Special allowances for mines; farm works = 20% in addition to other allowances claimed.
Essentially exempt.	Exempt	Exempt	Industrial, farm, hotel bldgs = 10% 1st yr, 5% annual allowances; machinery and equipment = 10-20% for 1st yr, 10–33% annual allowance.	
Tax paid on dividends before distribution is credited vs, recipient cos. tax liability.	Nigeria abrogated all tax treaties in 1979.	1st yr. allowance = 33.5%% for all equipment, 12.5% declining balance; ind'l bldgs = 25% + 10%; non-ind'l bldgs = 15% + 10%.	None.	Varying allowances on qualifying capital expenditures: eg. ind'l bldgs = 15% for 1st yr, 10% annually; plantations = 25% 1st yr, 15% annually.
No tax.	No tax.	No tax.	Deduct fair and reasonable amounts; 2% depreciation annually on bldgs; 100% on all mining capital expenditures; 25% per yr. for 4 yrs. allowance for scientific research, development.	
20% withholding tax, with recipient co. getting tax credit.	Taxed on remittances to Zambia; avoid double taxation by foreign tax credits.	No tax on bonus shares.	Initial allowances = 10% of ind'l bldgs; wear & tear allowance of 5% on ind'l bldgs, 2% on commercial bldgs, 30% on machinery.	
Tax exempt.	Relief from Zimbabwe tax.	Bonus shares, stock dividends exempt.	100% initial allowance for all bldgs, machinery.	15% for capital expenditures on rural growth points 5% for minerals.
Excluded from tax.	Tax on income received except tax credits provided under double taxation treaties.	May distribute some classes of stock free but if cash will be taxed as dividend income.	100% depreciation allowance on machinery except private cars; or 25% 1st yr, 25% per yr on declining balance.	Varying allowances for depreciation of natural resources properties.

Table 8–4 (continued)

Country	DEDUCTIONS *Operating losses*	*Payment to foreign affiliates*	*Other Items*
Botswana	Losses carried forward for 5 years except no time limit for farms, mines, prospectors.	Royalties, interest, service fees deductible if at arms length and have paid withholding tax.	
Kenya	May carry forward and offset losses only against future profits from source; no time limit.	May not deduct interest, royalties, or fees paid to head office.	1. Insurance cos. must hold reserves; 2. Must distribute 40% of after tax profits + 100% of capital gains and investment income.
Malawi	May carry forward net operating losses indefinitely.		May deduct costs of land, crop preparation, pre-production costs of manufacture, payments to charitable organizations, and interest.
Nigeria	None.	'Pioneer' co. profits = exempt for 3-5 yrs.	
South Africa	Indefinite carry over of losses (no carry back).	15% withholding tax unless abated by treaty. Deductions for royalties, management fees, interest if approximate arms length amounts.	100% deduction for training skilled workers; special allowance for exports = 75-100% of marketed expenditure.
Zambia	Carry back one year, forward unlimited time against income from same source.	Deductions for royalties, management services, interest	Tax on rural enterprise reduced 33.3% for 1st 5 years in business.
Zimbabwe	Carried forward indefinitely.	Deductions for royalties, interest, service fees of approximate arms' length amounts.	
United Kingdom	Losses carried forward indefinitely in same trade by same co. and carried back 1 year including losses of 75% owned affiliates.	Deductions for royalties, management fees, interest if approximate arms' length amounts.	No deduction for entertainment except for approved circumstances.

TAX INCENTIVES		OTHER TAXES
Inward Investments	*Capital Investments*	
Extra relief granted for projects considered beneficial to Botswana.	15% allowances on new industrial bldgs (including hotels); 25% on new machinery used in such buildings.	Withholding tax deducted from payments to non-residents; 15% for interest, dividends, royalties, management or consultant fees; 20% for certain contractual fees; 10% for entertainment.
	Capital allowances on new bldgs. on straightline basis; industry = 25%; hotels = 40%.	Sales taxes, varied between 15–20%; withholding tax deducted from payments to non-residents as follows: 15% from dividends, 20% from royalties, 30% from rents.
None	See deductions.	Double taxation treaties with Denmark, France, Holland, Kenya, Norway, South Africa, Sweden, Switzerland, United Kingdom, United States.
May repatriate approved investments together with dividends; may receive 5 yr tax holiday.		85% tax on profits from petroleum exports after oil firms' starting cost is fully amortized; 45% withholding tax on interest, royalties paid by one co. to another with some exceptions.
Special incentives for 'economic' development areas; 30% for new machinery; 20% for factory bldgs 10% for hotels.		Undistributed profits tax: = 33.3% of amount by which distributed income exceeds dividends distributed; Donations tax: = graduated, 3%-25% on cumulative value of donations; specified donations = deductible. Deduct 25% of cost of housing employees, up to R3000 per dwelling. Deduct all expenditures for specified scientific research. Withholding taxes: 15% for dividends, 10% for interest, royalties. Double tax agreements with specified countries.
Tax and other relief to new industries under specified conditions.	(See deductions).	Sales tax: 10%, 15% or 20% on locally manufactured goods; 20% tax on employment of non-Zambians; Undistributed profits tax = 35% in addition to normal profits tax.
	15% on new bldgs, farm improvements, machinery.	Export incentives paid by government, exempt from tax; 15% withholding tax on dividends to non-resident shareholders except in South Africa.
15% cash grant for development area investment; 22% for machinery and equipment.	100% 1st year depreciation; 50% on industrial bldgs.	Petroleum revenue tax=60% of total profits; Development Land Tax = 60% of value developed land on sale; Value added tax = 8%–15% on light hydrocarbons and many non-essentials; Local municipal taxes on property; Withholding taxes of varying amounts on income (interest, dividends, royalties) paid abroad limited by double taxation agreement.

Source: Price-Waterhouse, Information Guide to Corporate Taxes (1251 Avenue of Americas, New York N.Y., 10020), 1980; up-dated by Coopers and Lybrand, International Tax Summaries, 1983 (New York: John Wiley & Sons, 1983).

Governments often tax capital gains at lower rates than net profits, and sometimes not at all. Capital gains are gains made from buying shares of equity or real property of various kinds at one price, and selling them again at a higher price. For instance, Company A may buy shares worth $10,000 in another company, receiving a tax deduction for this new investment. It may then sell those shares for $15,000, but it will only pay the capital gains tax on the resulting $5,000 in added profits—say 30 per cent, instead of the corporate income tax rate of 45 per cent. Presumably, the government thus aims to stimulate investment. Unfortunately, however, it may also foster speculation. Furthermore, it may provide affiliated companies with another avenue for reducing overall tax revenues.

In Zimbabwe, for example, the pre-independence government imposed no tax at all on capital gains. In 1982, the new government imposed a 30 per cent capital gains tax, but exempted pension funds, local authorities, parastatals and welfare organizations. Pension funds, closely associated with industrial and financial groups (see Chapter 5), purchased buildings from industrial corporations and then charged them rent for their use. The industrial corporations paid only 30 per cent capital gains tax, and, if they invested the capital gained, could receive tax deductions for so doing. At the same time, they could deduct from their profits as costs all the rental payments they made to the pension funds for their buildings before they paid taxes. The pension funds, on the other hand, could sell the premises at a later date and retain the capital gains within the group, untaxed.

In many countries, companies pay no tax on interest obtained from loans to governments, local authorities, parastatals or post office savings banks. While providing companies with an incentive to lend to government agencies, this also substantially reduces their contribution to tax revenues.

Many governments permit a company that makes a loss one year to deduct that loss from its profits in subsequent years before paying tax. This is called "carrying the loss forward". Some governments permit companies to carry the losses forward indefinitely until they have been fully recovered, which may substantially reduce tax revenues in good years. Others set some limit. Some governments also allow companies to carry the losses back one or more years, providing a rebate on taxes in earlier good years. These provisions significantly reduce the taxes a corporation must pay on profits in a good year.

Some governments permit companies to deduct business expenses from net profits before tax. These deductions have, in some instances, provided elastic loopholes, which may be stretched to include parties for visiting officials and their wives, extensive trips abroad, the purchase of yachts for entertainment, and so forth.

In designing taxes to attract foreign capital, African states should not forget the potential benefits of double taxation treaties. These treaties are usually negotiated between the governments of developing and developed countries on a bilateral basis. They typically create incentives for investments in developing countries in one of two forms:

1. The capital-exporting country exempts all foreign income from tax. The developing country may, therefore, raise taxes to the level of that imposed in the developed country without discouraging investment.
2. The capital-exporting government deducts from its tax bill, levied on income from abroad, all taxes which the investor has paid on that income in the country where it was generated. If a transnational corporation has already paid a corporate tax in the developing country, it will receive a tax credit for that tax in its home country. If the developing country's corporate tax is less than the rate charged in the transnational's home country, however, the transnational will have to pay the difference to its home government. In effect, by reducing the corporate tax, the developing country provides a tax subsidy, not to the transnational's corporate affiliate, but to the developed home country government. As shown in Table 8.4, Britain's corporate tax rate in 1980 was 52 per cent. Therefore, any African government with a double taxation treaty with Britain that taxed British companies at a lower rate in effect provided the British government with a tax subsidy.

Japan, the United States and Britain, among others, have negotiated this kind of double taxation agreement with a number of African states. Readers may inquire from the Ministry of Foreign Affairs whether their government has negotiated such a treaty.

Individual Income Taxes: Most African governments levy some form of direct tax on individual incomes (see Table 8.5). Not surprisingly, individual income taxes provide a higher proportion of government revenues in countries, like South Africa and Zimbabwe, with very skewed income distributions. The amount of revenue they produce may also reflect the ruling group's willingness to tax itself.

Typically, governments graduate individual income tax: the higher the income, the higher the tax on the marginal increment of additional income. As Table 8.6 shows, the degree of graduation varies significantly from country to country. Usually, persons with very low incomes pay little or no tax. The more steeply graduated the tax, the more progressive it is considered to be.

Most African governments permit a married man to pay lower income tax than a single person. His wife's income is commonly taxed at the higher single rate, or her income tax return may be filed jointly with that of her husband so that both together pay a higher marginal rate. Women's groups argue that this difference in treatment is discriminatory. Most governments permit deductions of several hundred dollars per child for up to three children. Botswana, Kenya and South Africa, among others, do not. Permitting such deductions makes the tax liability more difficult to calculate. In addition, some governments may consider tax deductions for children as an unnecessary incentive to expand population growth.

Table 8.5
Individual Income Tax Revenues in national currency and as percent of total revenues of selected African States, 1972 and 1982

		1972		*1982*	
Country	*Currency*	*Natl. currency (mn.)*	*Tax revenue (%)*	*Natl. currency (mn.)*	*Tax revenue (%)*
Ghana	Cedi	35.8	9.6	693.80	16.5
Kenya	Shillings	36.0	1.7	601.00[a]	11.3[a]
Malawi	Kwacha	6.5	18.1	34.28	16.5
Nigeria	Niara	0.3	NA	3.70	0.01
Sierra Leone	Leone	4.1	4.4	20.00	11.4
South Africa	Rand	781.0	27.2	3440.00	24.3
Sudan	Pound	56.0	4.1	47.40	7.0
Swaziland	Emalangeni	2.4	15.4	21.43	17.7
Tanzania	Shillings	125.0	8.7	1012.00	12.4
Zambia	Kwacha	NA	NA	127.90	16.4
Zimbabwe	Dollars	NA	NA	373.60	27.3

Note: (a) Latest data available for Kenya is 1977.

Source: International Monetary Fund, Government Finance Statistics Yearbook, 1982 and 1984, Country tables.

Wages and salaries are the easiest income to tax. All employers of more than, say, ten workers, are responsible for deducting tax before paying their employees, and turning it over to the government. Often called Pay-As-You-Earn (PAYE), this tax usually accounts for the largest share of the individual income tax revenue. In 1980, in Zimbabwe, for example, PAYE accounted for 92 per cent of all individual income taxes. Yet, although over a quarter of the adult population received wages and salaries that year, less than 10 per cent paid income tax, because less than 10 per cent of all workers received half the entire wage and salary bill. The wages of the rest of the workers, all Africans, were below the taxable minimum of $2,000 a year.

African governments find it more difficult to tax the large amounts of wealth that individuals receive from sources other than wages and salaries. These include dividends, interest, professional fees and the profits of self-employed store-owners, farmers and other businessmen. Non-incorporated individuals' taxable income as reported in Zimbabwe in 1981, for example, totalled only about $50 million, only 10 per cent of the non-incorporated sector's reported gross operating profits of $504 million. Only one out of four of the nation's prosperous commercial farmers paid any income tax. This suggests that large numbers of non-incorporated individual businesses successfully evaded income taxes.

Wealthy self-employed individuals may avoid income taxes by various means. They may not report all income received. They may give funds to charity, deducting them for tax purposes. Thus, if they give a yacht to charity, it becomes tax deductible; but they may then use the yacht for their own purposes. They may form corporations into which they put their funds, or put their funds in trust with commercial banks, which may then use them to

Table 8-6 Graduated Individual Income Taxes in Selected African States, and the United Kingdom in U.S. SDR equivalents* for different levels of remuneration

	Botswana		Kenya		Malawi	
	Taxable income (SDRs)	*Rate of tax (%)*	*Taxable income (SDRs)*	*Rate of tax (%)*	*Taxable income (SRDs)*	*Rate of tax (%)*
Schedule	1st 2,479	10%	1st 2,080	10%	1st 1,357	10%
	next 3,306	20%	next 2,080	15%	next 1,357	20%
	next 3,305	30%	next 2,080	25%	next 1,357	30%
	next 4,959	40%	next 2,080	35%	next 2,715	32.5%
	next 6,612	50%	next 2,080	45%	next 2,715	35.0%
	next 16,532	60%	next 2,080	50%	next 5,430	37.5%
	over 37,197	65%	next 4,161	60%	next 12,219	40.0%
			over 16,470	65%	over 27,154	50.0%
Spouse	Husband and wife effectively taxed separately.		Liability on wife's income calculated separately, added to husband's income.		Married woman's income added to husband's for tax purposes, tho tax credit permitted if separate incomes would be in lower bracket.	
Deductions	Personal and other allowances for education, insurance, medical expenses, mortgage interest (none for children).		Life insurance premiums, mortgage relief, personal relief up to SDR200/family.		Marriage allowance, per child allowance up to 4 children, life assurance premium.	
Local income taxes	None		None		None	

Note: *To permit comparison, the income schedules are converted to SDR equivalent at 1983 rate of exchange as reported in International Monetary Fund, International Financial Statistics. This explains the seemingly odd categories.

Source: Coopers and Lybrand, 1983 International Tax Summaries—a guide for planning and decisions (New York: John Wiley & Sons, 1983).

Table 8-6 continued

	Nigeria		Zambia		Zimbabwe	
	Taxable income (SDRs)	*Rate of tax (%)*	*Taxable income (SDRs)*	*Rate of tax (%)*	*Taxable income (SDRs)*	*Rate of tax (%)*
Schedule	1st 2,552	10%	1st 781	5%	1st 1,728	10%
	next 2,552	15%	next 1,171	10%	rate rises 2% for each	
	next 2,552	20%	next 1,171	15%	additional 864 till	
	next 2,552	25%	next 1,952	20%	reaches 14,688;	
	next 2,552	30%	next 1,952	30%	over 14,688 = 45%	
	next 6,380	40%	next 2,434	45%	+ surcharge, starting	
	next 6,380	45%	next 2,434	60%	at 15% for 1st 864,	
	next 12,760	55%	next 3,905	70%	rising by 2% to 33%	
	over 38,280	70%	next 3,905	75%	at 10,368 and over.	
			over 19,525	80%		
Spouse	All individuals liable to tax.		All individuals liable to tax.			
Deductions	Allowances to men and women for children, dependent relatives; life insurance premiums, pensions, other retirement schemes.		Single: 507; married: 1,327. For children (up to 6), handicap, life insurance premiums.			
Local income taxes	None (income tax collected from residents by each state on a uniform basis).		None.			

Table 8-6 continued

	South Africa		United Kingdom	
	Taxable income (SDRs)	*Rate of tax (%)*	*Taxable income (SDRs)*	*Rate of tax (%)*
Schedule	187 to 5,471:	10%	1st 17,734	30%
	From 5,471 to 11,725:	Rises 2% per 781	next 3,186	40%
			next 5,542	45%
	From 11,725 to 26,577:	Rises 2% per 1,562	next 8,590	50%
			next 8,590	55%
	From 26,577 to 31,268:	Rises 1% per 1,562	Remainder: over 43,643	60%
	Over 31,268:	50%	(+15% surcharge on investment income over 8,659)	
Spouse	For married persons, reduce tax by applicable rebates. Single person pays 20% surcharge up to 21,887, over that pays 50% on all income.		Wife's income aggregated with husband's for tax purposes.	
Deductions	Deductions for up to 5 children, persons over 60, other dependants, insurance premiums.		Full tax relief for taxes paid outside UK. Deductions for up to 3 children.	
Local income taxes	None		None	

buy and sell securities. The government may tax the resulting profits only at the tax rate for capital gains which is typically lower than the tax rate on ordinary profits.

It is obviously difficult for governments to administer and monitor effective collection of individual income taxes other than PAYE. The difficulty of monitoring taxes imposed on individual incomes, other than wages and salaries, especially in Third World countries, probably constitutes the most important reason why they tend to be neglected. In addition, many mainstream theorists advocate low taxes on high incomes so as to encourage wealthy individuals to save and, they assumed, subsequently invest.

Indirect Taxes

A government may levy indirect taxes on commodities rather than wealth, for example through sales taxes, excise taxes, import duties, taxes on agricultural products, etc. Supply-side economists typically urge African governments to rely more heavily on indirect than direct taxes, leaving companies and high-income individuals free to invest their accumulated wealth. Demand-side economists, on the other hand, often hold that indirect taxes, especially those falling heavily on the lower-income groups, reduce the demand for goods, thus rendering investments unprofitable.

Who Pays Indirect Taxes? The burden of the indirect tax depends not only on the rate charged but on who pays it. As Diagram 8.1A illustrates, where the demand for the commodity taxed is inelastic, the producer may add the tax to the sales price so the customers pay it. The consumers pay most taxes on domestically consumed necessities because they must buy them.

If the demand for the commodity is elastic (see Diagram 8.1B), the producer cannot pass the tax on to the consumers without endangering sales. The producer may have to absorb some or all of the tax to keep sales up. In the case of taxes on exports, where the price is set on the world market, and demand for any one country's product is completely elastic (Diagram 8.1C), the local producers have no choice but to absorb the tax if they wish to sell their product.

Sales and Excise Taxes: Many African governments levy taxes on the sale of consumer goods, whether locally produced or imported. They collect the tax from retail traders, who usually pass them on to the consumer. Not infrequently, the traders explicitly add the tax on to the stated sales price, thus making clear to the consumer that the government tax has caused the resulting price increase.

Governments may introduce sales taxes because they are relatively easy to collect and cast a wide net, taxing many people who do not pay income taxes. In a country like Tanzania, with a large proportion of the population in rural areas or the informal sector, sales taxes may become the major source of revenue. In the 1970s, as Table 8.7 shows, several African governments raised sales taxes. By 1982, the Tanzanian government had increased its sales tax revenues almost twentyfold to provide 53 per cent of its total tax revenue;

Figure 8.1
Relative elasticity of demand

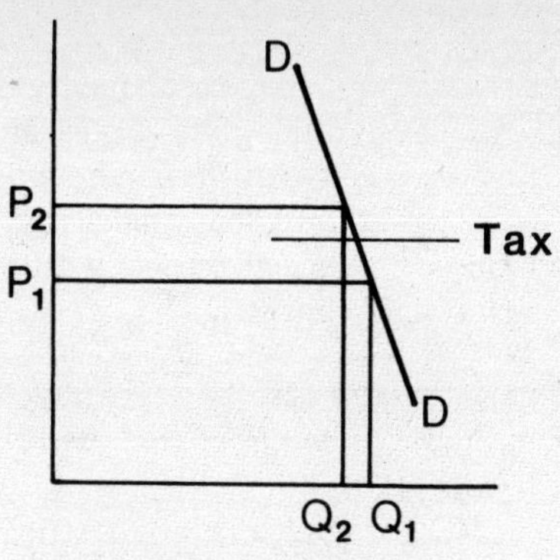

A. Inelastic demand

consumer usually pays the tax to obtain the needed commodity.

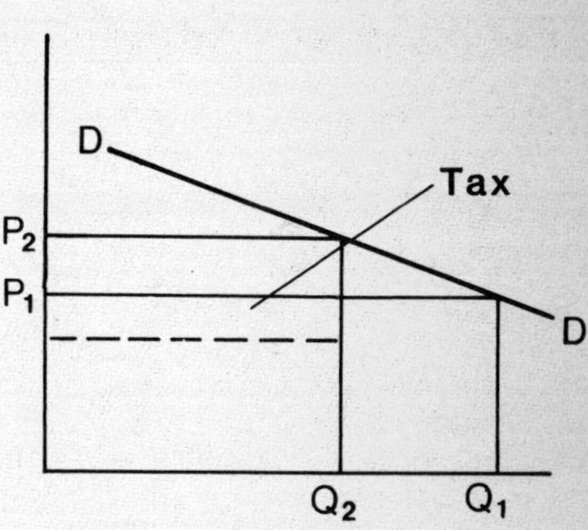

B. Relatively elastic demand

dotted line indicates sharing of tax burden between producer and consumers to keep prices down, sales up.

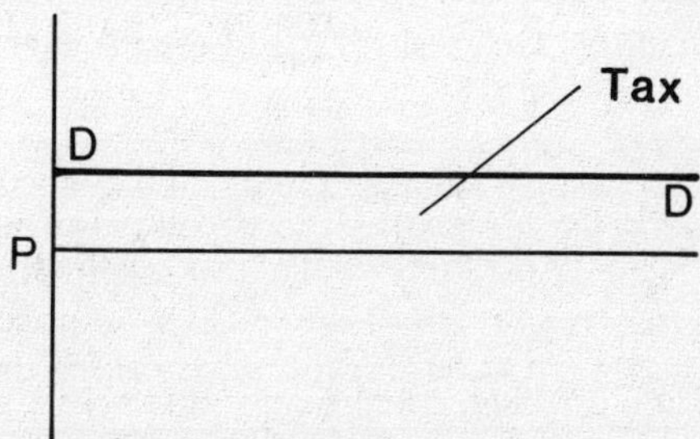

C. Completely elastic demand

producer absorbs tax to keep price down and sell produce –typical of export commodities.

and the Kenyan government had raised the sales tax to between 15 and 20 per cent of the value of the goods taxed to provide almost a third of its total tax revenue.

Table 8.7
Sales and Excise Taxes, in national currency units and as percent of total tax revenues, 1972 and 1982

A. SALES TAXES

		1972		*1982*	
Country	*Currency*	*Natl. currency (mn.)*	*Tax revenue (%)*	*Natl. currency (mn.)*	*Tax revenue (%)*
Ghana	Cedi	40.9	11.0	193.0	4.6
Kenya	Shilling	NA	NA	3896.0	28.8
Malawi	Kwacha	7.1	19.6	58.8	28.2
South Africa	Rand	181.0	6.3	2140.0	15.1
Tanzania	Shilling	219.0	15.3	4335.0	53.1
Zambia	Kwacha	NA	NA	118.6	15.3
Zimbabwe	Dollar	NA	NA	323.8	23.7

B. EXCISE TAXES

		1972		*1982*	
Country	*Currency*	*Natl. currency (mn.)*	*Tax revenue (%)*	*Natl. currency (mn.)*	*Tax revenue (%)*
Ghana	Cedi	74.4	20.0	1401.61	33.8
Kenya	Shilling	435.0	20.4	1293.00	9.9
Malawi	Kwacha	2.7	7.5	11.57	5.5
Nigeria	Niara	99.7	10.9	282.80	5.5
Sierra Leone	Leone	11.4	13.8	42.00	23.9
South Africa	Rand	513.0	17.9	1973.00	13.9
Sudan	Pounds	28.4	22.5	118.40	19.6
Tanzania	Shilling	243.0	16.4	8.00	0.1
Zambia	Kwacha	56.2	22.5	279.90	36.0
Zimbabwe	Dollar	NA	NA	745.80	10.6

Source: International Monetary Fund, Government Finance Statistics Yearbook, 1982, and 1984.

The impact of a sales tax depends on the kinds of consumer goods taxed, as well as the rate of the tax. A study in Tanzania showed[1] that a flat-rate sales tax falls most heavily on urban lower-income groups. Rural low-income groups produce about 40 per cent of their own essential consumption goods, notably food and drink (65 per cent) and housing (53 per cent). Urban low-income groups, in contrast, must buy almost all the goods they consume, and so must pay the taxes levied on them. Higher-income urban groups spend a smaller proportion of their income on essential consumption goods, so they pay a smaller percentage of their income in sales taxes

A government may reduce the impact of sales taxes on the urban poor by exempting basic necessities like staple foods, paraffin and children's clothing. However, this makes administration of the tax more complex. Few people, especially in lower-income brackets, know which items are exempt. Many may have difficulty in calculating the tax on a total bill in which some, but not all, items are exempt. Traders, seeking to maximize their profits, may manipulate prices without detection, implying that the sales tax has caused the resulting price increase.

Governments often levy higher sales taxes on durable consumer goods primarily purchased by higher-income groups, like furniture, refrigerators, television sets, radios and automobiles. They thus tax some of the higher incomes of non-wage workers not otherwise taxed. They may also discourage purchase of these items which are frequently imported with scarce foreign-exchange earnings. Of course, wage and salary workers taxed under PAYE will be doubly taxed to the extent that they, too, purchase such items.

Most African governments levy excise taxes on certain manufactured goods, like tobacco, spirits and luxuries. As Table 8.7B shows, these may provide significant amounts of revenue—about a third of total tax revenues in Zambia in 1980 for example. Many consumers, including lower-income families, habitually buy tobacco and spirits, providing a relatively inelastic demand for these items. A high tax on them, therefore, can reap high returns for government. Since these items may harm the consumers' health, any resulting reduction in consumption may be considered desirable. Excise taxes on luxury items like petrol for private cars may reduce consumption, hopefully encouraging savings which may be directed to more productive investment. When these items are imported, the economy also saves foreign exchange. If consumption persists, however, the government will at least receive the added tax revenues.

Import Duties: Most African governments levy duties directly on imports. The most important of these are custom duties, levied by customs officials on goods as they enter the country. Import duties on consumer items have much the same economic impact on customers as taxes on domestically produced goods. Depending on the elasticity of the demand for particular items, trading firms may pass them on to their customers.

African governments impose import duties for two primary reasons: first, they provide an important source of revenue in developing countries which depend significantly on imported goods. Table 8.8 shows that import duties provide a major share of tax revenue in several African states. In 1980, the relatively undeveloped economies of Botswana and Swaziland obtained over half their revenues in the form of customs duties collected and transferred to them by South African customs officials under the South African Customs Union Agreement. Second, customs duties may protect locally based industries against competitive imported goods. They may thus encourage domestic and foreign investors to produce goods locally instead of importing them. Local production may help provide local employment as well as save scarce foreign exchange.

To make domestic investment more attractive, the government may reduce duties imposed on imported machinery and equipment, as well as semi-processed materials to be manufactured into finished products in the country. This may reduce import revenues. Some critics maintain it provides an incentive for importing capital-intensive machinery and materials, rather than building more labour-intensive industries and using locally produced materials. Furthermore, if a manufacturer continues to import parts and materials once the factory is operating, the foreign-exchange savings to the country may be only marginal. As import industries succeed, of course, overall import duty revenues will inevitably decline, and governments may have to shift, as have Zambia and Kenya, to other revenue sources.

The duties that South African customs officials impose and collect on goods imported into Botswana, Lesotho and Swaziland, on the other hand, only protect the common market for South African manufacturers. The South African Customs Union does not protect infant industries, which Botswana, Lesotho or Swaziland might establish, from competition with the much larger manufacturing firms based in South Africa.

Table 8.8
Import Duties in Selected African States in national currency units and as percent of total tax revenue, 1972 and 1982

Country	Currency unit	1972 Natl. currency (mn.)	1972 Tax revenue (%)	1982 Natl. currency (mn.)	1982 Tax revenue (%)
Botswana[a]	Pula	8.3	65.3	114.32	52.4
Ghana	Cedi	59.7	16.1	569.61	13.6
Kenya	Shilling	630.0	29.4	3674.00	27.2
Malawi	Kwacha	10.5	29.2	52.49	25.3
Nigeria	Niara	182.7	19.9	1324.90	25.7
Sierra Leone	Leone	30.1	36.4	69.20	39.4
South Africa	Rand	138.0	4.8	686.00	4.9
Sudan	Pound	52.7	41.8	383.60	56.9
Swaziland[a]	Emalangeni	3.9	25.0	62.67	51.8
Tanzania	Shilling	337.0	23.5	656.00	8.0
Zambia	Kwacha	42.4	16.9	72.40	9.3
Zimbabwe	Dollars	NA	NA	168.30	12.3

Notes: (a) Botswana and Swaziland receive customs duties through the South African Customs Union.

Source: Calculated from International Monetary Fund, Government Finance Statistics Yearbook, 1982 and 1984, Country tables.

Agricultural Taxes: Existing and Potential

Why Agricultural Taxes?

Many tax experts hold that in underdeveloped countries the government must tax agriculture to obtain the essential funds to implement development plans for other sectors of the economy, as well as for agriculture itself. G.M. Meier summarized the argument succinctly:

> Unless the agricultural sector is taxed in order to expand the "agricultural surplus", the growth of the non-agricultural sector may be retarded. As development proceeds, the proportion of the working population engaged in non-food production increases; to make this possible, the marketable surplus from agriculture must also rise—that is, the proportion of food produced in the agricultural sector which is not consumed by the food producers must increase and be transferred to the non-agricultural sector. To accomplish this requires either taxes in money which impel greater deliveries to market, taxes in kind, or compulsory sales to the government or a deterioration in the terms of trade of the agricultural sector vis-a-vis the non-agricultural sector.
>
> Taxation of the agricultural sector may also serve as an important policy instrument in the underdeveloped countries: the incentive and distributional use of taxation may be utilized to redirect agricultural production, encourage the more efficient use of land, accomplish changes in land tenure, promote new productive investment in agriculture, and stimulate movement of redundant labour from agriculture to non-agriculture employment.[2]

Another tax authority, R.M. Bird, has observed, however:

> There is, it appears, no good example of a country successfully levying heavy direct taxes on agriculture as part of a conscious development policy apart from Meiji Japan and several Communist countries. When agricultural taxes are significant today, it is because most of the population is engaged in agriculture and there really is no other source of taxation.[3]

African governments' policies on taxing agriculture, and their consequences for the rest of the economy, vary widely, depending on historically shaped political and economic factors in each country. As Table 8.9 indicates, some governments—although by no means all—have imposed fairly heavy taxes on agriculture, typically either through the so-called "personal tax" or by taxing exports. African governments have seldom attempted to tax agricultural land, and almost never have taxed agricultural marketed products other than those for export.

The "Personal Tax"

At different times and places, African governments have imposed personal taxes in the form of poll taxes, hut taxes, village taxes, minimum taxes, graduated personal taxes (GPT) and income taxes. Usually, these aim to provide local finance for local government. Some governments view them as techniques not only to raise funds but also to ensure local fiscal responsibility.

Table 8.9
Patterns of Agricultural Taxation: Yield by Type of Tax as percentage of total tax receipts

Country	*Year*	*Personal*	*Export*	*Land*	*Produce*
Benin	1969	2	4	0	...
Burkina Faso	1968	15	1	1	...
Cameroon	1966	...	10	...	...
Central African Republic	1966	9	5	0	...
Chad	1969	9	10	0	...
Congo (Brazzaville)	1967	...	0	...	...
Egypt	1968	...	2	8	...
Ethiopia	1968	...	9	8	...
Gabon	1966	2	...	0	...
Ghana	1968	...	17	...	...
Ivory Coast	1966	...	20	1	...
Kenya	1968	2	0	0	...
Liberia	1969	5	2	0	...
Malagasy Republic	1969	12	6	5	...
Malawi	1968	12	...	...	...
Mali	1962	21	2	...	...
Mauritania	1968	1	...	...	...
Morocco	1969	2	2	6	...
Niger	1968	34	7	...	...
Nigeria	1963	6	18	...	3
Senegal	1968	3	7	...	...
Sierra Leone	1969	...	4	...	...
Somalia	1968	...	9	1	...
Sudan	1964	...	24	...	...
Tanzania	1965	3	16	...	2
Tunisia	1968	1	4	4	...
Uganda	1964	14	41	...	...
Zaire	1965	3	...	...	...

Note: ...signifies no information is available; 0 means the value is less than 0.5%. These figures were brought together from many different, sometimes incompatible sources, so the data are not strictly comparable. Some of the classifications of particular taxes are arbitrary. In most cases, only central government tax revenues are treated, except where major taxes treated are subnational. In some cases, figures shown for certain taxes refer to different years, or even different from the year indicated. The major problem in interpreting this table concerns the extent to which the taxes cited actually fall on agriculture. In some instances, special estimates have been made; in others, information, for example on exports where most exports were non-agricultural, were omitted. "Personal" taxes may in some instances have been paid primarily by urban workers.

Source: R.M. Bird, "Taxing Agricultural Land in Developing Countries" (Cambridge, Mass: Harvard University Press, 1974), appendix, pp. 299-301, compiled from R.J. Dhelliah, "Trends in Taxation in Developing Countries", IMF Staff Papers, XVIII (July, 1971), 270-271; R. Goode, G.E. Lent, and P.D. Ojha, "Role of Export Taxes in Developing Countries", IMF Staff Papers, XIII (Nov., 1966) 460; E.A. Arowolo, "The Taxation of Low Incomes in African Countries," IMF Staff Papers, XV (July 1968); IMF, Surveys of African Economies, 4 Vols., Washington, 1968-1971).

Colonial Hut and Poll Taxes: The colonial governments commonly imposed hut and poll taxes on the African populations, usually as a fixed tax per hut or per head. They aimed thus to coerce the Africans into the monetized economy. In peasant-based economies like those in West Africa, Africans could earn the money by producing export crops. The luckier ones, who lived in export cropping areas like the cocoa belt in Southern Ghana, owned their own farms. Hundreds of thousands of others migrated to work for them as sharecroppers, often leaving their home areas neglected and stagnant.

In settler colonial areas, like South Africa, Kenya and the former Northern and Southern Rhodesia now Zambia and Zimbabwe, commercial farmers and mining companies successfully persuaded the colonial government to push African peasants into infertile reserves and block their efforts to sell cash crops. This forced many, especially the able-bodied young men, to leave their farms and enter the low-paid wage labour force which rendered the settler-owned commercial farms and mines so profitable. For the most part, only women, children and old folk remained to scratch their living from the overcrowded, infertile and neglected areas "reserved" for the African population.

Post Colonial Innovation: At independence, most governments at first reduced or eliminated these widely unpopular taxes. A few, following the pattern earlier established in Uganda, transformed personal taxes into a "graduated personal tax", a hybrid between a poll tax and an elementary form of income tax. In the Buganda area of Uganda, the local authorities had based a graduated personal tax on a presumed gross income; the estimated gross yields from acreages cultivated, the number of coffee trees, and the size of the livestock herd. They divided these incomes into nine brackets, setting tax rates at 5 to 6 per cent on the minimum income in each bracket. Local committees, under the chief's authority, assessed the individual incomes.

In Nigeria, the state governments levied personal taxes which varied from state to state. In the north, for example, in 1962 the government integrated the personal tax, which pre-dated British rule, with the income tax. A person earning over £400 a year paid the income tax instead of the personal tax. The provincial authorities assessed a "community" tax on the rest of the community based on the number of adult males, the per capita rate roughly reflecting the estimated wealth of the district. The local authorities apportioned the tax on a graduated basis among the individuals not subject to the income tax. They imposed a cattle tax on the nomadic herdsmen, the Fulani, whose main wealth consisted of their cattle herds. Personal taxes provided an estimated 65 per cent of the Nigerian regional government taxes in 1964-65. About a fifth of this came from the community tax, and another 65 per cent from the cattle tax, both of which applied only in the rural areas. These taxes provided almost 90 per cent of the revenues of the local authorities which collected them.

The Issue of Equity vs. Local Finance: The use of personal taxes to finance local expenditure raises a fundamental issue of equity. Colonialism left behind the dualistic economies with major regions grossly underdeveloped. Dependence on local taxes, while perhaps encouraging local fiscal self-reliance, inevitably benefits the inhabitants of the more developed regions, leaving those living in the less developed areas to fall still further behind.

The Zimbabwean case provides an extreme illustration of this fiscal dualism. One author characterized the local financial system introduced by the pre-independence regime as "apartheid in public finance".[4] By law, the regime provided African councils for the 70,000 or so families crowded into the so-called Tribal Trust Lands reserved for the Africans. It established Rural District Councils for the 6,000 white commercial farmers who owned the most fertile half of the national land area. In urban areas, the government likewise divided the municipalities and town councils along racial lines, confining the Africans to segregated townships.

The local tax structure followed these lines. The central government required the African Councils in the Tribal Trust Lands to finance primary education, preventive health services, maintenance of local roads, agricultural services like dipping tanks, soil conservation and water supplies, and the operation of beer halls. The central government allocated 97 per cent of the funds for these through an African Development Fund financed by hut and poll taxes and levies raised by taxes on peasant produce marketed through the marketing boards. The levies reduced the returns to the peasants below those received by the commercial farmers, inevitably discouraging peasant cash crop cultivation. As a result, whereas the per capita tax revenues in the prosperous commercial farm areas (excluding the farm labourers who received none of the benefits) exceeded $90 a year, in the Tribal Trust Lands, they averaged less than 30 cents.

In the urban areas, the government required the African Affairs Account to finance the costs of housing, water, electricity (when provided), refuse collection, roads and sewerage services. The main sources of revenue included rents from houses (the law prohibited Africans from owning their own homes, viewing them primarily as rural dwellers sojourning in cities only as long as they worked for whites); charges for services; and profits from municipal enterprises like beer halls. Use of beer halls for revenues created the ironic situation in which the more beer the population drank, the higher the township's income! The white suburbs, in contrast, raised revenues through property taxes levied as set rates on the assessed value of land and buildings. Since the settler minority received most of the nation's cash income and annually invested 10 per cent of the national capital formation in their homes, these represented very high values and provided relatively high revenues—some 20 times the per capita revenues provided in the African townships.

After independence, the civil servants in the new Zimbabwe Ministry of Housing and Local Government revised the laws essentially by changing the names of the rural and urban areas to eliminate racial distinctions and to provide the Africans with the right to vote in elections.[5] The Tribal Trust Lands became the Communal Areas. The African townships became municipalities. The inhabitants of each area elected their own councillors. But the inherited tax structure remained largely intact. A few, more well-to-do Africans moved into the formerly all-white suburbs, changing the equality issue from one of race to one of class.

The lowest-income groups, the vast majority of the African population, remained in the Communal Areas. The post-independence central government alleviated their fiscal problems temporarily by directing part of the funds it borrowed from abroad to reconstruction and development in the Communal Areas. But in 1982 it announced that as borrowed funds were limited the local councils would need to become increasingly self-reliant. This again raised the issue of the inequitable consequences of relying on local taxes when a grossly distorted pattern of asset and income distribution has been inherited from the past.

Export Duties

Colonial governments, particularly in West Africa, collected export duties on agricultural crops, either directly or through the marketing boards which handled them. Export duties typically fall on the producers of export crops. Since many developing countries compete to sell their crops on the world market, the demand for any one country's produce is relatively elastic; the tax cannot be passed on to the foreign consumer. Thus export duties provided colonial governments with an effective means of taxing the African peasants who produced most of the export crops in West Africa. Post-independence governments typically continued this form of tax because of the revenue it produced, although they generally sought to introduce other revenue sources as well. In Sierra Leone, export duties dwindled in significance after iron mining began to provide a major source of national revenue. In Nigeria, export duties' contribution to revenue dropped dramatically in the 1970s as the oil exports and revenue boomed.

But as Table 8.10 shows, Ghana continued throughout the 1970s to obtain about a third of its tax revenues from export taxes, although most authorities agree that such high taxes tend to discourage peasant cultivation of export crops and may even encourage smuggling through neighbouring countries with lower export taxes or none at all.

In settler colonial countries, like Zimbabwe, Kenya and Malawi, the commercial farmers constituted a sufficiently powerful political force to thwart government proposals to impose export duties on their crops. Post-independence governments seldom introduced them.

The fact that export duties may discourage production of export crops suggests the need to search for alternative methods of taxing agriculture which stimulate production at the same time as producing revenue.

Land Taxes

Many Third World countries rely on land taxes, one of the oldest forms of taxation dating back at least to Babylonia in 3800 BC and Egypt in 3000 BC. But this form of taxation has never become widespread in sub-Saharan Africa.

Land taxation may take a variety of forms which cannot all be adequately considered here. A government may tax the capital value of land, plus improvements, or its rental value. It may tax the gross income produced from

Table 8.10
Export Duties of Selected African States, in national currency units and as percent of total tax revenue, 1972 and 1982

Country	*Currency*	*1972* Natl. Curr. (mn.)	*1972* Tax Revenue (%)	*1982* Natl. Curr. (mn.)	*1982* Tax Revenue (%)
Botswana	Pula	0.4	3.3	0.6	0.3
Ghana	Cedi	110.4	29.8	2800.0[a]	33.1[a]
Kenya	Shilling	9.0	0.4	106.0	0.8
Nigeria[b]	Niara	28.0	3.1	1.5	0.02
Sierra Leone	Leone	8.7	10.5	13.9	7.9
South Africa	Rand	13.0	0.4	25.0	0.2
Sudan	Pound	7.8	6.1	33.3	4.9
Swaziland	Emalangeni	0.02	0.1	12.3[c]	10.2[c]
Tanzania[d]	Shilling	45.0	3.1	215.0	2.6

Notes: (a) No data is reported for 1982; this data, for 1983, may include some 1982 export tax revenue. The percent figure is calculated on 1983 total revenue.
(b) Nigeria collected these export duties for its several states.
(c) Beginning in the 1970s, Swaziland imposed a levy on sugar produced and exported by transnational corporations in the lowveld.
(d) Over 80% of Tanzania's export duty revenue came from coffee exports in 1982.

Source; Calculated from International Monetary Fund, Government Finance Statistics Yearbook, 1982 and 1984, Country tables.

the land, or, with some allowance for expenses, the net land incomes. It may levy a periodic tax on increments in land value, or impose betterment taxes or special assessments in connection with the financing of public improvements. It may tax land as part of a more general wealth tax or capital levy on an annual or periodic basis. Finally, it may tax transfers of land, either through a special tax or under a more general capital gains tax.

Mainstream economists generally assert that rural land taxation in Africa is "just not possible . . . without definition and registration of land titles".[6] In the urban areas which are most influenced by European enterprise and ideology, local authorities did impose taxes on land and property. In West Africa, where the European presence was less pervasive, the lack of formally registered land titles and precisely demarcated boundaries allegedly hindered urban authorities from assessing the value of land itself; instead they imposed taxes on the rental value of buildings. But this tended to discourage construction, for improvements led immediately to higher taxes.

In East and Central Africa, the European settler governments introduced the practice of registering land and defining ownership title in commercial centres. In Kenya, urban local governments imposed taxes on the value of land alone. The then Rhodesian government imposed property taxes in urban European areas on both land and buildings, although at a lower rate on the latter. This practice may have stimulated construction of the high-rise modern buildings that etch the Nairobi and Harare skylines. Critics suggest that it encouraged investment in speculative real estate rather than in desirable development projects.

The introduction of the urban property taxes required the training of personnel capable of assessing the values of the relevant properties. Typically, they reassessed properties periodically so as to adjust tax revenues to inflation as well as local improvements. In former British colonies, these assessors exerted a conventional influence on post-independence thought about the appropriate ways to value agricultural property for tax purposes.

In countries elsewhere in the Third World, governments have successfully introduced taxes on land income in ways that stimulated productivity. As in Buganda (see p. 155), they frequently tax a presumed income based on the potential yield of a given area. The People's Republic of China,[7] for example, revived an ancient land income tax during the early transition period after the 1949 revolution. It set the tax (first with progressive, and later, after the completion of land reform, proportional rates) on the gross estimated normal income from land with differentials for the particular type of crops. The authorities took into account the natural capacity of the soil, the extent of irrigation, and the normal methods of cultivation when they assessed the tax. They collected about 90 per cent of the proceeds in kind to protect the tax yields against the potential depreciation of value due to inflation. This also gave the government direct control over allocation of basic foodstuffs.

In 1951, North Vietnam introduced a similar comprehensive agricultural tax, payable solely in kind, but levied on the community rather than the individual. The local taxpayers participated in assessing the tax. This required extensive popular education about the purpose of taxes and the necessity for fiscal responsibility for financing national development.

The involvement of local citizens in assessing land income taxes may reduce the necessity for demarcating boundaries and registering land titles in communally held land areas. The local people generally know who uses which pieces of land and what they are worth.

Governments might supplement local knowledge by developing cadastral surveys showing the allocation of areas of land throughout the nation, and estimating the value of different types. Governments today may obtain survey maps through aerial photography combined with sample field surveys. Relatively unskilled technicians, using a written manual prepared by a few skilled appraisers, can set the value of given pieces of land on the basis of a system of standard value units. They can make appropriate modifications for such factors as location, topography, availability of water, salinity, stoniness, erosion and drainage. Although these techniques may introduce elements of arbitrariness and approximation, they may make the taxing of land possible for low-income countries, especially when the local population participates in the assessment process.

Summary

African governments, after independence, generally sought to revise their tax structure to increase revenues and sometimes to distribute the burden more equitably.

Available data show that tax revenues constitute widely varying shares of the GDPs of African states, depending on such factors as the level and distribution of income as well as the tax structure itself. Mainstream theorists commonly tend to assume developing countries lack significant investable surpluses. Many argue that high taxes on wealthy groups will discourage investment of what little investable surplus exists, and scare away needed foreign capital. They advocate tax policies designed to attract foreign investment.

Marxists, in contrast, focus on what happens to the sometimes quite large investable surpluses generated locally. They urge the formulation of tax programmes designed primarily to capture and reinvest these surpluses to achieve economic reconstruction and finance a planned transition to social ownership of the means of production.

In practice, African governments tend to rely more heavily on indirect than direct taxes. In some countries, where large, often foreign-owned firms dominate the modern sector, company taxes may contribute a significant share of government revenue. In many countries, however, the tax laws specify various deductions which permit companies to reduce the effective tax rate to well below the nominal level stipulated by the law. These may also lead to unintended consequences such as increased capital-intensive production structures reinforcing externally dependent dualistic development.

Personal income tax usually provides a relatively small share of tax revenue, in part because of difficulties in collecting it from the large number of self-employed typical in most developing countries. Wealthy individuals, in particular, may take advantage of a variety of opportunities to reduce their tax liability.

Consequently many African governments rely heavily on indirect taxes as an easier source of revenue from incomes that might otherwise remain altogether untaxed. Supply-side economists often advocate indirect taxes in line with their argument that governments should encourage companies and wealthy individuals to invest. The elasticity of demand for particular commodities generally determines whether the producer or the consumer pays the tax.

Some African governments collect a major share of their revenues through taxes imposed on domestically sold goods. Sales taxes tend to fall most heavily on the urban poor, although necessities may be exempted to offset this. Taxes on luxuries affect wealthier groups that can better afford them. Excise taxes may aim to reap high revenues and, in some cases, reduce consumption of harmful items like alcohol and cigarettes. Governments may use customs duties, not only to raise revenues but also to reduce overall imports so as to save foreign exchange and protect local industries from competing imported goods.

In largely agricultural countries like those in Africa, many tax experts urge imposition of various kinds of taxes either to capture investable surpluses generated in the agricultural sector, or to stimulate agricultural productivity, or both. Colonial governments imposed hut and poll taxes on Africans primarily to force them into the monetized economy. After independence, most African states abandoned these unpopular measures, while some transformed them into an elementary form of rural income tax. Given the inherited dualistic economy typical of most African countries, however, the requirement that rural communities raise local taxes to finance their own development raises questions of justice. The already more developed regions have greater resources to finance their growth; whereas the underdeveloped areas, forced to remain self-financing, can only lag further behind.

In West African and other peasant cash-crop economies, colonial administrations imposed duties on agricultural exports as a means of taxing peasant incomes. After independence, some governments continued this form of tax, although if it becomes too high, it may discourage peasant cultivation of crops for export. Other governments shifted the burden of taxes to other sources.

Although various forms of land taxes have been widely used elsewhere in the world, in sub-Saharan Africa governments have seldom introduced them, in part because of the mainstream assumption that they presuppose private land ownership and registered land titles. Elsewhere, governments have introduced taxes on a presumed level of income based on the potential yield of given land areas. The farmers then keep whatever surpluses they produce beyond that level.

Notes

1. Huang, "Distribution of Tax Burden in Tanzania" in K.S. Kim, (ed) *Papers on the Political Economy of Tanzania*, 1975.
2. Meier, *Leading Issues in Development Economics*, 2nd ed., New York: Oxford University Press, 1970, pp. 198-9.
3. Bird, *Taxing Agricultural Land in Developing Countries*, (Cambridge, Mass: Harvard University Press, 1974, pp. 37-8.
4. Harris, "The Tax System from UDI to Independence", (paper presented to the Economic Symposium on Zimbabwe, Salisbury, Zimbabwe, September 8-10 1980).
5. Ndoro, "Local Taxes in Zimbabwe".
6. Bird, *Taxing Agricultural Land*, p. 58.
7. For further discussion of agricultural taxation in socialist countries, see Part IV.

Exercises and Research

1. What factors may determine the tax capacity of different African countries? Can you think of factors other than those indicated in the text?
2. Distinguish between direct and indirect taxes and give some of the reasons why many African states seem to rely more heavily on indirect than direct taxes.
3. On what basis do companies usually pay taxes? Compare the company tax provisions in different African countries and suggest reasons for the differences. Why are *effective* company tax rates as a percentage of profits often less than those stipulated by law? Why should African governments not neglect the possible benefits of double taxation treaties?
4. How are direct taxes collected in most African states? Why do only a relatively small proportion of wage and salary earners pay income tax through PAYE in most African states? Why do most African governments tax a relatively small share of the incomes of self-employed individuals (e.g. professionals, traders, farmers)? Compare the income tax rates of the African countries given in the text. What political and economic factors might explain the differences?
5. What determines who pays indirect taxes? Which income group is likely to be most affected by sales tax? What arguments can you give for and against raising the sales taxes on luxury goods as opposed to consumer necessities? What reasons can you advance for and against excise taxes?
6. Why do African governments often introduce import taxes? Who usually pays import taxes? What effect may import taxes have on domestic development, including the growth of local industry?
7. List all the arguments you can think of for and against the various kinds of taxes which might be imposed on agriculture. Who pays taxes imposed on agricultural exports? Why have many African governments imposed such taxes? What kind of tax would you recommend to stimulate agricultural productivity? Be sure to give your reasons.
8. Prepare a table showing the sources of tax revenue in your country over the last five years.
   a) Calculate the total tax revenues as a percentage of GDP for each year.
   b) Calculate the tax revenue obtained from each source as a percentage of total tax revenue for each year.
   c) Calculate the total company tax revenue as a percentage of Gross Operating Profit of all companies.
   d) Evaluate whether the overall tax structure is regressive or progressive. Be sure to give the reasons for your conclusions.
9. What theory offers the most adequate guide for explaining the overall tax structure in your country? Be sure to explain why.

Recommended Reading

(For annotations see bibliography at the end of the book)

Carlson *et al.*, *International Finance*
Clower *et al.*, *Growth without Development*
Cohen and Koehn, *Ethiopian Provincial and Municipal Government*
Daniels, *Corporate Financial Statements*
Dean, *Plan Implementation in Nigeria*
Due, *Taxation and Economic Development in Tropical Africa*
Elliott (ed.), *Constraints on the Economic Development of Zambia*
Harvey (ed.), *Papers on the Economy of Botswana*
Hazlewood and Henderson, *Nyasaland*
Houghton, *The South African Economy*
Illugbuh, *Nigeria's Experience in Domestic Financing of Development*
IBRD country reports
IMF Surveys of African economies
Jackson (ed.), *Economic Development in Africa*
Koneacki, An *Economic History of Tropical Africa* Vol. II
Lewis, *Reflections on Nigeria's Economic Growth*
Morton, *Aid and Dependence*
Odenigwe (ed.), *A New System of Local Government*
Okigbo, *Nigerian Public Finance*
Ord and Livingstone, *An Introduction to West African Economics*
Platt, *Tax Systems of Africa, Asia and the Middle East*
Robinson, *Economic Development for Africa*
Sabine, *A History of Income Tax*
Seidman, *An Economics Textbook for Africa*
—— *Planning for Development in SubSaharan Africa*
Teriba and Kayode (eds), *Money, Finance and Nigerian Economic Development*
UN Economic Commission for Africa, *Budget Planning and Management*
Uppal and Salkever (eds), *African Problems in Economic Development*
Wetham and Currie, *Readings in Applied Economics of Africa*, Vol. 2

Periodicals

The Economist Intelligence Unit, *Quarterly Economic Reviews*
IMF *Government Statistics*

Chapter 9: Public Finance in the Productive Sectors

The Growth of Subsidized Public Enterprise

Governments in Africa, as in other Third World countries, have long intervened to finance productive activities. From the colonial era, this intervention primarily took two forms. First, governments subsidized those private productive sectors they considered essential for the kind of development they envisaged; second, they established state enterprises to develop sectors which private enterprise found unprofitable.

After independence, many African governments further extended government finance through subsidies and public enterprise in the sphere of productive activities. Sometimes they acted for nationalist reasons, to reduce foreign enterprises' domination of what they perceived as crucial sectors of the economy. Sometimes they proclaimed their intention of effecting a transition to socialism.

Table 9.1
Subsidies[a] of Selected African Governments in Millions of National Currency Units and as Percentage of Tax Revenues and of National Debt, 1972 and 1982.

Country (Currency Unit)	*Subsidies, 1972*			*Subsidies 1982*		
	Millions of National Currency	*% of Tax Revenue*	*% of Debt*	*Millions of National Currency*	*% of Tax Revenue*	*% of Debt*
Botswana (Pula)	2.1	11.1	18.8	94.49[a]	43.4[a]	47.3[a]
Ghana (Cedi)	67.2	18.1	41.6	1,831.10	43.8	8.4
Kenya (Shilling)	320	14.9	56.5	3,353.00	24.8	12.7[b]
Malawi (Kwacha)	6.6	16.7	33.0	24.98	12.0	NA
South Africa (Rand)	464	16.2	71.1	5,325.00	37.0	23.5
Swaziland (Emalangeni)	1.7	8.8	36.9	4.16[c]	3.9[c]	NA
Tanzania (Shilling)	2	0.1	0.3	NA		
Zambia (Kwacha)	52.8	12.9	30.1	NA		

[a] Defined as "Subsidies and Other Current Transfers".
[b] 1978 is last date for which Kenya's total debt is reported; the subsidy data used to calculate that figure are also for 1978 (Ksh: 341 million).
[c] 1981 data.

Source: IMF, *Government Finance Statistics Yearbook*, 1982, 1984.

Table 9.2
Number of Public Enterprises[a] in Selected African Countries, by Major Category,[b] 1980

Country	Non-financial						Financial					
	Agriculture, Fishing, Forestry	Mining	Manufacturing and Equipment Suppliers	Trade & Transport	Public Utilities	Other	Monetary Banking	Agricultural Finance	Industrial Finance	Insurance & Pensions	Housing	Other
Ghana	4	2		7	4	10						
Lesotho		1	7[e]	5	5	3	1	1	1		1	
Kenya	6	3	43[f]	10	7			4				
Malawi	5	1	4	3	5	3	3					
Sierra Leone	3	3	4	5	6	1	3		2	1		
South Africa	4	4	7	1	3	2	3	2	7	3	1	8[d]
Tanzania	23	4	52	35	4	3	3	1	1	2	1	
Zambia[c]	11	6	37	23	7	16	4	1	1	5	1	

[a] Parastals; state corporations, with majority of government shares.
[b] Roughly estimated, based on title.
[c] Plus 195 local government public enterprises.
[d] Includes development corporations for Bantustans.
[e] Mostly handicrafts.
[f] Of which 14 are tea factories, rest mostly agricultural processing plants.

Source: IMF, *Government Finance Statistics Yearbook*, 1980.

By the 1980s many African governments, regardless of ideology, used subsidies to finance various aspects of production and distribution, even where private ownership remained predominant. As Table 9.1 shows, subsidies, as defined by the IMF, consumed a significant and growing percentage of many African governments' tax revenues and contributed significantly to their mounting debts.

Governments also expanded the activities of public enterprises (called either "state corporations" or "parastatals") to operate in a wide range of activities both financial and non-financial.

Table 9.2 provides a rough indication of the numbers and types of public enterprises created by several African states in 1980. The table, based on IMF data, includes only enterprises which that organization defined as "public". Although their activities seldom appear in government budgets, public enterprises significantly influence the pattern of investment, as well as governments' ability to regulate money supplies and foreign-exchange commitments.

This chapter aims first to elaborate briefly the major alternative theoretical explanations of the role of subsidies and state corporations in public finance; and, second, to discuss some of the available evidence concerning their actual impact.

Some Theoretical Considerations

Keynesian Prescriptions

Keynesian theory justifies, even for those devoted to the private enterprise system, government finance of productive activity. Where the private sector has failed to act, government should initiate desired investments to stimulate private activity. This theory provides a rationale for providing government subsidies to private firms until they can stand profitably on their own feet. Where subsidies alone are inadequate, the government itself enters into productive activities through public enterprise.

Under colonialism, and in some post-colonial African countries, governments typically interpreted Keynesian prescriptions to propose that, projects initiated by government should operate autonomously, as much like profit-maximizing private firms as possible, and once viable, should be restored to the private sector. In southern Africa, government publications commonly categorize parastatal finances under private-sector headings. Once a government has provided the initial subvention, the enabling legislation usually requires management to observe profit-maximizing criteria as in a private firm.

The Monetarist Objections

Monetarists generally object to this extension of state finance to support productive activities, pointing to subsidies' drain on the public purse and arguing that private enterprise should be capable of standing on its own two feet or should go under; private competition for profit should lead to the best possible allocation of resources where as government intervention, whether through subsidies or public enterprise, will foster deviation from the optimal pattern.

The Marxist Theory of State Capitalism

Marxist theorists explain the rapid growth of state financial intervention in productive sectors as an inevitable consequence of the inability of private enterprise to cope with the contradictions of capitalism in its imperialist phase. Particularly in African and other Third World countries, those contradictions express themselves in three main forms: the domination of distorted productive sectors by transnational corporate capital; extensive neglect of resources which could be developed to increase the population's living standards; and widespread and growing unemployment which fosters social unrest. The post-colonial capitalist state had to intervene in many ways, including financial, to overcome the consequences of these contradictions, and maintain and reproduce the capitalist productive systems. Such state capitalist intervention typically advantages the classes that control the machinery of state.

The colonial governments utilized the public purse to help finance the profitable growth of colonial private enterprise. They subsidized colonial firms in mining, agriculture and—to a limited extent—manufacturing, by providing low-cost infrastructure, hydroelectricity and irrigation projects, railways, roads, ports and telecommunications. In central and southern Africa, they even helped to keep down the cost of labour for the settler-owned mines, commercial farms and factories, by subsidizing the production and sale of foodstuffs (almost entirely produced on settler-owned commercial farms). They also established agricultural banks of one kind or another to provide low-cost, long-term credit to settler commercial farmers.

The newly independent African governments represented a broad spectrum of nationalist forces, typically led by petty-bourgeois elements: the intelligentsia, traders, well-to-do African farmers and, sometimes, trade union leaders. Colonial policies deliberately fostering underdevelopment outside a narrow enclave left few Africans as capitalists owning significant productive assets. Often the new governments claimed to be "socialist"; but in reality, they frequently sought to advance African—not infrequently their own—as opposed to foreign capitalist enterprises; and they redirected the inherited subsidies and public enterprises to achieve this goal. As directors of state enterprises and transnational corporate affiliates, they typically received lucrative salaries. In very few cases did the nationalist leadership genuinely seek to ally itself with the working class and poorest peasants, or to reorientate and expand the system of subsidies and public enterprise to achieve increasingly democratic social ownership of the means of production. Instead, they used state intervention to expand what has become widely known as a "bureaucratic" or a "managerial" bourgeoisie.

In short, Marxists explain, state capitalism, arising from the contradictions inherent in capitalist penetration of Third World countries, may go in one of two ways. The new ruling class may expand state intervention and financial assistance in the productive sectors, sometimes displacing, sometimes collaborating with foreign firms in an attempt to strengthen the emerging national capitalist class. Over time, given transnational corporate domination over the world capitalist system, this type of budding nationalist capitalist element must inevitably degenerate into a subordinate comprador bourgeois class, in close partnership with, but ultimately controlled by foreign capital.

On the other hand, only when the nationalist political leadership consciously and continuously strengthens its alliance with the mass of the workers and poor peasants will it exercise state intervention to implement plans to achieve the practical transition to socialism. This would require redirection of subsidies to finance genuine improvements in the living standards of the lowest-income groups; and the establishment of new forms of state enterprise, closely integrated into national plans, to redirect investable surpluses to expand productive employment opportunities in the context of a more self-reliant, balanced and integrated national economy. (For a fuller discussion, see Part IV.)

The remainder of this chapter presents evidence on Zimbabwe and other African states to help the reader begin to assess the likely consequences of subsidies and state enterprises in different circumstances.

Subsidies

For reasons of space, this section merely attempts to illustrate the main issues, and their implication for public finance, pertaining to government subsidies in the productive sectors of African economies.

Definitional Problems

A.R. Prest wrote an entire monograph simply trying to define the term "subsidies", as used in the United Kingdom.[1] These may include anything from outright payments for particular activities and construction of infrastructure for favoured sectors of the economy to provision of low-cost credit and tax deductions. A great deal of study is essential to determine the nature and impact of subsidies in any given country. An analysis of subsidies in one country, Zimbabwe, illustrates the complex issues involved. A cursory analysis of available Zimbabwe data indicates the one-sided impact of pre-colonial subsidies, and the extent of the newly independent government's initial efforts to shift the benefits from the minority to the African majority.

Subsidies in Zimbabwe

At independence, Zimbabwe inherited a number of subsidies, only some of which were explicitly identified in the government budget (see Table 9.3). If one adds grants and loans, presumably at relatively low rates of interest not elsewhere available, the total element of subsidies constituted between 10 and 12 per cent of total public expenditure. They consumed a significantly greater share of total tax revenues, 24.2 per cent in 1981-82 and an estimated 16.4 per cent of much greater revenues in 1982-83.

Table 9.3
Selected Zimbabwe Government Subsidies, Loans, and Grants, Explicitly Identified in the National Budget, 1981-82 and 1982-83 (est.)

	1981/82 (actual) Z$	*1982/83 (estimated) Z$*
Subsidies		
Agriculture	43,738,000	75,906,000
Transport	43,919,000	31,000,000
Trade and Commerce	79,000,000	36,000,000
Sub-total	166,657,000	142,906,000
Grants		
Agriculture	2,325,000	2,303,000
Mining	—	846,000
Tourism	550,000	600,000
Natural resources	1,855,000	1,833,000
Sub-total	4,730,000	5,582,000
Loans		
Agriculture	9,081,000	15,210,000
Mines	—	500,000[a]
Transport	67,760,000	79,050,000
National Housing Fund	—	59,500,000
Sub-total	76,841,000	154,260,000
Grand Total	*248,228,000*	*302,748,000*
% of total expenditure	11.6	10.8
% of total tax revenues	24.2	16.4

[a] By mid-1983 the government reported lending roughly ten times that sum to mining companies to offset losses due to the international recession. In the event of the companies failing to repay the loans, the government reportedly would acquire shares in the mines on a dollar-for-dollar basis (*Financial Gazette*, 8 April 1983).

Source: *Estimates of Expenditure for the Year Ending June 30, 1983*, (Harare: Government Printer, 1982).

Agricultural Subsidies: Examination of the particular kinds of subsidies, grants and loans made in Zimbabwe in the early years after independence suggests whom they may have benefited, as well as the nature of the government's efforts to alter them. For example, the Agricultural Ministry for decades subsidized the minority-owned beef, dairy and maize farms. It was mainly high-income urban groups, as well as the handful of settler colonial farmers, who benefited from the resulting low dairy and beef prices, since African wage earners and peasants could not afford them until the post-independence government raise the minimum wage. In 1981-82, subsidies on these accounts totalled Z$43 million; in 1982-83 they increased to an estimated Z$74 million, in part because the Agricultural ministry redirected some of the funds to finance the purchase of peasants' cattle which were suffering severely from the drought.[2]

In 1982-83, the Ministry of Agriculture budgeted an additional subsidy to cover the Agricultural Finance Corporation's anticipated losses of Z$1,340,000. It also gave that corporation an outright grant of Z$1.5 million, in an attempt to encourage it to lend at least a small percentage of its funds to the African peasants, despite management fears that they would be unable to repay.

The Agricultural Ministry gave a quarter of its grant funds to the Tobacco Research Board, initially established to conduct research primarily to assist the 1,260 settler commercial farmers who grew almost all the nation's flue-cured tobacco. In 1981-82, following independence, the ministry granted Z$950,000 for the establishment of co-operative unions and for assistance to peasants. The next year, it reduced funds for this purpose to Z$50,000.

The Agricultural Ministry also loaned funds to the Agricultural Finance Corporation, the agricultural marketing organizations, and the Tobacco Research Board. The previous government had created these institutions to assist the 6,000 settler commercial farmers. How effectively they might assist the nations 850,000 peasant farmers after independence depended, of course, on how adequately they were restructured. (The Agricultural Finance Corporation is discussed briefly on pp. 173-4.)

The Ministry of Trade and Commerce provided heavy subsidies, Z$79 million in 1981-82, for foodstuffs, primarily wheat and maize. It presumably aimed to hold down the prices of these essential foodstuffs for low-paid urban workers while ensuring a high return to the growers. Commercial farmers, owning large irrigated fields, produced the wheat. Even after independence, they also produced about two-thirds of the marketed maize. In 1982-83, the ministry dramatically reduced these subsidies to Z$36 million, leading to an immediate increase in consumer prices of both wheat and maize. Unfortunately, no detailed study was published to reveal the impact of these changes on the profit margins and marketed output of commercial as compared to peasant farmers. The rising prices, however, seriously eroded the benefits of the minimum wage increases introduced after independence.

Transport Aid: The Ministry of Transport regularly subsidized the National Railway's losses, incurred because tariffs for agricultural and mineral produce were set at less than economic rates. In 1982-83, it proposed a Z$31 million subsidy to cover its expected losses. Initial investigations suggest that throughout the colonial and UDI period the government had in this way extensively subsidized the bulk transport of settler farm crops and transnational firms' minerals for export. Representatives of these industries on the National Railway's board of directors helped to shape this long-standing policy. In addition, the Transport Ministry loaned the railways large sums (estimated at Z$69 million in 1982-83). It also loaned funds (Z$3 million in 1981-82, and an estimated Z$2.2 million again in 1982-83) to a private air cargo firm, Affretair.

Tourism and Natural Resource Development: The Ministry of Natural Resources and Tourism granted funds to several private conservation committees, natural resource societies and national park managements, as well as for the overall development of tourism. Tourists could use these parks and facilities at a very low cost. Until independence, racist administrative policies had restricted their use almost entirely to the white minority. After independence, the new government urged Africans to participate in internal tourism, but few could afford it even though prices remained relatively low; and very few owned a car and so could not reach the remote resort areas.

New Low-Cost Housing Aid: After independence, the newly created Ministry of Housing established a new National Housing Fund and loaned it Z$59.5 million to finance new high-density housing schemes for lower-income groups. Presumably, these loans were to be recovered from the tenants' rents. As the economic crisis deepened the following year, however, the government withdrew its funds.

Other Government Aid: The subsidies, grants and loans outlined above and identified in the government budget by no means exhaust the list of financial contributions made by the Zimbabwe government to assist particular private-sector activities. For example, the government continued the practice of financing half the cost of mine access roads. In 1981-82, the Ministry of Roads and Road Traffic spend Z$1.2 million on the construction of an access road for Renco Mine, owned by the British firm, Rio Tinto Zinc. The ministry paid Z$45 million to help finance several more mine roads in 1981-82, although the next year it reduced the amount to Z$15 million.

The decision to finance water supplies and conservation works with taxpayer funds in one area and not in others constitutes a decision to subsidize water users of one area and not others. In 1982-83, the Ministry of Water Resources and Development planned to construct large water supply schemes and water conservation works costing an estimated total of Z$26 million for urban areas, commercial farms and resettlement areas. It proposed to spend only Z$667,000 on what it designated as Rural Water Supplies for the Communal Areas inhabited by 60 per cent of the African population.

These examples illustrate only some of the complex factors involved in analysing the kinds of subsidies a government may provide, and the issues involved in determining who benefits. Clearly, only carefully designed, detailed research can reveal the full implications of such public subsidies, grants and loans. Nevertheless, such expenditures, constituting a signficant share of the national budget, clearly affect the national pattern of investment and income distribution and require careful monitoring to assess the impact of a government's financial plans.

Public Enterprise Growth

The Implications

Experts have written entire books on the complicated questions involved in creating and financing public enterprises in state capitalist economies like those in Africa. The typical form of state corporation or parastatal—operating autonomously in accordance with mainstream prescriptions—hampers government efforts to monitor its own expenditures, regulate the money supply, control foreign-exchange allocations, and influence investment and income distribution patterns. This is so for several reasons.

First, unless the government spends tax revenues directly on particular enterprises—either as subsidies, grants or loans—the financial activities of state corporations as such generally do not appear in the budget. As a result their activities are seldom subject to public scrutiny.

Second, the managers and boards of directors of public enterprises, including those appointed by government, generally conduct their financial activities as much as possible like those of private firms. The government typically grants them the power to negotiate contracts for almost all their business activities. These may or may not be subject to agreement by the minister. Ordinarily, public enterprises employ labour, carry on their productive activity, and even spend foreign exchange or lend money to other public or private enterprises, with no controls other than those imposed on the private sector. Thus, operating outside the constraints of government plans, they make decisions which may profoundly affect the pattern of production and distribution.

Third, the government frequently owns only some part of the capital of individual statutory corporations—often, but by no means always, a majority. It commonly pays fees to the private partner, usually a transnational corporate affiliate, to provide the management, technology, essential inputs and markets. The management often conducts negotiations for funds with commercial banks or other industrial or financial corporations, both inside the country and abroad. Government-appointed directors, often sitting on as many as a dozen or more boards, frequently lack the time or essential knowledge to do more than rubber-stamp the management's decisions.

Fourth, state corporations often lose money and require government subsidies. Investigations have suggested a number of possible causes for this. Governments often create a public enterprise to bail out failing companies so that almost inevitably, at least initially, they lose money. Seeking to reduce expenditures, government may restrict the working capital the enterprise requires to function efficiently. Foreign-exchange constraints may hinder acquisition of essential parts and materials. Government and political personnel may view lucrative posts on boards of directors and in supervisory positions as the rewards of office. Workers may expect continued employment even when demand for the commodities produced has declined. Transnational corporate partners, contributing managerial services, may use various transfer pricing techniques to ship abroad undetected profits. To determine whether any or all of these factors operate in the case of any particular public enterprise would require a thorough on-the-spot investigation. The widespread problem, however, underscores the necessity of careful monitoring of all public enterprises to ensure that they play the desired role in the development process.

African Experiences

The experiences of African countries adopting different ideological perspectives illustrate some of the factors that may limit the potential contribution of the typical autonomous public enterprises to integrated national development. This section summarizes the evidence from three countries: Zimbabwe, Kenya and Tanzania.

Zimbabwe: Prior to independence in Zimbabwe, the settler-colonial government intervened extensively in the economy through the typical array of state corporations. The operation of the three parastatals described here—the Agricultural Finance Corporation (AFC), the Zimbabwe Iron and Steel Corporation (ZISCO), and the Industrial Development Corporations (IDC)—illustrates some of the difficulties the new government confronted in attempting to redirect this type of state intervention to facilitate more balanced national development.

1) The AFC: The Zimbabwean Agricultural Finance Corporation is a lineal descendant of the colonial Land Bank, set up before World War I to help finance settler commercial estate agriculture. During the 15-year period of UDI, the government restructured the AFC to help the 6,000 minority-owned commercial farms weather the impact of UN sanctions and the liberation war. After independence, the new government directed the AFC to make much larger amounts of credit available to African peasants. Its board of directors, appointed by the previous government and still representing primarily commercial farm and banking interests, responded slowly to this initiative, although the corporation expanded its overall loans rapidly. In the first post-independence year, the AFC provided only 5 per cent of all its loans to 18,000 peasant farmers, barely 2 per cent of the 850,000 peasant farming families in the country. The new government appointed new directors with the explicit requirement that they increase loans to peasants in resettlement schemes and the former Tribal Trust Lands (renamed Communal Areas). It also increased the amount of funds available to the corporation to enable it to fulfil this mandate (see pp. 169-70) but the increment still constituted only a small fraction of total AFC loans. Two primary difficulties hampered the expansion of AFC credit to the peasants. First, when the Central Bank raised the bank rate, the AFC raised the interest charged on its loans to 13 per cent. This consumed most of the average peasants' profit, rendering it uneconomic for them to take loans.

Second, the overcrowded infertile lands and low productivity of large parts of the Communal Areas imposed severe constraints on most peasant's ability to use credit productively. Only a few more wealthy ones could meet the new criteria for credit set by the AFC. Until the government provided more land through further land distribution, and ensured they had access to farm inputs, extension education and markets, the majority of peasants could not increase production sufficiently to repay the loans. This reality was underscored during the drought which especially hit crops in the ill-watered southern Communal Areas: many peasants who managed to qualify for credit could not repay at all.

In other words, the publicly held AFC constituted only one feature of an institutional structure shaped over almost a century of colonial rule to support a handful of (white) commercial farmers. To change its role to providing credit to the mass of the peasantry, the new government faced a double challenge: it not only had to replace the directors and managers of the corporation itself, and require them to revise the criteria for granting credit; it also had to carry through an adequate land reform, supported by the provision of appropriate inputs, extension education and marketing institutions, to enable the peasants to increase their marketed output.

2) ZISCO: During World War II, the colonial settler government set up an Iron and Steel Commission, RISCOM, to construct an iron and steel works near Kwekwe. Despite the existence of high-grade iron ore and limestone deposits, British steel firms had rejected proposals to set up a steel works in competition with their plants in England and South Africa. After the war, the government financed the expansion of RISCOM to produce steel inputs for the Federation of Rhodesia and Nyasaland. In 1956, when RISCOM emerged as a profitable enterprise, the government sold a majority of its shares to several British South African steel companies, including the Anglo-American Group. The government retained 11 per cent, ensuring its continued favourable treatment of the project.

During Federation, RISCO, as it became known, almost tripled its output to 165,000 tonnes of steel a year. As the Federation era drew to a close, it expanded its blast furnace capacity.

During UDI, despite UN sanctions, RISCO continued to grow, once again with major government assistance. It built a pipeline from the Sable Chemical plant (jointly owned by a locally held conglomerate, TA Holdings, and a British firm, Oxyco) to supply oxygen for a more efficient oxygen steel conversion process. In the mid-1970s, the government invested Z$8.5 million to rescue the company from the double impact of reduced domestic demand and the recession in the world steel market. This once again increased government's share in the company to 49.74 per cent.

RISCO's steel output expanded steadily from Z$24.7 million in 1964 to reach Z$167.9 million in 1978. The company's managers, primarily provided by the foreign partners, formulated price and output policies designed to provide relatively low-cost steel inputs to commercial farming, mining, manufacturing and construction in the modern sector. In addition, despite UN sanctions, RISCO's transnational corporate partners helped it to export between a third and a half of its output to developed capitalist countries. The economy still had to import more specialized types of steels, however, because RISCO could not take advantage of the economies of scale required to produce them.

The post-independence Zimbabwe government sought to restructure the company, renaming it ZISCO. The old board of directors and management argued that rising minimum wages, transport difficulties and persistent recession in the developed capitalist countries threatened it with insolvency. The government imported a new manager from Austria. Continued growth required a broader market, perhaps within the SADCC region. Whether this could be realized depended on the extent to which Zimbabwe and its neighbours could plan and implement a mutally beneficial regional industrial strategy, ensuring complementary specialization in various basic industries. Otherwise, other SADCC member countries seemed unlikely to forgo their own possibilities of constructing this basic capital goods industry.

3) IDC: In 1963, during the last days of the Federation of Rhodesia and Nyasaland, the settler controlled government established the IDC, primarily to assist private firms especially in the manufacturing sector to start or continue operating. Government provided 80 per cent of the IDC's initial capital of Z$10 million. The four foreign-owned commercial banks, together with the South African Mutual Insurance Company (see Chapter 5), a predominantly locally held firm, Delta, and an Anglo-American Group affiliate, Security Nominees, provided the rest. The private participants, although providing only a fifth of the capital, appointed four of the nine directors.

The IDC's terms of reference directed it to establish industrial undertakings deemed to be in the national interest, and conduct them on the basis of their "economic merit". By independence in 1980, the IDC had invested Z$23 million. It had spent about half this amount on taking over failing mines. This typical governmental rescue operation ensured that the mines continued to earn foreign exchange and that workers retained their jobs. In addition to getting their investment back, the private firms continued to provide the management. The IDC invested another fifth of its funds in motor car assembly, taking over the assets of transnational auto firms which, apprehensive about the impact of UN sanctions, withdrew from the country. The IDC reorganized its assembly plant capacity to produce cars from kits imported despite sanctions, primarily from France and Japan. It invested about 10 per cent of its funds in textiles. It purchased a small holding in Lonrho's David Whitehead subsidiary which dominated the national textiles industry. This apparently reflected Lonrho's policy of drawing on local capital to finance its domestic expansion, as well as gaining support from the government of the day. The IDC invested the remainder of its capital in metal products, financial services and engineering.

Like development corporations elsewhere in Africa, the IDC tended to grant its financial assistance primarily to larger firms. One year after independence, its managers reported that IDC affiliates expressed reluctance to invest in rural projects because this might hinder maximization of profits. The IDC did, however, assist in setting up the Chisumbanje sugar scheme in which some peasants participated, growing crude sugar for the Anglo-American Group's Lowveld mills.

These three Zimbabwean parastatals illustrate the way local and transnational corporate capital may co-operate with the government to finance projects which private firms alone would find insufficiently profitable to undertake.

The transnational corporate partners provide managerial and technical skills and, if required, external markets for more complex operations like those undertaken by ZISCO; and supply the necessary imported parts, machinery, equipment and semi-processed materials for manufacturing projects like those of the IDC. They typically operate according to profit maximizing criteria, often as viewed by the foreign partners. Unless the government exerts more direct controls over their operations, including their finances, such state corporations are unlikely to contribute significantly to restructuring, and may even aggravate the distortions of, an inherited, externally dependent economy.

Kenya: After achieving independence, other African governments also confronted the task of restructuring inherited public-enterprise institutions and integrating them into their physical and financial planning structures. At the same time, they frequently expanded government holdings. A brief review of the longer and seemingly different approaches to public enterprise, those of Kenya and Tanzania, may shed further light on some of the factors shaping their impact on national development.

After World War II the colonial government set up the Industrial and Commercial Development Corporation (ICDC) to assist Kenyan businessmen. Initially, the ICDC had functioned much like Zimbabwe's IDC, primarily working in concert with transnational corporate affiliates. In 1967, the newly independent government shifted the ICDC's focus to Africanization, seeking primarily to aid Kenyan small businessmen. It directed one ICDC subsidiary, the Development Finance Company of Kenya—partly owned by British, Dutch and German institutional investors—to continue to finance larger industrial and commercial undertakings, often in collaboration with foreign partners. A second subsidiary, the ICDC Investment Company, aimed to help wealthy Kenyans to acquire shares in private industries. Eventually, with World Bank assistance, the government established an Industrial Development Bank, in which the ICDC held an important share, to finance larger-scale private industrial projects.

Thus the post-independence Kenyan government expanded its parastatal sector to provide additional ways of mobilizing local capital to co-operate with transnational corporate investors in promoting industrial development. By the early 1970s, however, the Kenyan industrialization programme faced acute foreign-exchange difficulties. The ICDC turned over a substantial part of its activities to a new development bank. It reserved for itself the primary task of financing smaller, predominantly African, private enterprise.

Tanzania: Following the 1967 Arusha Declaration that it aimed to achieve socialism, Tanzania took over the foreign-held commercial banks and expanded the holdings of its inherited National Development Corporation by purchasing a majority of shares in the few larger existing industrial projects. By 1980, as Table 9.2 (p. 165) shows, its public-enterprise sector encompassed a wide range of activities.

As mainstream theory would recommend, however, the Tanzanian government left the National Development Corporation under the governance of an autonomous board of directors. It did not attempt to plan the Corporation's investments according to a long-term industrial strategy to restructure the national economy. Instead, the managers and directors of each subsidiary—many of them still including transnational corporate partners—tended to make decisions in the light of their own perceptions, at most only partially influenced by vague national welfare criteria other than overall profit maximization.

Although the government had nationalized the banks, it did not encourage them to play a significant role in monitoring the National Development Corporation's subsidiaries. The nationalized commercial banks could not initiate investment projects. The development banks and planning departments of the ministries supposedly performed that function, but they had not formulated a cohesive overall industrial strategy. Inter-enterprise lending took place between the National Development Corporation's subsidiaries through an internal bank, which charged lower lending rates and offered higher deposit rates than the nationalized commercial bank. This made it attractive for them to avoid the national bank, thus eliminating its potential role in monitoring their expenditures. The National Co-operative Bank, too, began to attract public-sector customers away from the National Commercial Bank.

Neither the government nor the Bank of Tanzania attempted to discourage these developments. As one expert, who had worked closely with the banking system following nationalization, declared:

> The likely outcome of this duplication of banking facilities is loss of financial control over public sector enterprises, encouragement of inefficient enterprises, competition for bank staff and a general rise in banking costs to the nation as a whole. It also runs directly contrary to the attempts to introduce more planning in this field.[3]

He particularly objected to the underlying ideology which fostered this competitive duplication:

> What is most disappointing . . . is the view held in some quarters that without competition we cannot allocate resources rationally neither can we guarantee efficiency of operation of the public sector, a view which has long been discarded even in Western capitalist countries where monopoly enterprises dominate.

In the early 1970s, the Tanzanian government confronted serious foreign-exchange difficulties and, seeking to redirect funds to its villagization programme, declared the need for a period of consolidation of its public enterprise activities. In the 1980s, the world economic crisis forced Tanzania's productive-sector public enterprises—still dependent on foreign exchange to import machinery, spare parts and materials—to a virtual standstill.

Summary

African governments, both before and after independence, intervened extensively in the productive sectors, both indirectly through subsidies to private enterprise and directly through state corporations. These forms of state intervention, promoting productive activities outside the framework of government plans, have significant implications for governments' efforts to regulate national money supplies and influence investment patterns.

Keynesian theories provide some justification for state intervention to stimulate the private sector. Monetarists, however, generally object that it wastes public funds and hinders the free interplay of market forces required to achieve optimal investment patterns. Marxists maintain that state capitalist intervention reflects the private sectors' inability to deal with the intensified contradictions characteristic of the era of monopolistic finance capital.

Colonial governments unabashedly introduced subsidies and created public enterprises to aid colonial companies and settler farmers. The nationalist governments that took power after independence only marginally altered these inherited forms of state capitalist intervention. Often, despite proclamations of "socialist" goals, the emergent bureaucratic bourgeoisie sought to redirect subsidies and state corporations to advance their own, as opposed to transnational corporate and (where they exist, as in Kenya and Zimbabwe) settler, interests. Few governments genuinely sought to involve the workers and peasants in reorientating these inherited institutions to achieve increasingly democratic socialist ownership of the means of production.

Independent African governments expanded the number and scope of public enterprises into a wide range of productive, financial and distributive activities. However, few succeeded in incorporating these expanding public enterprises into meaningful plans to restructure the national economy. The experiences of Zimbabwe, Kenya and Tanzania, all pursuing quite different, explicitly formulated development strategies, suggest that, unless fundamentally changed, the inherited autonomous corporate form itself will hamper efforts to implement more coherent plans.

Notes

1. Prest, *How Much Subsidy? A Study of the Economic Concept and Measurement of Subsidies in the United Kingdom*, Institute of Economic Affairs, London, 1974.
2. Many peasants' cattle died in 1982-83 of old age and lack of adequate water. The funds actually allocated for stock watering in low-rainfall areas initially, however, totalled only Z$30,000.
3. Loxley, in Cliffe and Saul, *Socialism in Tanzania*, Vol. 2, p. 109.

Exercises and Research

1. Compare mainstream and Marxist theories for state intervention in the productive sectors.
2. What conclusions can you draw about the role of subsidies in Zimbabwe? a) What factors determine who benefits? b) Should a newly independent government abolish subsidies or take steps to ensure that subsidies benefit the lower-income groups?
3. In what ways does typical government policy on public enterprises in the productive sectors in Africa tend to make coherent financial planning difficult? Illustrate from African experiences.
4. Which body of theory do you think most adequately explains the diverse patterns of Zimbabwean, Kenyan and Tanzanian state intervention in the productive and financial sectors of the economy? Explain why.
5. Examine state budget estimates and government reports to estimate the extent of subsidies as a percentage of government expenditures in your country. Attempt to determine who benefits. How would you suggest the subsidy programme be altered and why?
6. List the major public enterprises active in the productive and financial sectors of your country. Select an important one for detailed study: a) What percentage of the shares does government own? What interests do the members of the boards of directors represent? How is management selected?
   b) By what criteria does the enterprise make its investment decisions? Evaluate the role of the enterprise in the economy. How does it affect the allocation of resources and the distribution of incomes?
7. In view of the evidence you have discovered, determine which theory seems "best" to explain the role of subsidies and public enterprise in your country.

Recommended Reading

(For annotations, see bibliography at the end of the book)

Aromolaran, *West African Economics Today*
Clower *et al.*, *Growth without Development*
Falkena, *The South African State and its Entrepreneurs*
Fitzgerald, *Public Sector Investment Planning*
Ghai (ed.), *Economic Independence in Africa*
Hartman, *Enterprise and Politics in South Africa*
Hazlewood and Henderson, *Nyasaland*
Houghton, *The South African Economy*
Illugbuh, *Nigeria's Experience in Domestic Financing of Development*

IBRD country reports
Marris and Somerset, *African Businessmen*
Nnoli, *Path to Nigerian Development*
Okigbo, *Nigerian Public Finance*
Public Enterprise in Nigeria, *Proceedings of the 1973 Annual Conference of the Nigerian Economic Society*
Report of a Working Party, *Who Controls Industry in Kenya*
Robinson (ed.), *Economic Development for Africa South of the Sahara*
Seidman and Makgetla, *Outposts of Monopoly Capital*
Teriba and Kayode (eds), *Industrial Development in Nigeria*
UN Economic Commission for Africa, *Budget Planning and Management*
US Department of Commerce, *Investment in Nigeria*
—— *Investment in the Federation of Rhodesia and Nyasaland*
Wetham and Currie, *Readings in Applied Economics of Africa*, Vol. 2
Williams (ed.), *Nigeria*

Periodicals
The Economist Intelligence Unit, *Quarterly Economic Reviews*
IMF, *Government Statistics*
Public Enterprise

Chapter 10: Expanding Domestic Public Debt

Widespread Government Borrowing at Home

Across the continent, independent African governments' failure to increase taxes sufficiently to finance rising expenditures forced them to borrow heavily, both domestically and abroad. Table 10.1 illustrates the extent to which, in the 1970s, selected African states expanded their public debt. Ghana's debt, for example, multiplied from 1972 to 1976 2.4 times; Kenya's from 1972 to 1980, 2.7 times, and Sierra Leone from 1974 to 1980, 6.2 times.

Many African governments borrowed at home to finance an increasing share of their rising public debt. Among independent[1] sub-Saharan countries, Ghana borrowed by far the highest proportion of its funds internally (82.4 per cent in 1980); but, as Table 10.2 shows, other independent African states also borrowed a growing share of their public debt from domestic sources.

This chapter will first review the theoretical debate concerning the impact of domestic borrowing, then summarize some of the evidence as to how domestic debt affected Zimbabwe's political economy as a fairly typical experience, and briefly discuss the more extreme Ghanaian case. Part III will consider the issue of foreign borrowing in more detail, in the context of an analysis of the international monetary system.

The Theoretical Debate

Mainstream economists disagree as to the causes and consequences of many aspects of public debt. In so far as it holds that the state may borrow to finance expenditures designed to start the wheels of private enterprise turning, the Keynesian approach provides some theoretical justification for the expansion of public debt. Government borrowing may provoke a degree of inflation. This will reduce the real wages of workers and increase the profits of private firms, thus stimulating them to invest, leading to desirable multiplier effects. Through the sale of treasury bills, moreover, governments expand the domestic money market. This facilitates the central bank's efforts to utilize indirect monetary techniques to help stabilize the economy.

Monetarists, however, maintain that expanded governments deficits and

Table 10.1
Total Outstanding Debt as Percent of Tax Revenues and Gross Domestic Product, Selected African states, 1972 and 1982

		1972					1982				
Country	*National Currency*	*Debt (mns.)*	*% Domestic*	*% Foreign*	*% of tax revenues*	*% of GDP*	*Debt (mns.)*	*% Domestic*	*% Foreign*	*% of tax revenues*	*% of GDP*
Botswana	Pula	NA	NA	NA	NA	NA	199.80	0.2	99.8	91.7	27.1
Ghana	Cedi	1156.4	80.3	19.7	276.1	NA	21,570.10	81.1	18.1	516.0	
Kenya	Shilling	3886	45.4	54.6	147.7	NA	10.524.00(a)	53.9(a)	46.1(a)	132.0(a)	25.6(a)
Sierra Leone	Leone	115(c)	38.3(c)	61.7(c)	139.2(c)	20.1(c)	829.30(b)	52.2(b)	47.8(b)	416.9(b)	48.6(b)
South Africa	Rand	NA	NA	NA	NA	NA	18,687.00(d)	96.4(d)	3.6(d)	196.8(d)	39.2(d)
Sudan	Pound	263.7(c)	47.7(c)	52.3(c)	167.5(c)	17.4(c)	NA	NA	NA	NA	NA
Zambia	Kwacha	NA	NA	NA	NA	NA	2,089.70(a)	69.7(a)	30.3(a)	426.8(a)	93.2(a)
Zimbabwe	Dollars	636	80	20	122.5(e)	47.6	2,478.60	66.0	44.0	181.6	49.5

NA = not available; (a) 1978; (b) 1981; (c) 1974; (d) 1980; (e) 1975

Source: International Monetary Fund, Government Finance Statistics Yearbook, 1982 and 1984, Country tables

Table 10.2
Outstanding Central Government Domestic Debt of Selected African States (by types of debt holders and debt instruments as % of domestic debt, 1982(a))

Country	*Type of Debt Holder (as % of domestic debt)*					*Type of Debt Instrument (as % of domestic debt)*		
				Other Domestic[a]				
	Monetary authorities	*Other govt levels*	*Deposit monetary banks*	*Other fin'l insts.*	*Non-fin'l (private)*	*Short term*	*Long term*	*Other liabilities*
Ghana	37.8	—	—	4.8	57.4	75.7[b]	22.5[b]	1.8[b]
South Africa	0.1[c]	3.7[c]	12.8[c]	66.1[c]	17.2[c]	82.3[c]	17.7[c]	—
Zambia	65.9[d]	0.4[d]	3.8[d]	20.9[d]	2.9[d]	72.2[d]	26.0[d]	1.8[d]
Zimbabwe	24.9	9.5	13.8	41.2	10.6	13.5	84.6	1.9

[a] totals may not equal 100% due to rounding;
[b] 1983 estimated data (1982 data not available);
[c] 1981 data; [d] 1978 data.

Source: International Monetary Fund, Government Finance Statistics Yearbook, 1984.

domestic debts have been a major cause of the inflationary trends apparent in Africa and the rest of the Third World. Rising wages may also introduce a cost-push element. Eventually, as government borrowing continues, inflationary pressures may—as in Ghana—get out of hand, undermining and distorting the normal functioning of the entire economy.

Some structuralist explanations of inflation tend to reinforce the monetarists' arguments. Inherited institutional structures obstruct the Keynesians' anticipated multiplier effects. Local entrepreneurs lack capital and skills essential to expand local production and employment in response to increased demand. Foreign firms may hesitate to risk new investment in apparently unstable nationalist environments. Foreign exchange controls hinder the import of goods, despite expanded domestic demand. Oligopolistic firms, therefore, can take advantage of the increased demand stimulated by government borrowing to raise their prices and increase their profits.

The monetarists call on governments to balance their budgets, if necessary by reducing welfare expenditures and raising taxes on lower-income groups. They recommend that the central bank raise the interest rate to reduce private borrowing since all borrowing increases the money supply and hence inflationary pressures. To overcome what they view as structural obstacles, monetarists recommend that foreign-exchange controls be reduced, opening domestic markets to international competition. They urge the government to create a more attractive environment for foreign investment. Part III will consider the international features of these arguments; this chapter focuses primarily on the domestic aspects.

Marxists theorists agree that structural obstacles hinder the spread of Keynesian-type multiplier effects, but they emphasize that decades of imperialist rule embedded these obstacles in the externally dependent African political economies. In this context, the Keynesian policy of expanding domestic debt inevitably has two negative consequences. First, especially as state capitalist governments typically borrow primarily to finance non-productive activities, the growing domestic debt does foster inflationary pressures. These also reflect the unplanned growth of the money supply and the accumulation of private profits without regard to the inherent features of the political economy which thwart the spread of productive employment activities. The resulting inflation reduces the real wages and other relatively fixed incomes of the working class, peasants and petty bourgeoisie.

Second, expanded domestic borrowing typically aggravates the skewed pattern of domestic income distribution. Governments usually borrow primarily from banks and associated financial institutions. They must repay these loans, with interest, from tax revenues. To the extent that the typical state capitalist government imposes taxes that weigh heavily on lower-income groups, this repayment tends to shift income from them to augment the profits of finance capital. It strengthens the concentrated financial sector's control over national savings, enhancing its power to determine whether and how they should be reinvested. To maximize their profits, the financial institutions tend to reinvest in unplanned expansion of production in the so-called "modern enclave", or remit funds to their corporate parents.

Marxists also reject the monetarists' undifferentiated aggregative approach to reducing expenditures and balancing the budget. Simply slashing welfare spending and cutting government employment and wages reduces the few benefits that independence has brought to the lower-income population. The unplanned reduction of incomes and employment of the working class and peasants aggravates the underlying contradictions arising from the accumulation of profits which cannot be reinvested because the local market cannot absorb the expanded output. Raising interests rates to reduce inflation further augments the flow of incomes to the financial sector and undermines emerging small businesses which cannot afford to pay higher rates; this accelerates the concentration and centralization of control over the means of production, distribution and finance by the largest firms, typically the transnational corporate affiliates.

Monetarist measures, in short, cannot resolve the underlying crises confronting the Third World countries. They simply throw the burden of the crises on to the impoverished population. When the workers and peasants object, the state capitalist governments inevitably adopt increasingly repressive measures to retain power.

Marxists maintain that Third World governments which seek to make a transition to socialism must plan the gradual expansion of social welfare programmes within the capacity of the growing national product to finance them. (See Part IV.)

Some Evidence from Zimbabwe

By the 1970s, most African governments, having increased domestic borrowing to cover the rising costs of their expanded administrative and social welfare programmes, began to experience increased inflationary pressures. Only research in each country can determine the extent to which the expansion of public debt caused rising prices. Evidence from Zimbabwe may suggest some possible lines of fruitful investigation.

Despite the fact that the pre-independence regime budgeted little for social welfare for the African population, it did borrow domestically, especially to finance its soaring military costs. Taxation covered only about 80 per cent of state expenditures until the late 1970s. In the early years of the UDI period, after UN sanctions restricted commercial banks' ties to their overseas parents, the Central Bank issued treasury bills to soak up excess commercial bank liquidity. It kept the interest rate at a low 4.5 per cent, using treasury bills to strengthen its role in the money market. However, over time, despite sanctions, expanded international trade and the growing use of other forms of short-term paper rendered this role of treasury bills less significant. The regime mostly borrowed domestic funds on a long-term basis. Under these conditions, it succeeded in keeping inflation below 10 per cent a year, though even this eroded the real incomes of the Africans whose money wages were essentially frozen.

Although it increased tax revenues in the last years of the liberation war, the regime had to borrow more and more heavily to finance its increased military expenditures. It almost tripled its annual deficit from 1977 to 1979. By 1980, its total domestic debt equalled almost half the national income.

After independence, the new government's rapidly growing expenditure on post-war reconstruction and new social welfare programmes further outpaced increased tax revenues. As a result, domestic debt rose 40 per cent more from 1979 to 1981, before it levelled off as the government turned to borrowing from foreign sources.

As Table 10.3A indicates, in Zimbabwe (as in other African countries) the government borrowed primarily from financial institutions controlled by the commercial banks and transnational corporations. Since, in Zimbabwe, interest payments on government debt are tax-free, they constituted clear profit for these institutions.

Table 10.3A
Zimbabwe Government's Stocks, Bonds and Treasury Bills (1979, 1980 and 1981)
Increased Monetary Banking Sector's Holdings of Government Stock and Treasury Bills, 1979-1981

	Total Bank Assets Z$m	*% Increase in Banhas per year*	*Central and Local-government Stock Z$m*	*Treasury Bills Z$m*	*% of Government Stock and Treasury Bills as Assets each year*
1979	2,017	11	472.7	57.5	26
1980	2,421	20	610.6	99.0	29
1981	2,710	12	545.2	52.9	22

Source: *Zimbabwe Monthly Digest*, June 1982, p. 69.

Table 10.3B
Institutions Subscribing to Government Debt (excluding Treasury Bills) in Zimbabwe Each Year, 1979-81 (% of total stock and bonds held by each Institution)

	Monetary Bank Sector[a] %	*Building Societies* %	*Post Office Savings Bank* %	*Insurance Companies* %	*Pension Funds* %	*Other*[b] %	*Total Z$m*
1979	25	11	17	21	16	7	188.9
1980	34	8	25	25	6	17	352.7
1981	21	6	16	12	7	37	309.8

[a] Commercial banks, discount houses, merchant banks
[b] Finance houses, companies, trade unions, government sinking funds, non-residents

Source: *Reserve Bank Quarterly*, Feb 1983, p. 30.

Table 10.3B shows that during UDI commercial banks and insurance firms had become increasingly important sources of government borrowing. After independence in 1980, "others" grew rapidly. The new government permitted transnational corporate affiliates, whose profits had been blocked during UDI, to invest them in six-year bonds which it promised to repay as they became due with relatively low rates of interest.

A government must repay its debt out of revenues collected from taxpayers. It may, of course, roll the debt over (borrow new funds to pay back the old debt). But then it must continually borrow more to finance new deficit expenditures, as well as the increasing interest costs. As a result, the financial sector obtains a growing percentage of the taxpayers' contribution to government. To the extent that the pre-independence regime in Zimbabwe imposed regressive taxes, taxes on the poor helped to finance repayments plus interest to the private financial institutions and their transnational parent corporations.

After independence, in line with IMF advice, the Zimbabwe Reserve Bank raised the bank rate from 4.5 to 9.5 per cent. The average tender rate for 91-day bills more than doubled, from 3.57 to 8.18 per cent. This raised the repayment cost for the increased issuance of treasury bills from Z$5 million in 1979 to Z$18 million in 1981. The interest rate on three-year government stock rose from 4.85 to 9.05 per cent, while that of 25-year stock rose from 9.5 to 13 per cent. The cost of repaying the increased government debt in the form of stocks and bonds almost tripled from $53 million 1978-79, about 6 per cent of taxes, to $136 million, or 8 per cent of significantly higher tax revenues in 1981. Except for education and defence, debt repayment became the largest single item of government expenditure.

Rising interest rates also imposed an increased burden on private-sector firms which had to borrow to finance productive activities. One sample study[2] showed that from 1980 to 1982 average depreciation and bank charges paid by manufacturing firms rose 45 per cent. This tended to adversely affect the smaller (particularly emergent African) businesses which relied heavily on borrowed funds for working capital expenditures.

As domestic public debt expanded to finance primarily non-productive activities, it contributed to inflationary pressures by increasing the money supply without expanding the production of real goods. In Zimbabwe, from 1979 to 1981, total bank assets rose over 40 per cent, reflecting the growing money supply. Government long- and short-term borrowing contributed about a quarter of this expansion. At the same time, prices began to rise at an accelerating rate. In 1980, the low-income consumer price index rose 14.6 points; in 1981, it rose 25 points; and in 1982, it rose 34.3 points.

Business spokesmen widely blamed increased minimum wages introduced by the new government as a cost-push factor causing inflation. The available evidence does not support this claim. As Table 10.4 shows, at a micro level wages in manufacturing sectors increased only marginally as a percentage of total input costs. Significantly, wages in the foodstuff industry actually declined as a percentage of total costs; yet foodstuff prices rose more rapidly than most other components of the low-income consumer price index (except household goods and transport).

Table 10.4
Percentage Contribution of Raw Material Purchases and Wage and Salary Costs to Total Input Costs, 1980, 1981, 1982

Sub-Sector	*1980*			*1981*			*1982*		
	RM Purchases as % Total Input Costs	Wage Costs as % Total Input Costs	RM & Wages as % Total Input Costs	RM Purchases as % Total Input Costs	Wage Costs as % Total Input Costs	RM & Wages as % Total Input Costs	RM Purchases as % Total Input Costs	Wage Costs as % Total Input Costs	RM & Wages as % Total Input Costs
Foodstuffs	75.5	12.4	87.9	75.5	12.2	87.7	74.5	12.2	86.7
Drink and Tobacco	45.3	23.8	69.1	46.4	25.7	72.0	48.6	24.4	73.0
Textiles	57.7	19.2	76.9	58.9	22.3	81.2	53.8	24.5	78.3
Clothing & Footwear	56.8	22.1	78.9	58.7	22.2	80.9	51.1	25.9	77.0
Wood & Furniture	60.7	22.9	83.6	57.9	23.6	81.5	53.7	26.3	80.0
Paper, Printing & Publishing	65.3	23.8	89.1	60.7	27.4	68.1	60.5	24.3	84.9
Chemical & Petroleum Products	64.9	14.0	78.9	64.1	14.9	79.0	60.5	16.2	76.7
Non-Metallic Mineral Products	18.8	24.9	43.7	21.4	24.9	46.8	19.6	30.0	49.6
Metals & Metal Products	53.5	25.6	79.1	52.1	26.2	78.3	50.4	27.5	77.9
Transport & Equipment	46.7	31.2	77.9	38.5	34.6	73.1	24.2	42.4	66.6
Average	*54.5*	*22.0*	*76.5*	*53.4*	*28.4*	*76.8*	*49.7*	*25.4*	*75.1*

Source: R. Riddell and D.F. Nsiyaludzu, *Turnover, Inputs and Inputs Costs in the Manufacturing Sector, 1980-1982: Findings of a Confederation of Zimbabwe Industries Survey*. Confederation of Zimbabwe Industries, 1983.

Table 10.4 unfortunately does not indicate the distribution of wage and salary payments by income group. Income tax data, however, reveal that half the wage and salary bill in Zimbabwe, as in most African countries, goes to the less than 10 per cent of all wage earners in highly skilled, administrative and supervisory posts. Using the 1982 average wage cost indicated in Table 10.4 then, minimum wages would affect less than 13 per cent of total costs. Thus, if minimum wages rose 30 per cent, they would increase total costs by less than 4 per cent—far less than the cumulative price increase of nearly 75 per cent in the three post-independence years.

Additional micro-level research is required to determine the impact of rising profits, as opposed to wages, on price levels. For example, in the labour-intensive tobacco-farming industry, where minimum wages rose from less than Z$20 to Z$50 a month, the 76,000 workers' wage income actually declined as a percentage of the total industry's product, from 22.1 per cent in 1980 to 17.8 per cent in 1981. Barely more than a thousand commercial farmers reaped in net income more than twice as much as the total amount they paid the workers in both years. The farmers might well have absorbed some of the wage increase by accepting somewhat smaller profits.

On a macro level, from 1979 to 1981, total wages and salaries paid in Zimbabwe actually dropped from 55 to 53 per cent of national income, while the share going to operating profits increased commensurately. By 1982, as inflation eroded the real wages of the workers, effective demand for consumer goods, like clothing and shoes, noticeably declined. This suggests that, far from causing inflation, the lowest-paid workers, in particular, suffered because of it. Furthermore, declining demand led to reduced output and employment in the consumer-goods industries.

Other factors may have contributed significantly to rising prices. In Zimbabwe, as elsewhere in Africa, oligopolistic firms, many of them transnational corporate affiliates, could take advantage of initially increased demand spurred by the growing money supply to push up prices. Table 10.5 reveals that in several key industries the impact of the liberation war and international recession in the last years of UDI had allowed a declining number of large firms to increase control of their sectoral output.

Table 10.5
Oligopolistic Tendencies in Several Key Zimbabwean Industries 1975-78

	Year	*Numbers of Large Firms (over $50,000 in Assets)*	*Percentage of all output Large firms output as*
Grain Mills	1975	5	75
	1978	3	74
Textiles	1975	26	63
	1978	15	53
Wood Products	1975	22	53
and Furniture	1978	7	21
Fertilizers	1975	4	80
	1978	3	74
Rubber	1975	8	66
	1978	7	53
Electrical Mech.	1975	17	45
	1978	11	35

Source: *Census of Production*, (Salisbury: Government Printers Office) 1976/7, 1978/9.

The rising costs of imported goods, reflecting the impact of international inflation, aggravated inflationary pressures in Zimbabwe as elsewhere in Africa. The biggest jump in prices per unit of imports in Zimbabwe, about 7 per cent, took place between 1979 and 1980. After 1980, with the end of

UN sanctions, prices per unit of imports actually declined slightly, rising again between 1981 and the first half of 1982 by about 4 per cent. These increases undoubtedly aggravated rising domestic prices, but could hardly have caused the 23 per cent rise in domestic prices that occurred during that 18-month period.

This evidence suggests that in Zimbabwe, government's increased domestic borrowing to finance non-productive activities may have been an important factor contributing to inflationary pressures. As demand expanded, stimulated by government spending, oligopolistic firms raised prices to maximize profits.

The Case of Ghana

The Ghanaian experience underscores the dangers of heavy domestic borrowing. The Ghanaian government failed, in the 1970s, to increase taxes sufficiently to finance its mounting expenses. Instead, as Table 10.2 shows, it relied increasingly on expanding its domestic debt. It borrowed half of this debt from monetary authorities, directly augmenting the money supply. The productive sectors tended to stagnate. By the end of the 1970s, runaway inflation had gripped the economy.

Summary

African governments' failure to raise taxes to match increasing expenditures forced many of them to acquire heavy domestic debts. Keynesian doctrine partially justifies domestic borrowing to finance expenditures to stimulate private investment. Monetarists object that such borrowing stimulates inflationary pressures, and urge retrenchment of government spending and central bank policies to restrict money supply expansion. Marxists agree that domestic government borrowing, especially for non-productive expenditures, may generate inflationary pressures which undermine the real living standards of the workers while channelling added surplus value to the finance capitalist sector. Monetarist proposals, however, simply throw the burden of the inevitable crises on the workers and peasants. Marxists advocate, instead, that the state, implementing a step-by-step transition to socialism, use planning to ensure expanding employment and production to increase funds allocated to finance expanding social welfare (see Part IV).

The case of Zimbabwe provides some evidence as to the impact of domestic borrowing as well as other factors on inflationary pressures. That evidence suggests that increased public debt, primarily directed to non-productive expenditures, in the context of oligopolistic control over major productive sectors of the economy, leads to rising prices. At the same time, a central bank's efforts to control inflation by raising interest payments imposes an increasing burden on taxpayers, while channelling additional funds to the financial sector; and tends to hinder small business efforts to expand output.

Notes

1. International opposition to apartheid restricted South Africa's efforts to borrow abroad, which explains, in part, the rapid growth of its domestic debt, especially to finance its growing military expenditures.

2. Riddell and Nsiyaludzu, *Turn-over, Inputs and Input Costs in the Manufacturing Sector, 1980-1982: Findings of a Confederation of Zimbabwe Industries Survey*, Confederation of Zimbabwe Industries, April 1983.

Exercises and Research

1. What are the main arguments in the theoretical debate over domestic debt?
2. Looking at the Zimbabwean case, what do you conclude from the evidence relating to:
   a) the impact of government borrowing and repayment of debt on the distribution of income?
   b) the effect of an increase in the interest rate on the cost of government borrowing and on smaller businesses?
   c) the impact of government borrowing on inflationary pressures? (Be sure to consider the evidence concerning other possible causes of inflation.)
3. Can you formulate any tentative conclusions as to which theory offers the "best" explanation of the impact of domestic debt?
4. Examine the extent of your government's domestic borrowing:
   a) From what individuals and institutions does the government borrow?
   b) What is the annual cost of repaying the domestic debt? What percentage does it constitute of total government spending? What factors determine this cost?
   c) Try to estimate the effect of repayment on income distribution and the pattern of accumulation and reinvestment of capital in your country.
5. Evaluate the probable impact of government borrowing on inflationary pressures in your country's economy.

Recommended Reading

(For annotations, see bibliography at the end of the book.)

Ahmad, *Deficit Financing, Inflation and Capital Formation*
Allen and Kenen, *Asset Markets, Exchange Rates and Economic Integration*
Cline and associates, *World Inflation and the Developing Countries*
Eshag, *Fiscal and Monetary Policies and Problems*
Ord and Livingstone, *An Introduction to West African Economics*
Seidman, *Ghana's Development Experience*
—— *Planning for Development in SubSaharan Africa*
Truu (ed.), *Public Policy and the South African Economy*
Wetham and Currie, *Readings in Applied Economics of Africa*

Periodicals

The Economist Intelligence Unit, *Quarterly Economic Reviews*
IMF, *Government Statistics*
Bank for International Settlements
Government Statistical Digests.

Part III: The International Monetary System

Chapter 11: African Trade and Payments and the International Monetary Crisis

The Significance of the International Monetary System for African Economies

Colonialism enmeshed the economies of the independent African states into the Western trade and monetary system. Therefore, to comprehend fully the causes of the problems of money, banking and public finance in Africa requires an understanding of that interrelationship, in particular, of how the prolonged monetary crisis that gripped the western system in the 1970s and early 1980s profoundly affected the African countries' efforts to attain higher levels of investment and development.

Part III examines how the underlying features of the international monetary system aggravated the difficulties confronting the independent African states as they tried to expand foreign trade and obtain additional investment capital. Chapter 11 reviews the necessary tools of analysis and uses them to explore the dimensions of the problems confronting African states as the international monetary crisis deepened. Chapter 12 considers the alternative explanations and solutions offered by mainstream and Marxist theorists. Chapter 13 describes the role of transnational banks and the Eurocurrency market. Chapters 14 and 15 provide evidence to enable readers to evaluate the way the institutional structures of the international monetary and financial system, largely shaped by mainstream theories, have both affected and been influenced by the financial difficulties engulfing African and other Third World economies.

African Trade and Payments

For international trade to expand, participating countries must agree on an international medium of exchange. That medium must have characteristics similar to those of money outlined in Chapter 2. In particular, the stability of international currency stands out as crucially important for the continued growth of international trade and payments.

A Review of Concepts

A review of the concepts of the balance of trade and payments helps to explain the importance of maintaining the stability of the international currency, as well as to delineate the scope of the problems confronting African states as the international monetary crisis developed.[1]

Table 11.1A
The Terms of Trade of Selected African States by Export Category[a]

	Average Annual Rate of Growth			
	Purchasing Power of exports		*Export Volume*	
Category	*1961-70*	*1970-79*	*1960-70*	*1970-79*
1. Oil Exporters[b]	7.7	12.6	7.2	−2.0
2. Mineral Exporters[c]	11.1	−7.7	4.6	−0.7
3. Other Primary Exporters[d]	4.9	1.1	4.7	−2.1
Sub-total, oil importers (Categories 2 & 3)	7.6	−2.7	4.7	−1.5
For all sub-Saharan Africa	*7.6*	*1.0*	*5.3*	*−1.6*

[a] Country group averages are weighted by value of country merchandise exports in 1970.
[b] Angola, Congo and Nigeria
[c] Liberia, Mauritania, Niger, Sierra Leone, Togo, Zaire and Zambia
[d] Benin, Cameroon, CAR, Chad, Ethiopia, Ghana, Ivory Coast, Kenya, Madagascar, Malawi, Mali, Rwanda, Senegal, Somalia, Sudan, Tanzania, Uganda and Upper Volta

Source: UNCTAD, *Handbook of International Trade and Development Statistics*, 1980, cited in IBRD, *Accelerated Development in SubSaharan Africa*

Table 11.1B
Changes in Terms of Trade and the Associated Loss of Income in Sub-Saharan Africa, 1980-82

Country Group	*Percentage Change in Terms of Trade between 1980 and 1982*	*Associated Loss of Income in 1982 over 1980[a] (Percentage of GDP)*
Low-income countries	*−14.5*	*2.4*
Low-income semi-arid	*− 2.6*	*0.5*
Low-income other	*−16.0*	*2.6*
Middle-income oil importers	*−11.1*	*3.0*
Middle-income oil exporters	*1.8*	*−0.5*
Total	*− 4.7*	*1.2*

[a] Calculated by multiplying the percentage of decline in terms of trade by the share of exports in GDP. Minus sign denotes income gain.

Source: IBRD, *Toward Sustained Development in Sub-Saharan Africa.*

The balance of trade shows the relationship between the money prices of the actual goods a country trades; that is, it summarizes the money value of nation's visible exports minus the money value of its visible imports. Most African countries enjoyed a balance of trade surplus until the mid-1970s, since the value of their exports exceeded the value of their imports. At the end of the year they generally had earned a net surplus of foreign exchange from their trade in goods.

The terms of trade affect a country's balance of trade. The terms of trade show, given existing money prices, how many units of a country's imports a given unit of its exports will buy. A country's terms of trade, then, reflect the prices of imports compared to exports.

In the 1970s and early 1980s, most African countries, like other Third World countries—initially excepting those exporting oil—confronted worsening terms of trade as prices of their imported goods rose compared to the prices of their exports. As Table 11.1A shows, mineral exporting countries were especially affected. The export volumes of all countries declined, however, reflecting the impact of the international recession in reducing the demand of developed countries for most African states' crude exports. As a result, sub-Saharan African countries' export earnings failed to keep pace with their growing import requirements. At the end of the decade, they more and more frequently experienced balance of trade deficits. In the early 1980s, the terms of trade of all sub-Saharan countries worsened still further causing significant losses in GDP (see Table 11.1B).

A country's balance of payments adds the balance of trade to the net balance of invisible exports minus invisible imports. Invisible items include all cash payments for services, including freight, insurance and travel abroad; and the flow of income, including corporate profits, interest and dividends, salaries and management fees for expatriate personnel, etc.

Since independence, most African countries' net invisible trade has ended up in deficit. Transnational affiliates typically own or control crucial shares of their productive, distributive and financial sectors. Therefore, the countries typically pay out more than they receive in new investments for services and in remittances of profits, interest and dividends, high salaries and fees to transnational corporations. As a result, in the post-independence era, most African countries, even if they enjoyed a balance of trade surplus, ended the year with balance of payments deficits.

By the late 1970s, worsening terms of trade, added to losses on invisible items, imposed increasing balance of payments deficits on most independent African states. More and more had to borrow international funds, not to finance development, but simply to pay their overseas debts.

The Relative Exchange Value of National Currencies

The relative exchange value of a country's national currency, compared to the value of the currencies of its trading partners, influences its balance of trade and payments. Producers of goods for international trade may use their country's own national currency to pay all local costs. When they sell those goods abroad, their earnings will be influenced by the value of their national currency compared to those of the countries buying their goods.

To illustrate, using a hypothetical Zimbabwe case; assuming an exchange rate of Z$1 = US$1.30. Suppose Company A mines copper in Zimbabwe. Company A draws on its deposit in a commercial bank to obtain Zimbabwe dollars to pay its labourers' wages, say Z$300,000. It spends another Z$350,000 on dynamite, fuel for its machines, depreciation, interest on loans, and managerial costs. Company A then sells the copper it has produced to a US firm for Z$1,000,000. The US firm pays US$1,300,000 by cheque made out to Company A. Company A deposits the cheque in its commercial bank account in Zimbabwe. The commercial bank turns the foreign exchange over to the Zimbabwe central bank which adds it to the country's reserves. It deposits an equivalent amount of Zimbabwe dollars, Z$1,000,000, in Company A's account in the commercial bank. Company A has now recovered its costs (Z$650,000) plus its profits (Z$350,000).

Suppose Company A now wants to buy Z$1,000,000 worth of mining machinery from a US manufacturer. Company A goes to its bank to obtain a US dollar cheque to pay for the machinery. If the central bank exercises exchange control, as it does in Zimbabwe and most other African states, Company A must obtain an import licence from the appropriate ministry. The commercial bank helps Company A to obtain permission from the central bank to draw on the country's foreign-exchange reserves to cover the cheque. (In Zimbabwe, the Reserve Bank has formulated overall regulations within the framework of which it permits commercial banks to decide whether its clients may draw on the foreign reserves.) Once it has permission, the commercial bank provides Company A with a cheque for US$1,300,000 which draws on the country's foreign-exchange reserves.

All this is fairly straightforward. Company A, with the aid of the bank, has essentially traded copper for machinery, using two currencies with a predetermined rate of exchange between them as the necessary medium of exchange.

The Effect of Devaluation

Mainstream theorists often argue that devaluation of a nation's currency enables exporters to reduce the prices of their export so they can expand their overseas sales. Suppose the exchange value of the Zimbabwe dollar changes, as it did at the end of 1982. For simplicity, suppose the new exchange rate is Z$1 = $US1; that is, the Zimbabwe dollar is devalued by 23 per cent. Company A in Zimbabwe pays its labourers Z$300,000 and spends Z$350,000 on its other requirements, as before. It sells its copper for Z$1,000,000 as before, but now the US buyer only pays US$1,000,000. In other words, the devaluation reduced the cost of the copper to the foreign buyer by 23 per cent.

But when Company A wants to purchase goods from other countries, it must pay 23 per cent more in Zimbabwe dollars to cover the foreign-exchange costs. Thus, when Company A decides to import the same amount of machinery from the United States, it will have to spend, not Z$1,000,000 as before but Z$1,300,000. Devaluation of Zimbabwe's currency by 23 per cent will raise the payments the country must make for all visible and invisible imports by 23 per cent. It will, in other words, reduce the country's purchasing power for imports by 23 per cent.

The importers usually pass on the increased cost of imports to the final consumers inside the country in the form of higher prices, ultimately reducing their real incomes.

The story does not necessarily end there. Company A's managers may conclude that reducing its export price in terms of US dollars, as implied by devaluation of the Zimbabwean currency, is unnecessary because of the inelastic world demand for copper. Therefore, it may raise the Zimbabwe dollar price and charge the US buyer the same price as before, US$1,300,000. Now, when the US dollar is translated back into Zimbabwe dollars, Company A will receive Z$300,000 more than before, raising its profits in Zimbabwe dollars to Z$650,000, almost double what it received before. The value of the real wages of the workers, on the other hand, will eventually be reduced by rising domestic prices. To the extent that the Zimbabwe central bank permits Company A to remit 50 per cent of its additional after-tax profits to its parent firm abroad, of course, the net national income and the foreign exchange available for the needs of the national economy will also fall.

Another option is open to Company A if the US buyer is its transnational corporate parent. It may sell its Zimbabwe copper to its parent firm for US$1,000,000. The parent firm may, in turn, sell that copper to the final customer in the US at the original price, US$1,300,000, keeping the extra profit in US dollars. This constitutes a transfer pricing technique. Since Company A's overseas parent simply retains the extra profit, the Zimbabwe central bank has no say in whether or not Company A may remit it.

In short, devaluation, by raising the prices of imported goods, may, in so far as its imports affect the general price level, eventually reduce the real incomes of the local population. This will reduce the real wages of the workers, whom Company A and all other employers still pay at the same rate in Zimbabwe dollars. The companies engaged in exporting goods, however, instead of accepting a reduced dollar price for their exports, may simply take in greater profits on the same amount of goods sold. Depending on what the local companies do with their profits, they may reduce net national income and the nation's foreign-exchange earnings.

Table 14.1 (p. 239) shows, in the late 1970s and early 1980s, many African countries had to devalue their currencies. As suggested above, this had a very real impact on their domestic price levels and the living standards of their populations. Thus the issue of what factors determine the relative exchange value of a nation's currency has vital significance for the peoples of African and other Third World countries.

Fluctuating Exchange Rates

As a consequence of—and also a factor behind the international monetary crisis of the 1970s, the developed capitalist nations agreed to allow the exchange values of their respective currencies to float, that is to fluctuate in response to demand and supply in the international market. As a result African countries which depend on their exports to earn the necessary foreign exchange to buy imports could never be certain, in advance, of the real purchasing power of the currencies they earned. Through no action on their part, the value of their currency in terms of US dollars, English pounds, French francs, German deutschmarks, Japanese yen or any other currency—except the one to which it was formally linked—might change dramatically. Given their crucial dependence on foreign trade and payments, the fluctuating exchange rates accompanying the international monetary crisis aggravated the serious problems already plaguing their efforts to develop.

The Rising Cost of International Capital

The international monetary crisis not only aggravated African balance of trade and payments problems; it also hampered their efforts to obtain capital to implement long-term development plans. On the one hand, transnational corporations showed greater reluctance to invest in independent African states, especially those that relied on imported oil. As Table 11.2 shows, in the 1970s, transnational corporations actually reduced their direct annual investments in non-oil exporting African countries from US400 million to US$300 million. As a share of the total funds available to African countries to offset their deteriorating payments balances, private direct investment fell far more dramatically, from 27 to 3 per cent.

Growing balance of payment deficits have forced African and other Third World countries to borrow heavily from transnational corporate banks at rising rates of interest. African governments, as well as the banks' home governments, often guarantee those loans, providing security for transnational corporate bank loans not available for direct investments. Table 11.2 illustrates that in the late 1970s, as direct private investment declined, African oil-importing countries almost tripled their foreign commercial debt.

Table 11.2
Private investment and commercial loans to oil-importing African countries in U.S.$ billions and as per cent of current account deficit, 1970-1980

	1970		*1975*		*1980*	
Item	*$ bil.*	*% def.*	*$ bil.*	*% def.*	*$ bil.*	*% def.*
Private direct investment	0.4	26.6	0.4	6.3	0.3	3.8
Commercial loans	0.8	53.3	1.9	29.7	2.1	26.3

Source: Calculated from World Bank, *Accelerated Development in Sub-Saharan Africa: An Agenda for Action,* p. 17.

Scarce Direct Investment Capital

Even before the 1970s, transnational corporations had relied where possible on mobilizing local capital instead of bringing in new funds. During UDI in

Zimbabwe, the transnationals had increased their holdings to about three-quarters of the assets of the expanding modern sector. They did this not by bringing in and investing their own funds from outside, but by collaborating with local financial institutions to mobilize locally generated surpluses.[2] After independence, the Zimbabwe government joined the many other African and Third World countries competing to attract foreign capital investments. It altered the inherited foreign-exchange controls to permit existing firms to remit half of their after-tax profits. It left corporate taxes relatively low. These measures helped to boost the officially reported annual profit outflow from Z$82.9 million in 1981 to Z$143.7 million in 1982. Together with probable transfer pricing on visible items estimated at Z$150 million a year, and another Z$50 and Z$75 million on invisibles, this probably brought the annual outflow of capital to over Z$350 million. The estimated inflow of new capital totalled less than a tenth of that amount. The Zimbabwe government began to borrow increasingly heavily from transnational banks at high rates of interest. This trend was repeated throughout Africa. In the competition to attract new foreign investment, South Africa emerged the clear winner. As Table 11.3 shows, for example, USA transnationals—the largest investors in Africa after World War II—invested far more heavily in all fields except petroleum (see note b to Table 11.3) in South Africa than in any independent state. In manufacturing and trade, they invested more in South Africa than in all the independent African states combined.

Table 11.3
US Investment in South Africa as a Percentage of US Investment in all of Africa, 1968, 1974

	1968 %	*1974* %	*1982* %
Mining	20.1	28.4	30.9
Petroleum[a]	9.3	12.0	NA[b]
Manufacturing	83.0	76.6	70.6
Finance & Insurance	NA	41.1	NA[b]
Trade	NA	68.1	78.8

[a] South Africa has no known oil deposits, but the oil transnationals invest largely in building the largest refining capacity on the continent as well as regional distribution network for refined output.
[b] The US government stopped reporting oil and bank investments in South Africa to "avoid disclosure of data of individual companies".

Source: US Dept of Commerce, *Survey of Current Business* (Washington DC, August 1970, August 1976, August 1984.

As Tables 11.4A and 11.4B illustrate, until the 1980s, US firms reported that rates of profits in South Africa significantly exceeded their profits elsewhere on the continent. This reflected in part the apartheid regime's low wages and taxes. In part, the firms' use of transfer pricing to avoid local taxes and exchange controls may have reduced the rate of profit they reported on their investments in independent African countries. In the 1980s, the international recession affected South African mining. Growing domestic and international protest against apartheid may also have affected the companies' reports on their South African investments income. The changed method of calculating investment income in the Survey may have also influenced the results.

Table 11.4A
US Firms' Profits in South Africa as a Percentage of US Firms' Profits in All Africa, 1968, 1974, 1982

	1968 %	*1974* %	*1982*[b] %
Mining	44.9	52.1[a]	—[c]
Manufacturing	88.0	90.1	62.2
Finance & Insurance	NA	40.0	—[c]
Trade	NA	56.2	85.5

Table 11.4B
US Firms' Rates of Profit in South Africa Compared to the Rest of Africa, 1968, 1974, 1982

	1968		*1974*		*1982*[b]	
	South Africa %	*Africa* %	*South Africa* %	*Africa* %	*South Africa* %	*Africa* %
Mining	39.7	12.3	22.8[a]	8.3[a]	—[c]	3.5
Manufacturing	11.1	7.3	15.4	6.2	6.5	9.6
Finance & Insurance	NA	NA	29.7	11.3	—[c]	—[c]
Trade	NA	NA	11.5	19.2	11.7	7.4

[a] These are 1973 data, since the US Department of Commerce did not publish mining figures for 1974 for "other Africa" to avoid possible identification of particular firms.
[b] The Department of Commerce altered its method of calculating investment income, so these figures are not precisely comparable to earlier ones.
[c] Reported an overall loss for the sector.

Source: US Dept of Commerce *Survey of Current Business* Washington DC, August 1970, August 1976, August 1984.

Foreign Loans

Unable to attract more foreign investment in the 1970s, most independent African states had to borrow increasing funds at rising interest rates from transnational commercial banks through the Eurodollar market. (For explanation of Eurocurrency market, see ch. 13) Table 11.5 illustrates the increased reliance of African countries on borrowing abroad in the 1970s and early 1980s.

Table 11.5
Outstanding External Debt of Sub-Saharan Africa, 1970-82

	1970		*1975*		*1980*		*1982*	
	$ million	*%*	*$ million*	*%*	*$ million*	*%*	*$ million*	*%*
Total Concessional Bilateral	2,377	43.9	5,319	37.8	10,173	25.0	11,566	24.1
Total Official Export Credits	324	6.0	927	6.5	5,505	13.5	6,187	12.9
Total Multilateral Loans	842	15.5	2,529	17.9	8,443	20.8	11,414	23.7
Total Private Publicly Guaranteed Loans	1,876	34.6	5,330	37.8	16,521	40.6	18,895	39.3
Total	*5,419*	*100.0*	*14,105*	*100.0*	*40,647*	*100.0*	*48,662*	*100.0*

Source: IBRD, Toward Sustained Development in Sub-Saharan Africa.

Traditionally, from the point of view of African and other Third World countries, the terms of repayment constituted the primary distinction between loans and direct private investments. A country had to repay direct private investments in the form of unknown amounts of profit for an indefinite period. The future burden on the country's balance of payments of repayment for any particular investment depended on the profitability of the project, as well as the taxes and foreign-exchange controls imposed by the government. Transnational corporations typically anticipated an annual return of at least 25 per cent before making an investment in independent African countries. In contrast, governments traditionally had to repay commercial loans in the form of predetermined fixed annual payments of principal and interest. This implied a known future balance of payments burden.

In the 1970s, however, changed international lending practices, responding to the inflationary pressure caused by the international monetary crisis, blurred the distinction between repayments for investments and loans. By the 1970s and 1980s, the terms on which African governments could secure loans varied from the traditional form in several respects.

The Grace Period: This is the length of time before repayment of the loans begins. Government negotiators typically seek as long a grace period as possible to ensure effective operation of the overall project and increased revenues and foreign-exchange earnings before beginning repayment. Private commercial firms providing suppliers' credits, that is credit to finance the import of goods, machinery or equipment, typically expect repayment to begin almost immediately. Some bilateral foreign government or international agency loans, in contrast, provide grace periods of eight to ten years.

The Length of Repayment Period: From the African country's perspective, a longer repayment period, if the interest rate is not too high, reduces the annual cost of the loan. This may enable the government to repay it more easily out of current income which presumably rises as the project begins to operate more effectively. Suppliers' credit, typically due in three to six months, imposes an immediate burden on foreign-exchange earnings. Transnational commercial banks or other foreign firms, providing ordinary or Eurocurrency commercial loans, usually expect repayment in three to five years. Most capital projects take at least that long to get off the ground, so the economy must finance the loans out of previously generated income. Bilateral and multilateral agencies may provide longer repayment periods of 10 to 40 years, by which time the project financed by the loan can contribute significantly to increasing the national income.

Interest Rate: The higher the rate of interest, the higher the cost of repaying the loan. Transnational commercial banks tend to charge lower rates for shorter-term loans and higher rates for longer-term loans. They generally relate the interest rate charged to Third World countries to the prime rate of interest charged in their home country financial markets. By the late 1970s and early 1980s, as international inflationary pressures spread, transnational banks had begun to charge rates ranging between 14 and 20 per cent. For the commercial banks, this resulted in a significant increase in real interest rates, that is, rates adjusted for the effect of inflation. From 1963-1973, real interest rates ranged from 1.75 to 2.75 per cent. In the late 1970s and early 1980s, real interest rates charged by US banks averaged 4 per cent, and at times exceeded 6 per cent. For the developing country, however, a nominal 15 per cent rate of interest doubles the cost of repaying a loan in a little over six years. A nominal 20 per cent rate doubles its cost in five years.

Developed capitalist governments and multilateral agencies charge somewhat lower rates, although in general they relate them to private commercial rates which hovered between 7 and 10 per cent in the late 1970s and 1980s. Such agencies made only a small proportion of their total loans available at significantly lower rates.

By the late 1970s and 1980s African and other Third World countries borrowed an increasing share of their international capital from the Eurocurrency market at floating rates adjusted to the London Interbank Offered Rate (LIBOR). Since LIBOR rises and falls in response to international money market pressures, the Eurocurrency rate charged on any given loan also fluctuates. In 1977, Eurobonds carried an average 8.5 per cent interest rate. By the second half of 1981, the rate had risen from 14 to 15 per cent.

Typically, the transnational commercial banks set Eurocurrency interest rates at LIBOR plus a spread (that is, an additional percentage determined by the transnational banks' evaluation of the risks involved in making loans to a particular country). In 1981, for example, oil-rich Nigeria paid a spread of 3/4 to 7/8 above LIBOR. Newly independent Zimbabwe paid 1 1/8 to 1 3/8 above LIBOR. South Africa, in contrast, despite its apartheid policies and the growing liberation struggle, paid 5/8 to 3/4 above LIBOR.

Because LIBOR itself fluctuates, countries contracting for Eurocurrency loans cannot know what their future interest burden may be. In this respect, debt repayments have come closer to profits remitted to foreign investors.

Table 11.6
The Five Largest African Eurocurrency Borrowers in 1981

Country	*Eurocurrency Debt (in US$ millions)*
Nigeria	3,026.7
Morocco	722.8
Algeria	500.0
South Africa	374.1
Zimbabwe	357.4

Source; *Euromoney*, February 1982.

Rising Debt Costs

In the late 1970s, as terms of trade deteriorated and balance of payments deficits mounted, African countries' foreign debts mounted rapidly. Total Third World debt multiplied almost five times from 1973 to 1981, when it reached US$540 billion. By 1982, African countries owed foreign lenders almost US$50 billion in accumulated public and publicly guaranteed debt. Twenty-three African states had borrowed US$8.2 billion in 1981 from the Eurocurrency market. (See Table 11.1A in Appendix to this chapter for details.) This represented a small share, 4.5 per cent of the "Euro-pie" but a 116 per cent increase over 1980. Table 11.6 shows the five biggest African Eurocurrency borrowers that year.

The repayment of these debts represented an increasing burden for African states. In 1980, Third World countries spent $1.50 out of every $3 borrowed simply on repaying loans. As borrowing continued to increase during the 1980s, this was expected to rise to $2 out of $3.

Debt servicing rose even more rapidly than borrowing, reflecting the rising interest costs as well as the deteriorating terms of trade. The debt service ratio is the ratio between the annual cost of repaying foreign loans and annual export earnings. It reflects both the debt costs and the state of the national exports.

$$\text{debt service ratio} = \frac{\text{annual repayments of principal and interest on foreign debt}}{\text{annual export earnings}} \times 100 = x\%$$

From 1976 to 1980, both Kenya and Zambia borrowed heavily abroad. Kenya's debt service costs increased almost twice as rapidly as its external debt, but its export earnings rose rapidly. Therefore, although Kenya's actual debt far more than doubled, its debt service ratio only doubled. In constrast Zambia's export earnings rose only very slowly in the same period, reflecting the fall in world copper prices. Therefore, although Zambia's total debt increased far less than Kenya's, its debt service ratio more than doubled.

In the late 1970s and the early 1980s, most Third World countries had to borrow increasingly heavily on the Eurocurrency market, since developed countries and multilateral agencies failed to provide enough funds. Despite western governments' promises to help finance post-independence reconstruction, even Zimbabwe found it necessary to rely heavily on high-cost transnational bank loans. Its external debt expanded rapidly. It organized a widely-publicized Zimcord conference where potential donor countries pledged Z$2 billion in aid. In the event, however, it found commercial loans much easier to obtain. As Table 11.7A shows, official "soft loans" fell far below expectations.

Table 11.7A
Zimbabwe's External Debt, 1980-81 to 1982-83

	Commercial Loans		*Aid (Soft Loans)*	
	Actual (Z$ million)	*Estimated*	*Actual (Z$ million)*	*Estimated*
1980-81	40		8.1	
1981-82	311	308	20	123.6
1982-83		300-400		296.9

Table 11.7B
Zimbabwe's Debt Servicing, 1978-79 to 1982-83 (est)

	Debt Service (Z$ million)	*Debt Service Ratio (% of exports)*
1978-79	9.2	1.5
1979-80	33.0	4.6
1980-81	34.0	3.7
1981-82	50.5	5.2
1982-83 (est)	188.6	18.8

Debt servicing costs rose sharply. As Table 11.7B indicates, when exports failed to expand at a corresponding rate, Zimbabwe's debt service ratio jumped dramatically. A country's debt servicing costs are usually fixed in terms of the currencies of the lender. When a developing country devalues its currency, it automatically increases its debt servicing costs. Thus when Zimbabwe devalued its currency in 1982-83, it automatically raised its debt servicing costs by approximately the same percentage. In 1983, the Finance Minister estimated its debt service ratio would rise to 30 per cent in 1984, well above what most authorities consider the danger level.

Government debt service ratios, like those given for Kenya, Zambia and Zimbabwe, do not include the rising costs of repaying private foreign loans. In most African states, the inherited banking and governmental structures seldom provide for adequate monitoring of private foreign debts. The private commercial banks which often arrange private-sector loans typically shroud their activities with confidentiality. Transnational corporations may arrange their own financing either through (sometimes affiliated) commercial banks or directly with their parent or other affiliated companies based abroad. The government often simply does not know the extent of the private sector's external debt.

The Zimbabwe case illustrates the potential debt servicing implications of additional external private debt. While the Zimbabwean government expanded its external debt after independence, the private sector also took advantage of the end of UN sanctions to borrow heavily, instead of bringing in direct capital investment. The South African-based Anglo-American Group, for example, proceeded to build a thermal power plant to use coal from its Hwange colliery.[3] Government estimated the cost of the thermal plant would exceed Z$1 billion. Standard Bank arranged international loans to cover the cost, involving the International Finance Corporation (a World Bank affiliate)[4] the US Citibank and suppliers' credits. Depending on the interest rates and the due dates fixed, these loans alone might double Zimbabwe's debt service ratio.

Summary

The newly independent African states, integrated into the world capitalist system by colonial rule, confronted aggravated financial problems because of the prolonged monetary crisis of the 1970s and 1980s. For many, their balance of trade began to show serious deficits, reflecting the deterioration of terms of trade. Even more suffered chronic and growing balance of payments deficits because of the heavy outflow of payments for invisible imports, including net income payments remitted to transnational corporate investors. In the 1970s, the fluctuating exchange rates for the currencies of major capitalist countries introduced gross elements of uncertainty. Not only did these factors thwart African countries' efforts to expand trade and increase foreign-exchange earnings required to import machinery and equipment for development, they also raised the cost of obtaining foreign capital either as investments or loans, to offset balance of payments deficits and finance desired growth. Increasingly, independent African governments were forced to turn to transnational commercial banks which charged high rates of interest. Their debt service ratios rose rapidly as their export earnings stagnated and the values of their national currencies fell. Private external borrowing threatened to further increase their debt service ratios by an unknown additional amount.

Notes

1. This introductory text assumes students have studied these concepts in economics and analysed them in depth in international trade courses. It aims only to relate them to an understanding of the international monetary system.

2. See Part I, esp. Chapters 4 and 5.

3. The government apparently accepted the argument that Zimbabwe should not rely on imported electric power from Zambia or Mozambique for more than 15% of its electricity requirements, although throughout the latter years of UDI it had relied on Zambia for almost a third of its power. The Anglo-American Group stood to gain, both because the government guaranteed a 12.5% rate of profit for every ton of coal it sold to the plant, and because it expected to participate in the profit of the Hwange plant as part owner and manager of the project.

4. The IFC reported that its loan for this project constituted its biggest loan in Africa.

Appendix A

External Public Debt and Debt Service

External Public and Publicly Guaranteed Debt Outstanding and Disbursed (US$ millions)

	Official Sources		Private Sources		Total		Debt Service	
	1970	*1982*	*1970*	*1982*	*1970*	*1982*	*1970*	*1982*
Low-income economies	1,950.1	15,408.4	827.8	4,763.6	2,777.9	20,172.0	188.4	1,475.0
Low-income Semi-arid	387.6	2,666.4	16.5	260.4	404.1	3,026.8	8.6	165.3
Chad	24.6	157.6	7.5	31.8	32.1	189.3	2.7	0.2
Mali	231.5	807.8	6.1	14.2	237.6	822.0	0.7	8.1
Burkina Faso	20.2	308.0	0.3	26.8	20.5	334.8	1.9	20.0
Somalia	74.9	884.5	2.2	59.5	77.1	944.0	0.9	19.8
Niger	31.2	390.6	0.5	212.0	31.7	602.6	2.3	110.2
Gambia, The	5.1	117.9		16.1	5.1	134.0	0.1	7.0
Low-income other	1,562.4	12,742.0	811.3	4,403.2	2,373.7	17,145.2	179.8	1,309.6
Ethiopia	140.2	792.4	28.7	82.2	168.9	874.6	21.1	54.8
Guinea-Bissau		101.2		24.6		125.8		2.5
Zaire	95.3	2,750.0	215.8	1,290.3	311.1	4,040.3	36.8	81.2
Malawi	89.1	491.1	33.3	197.7	122.4	691.8	5.9	64.3
Uganda	107.8	552.9	29.7	40.9	137.5	593.8	7.9	132.1
Rwanda	1.5	189.3	0.4		1.9	189.3	0.3	5.2
Burundi	5.8	196.3	1.5	4.6	7.3	200.9	0.6	5.2
Tanzania	152.7	1,550.5	95.8	81.1	248.5	1,631.6	15.7	112.6
Benin	29.2	252.9	11.3	303.5	40.5	556.4	1.7	46.4
Central African Republic	17.8	160.4	6.1	61.6	23.9	222.0	2.9	4.5
Guinea	277.4	1,045.3	36.7	184.6	314.1	1,229.9	14.5	78.5
Madagascar	85.0	1,002.9	7.6	561.9	92.6	1,564.8	6.9	112.2
Togo	32.0	546.2	7.8	272.8	39.8	819.0	2.3	33.7
Ghana	264.3	949.3	225.1	166.3	489.4	1,115.6	23.7	65.1
Kenya	232.0	1,572.7	84.3	828.9	316.3	2,401.6	27.4	376.2
Sierra Leone	32.4	229.8	27.0	73.1	59.4	302.9	12.0	40.6
Mozambique		356.0		229.0		585.0		94.4

Appendix A (continued)

External Public and Publicly Guaranteed Debt Outstanding and Disbursed (US$ millions)

	Official Sources		*Private Sources*		*Total*		*Debt Service*	
	1970	*1982*	*1970*	*1982*	*1970*	*1982*	*1970*	*1982*
Middle-income oil importers	909.9	10,285.1	894.9	6,810.3	1,804.8	17,095.4	176.3	1,683.3
Sudan	272.5	3,772.8	46.2	1,320.7	318.7	5,093.5	34.6	79.3
Mauritania	19.4	890.8	7.9	109.9	27.3	1,000.7	3.3	39.7
Liberia	124.0	498.1	33.9	143.1	157.9	641.2	17.6	33.2
Senegal	78.4	1,082.1	19.6	246.4	98.0	1,328.5	6.7	101.9
Lesotho	7.6	128.9	0.5	9.7	8.1	138.6	0.5	8.0
Zambia	119.4	1,732.5	503.1	648.1	622.5	2,380.6	59.0	184.3
Zimbabwe	88.1	276.5	144.6	944.3	232.7	1,220.8	9.4	145.8
Botswana	14.1	174.8	0.6	34.2	14.7	209.0	0.6	13.4
Swaziland	20.9	165.4	16.1	12.3	37.0	177.7	3.3	17.7
Ivory Coast	144.1	1,343.9	112.0	3,193.4	256.1	4,537.3	38.5	996.7
Mauritius	21.4	219.1	10.3	148.3	31.7	367.4	2.9	63.1
Middle-income oil exporters	683.2	3,474.6	153.0	7,321.4	836.2	10,796.0	84.5	2,305.7
Nigeria	383.4	1,144.0	96.2	4,940.7	479.6	6,084.7	55.7	1,339.5
Cameroon	119.6	1,310.1	11.6	601.8	131.2	1,911.9	8.6	264.2
Congo, People's Republic	113.8	618.9	20.8	751.0	134.6	1,369.9	8.8	272.9
Gabon	66.4	321.5	24.4	549.9	90.8	871.4	11.3	288.1
Angola		80.0		478.0		558.0		141.0
Sub-Saharan Africa	*3,543.1*	*29,168.0*	*1,875.7*	*18,895.4*	*5,418.8*	*48,063.4*	*449.1*	*5,464.0*
Sub-Saharan Africa as a percentage of all developing countries	9.7	15.3	9.6	7.9	10.0	11.3	6.8	8.1

Appendix B

Balance of Payments, Debt Service, and International Reserves

	Current Account Balance (US$ millions)		Interest Payment on External Public Debt (US$ millions)		Debt Service: As Percentage of GNP		Debt Service: As Percentage of Exports of Goods & Services		Gross International Reserves: Amount (US$ millions)		Gross International Reserves: In Months of Import Coverage
	1970	1982	1970	1982	1970	1982[a]	1970	1982[a]	1970	1982[a]	1982[a]
Low-income economies					*1.3w*	*1.7w*	*4.9w*	*12.4w*			*1.7w*
Low-income semiarid					0.5w	2.9w	2.9w	4.8w			0.6w
Chad	2	19	(.)	(.)	1.0	0.1	3.9	0.4	2	18	2.0
Mali	−2	−113	(.)	5	0.2	0.8	1.2	3.5	1	25	0.7
Burkino Faso	9	..	(.)	7	0.6	1.7	4.0	..	36	67	..
Somalia	−6	−177	(.)	10	0.3	1.6	2.1	7.2	21	15	0.3
Niger	(.)	..	1	44	0.6	7.3	3.8	..	19	35	..
Gambia, The	1	*−47*	(.)	4	..	3.4	0.6	*6.5*	8	8	*0.3*
Low-income other					1.4w	1.5w	5.0w	13.4w			1.8w
Ethiopia	−32	−196	6	22	1.2	1.2	11.4	9.5	72	277	3.6
Guinea-Bissau	..	..	..	1	..	1.9	..	..	..	..	..
Zaire	−64	−375	9	72	2.1	2.6	4.4	..	189	312	1.8
Malawi	−35	−78	3	32	2.1	4.5	7.1	22.8	29	29	0.9
Uganda	20	−256	4	10	0.6	0.9	*2.7*	*22.3*	57	73	0.1
Rwanda	7	−90	(.)	2	0.2	*0.2*	1.3	3.2	8	128	4.3
Burundi	..	..	(.)	2	0.3	0.4	..	..	15	37	..
Tanzania	−36	*−268*	6	33	1.2	1.1	4.9	*5.1*	65	*19*	*0.2*
Benin	−1	..	(.)	28	0.7	4.8	2.2	..	16	10	..
Central African Republic	−12	−39	1	2	1.7	0.7	4.8	2.9	1	52	2.3
Guinea	..	..	4	24	2.2	4.9	..	..	..	..	
Madagascar	10	−369	2	42	0.8	4.1	3.5	..	37	20	0.3
Togo	3	−152	1	22	0.9	4.3	2.9	..	35	173	5.6
Ghana	−68	83	12	27	1.1	0.2	5.0	6.8	58	318	4.0
Kenya	−49	−509	12	147	1.8	5.4	5.4	20.3	220	248	1.4

	Current Account Balance (US$ millions)		Debt Service: Interest Payment on External Public Debt (US$ millions)		Debt Service: As Percentage of GNP		Debt Service: As Percentage of Exports of Goods & Services		Gross International Reserves: Amount (US$ millions)		Gross International Reserves: In Months of Import Coverage
	1970	1982	1970	1982	1970	1982[a]	1970	1982[a]	1970	1982[a]	1982[a]
Sierra Leone	−16	−158	2	2	2.9	0.9	9.9	*20.8*	39	0.4	0.4
Mozambique	..	..	..	..	..	..	..	..	..	..	
Middle-income oil importers					2.0w	5.6w	6.2w	16.9w			1.1w
Sudan	−42	−248	13	11	1.7	*0.8*	10.7	7.5	22	21	0.2
Mauritania	−5	−252	(.)	24	1.7	5.8	3.1	11.8	3	144	2.7
Liberia	..	*−79*	6	14	5.5	3.5	..	*5.1*	..	*8*	*0.2*
Senegal	−16	..	2	64	0.8	4.2	2.7	..	22	25	..
Lesotho	..	−50	(.)	3	0.4	1.2	..	2.0	..	48	1.2
Zambia	108	−252	26	88	3.5	5.1	5.9	17.4	515	157	1.5
Zimbabwe	..	−706	5	95	0.6	2.3	..	9.2	59	320	1.7
Botswana	..	−61	(.)	10	..	1.6	..	*1.4*	..	293	*3.1*
Swaziland	..	−69	2	9	..	3.9	..	*3.6*	..	76	*1.9*
Ivory Coast	−38	15	11	476	2.8	14.9	6.8	36.9	119	23	0.1
Mauritius	8	−43	2	34	..	6.0	2.9	12.4	46	55	1.1
Middle-income oil exporters					0.7w	2.5w	4.2w	10.9w			1.0w
Nigeria	−368	−7,324	20	722	0.6	1.9	4.2	9.4	223	1,927	1.1
Cameroon	−30	−525	4	121	0.8	3.7	3.1	15.6	81	81	0.5
Congo, People's Republic	..	−320	3	92	3.3	13.4	..	22.6	9	42	0.3
Gabon	−3	680	3	97	..	10.1	5.5	*12.6*	15	318	*1.1*
Angola	..	..	..	..	..	..	..	..	..	..	..
Sub-Saharan Africa					1.2w	2.7w	5.1w	12.6w			1.1w
All low-income countries					1.1w	1.1w	11.3w	8.8w			7.3w
All lower middle-income countries					1.6w	3.7w	9.2w	16.8w			3.9w
All upper middle-income countries					1.5w	4.4w	10.7w	16.9w			5.1w
Industrial market economies					..	..	..	..			5.6w

[a] Figures in italics are for 1981, not 1982.

Source: IBRD, *Toward Sustained Development in Sub-Saharan Africa*.

Exercises and Research

1. List all the possible ways in which the international monetary system may affect the monetary and public finance problems of the typical African economy.
2. How does a country's balance of trade and payments affect its money, banking and public finance?
   a) What effect have the worsening terms of trade in the 1970s had on many African countries' balance of trade?
   b) Why have most African states experienced balance of payments deficits in the 1970s and early 1980s?
   c) What effect may devaluation have on prices and living standards in the typical African country? Explain why.
   d) In what way may fluctuating exchange rates introduce problems for African economies?
3. What effect has the international monetary crisis had on the flow of investment capital in the typical African country?
   a) In what African country have transnational companies invested the most in manufacturing? Why?
   b) What factors must independent African states consider when borrowing funds from abroad?
   c) What is the debt service ratio, and why did it increase for most African countries in the late 1970s and early 1980s?
   d) What effect will devaluation have on the debt service ratio of most African economies? Explain why.
4. Explain your country's balance of trade and payments over the last five years.
   a) What factors determine whether your country has a balance of payments deficit or surplus?
   b) What has happened to your country's debt service ratio over the last five years? Show what factors have affected it.
   c) If your country has devalued its currency, what has been the effect on the balance of trade and payments, the cost of living and the relative share of the GDP going to a gross operating profit, compared to that paid in the form of wages and salaries?
   d) What theory do you think provides the best explanation of your country's balance of trade and payments?

Recommended Reading

(For annotations, see bibliography at the end of the book.)

Ayida (ed.), *Reconstruction and Development in Nigeria*
Brenner, *The Politics of International Monetary Reform*
Carlson *et al.*, *International Finance*
Chachaoliades, *International Monetary Theory and Policy*

Cline and associates, *World Inflation and the Developing Countries*
Dell and Lawrence, *The Balance of Payments Adjustment Process*
Edwards, *Export Credit*
Green and Seidman, *Unity or Poverty?*
Hansen and Marzouk, *Development and Economic Policy in the UAR*
Henning, Pigott and Scott, *International Financial Management*
Heywood, *Foreign Exchange and the Corporate Treasurer*
IBRD, Surveys of African Economies
Killick (ed.), *Adjustment and Financing in the Developing World*
Kindleberger and Laffargue, *Financial Crises*
Llewellyn, *International Financial Integration*
Lozoya and Bhattacharya, *The Financial Issues of the New International Economic Order*
OECD, *International Investment and Multinational Enterprises*
—— *Investing in Developing Countries*
Seidman and Seidman, *US Multinationals in South Africa*
Seidman and Makgetla, *Outposts of Monopoly Capital*
Truu (ed.), *Public Policy and the South African Economy*
Van Biljon, *State Interference in South Africa*
Weisweiller, *Introduction to Foreign Exchange*
Willett, *Floating Exchange Rates and International Monetary Reform*

Periodicals
IBRD, *Annual Reports*
IMF, *Annual Reports*
—— *International Financial Statistics* (monthly)
IMF *Survey* (weekly)

Chapter 12: Theoretical Considerations

The Underlying Argument

Mainstream theorists and Marxists offer qualitatively different explanations for the international monetary crisis and its impact on the inhabitants of Third World countries. Mainstream economists tend to blame the crisis on such factors as rising oil prices and excessive governmental intervention thwarting the free interplay of international market forces. Although they argue among themselves as to the appropriateness of particular policies they generally agree that multilateral financial institutions like the IMF and the World Bank should facilitate investment by free private enterprise to expand world trade and promote development.

Marxists, on the other hand, maintain that mainstream theories fail to identify the basic causes of international monetary crises which lie in the contradictions inherent in imperialism, termed by Lenin "the highest stage of capitalism". Therefore, they cannot provide an adequate guide for the policies to overcome them. At best, they may propose measures to reduce their impact. At worst, their policies will thrust the burden of the crisis on to the working class and peasantry in both the developed and the developing countries.

This chapter outlines some of the more significant debates within and between these sets of theories as they relate to international monetary and financial problems.

Mainstream Explanations

Basic Premises

On the international as on the national level, most mainstream economists hold that the free competitive play of market forces should lead to the best allocation of international resources, including capital. Under competitive conditions, trade will develop and capital investments will flow to enable each national economy to produce those exports for which it enjoys a comparative advantage. Attainment of this goal requires a stable international medium of exchange.

Mainstream theorists initially maintained that the gold standard provided the necessary stability. The exchange values of national currencies, based on the gold standard, automatically adjusted in the international market at the point of balanced payments equilibria. However, the two world wars and the Great Depression disrupted the smooth operation of the gold standard. Mainstream economists concluded it was too rigid to accommodate the necessary readjustments. They sought to devise a more flexible mechanism to restore the conditions necessary for the desired automatic adjustment at the equilibrium point.

The World Bank and the International Monetary Fund

Keynes himself attended the Bretton Woods Conference which, meeting after World War II, designed the International Monetary Fund (IMF) and the International Bank for Reconstruction and Development (IBRD), otherwise known as the World Bank. The conference participants anticipated that the World Bank would help to mobilize long-term capital funds to reconstruct the war-ravaged countries and stimulate world-wide development. In a sense, the founders of the Bank expected it to play the role of an international pump primer, helping to create the conditions in which private investment could achieve desired development goals. They believed the IMF would provide complementary short-term assistance to enable national economies to overcome the imbalances introduced by World War II. Eventually, they thought, all countries would succeed in adjusting their currencies' rates of exchange at an equilibrium point where each would produce and export those goods for which it had a comparative advantage. Gradually, all countries would eliminate the import licensing and foreign-exchange controls which impeded the free flow of goods and capital. Competitive private enterprise would then resume its role in expanding international investment and trade, stimulating a multiplier effect to spread development throughout the world.

The Monetary Crisis

The beginning of the international monetary crisis in the 1970s, however, led to renewed debate among mainstream theorists as to how to restore international monetary stability. Some urged creation of a centralized monetary authority with greater powers to regulate the international money supply. This, in turn, engendered arguments over the form and extent of each nation's participation in the proposed monetary authority. Others argued for restoration of some sort of international monetary standard which, like the gold standard, might function automatically, thus avoiding the perplexed issue of shared national participation in a centralized authority.

Not a few mainstream theorists viewed the Organization of Petroleum Exporting Countries (OPEC) decision to raise oil prices in 1973 and 1978 as a central cause of the monetary crisis. Rapidly rising oil prices, they maintained, introduced major destabilizing influences. These constituted a primary cause of the mounting balance of payments deficits which plagued developed as well as developing countries. Oil-producing states accumulated vast amounts of capital which they injected into international money markets, aggravating their instability. To overcome these destabilizing effects, governments should introduce measures to reduce oil consumption and, where possible, increase oil production outside OPEC control. Meanwhile, the IMF should find ways of drawing on the oil countries' accumulated capital to provide additional funds to aid countries suffering chronic payments deficits.

The Debate over Third World Policies

Mainstream economists do not always agree on the appropriate Third World response to the international money crisis. Most agree that since they lack capital, developing countries need to devise measures to attract foreign investment. Some urge Third World governments to increase exports as an initial engine for growth. This should set off multiplier effects, leading to growth throughout the national economy. Others maintain that developing countries should temporarily impose tariffs, import licensing and foreign-exchange controls to protect new national industries. By guaranteeing a protected national market, they can more easily persuade transnational manufacturers to invest in domestic industries.

Mainstream theorists disagree over whether and for how long developing countries should retain these forms of protection. Some, including most IMF advisers, argue that such devices as tariffs, import licensing and foreign-exchange controls grant manufacturing firms monopolistic control over relatively small national markets, thus enabling them to raise local prices. This tends to divert the national economy away from production of commodities in which it enjoys a comparative advantage. Foreign-exchange controls, furthermore, foster overvalued national currencies which hinder domestic industries from selling manufactured or other exports competitively on world markets. Therefore, governments should eliminate these protections and expose domestic industries to international competition which will stimulate them to achieve efficient, low-cost output.

Others maintain that developing countries must continue to protect domestic firms in order to industrialize. Without protection, domestic firms can never compete with much more efficient transnational corporations based in the developed countries and using the most advanced technologies. Cental banks must retain foreign-exchange controls to reserve scarce foreign currencies for the purchase of the machinery and equipment essential for continued industrial growth. A government's failure to retain protection and allocate foreign exchange to balanced industrial and agricultural development condemns its national economy to permanent dependence on the sale of low-priced raw materials on uncertain world markets.

Another mainstream debate centres on the issue of expanded IMF assistance. Some economists, like the members of the Brandt Commission,[1] urge the IMF to increase funds to help developing countries overcome their mounting balance of payments deficits. Others recommend that developing countries pursue a more self-reliant path, developing their own resources to expand exports.

Mainstream economists argue about the conditions the IMF imposes on developing countries before granting them assistance. Some recommend that, in line with monetarist prescriptions, the IMF should require developing countries to restructure their economies by imposing austerity measures, devaluing their currencies, and dismantling protective devices. Austerity measures aim to reduce government borrowing, thus reducing inflationary pressures which render national exports uncompetitive on world markets. Devaluation enables exporters to reduce their prices in terms of foreign buyers' currencies, enhancing their competitiveness abroad. Dismantling protective measures and foreign-exchange controls subjects domestic producers to the discipline imposed by foreign competition, and expands the range of goods available to consumers at lower prices.

Other theorists, more influenced by the Keynesian emphasis on national income and demand, claim these measures may undermine national efforts to attain self-reliant development and expand domestic employment and income.

The Marxist Analysis

Marxist theorists generally hold that the exchange of commodities for money on an international, as on a national scale, tends to veil the exploitative relations revealed by the labour theory of value. Marxists reject mainstream notions that the international monetary crisis can be overcome by adjustments in international trade and payments mechanisms. That crisis, they hold, stems from the contradictions inherent in the imperialist phase of capitalism (see pp. 24-25, and 124-7).

Changing Forms of Exploitation in the Third World

Marxists reject the mainstream proposition that the international market resulting from the growing international division of labour and trade is or can be in any sense "free". Finance capital—interlinked oligopolistic transnational industrial corporations and commercial banks—dominates capitalist world markets. African and other Third World countries inevitably confront worsening balance of payments difficulties because transnational finance capital continually extracts surplus value from them in two forms.

First, transnationals directly expropriate and export through Third World countries' invisibles accounts the profits, interest, dividends and other forms of income they accumulate through the ownership of the basic means of production and distribution. Secondly, transnationals extract surplus value indirectly, through terms of trade differences: the low prices they pay for Third World exports of raw materials and the high prices they charge for Third World imports of manufactured goods. In both cases, transnational corporate affiliates manipulate transfer pricing techniques[2] to shift hidden profits out of the country to their parent companies and so evade local taxes and exchange controls.

After World War II, as more Third World nations became independent, transnational finance capitalists altered the form of their domination from direct ownership of their means of production to controls over management, technology, trade and long-term international loans arranged by associated commercial banks. Thus, increasingly they shifted from direct to indirect techniques of extracting surplus values. The resulting deterioration in their terms of trade, including the impact of transfer pricing, deprived developing countries of the balance of trade surpluses which formerly tended to offset their direct losses of surpluses through their invisibles accounts. In addition, transnational commercial banks charged rising interest rates to Third World countries for their expanding foreign debt, thus creaming off additional shares of locally generated surpluses.

Growing Contradictions and the General Crisis of Capitalism

Over the post-war years, transnational finance capitalist groups, based in core capitalist nations, competitively accumulated increasing amounts of capital—including the surplus value extracted from Third World countries—and reinvested much of it in their unplanned expansion of industrial production at home. Immediately after World War II, the then dominant US companies invested heavily in buying up shares in European and Japanese firms, gaining control over major sectors of entire industries. Through their British and French holdings, they acquired access to mines, trading firms and financial institutions with assets in Africa and other former colonial regions. US government support ending colonial rule in Africa helped to facilitate US transnational corporate access to African agricultural and mineral riches.

Once they recovered from the worst ravages of the war, however, the largest finance capitalist groupings of Europe and Japan, strongly backed by their respective capitalist governments, mobilized their forces to thwart continued US transnational corporate expansion. The resulting competitive battle among these industrial-financial giants brought two contradictory sets of results. On the one hand, their efforts to amass the capital necessary to finance increasingly capital-intensive technological innovations led to further concentration and centralization of control among national finance capitalist groupings. At the same time, the rapid expansion of technologically advanced machinery and equipment and the relative decline in the employment of labour per unit of output accelerated the tendency for their average profit rates to fall. Yet they had to intensify their efforts to sell their expanding output even to realize those declining rates of return. They entered an increasingly aggressive competition in the Third World to find more crude materials to feed their growing industries; expanded markets for their multiplying industrial output; and new sources of higher rates of profit.

On the other hand, drained of investable surpluses and confronting worsening terms of trade, Third World countries imposed tariffs, import licensing and foreign-exchange controls to reduce their imports—simultaneously narrowing the markets in which transnationals could sell their manufactures. The establishment of socialism in a third of the world, accompanied by intensifying struggles for colonial liberation, hindered the transnationals' further expansion at the high rates of profit to which they had become accustomed.

To offset their falling rates of profit at home, transnational finance capitalist groupings began to invest in manufacturing capacity in oppressive regional sub-centres like South Africa and Brazil. Simultaneously, transnational industrial firms laid off higher paid workers in basic industries in their home countries, forcing growing numbers into unemployed labour reserves. Transnational commercial banks expanded their loans through the Eurocurrency market to escape controls imposed by their national governments. Increasingly, they loaned their vast and still growing accumulations of capital at high government-guaranteed rates of interest to eager Third World borrowers seeking to offset balance of payment problems and finance development. The expanding international money supply, fuelled by speculative shifts of funds by transnational banks from one to another currency, aggravated inflationary pressures. These further hindered national central banks' efforts to stabilize their own monetary systems. Repeated "recessions" reflected inevitable crises of overproduction as manufacturing industries discovered they could not sell all of their continually expanded outputs.

This competitive process of international accumulation and reinvestment of the surplus value extracted from workers in both the developed capitalist states and the Third World inevitably aggravated mounting international contradictions. For years, US involvement in the Korean war and the more prolonged Vietnamese war further intensified these contradictions while concealing them behind an illusion of prosperity financed by billions of dollars, borrowed to be squandered on military destruction. Nevertheless, as the Vietnamese finally won their struggle for liberation, the contradictions culminated not only in the widely recognized international monetary crisis, but also the re-emergence of the general crisis of capitalism.

The IMF and the World Bank as Instruments of Finance Capital

In this context, most Marxists view international agencies like the IMF and the World Bank as the joint creation of the major capitalist governments and transnational corporate finance capital. That the state capitalist governments had to collaborate with each other to establish these agencies reflects the growing international socialization of the processes of production and distribution of goods under the increasingly concentrated control of competitive national finance capitalist groupings. The failure of the core states to agree on a "solution" to the international monetary crisis stems from that underlying oligopolistic competition.

Despite repeated efforts, the major capitalist governments, together with the IMF, have failed to restore an automatically adjusting international medium of exchange for two primary reasons. First, the major competing capitalist member states could not agree on any one currency to take the place of the US dollar. They did not want any single nation to achieve the dominant status enjoyed by the US for the first decades after World War II. They could not agree on how to establish an effective international central bank because they could not resolve their conflicts over how to share in its operation.

Second, the dominant capitalist governments and the international finance groupings view the IMF as an instrument for ensuring that Third World countries will repay their growing foreign debt, including interest at increasingly high rates—another way of extracting surplus value. On the other hand, the Third World countries will continue to object to the IMF's insistence on reforms which they reject as unpalatable. Behind this debate lies the underlying reality: finance capital's continued extraction of surplus value from Third World economies inevitably deepens the contradictions, aggravating not only the international monetary crisis but also the deepening general crisis of capitalism.

The Alternative

Despite these criticisms, some socialist states have become members of the IMF in the hope of gaining easier access to the capital and technology of the developed capitalist states. They believe that state control over their banking system and their participation in foreign trade will protect them from undue adverse consequences. In the longer run, however, most Marxists maintain that only social ownership of the means of production and distribution at the national level can build a more solid foundation for co-ordinated control and planned participation in international trade.

As national governments assert increased control over their own banks and foreign trade institutions, they should co-operate to create regional monetary and financial institutions to co-ordinate the accumulation and investment of their combined locally generated surpluses in planned national development. This would help them to reduce their dependence on such international state capitalist agencies as the IMF and the World Bank, as well as transnational corporate finance capital. Over time, it would lead to more balanced agricultural and industrial projects directed to raising regional living standards as well as participating in a more equitable pattern of world trade.

Summary

Most mainstream theorists, extending their basic analytical framework from the national to the international sphere, tend to attribute international monetary crises primarily to unwarranted interference in the free interplay of international market forces. These include OPEC's pressure to raise oil prices as well as governments' introduction of tariffs, import licensing and foreign-exchange controls. Although they may question specific programmes and recommendations, they generally agree that the IMF and the World Bank provide useful instruments for alleviating and eventually resolving that crisis by encouraging the creative forces of competitive private enterprise.

Marxists claim that the international monetary crisis stems from the contradictions inherent in and aggravated by the imperialist stage of capitalism. Relying increasingly on indirect rather than direct forms of extraction of surplus value, competitive finance capitalist groupings, backed by their respective governments, continue to exploit Third World countries. Their reinvestment of their accumulated capital to finance an ongoing technological revolution at home impels them to seek new sources of raw materials, markets and profits in the Third World. Reconstruction following World War II, and the vast military expenditures occasioned by the Korean and Vietnam wars, created an illusion of prosperity. In reality, however, they aggravated contradictory tendencies which eventually culminated in the re-emergence of the general crisis of capitalism, partially reflected in the international monetary crisis. The IMF and the World Bank, created and run jointly by the developed capitalist states, are incapable of resolving the underlying contradictions that created that crisis.

Marxists generally contend that only by a transition to socialism can Third World countries end finance capitalist exploitation. If they can co-operate to develop regional mechanisms for trade and payments, they may more quickly reduce dependence on finance capital by implementing complementary regional plans for balanced industrial and agricultural development.

Notes

1. Established under the chairmanship of former West German Chancellor Willie Brandt, this Commission made repeated pleas for expanded IMF assistance in the 1970s and 1980s.
2. For details, see Murray, *Multinationals beyond the Market.*

Exercises and Research

1. What basic theoretical assumptions underlie mainstream proposals to achieve a stable international medium of exchange?
2. What explanations do mainstream theorists offer for the international monetary crisis of the 1970s and 1980s?
3. What is the substance of the debate among mainstream economists over the measures developing countries should take to overcome the effects of the international monetary crisis?
4. In what way do Marxists suggest that finance capital has altered its methods of exploiting Third World countries?
5. What do Marxists hold to be the causes underlying the contradictions that have culminated in the general crisis of capitalism, of which the international monetary crisis is a part?
6. How do Marxists generally explain the role of the World Bank and the IMF?
7. What implications does the Marxist explanation of the international monetary crisis have for Third World countries' policies?
8. Read at least two mainstream and two Marxist authors' analyses of the international monetary crisis and compare the arguments they offer with those offered in this text.

Recommended Reading
(For annotations, see bibliography at the end of the book.)

Amin, *Accumulation on a World Scale*
—— *Imperialism and Unequal Development*
Anderson, *Studies in the Theory of Unequal Exchange*
Bailey, *Africa's Industrial Future*
Brenner, *The Politics of International Monetary Reform*
Carlson *et al.*, *International Finance*
Chachaoliades, *International Monetary Theory and Policy*
Ewusi (ed.), *The New International Economic Order and UNCTAD*
Green and Seidman, *Unity or Poverty?*
Hansen and Marzouk, *Development and Economic Policy in the UAR*
Harvey (ed.), *Papers on the Economy of Botswana*
Henning, Pigott and Scott, *International Financial Management*
Killick (ed.), *Adjustment and Financing in the Developing World*
Kindleberger and Laffargue, *Financial Crises*
Lees and Eng, *International Financial Markets*
Leipziger, *The International Monetary System and Developing Nations*
Lenin, *Imperialism, the Highest Stage of Capitalism*
Lozoya and Bhattacharya, *The Financial Issues of the New International Economic Order*
Marcus, *Investment and Development Possibilities in Tropical Africa*
Mikesell, *Foreign Exchange in the Postwar World*
Nkrumah, *Neo-colonialism*
Rowan *et al.*, *Investment and Development*
Seidman and Seidman, *US Multinationals in South Africa*
Seidman and Makgetla, *Outposts of Monopoly Capital*
Swiderowski, *Exchange and Trade Controls*
Thomas, *Capital Accumulation and Technology Transfer*
Thomas *et al.*, *Importing Technology into Africa*

Periodicals
Development and Peace
IMF, *Annual Reports*
IMF, *International Financial Statistics*
IBRD, *Annual Reports*
Monthly Review
Review of African Political Economy

Chapter 13: Transnational Banks and the Eurocurrency Market

In the 1970s, African governments seeking new sources of funds to finance growing balance of payments and budget deficits began to borrow heavily on the Eurocurrency market. That market, dominated by transnational commercial banks, emerged in the post-World War II era, outside the control of national monetary authorities, as a prominent feature of the international financial system.

This chapter first describes how the post-war technological revolution enhanced the role of national commercial banks in the accumulation and reinvestment of vast amounts of capital in the major developed countries. Second, it shows how those banks, closely intertwined with nationally based industrial conglomerates, expanded in search of profitable new sources of raw materials and markets. Third, it portrays the characteristics of the resulting Eurocurrency market. It focuses on the way international banking consortia, unable to dispose of their growing accumulations of capital in their stagflation-ridden home economies, pressed vigorously to make government-guaranteed loans in the Third World, including Africa.

Capital Accumulation and the Technological Revolution

World War II spurred the invention of new technologies like computers and aeronautical equipment, which in the post-war era formed the basis for the rapid growth of sophisticated industries in the core developed countries. After an initial reconstruction period, European and Japanese firms began to compete with US companies in the development of new products. The resulting technological revolution led to rapid increases in productivity. From 1960 to 1970, output per work hour rose 34 per cent in the US, 43 per cent in the UK, 74 per cent in Federal Republic of Germany (FRG) and 289 per cent in Japan.

A few examples illustrate the impact of technological innovation. In Japan, Mitsubishi developed a new method of smelting copper which eliminated 30 per cent of the labour traditionally employed by introducing continuous processing and automation. In the United States, about half of all new machine tools produced in the 1970s were computerized and "numerically controlled".

These new processes involved ever larger—and more expensive—economies of scale. By the 1970s, steel plants, in an industry always characterized by large size, required an annual production of at least six million tons to achieve optimum scale.

The technological revolution also facilitated a fundamental shift in the international division of labour. Dramatic advances in distribution and communications technologies made possible the transfer of entire manufacturing plants to remote, low-wage regions. Air freight and improved telecommunications systems increased the flexibility of world trade. Containerized shipping reduced the cost and facilitated the expansion of bulk international trade.

New technologies involving rising economies of scale required vast investments. The average contract for transnational corporate engineering and construction firms rose from $13 million in the mid-1960s to $100 million a decade later.

The huge size and capital expense of new projects designed to take advantage of new technologies pressured transnational corporations to form consortia and joint ventures. An increasingly oligopolistically competitive pattern emerged, involving not simply individual firms, but huge corporate alliances.

The heavy costs of the technological revolution stimulated the continuous expansion of transnational financial institutions, especially the commercial banks. By the mid-1970s, some 30 or 40 transnational banks dominated the international banking market. The top ten banks held almost a fifth of the assets of the 300 largest banks in the world; the top five banks' assets exceeded the combined assets of the bottom 100.

The transnational corporations' growing capital requirements strengthened their close alliance with at least one or two of the largest banks which dominated their home economies. The particular linkage mechanism varied in each country, depending on national legal requirements. In the US and Britain, industrial firms and banks typically shared directorships. In the FRG, the law permitted banks to own stocks in industrial firms. In Japan, the largest banks joined massive industrial groups. Whatever the particular form of relationship, the banks played a major role in organizing consortia to finance the costs of huge new projects.

Transnational Commercial Banks and the Eurocurrency Market

The transnational banks' activities both reflected and contributed to the expansion of what came to be known as Eurocurrency or Euromoney markets. The shrinkage of time and space brought about by the technological advances in transportation and global communications systems facilitated the shift of bank capital from the US to Japan and Europe, and from Europe and Japan to finance expanding corporate activities in Africa.

The US Transnational Banks

Immediately after World War II, the largest US banks co-operated closely with US transnational corporations to penetrate the near-prostrate economies of Europe. For example, Chase Manhattan Bank, the third largest in the world and closely knit into the Rockefeller network,[1] shared directors with some of the biggest US firms which dominated their respective home markets: Firestone, General Motors, Chrysler, Exxon, General Electric, American Telephone and Telegraph, US Steel and other domestic US companies. Representatives of foreign firms sitting on Chase's international advisory board included the Japanese Mitsubishi group, the Italian Fiat, the Swiss-owned Nestlé, the British Dunlop, the Royal Dutch Shell and the Swedish company, Volvo.

The US banks opened overseas branches to service their industrial clients' expansion abroad. In the 1960s, as the United States began to experience growing balance of payments deficits, the Federal Reserve Bank (the central bank of the US) imposed regulations designed to prevent companies from investing more funds abroad. The regulations prohibited banks from re-exporting funds returned to the US from their overseas operations. The banks responded by depositing capital they had accumulated abroad in their European branch banks. This enabled them to mobilize increasing amounts of credit for further overseas investments outside US government controls. It stimulated the rapid growth of the Eurocurrency market.

A few highly concentrated US transnational commercial banks dominated this expanding foreign business. By the mid-1970s, 20 banks controlled about a third of all banking assets within the US itself. These same banks held over 90 per cent of all US banks' foreign-branch assets. They also held a majority of shares in over 50 European banks and almost 30 banks elsewhere in the world, giving them control over more than a third of the financial entities operating in the Euromoney market.

In the 1970s, as growing unemployment and inflation spread simultaneously throughout the US economy, the biggest US banks, seeking more profitable outlets for their accumulated funds, began to expand abroad more rapidly. Between 1970 and 1975, US banks' foreign assets rose from 8 to 18 per cent of their domestic assets. They expanded international credit by about 30 per cent, more than three times the rate at which they increased loans in the US itself. By the mid-1970s, the overseas activities of the largest US banks exceeded their domestic business. By the late 1970s, Citibank, then the second largest US bank, held over half its assets and earned over 80 per cent of its profits outside the US. By the 1980s, Citibank, together with its transnational holding company Citicorp, had emerged as the largest bank in the world.

Gradually, US banks shifted their foreign financial headquarters from Europe to "financial centres" in places like the Caribbean where they faced neither severe government regulations nor high taxes. By the mid-1970s, still considered part of the Eurocurrency market, the Caribbean branches conducted three-quarters of the US banks' overseas business.

As they expanded their Eurocurrency activities, the largest US banks also began to extend loans in Africa, sometimes directly through their own branch activities, more often indirectly through British and French associates. Chase Manhattan and Citicorp established branch networks in South Africa and opened offices in the largest independent African countries, Egypt, Nigeria and Zaire. Elsewhere, they operated primarily through British[2] and French affiliates. In the 1960s, Citicorp purchased 49 per cent of the French Banque d'Afrique de l'Ouest, which had branches in nearly every Francophone African country. It also bought 49 per cent of the British bank Grindlays which had long been active in East and Central Africa. Chase Manhattan, the third largest US bank, formed ties with another large French bank, Société Générale de Banque, and established close links with the British-owned Standard Bank, the second largest in South Africa with branches in almost every former British colony.

Bank of America, in the 1980s the second largest bank in the world, joined the British Barclays Bank in a consortium, the Société Financière Européene. It also established direct ties with another British bank, Kleinwort Benson Lonsdale. This latter connection provided the Bank of America with outlets in South Africa through two South African affiliates, and with the British Midlands and International Banks consortium, which included Standard Bank.

The German Grossbanken

The US banks' penetration of the European market did not go unchallenged. By the 1970s, despite initial weaknesses due to national defeat in World War II, the banks of both the FRG and Japan had re-emerged, closely integrated with their nation's dominant industrial conglomerates, and plunged into vigorous competition.

In the FRG, the Deutsche Bank, Dresdner Bank and Commerzbank collaborated with the post-war government to help the largest German corporations to become, once again, industrial giants on the world scene. As one observer explained:[3]

> The rise of high finance [in the FRG] is not the result of the economic miracle alone. It has a system. Although the allies broke up the German banking concern after the War, the parts soon rejoined each other.
>
> Today these institutions are centralized and universal, financially strong and aggressively managed, equalled by only a few banking giants around the world. The freedom of action of German Grossbankiers is much larger than that of their colleagues in most other countries.

Another authority added: "A vast number of large German companies are closely controlled today by a relatively small number of financial institutions and organizations. These groups . . . enjoy great influence over every aspect of the development of West German industry.[4]

In one sense, the wholesale destruction of German factories by British bombers during World War II gave FRG industry an advantage. Its managers could invest in totally new plants, incorporating the latest technological advances, including those transferred into the country in the immediate post-war period by US industrial investors. Concentrated industrial control and government assistance enabled FRG firms, working closely with the banks, to mobilize the necessary know-how and financial backing to adapt and utilize the most advanced industrial plant and equipment. As FRG industry expanded in the 1960s and 1970s, an increasing share of its output was sold abroad and its foreign investment expanded even more rapidly. Between 1967 and 1977, FRG holdings abroad multiplied almost seven times to reach $20.5 billion (excluding reinvestments by subsidiaries, which would probably boost total foreign investment to closer to $30 billion).

In the same period, FRG banks expanded their foreign activities, facilitating FRG industrial firms' growing foreign investments. The Grossbanken organized bank consortia to finance the massive expansion of FRG exports. Frequently, the FRG government underwrote the banks' financing packages for overseas sales.

As the international monetary crisis matured, the strength of the Deutschmark enabled the FRG banks to assume an increasingly important role in the Euromoney market. The growth of Deutschmark Eurobonds, monopolized by the Grossbanken, reflected their new international strength. By the late 1970s, the FRG banks' foreign loans were multiplying more than twice as fast as their domestic business. About a third of the total profits of the Grossbanken came from their foreign business.

Even more than their American counterparts, FRG banks conducted their financial arrangements on a wholesale basis outside their country. Each of the Grossbanken participated in an international consortium: the Deutsche Bank joined European Banks International (EBIC); the Dresdner Bank, the Société Financière Européene (SFE); and Commerzbank joined Credit Lyonnais and the Banco di Roma. Through these consortia, the banks could draw on greater resources and contacts outside the FRG to finance new investments. In developing countries the Grossbanken usually operated through affiliates. Unlike the US banks, they did not buy major shareholdings in British or French banks operating in Africa. In West and North Africa, they bought minority shares—from 0.4 to 18 per cent—of locally based banks. They opened representative offices, or used consortia offices, to collaborate with local banks in conducting their expanding business with South Africa.

The Japanese Industrial-Financial Groupings

The largest Japanese banks expanded their post-war activities in a pattern remarkably similar to that of the Grossbanken in the FRG. By the end of the 1960s, a handful of huge Japanese-owned industrial finance groups had succeeded in restoring their dominant position in the national economy. For example, the member companies of Mitsubishi, one of the three largest, engaged in finance, brewing, rayon, paper, chemicals, petrochemicals and plastic, glass, mining and cement, aluminium and steel, electrical equipment, transport equipment and real estate. Each group's financial institutions helped it to accumulate the vast sums of capital required to finance new technological innovations. A Japanese financial journal declared, "Most industrial companies are actually run by the banks from which they borrow."[5]

As in the FRG, close co-ordination of industrial corporations, government and the banks helped Japan become one of the world's major industrial powers. Its modern technology gave it an edge over its rivals on the international scene in several sectors. For example, from 1964 to 1975, thanks to its modern oxygen blast furnace system, Japanese steel output rose 166 per cent, compared to 17.5 per cent in the US. In 1975 Japanese steel workers produced about 9.35 tonnes of finished steel per 100 work hours, compared to 8.13 tonnes in the US.

By the 1970s, the Japanese island economy required huge amounts of imported raw materials, as well as growing export markets for its burgeoning industrial output. Japanese transnationals began to invest abroad to secure their hold on vitally needed sources of raw materials, as well as markets for their domestically manufactured goods. Their overseas investments multiplied.

A handful of Japanese groups largely controlled the flow of Japanese capital abroad. Five commercial houses—Mitsui, Mitsubishi, Marubeni, C. Itoh, and Sumitomo—controlled almost half of the foreign investments and loans of the 50 largest Japanese companies. Japanese banks, like those in the US and the FRG, extended their operations in line with the commercial groups and contributed to the rapid growth of foreign investment. From the early 1970s, Japanese banks also entered the international money market through minority participation in banking consortia, mostly formed with European partners. They established even fewer overseas banks than did the FRG's Grossbanken. They operated almost solely at the wholesale level. They created jointly owned merchant banks with European banks: Sumitomo Bank with the British-Swiss Bank, Credit-Suisse-WhiteWeld; Mitsui Bank with the British Hambros; and the Industrial Bank of Japan with the FRG Deutsche Bank. The Mitsubishi Bank participated in the Orion Bank, a consortium controlled by the US Chase Manhattan Bank in which the British Standard Bank also participated.

Increased representation on the London Metal Exchange reflected the growing involvement of Japanese industrial finance groups in overseas mining projects. Until 1973, North American, European and South African companies constituted the main brokers on the Exchange. By the late 1970s, Sumitomo had obtained representation by purchasing a 50 per cent share of the aluminium division of the American firm AMAX; Mitsui had bought shares in the South African Anglo-American Group; Mitsubishi acquired shares in British Triland Trading, as well as acquiring shares through a group affiliated with the FRG firm Metalgesellschaft; and Marubeni, together with Consolidated Gold Fields, a British firm with massive South African holdings, controlled Tenant Trading.

The growing competition of Japanese and FRG banks began to erode the US bankers' predominant position in international finance. By the mid-1970s, the US banks' share of assets of the world's biggest 300 banks had declined, while the Japanese share rose to 18 per cent and the West German to 11 per cent. Combined, the transnational banks based in these three countries held over two thirds of the top 300 banks' assets. Only French-based banks, with 7 per cent of the assets, ranked next, but as already noted, some of the larger French banks had become closely allied with those based in the US.

The Eurocurrency Market and the International Monetary Crisis

As the international monetary crisis developed in the 1970s, transnational corporate banks from the three leading capitalist countries continued to expand and compete abroad, seeking profitable new outlets for their growing accumulations of capital. Oil-producing countries added their mounting surplus capital to funds at the disposal of these banks. As their national economies began to feel the pinch of growing inflation and unemployment, the transnational corporate bankers welcomed the Third World's growing demand for loans at high rates of interest. They apparently viewed the higher-income developing-country borrowers, backed by government guarantees, as fairly safe risks.

In the 1980s, however, as renewed recession gripped the developed capitalist countries, world trade stagnated. Third World borrowing countries found it increasingly difficult to expand their exports at the 5 to 6 per cent rate necessary to enable them to pay their rising debt service costs. For the first time in five years, the transnational commercial banks began to cut back on credit to developing countries. This tended to aggravate further the factors hindering the necessary growth of world trade. Increasing numbers of countries—both lenders and borrowers—looked to the IMF to help them overcome their mounting financial difficulties. Fears were expressed that massive defaults might bankrupt some of the world's largest transnational financial institutions and further undermine the already shaky international monetary system.

Summary

The post-World War II technological revolution required investment of vast sums of capital. This increased the importance of the transnational commercial banks' role in nationally-based industrial-financial groups. As these groups expanded competitively in search of profitable new sources of raw materials and markets in Africa and elsewhere, the transnational banks increased their holdings of surplus capital in Euromarket banks, outside the control of their respective central bank authorities. As their home economies stagnated, the transnational banks welcomed the opportunity to lend increasing amounts of surplus funds, accompanied by government guarantees and high interest rates, to African and other Third World nations. By the 1980s, as renewed recession gripped the major capitalist countries both lenders and borrowers looked to the IMF for assistance to overcome the dangers of growing monetary instability and stagnating world trade.

Notes

1. The Rockefeller group which emerged from the war as one of five financial groups that dominated the US economy originally grew out of the Rockefellers'

accumulation and reinvestment of vast amounts of capital through the Standard Oil Company and its affiliates.

2. For more detailed descriptions of Barclays and Standard Banks, see Chapter 4.

3. *Capital* (Cologne), August 1978, No. 8.

4. Vogl, *German Business After the Economic Miracle* (New York: John Wiley & Sons, 1973), p. 32.

5. Cited in *South African Financial Mail*, Japan Survey, 12 November 1976.

Exercises and Research

1. How did the post-World War II technological revolution affect capital accumulation and the role of international banks?
2. Analyse the competitive role of US, West German and Japanese banks in the development of the Eurocurrency market.
3. How did the international monetary crisis affect Eurocurrency loans to the Third World countries?
4. Find out whether and how much your country's government has borrowed on the Eurocurrency market and from other sources in the last five years. Compare the terms of the loans, including the rates of interest. Find out how much and on what terms the private sector in your country has borrowed from the Eurocurrency market.

Recommended Readings

(For annotations, see bibliography at the end of the book.)

Akinlan, *The Law of International Economic Institutions in Africa*
Angelini, Eng and Lees, *International Lending, Risk and the Euromarkets*
Brenner, *The Politics of International Monetary Reform*
Carlson *et al.*, *International Finance*
Channon, *British Banking Strategy and the International Challenge*
Curran, *Banking and the Global System*
Davis, *The Management Functions in International Banking*
Duffy and Giddy, *The International Money Market*
Ewusi (ed.), *The New International Economic Order*
Germidis, *International Subcontracting*
Havrilesky and Boorman, *Current Perspectives in Banking-operations,*

Management and Regulation
Henning, Pigott and Scott, *International Financial Management*
Heywood, *Foreign Exchange and the Corporate Treasurer*
Hudson, *Money and Exchange Dealing in International Banking*
Kindleberger and Laffargue, *Financial Crises*
Lees and Eng, *International Financial Markets*
Livy (ed.), *Management and People in Banking*
Lozoya and Bhattacharya, *The Financial Issues of the New International Economic Order*
Payer, *The Debt Trap*
Seidman, *US Multinationals in South Africa*
Seidman and Makgetla, *Outposts of Monopoly Capital*
Wellons, *Eurocurrency Loans*
Wood and Byrne, *International Business Finance*

Periodicals

Bank for International Settlements
Monthly Review
Moody's Banks and Financial Manual
Review of African Political Economy
Who Owns What in World Banking
Annual reports of major commercial banks

Chapter 14: The International Monetary Fund

The International Monetary Fund (IMF) was created shortly after World War II. It became the primary international agency attempting to shape a workable international monetary system, especially for capitalist and Third World countries. To enable the reader to evaluate the role of the IMF, this chapter first briefly outlines the history leading up to its formation. It then examines how the IMF functions. Finally, it considers the IMF's response to the international monetary crisis, and the criticisms levelled at it by African and other Third World governments.

A Brief History of the International Medium of Exchange

The history of efforts to regulate the international monetary system sheds light on the current international monetary crisis, characterized by floating rates of exchange between currencies and increasing Third World foreign debts. Until World II, as the capitalist system spread throughout Europe and most of the rest of the World, the major international trading countries relied on a gold standard; that is, they accepted gold as the international medium of exchange. Each government fixed its currency's value in terms of the number of currency units required to buy a fixed amount of gold. If country A's dollar represented a fifth as much gold as B's pound, the par rate of exchange would be: \$5 = £1.

The value of national currencies fluctuated between narrow limits called "gold" points. A's demand for B's goods determined A's demand for B's currency to buy those goods. Otherwise, A would have to ship gold to B to cover its purchases. A would be willing to increase the price it would pay in terms of its currency for B's currency to the point where the price reached the cost of insuring and shipping actual gold. That is, gold acted as the regulator of exchange.

In accordance with the then mainstream theory, a country operating on the gold standard would ship gold to cover its balance of payments deficits with the rest of the world. This would reduce its own gold reserves, and automatically reduce its money supply, since the latter would be linked by the central bank to the available gold reserves. According to the then widely accepted quantity theory of money, the reduced money supply would automatically lead to lower domestic prices. The prices of imports, in contrast, would become relatively more expensive, so consumers in the country would buy less of them. This would automatically lead to a correction of the balance of payments.

During World War I, the combatants suspended the gold standard. To the extent that they continued to trade with their allies, they adopted fixed rates of exchange between them. After the war, the exchange rates fluctuated, until the resulting difficulties in expanding trade led the major capitalist countries to return to the gold standard for international transactions. Some countries tied their internal money supply directly to their gold reserves as before the war. The British government required its African and other colonies to hold their reserves in pounds sterling, thus acquiring additional backing for the British currency. (See the discussion of the African currency boards, Chapter 2.)

The Great Depression of the 1930s disrupted international trade and payments among the capitalist states. As international trade declined, Britain's exports and income from invisible items fell, until it found it could only cover its balance of payments deficits by borrowing abroad. When Germany's banks collapsed in the early 1930s, Britain's creditors, mainly in the United States, feared the British banks might fail too, so they demanded gold in payment. As a result the British authorities decided to leave the gold standard. The other major capitalist countries followed suit. All the colonial currencies dependent on the British pound and the French franc likewise went off the gold standard. In 1936, the United States, Britain and France reached a tripartite agreement to buy back their own currencies from each other in exchange for gold, thus re-establishing a modified form of gold standard.

With the onset of World War II in 1939, Britain imposed strict exchange controls to protect the pound sterling. The war pushed domestic prices up, causing overvaluation. Its foreign-exchange controls enabled the British government to keep the costs of imports, including raw materials bought from its colonies, at an artifically depressed level. With its economy mobilized for war production, it could not expand exports sufficiently to pay higher prices for its required imports. After the war, it used exchange controls to hold down the prices of raw materials from its colonies in order to boost its production and export of manufactured goods. The British central bank rigorously restricted the supply of US and other currencies it made available to commercial banks, both at home and in the colonies, for the import of competitive goods.

During the war, the US, on the other hand, had become the major creditor of its allies. As long as they could, they paid off their debts with gold, enabling the US to accumulate most of the world's gold in Fort Knox.

The Founding of the IMF

In 1944, as the end of the war neared, the US government invited its allies to the Bretton Woods Conference to discuss proposals for a new monetary system. These resulted in the establishment of the IMF and the World Bank. At the outset, for the most part, the socialist countries remained outside these institutions. They declared their desire to regulate their own currencies, and carry on trade among themselves without the economic fluctuations characteristic of capitalist countries.

The IMF began operations in 1947 along lines consistent with mainstream, predominantly Keynesian, monetary theory. The US, having emerged from the war with most of the capitalist world's gold, dominated the Bretton Woods Conference, influencing the decisions shaping the basic features of the IMF. Its founders agreed on certain key principles. The Fund should seek to: 1) eliminate bilateral trade which might interfere with free competitive international trade; 2) establish stable exchange rates between currencies to give traders confidence in the stability of the international medium of exchange; and 3) end restrictions on traders' acquisitions and free expenditure of foreign currencies, that is, eliminate exchange controls.

Basically, these principles reflected the then mainstream conclusion that the gold standard, alone, had become too rigid. Fluctuating exchange rates, on the other hand, while giving domestic policy-makers freedom to adjust money supplies in terms of national policy needs, hindered the free flow of trade.

Rate of Exchange

The participating countries declared the rate of exchange for their currencies, that is, their currency's par value, in terms of US dollars and gold. The conferees agreed that an ounce of gold would equal US$35. Britain established the par value of the pound at £1 = US$4.03, thus initially retaining the overvalued rate it established during the war. It continued to impose that rate on the colonies.

All members agreed to consult the IMF before altering their exchange rates. According to mainstream tenets, if they suffered long-term balance of payments deficits, they should devalue, thus achieving an automatic adjustment. If they had a long-term balance of payments surplus, they should revalue. The IMF founders assumed that, following such adjustments, all currencies would eventually become freely convertible. This would leave the world's market forces free, once again, to adjust the supply and demand for money in accordance with the requirements of international trade.

The Pool

The participants agreed to set up a pool or fund (the basis of the IMF's name), consisting of gold plus a quota of the currencies of all members determined by each member's GDP per capita and gold reserves. Each member provided 75 per cent of its quota in its own currency, and the rest in gold or US dollars. They deposited these funds in their own national central banks in an account on which the IMF could draw as required.

Initially, a member could use its own currency to purchase from the Fund an equivalent amount of foreign currency, up to 25 per cent of its own quota, to help cover annual balance of payments deficits. To discourage excessive purchases of foreign currencies from the Fund, members had to pay charges when their own currency in the Fund exceeded 25 per cent of their quota. Initially, a member could not draw foreign currencies totalling more than two times its own quota at one time; beyond that, it had to pay for additional foreign currency with gold.

The Fund aimed to permit countries to have balance of payments deficits for a limited period; the founders expected that the country would then experience an outflow of gold and so would take steps to restore the payments equilibrium. If a country had a persistent deficit, the Fund managers could make further assistance contingent upon the country's government accepting Fund advice. Over the years, the IMF board of governors have increased the members' quotas, thus increasing the Fund's financial resources.

Special Drawing Rights

In 1969, as more and more countries, including core capitalist nations, experienced persistent balance of payments deficits, the Fund created Special Drawing Rights (SDRs); under this system a government may exercise special rights to draw additional foreign exchange to cover balance of payments needs or if it confronts difficulties in relation to gold, foreign exchange or its Fund position. Over the next years, the IMF managers expanded the SDRs. They retained the right to impose conditions which a country must accept before it could avail itself of these expanded SDRs.

Operation of the International Monetary Fund

Reflecting the strong influence exerted by the United States, the member nations located the IMF's headquarters in Washington, DC. Members voted on IMF policy and elected IMF directors according to the size of their quotas in the pool. The US alone had about a quarter of the votes, based on its creditor status at the end of World War II. By the 1980s, the US share had declined to about 20 per cent of the total votes, reflecting the relative decline of its quota in the Fund. However, the major European states, together with the US could still determine the outcome of any vote. Most African states joined the IMF upon attainment of independence, but each received only a fraction of the total vote.

The IMF and the International Monetary Crisis

By the 1970s, worsening balance of payments deficits culminated in the prolonged monetary crisis which not only seriously aggravated the difficulties of developing countries, but also threatened the stability of the monetary system shaped at Bretton Woods.

The Impact of the US Devaluation of the Dollar

By the end of the 1960s, the United States confronted persistent payments deficits because of growing transnational corporate involvement abroad and its heavy military expenditure in Vietnam. In 1971, without consulting the IMF or its own allies, the US devalued the US dollar by 15 per cent. All countries automatically lost 15 per cent of the value of their foreign-exchange reserves held in the form of US dollars. This set off a series of devaluations among other countries. At the same time, the US pressured a few developed countries, particularly the Federal Republic of Germany and Japan, to revalue. US spokesmen insisted that both had achieved an unfair competitive advantage in world markets by undervaluing their currencies; revaluation would reduce that advantage by raising their relative costs of production, including the real wages of their workers. Devaluation of the US dollar, by the same token, relatively reduced the real value of US workers' wages which ceased to be the highest in the capitalist world.

The adjustments of currencies following the US devaluation ultimately led to the situation of flexible or floating exchange rates which still persists as this text goes to press. Far-reaching consequences flow from the resulting instability of the international medium of exchange. First, fluctuating currency rates pose problems for international traders seeking to arrange long-term contracts. They can never be sure that the price paid in a particular currency on a due date a year or more ahead will be worth the same amount as on the day the contract was written. For example, in the early 1970s, OPEC initially agreed to establish oil prices in terms of US dollars. When the value of the US dollar declined, the OPEC countries confronted declining real payments for their oil. As a result, they pressed for the second round of major oil price hikes in the late 1970s which aggravated the balance of payments problems of all oil-importing countries. Uncertainty as to the real value of contracts for trade in goods to be produced and shipped some time in the future, most economists agree, inevitably hinders the expansion of world trade.

Second, transnational commercial banks, using complex communications techniques (including telexes and telephones), can shift bank balances in the Eurocurrency market from one currency, with a declining value, to another with a rising value, thus realizing profits. Some of the largest commercial banks reported in the late 1970s that they realized 10 to 15 per cent of their profits abroad from these international currency operations. But these speculative movements also aggravate the fluctuations of currency values: as increasing numbers of banks move their funds out of one currency into another, they may aggravate the swings in value, competitively bidding up those that are rising, while aggravating the downswings of those that are falling. Central banks might intervene to defend their own weak currency by buying it in the open market; but by the 1980s this had become prohibitively expensive. In 1983, an American economist asserted,

> The days when a government could hold the line on its currency are over. Speculators have more money than governments. No country, not even the United States or Germany, has enough resources to fight market trends. They're just giving taxpayers' money to currency traders when they do.[1]

Third, the lack of a fixed, agreed medium of exchange and centralized control over transnational commercial banks' powers to extend loans tends to foster international inflationary pressures. The banks may extend loans without regard to whether they contribute to production. To the extent that the international money supply expands without a coincident expansion of output, international prices will tend to rise.

The US devaluation of its currency also ended any pretence that the international community accepted gold as an international medium of exchange. Even before the US devalued, many countries had accepted two values for gold: they accepted US$35 = an ounce of gold for the valuation of their foreign-exchange reserves; but, for the purposes of private trade, they left the value of gold subject to market forces which pushed its price steadily higher. With the establishment of floating exchange rates, one country after another revalued its gold reserves at the current higher rate. In the late 1970s, speculation pushed the value of gold over US$1000 an ounce. This created a boom for the South African mining finance houses like the Anglo-American Group, and rescued the South African economy from the severe economic crisis it confronted as a result of the Soweto uprisings and the international recession. It also enabled the South African regime to buy military equipment and oil, despite UN and OPEC sanctions. When the world gold price fell back to between US$300 and US$400 in the early 1980s, however, South Africa once again faced serious economic difficulties. In 1982, the South African government requested a billion-dollar loan from the IMF which was granted despite widespread international opposition.

SDRs: A Compromise

Unable to arrive at a satisfactory arrangement for a stable international medium of exchange, the IMF member states agreed to a compromise by establishing the SDRs as a partial substitute. They set the SDRs' value in relation to a basket of different currencies, weighted by the relative importance of their respective countries. Until 1977, the 16 currencies in the SDR basket included the South African Rand. Since then, the IMF has reduced the number of currencies and changed the composition of the SDR backing. In 1983, the value of the SDR was fixed in terms of the US dollar value, based on the market exchange rates of specified quantities of five currencies: the Deutschmark, the French franc, the Japanese yen, the British pound sterling and the US dollar. Many African countries linked the value of their currency's exchange rate to the US dollar. Increasing numbers set their currencies' values in terms of the number of currency units per SDR. Table 14.1 shows their value, in 1978 and 1985 (October) as translated into the number of each country's national currency units that equalled one SDR on those dates. That in most cases one SDR equalled more national currency units in 1985 than in 1978, reflected the fact that most African states had had to devalue in the interim.

Member countries may draw on SDRs and use them as foreign exchange in accordance with the weighted value of currencies included in the basket. In this sense, SDRs have acquired the status of a limited kind of medium of exchange with somewhat fluctuating values determined by the changing rates of the basket of currencies of which they are composed.

Table 14.1
Exchange rates of African countries, 1978 and Oct., 1985, (units of national currency per SDRs/Special Drawing Rights)

Country	*Currency Unit*	*Units per SDR*	
		1978	*Oct. 1985*
Algeria	Dinar	4.9955	5.2120
Benin	Franc[a]	272.28	427.27
Botswana	Pula	1.0319	2.2227
Burkina Faso	Franc[a]	272.28	427.27
Burundi	Franc	117.25	122.70
Cameroon	Franc[a]	272.28	427.27
Central African Republic	Franc[a]	272.28	427.27
Chad	Franc[a]	272.28	427.27
Congo	Franc[a]	272.28	427.27
Egypt	Pound	0.5097	0.7501
Ethiopia	Birr	2.6968	2.2183
Gabon	Franc[a]	272.28	427.27
Gambia	Dalasi	3.2894	3.4000
Ghana	Cedi	3.436	64.102
Ivory Coast	Franc[a]	272.28	427.27
Kenya	Shillings	9.660	17.738
Lesotho	Loti	1.1328	2.7616[c]
Liberia	Dollar	1.3028	0.9802
Libya	Dinar	0.3856	0.2901
Malawi	Kwacha	1.0541	1.8185
Mali	Franc[a]	272.28	427.27
Mauritania	Ouguiyas	60.130	81.745
Morocco	Dirham	5.063	10.630
Niger	Franc[a]	272.28	427.27
Nigeria	Naira	0.8435	0.9773[b]
Rwanda	Franc	120.95	102.71
Senegal	Franc[a]	272.28	427.27
Seychelles	Rupees	8.5380	7.2345
Sierra Leone	Leone	1.3668	5.7405
Somalia	Shillings	8.201	43.518
South Africa	Rand	1.1328	2.7616
Sudan	Pound	0.5211	2.6483[b]
Swaziland	Lilangeni	0.8827	2.7616[c]
Tanzania	Shilling	9.660	17.854
Togo	Franc[a]	272.27	427.27
Tunisia	Dinar	0.5255	0.8500
Uganda	Shilling	9.66	739.44
Zaire	Zaire	1.313	56.731[b]
Zambia	Kwacha	1.0242	7.5018
Zimbabwe	Dollar	0.8795	1.7972

Notes: [a]Members of the franc zone dominated by France; [b]September; [c]Still exchanged at parity with the South African rand.

Source: *Calculated from the International Monetary Fund, International Financial Statistics*, December 1985, country tables.

The Expanding Role of the IMF

As the international monetary crisis deepened, the IMF members established a committee of 22, including representatives of Third World countries, to consider how to create a new international monetary system. Although it met regularly, it failed to achieve any lasting solution. In the 1970s, the oil-exporting countries, which contributed some of their surplus oil money to the Fund, demanded and obtained a somewhat larger share of the voting power in the IMF. Nevertheless, the big ten, led by the United States, the Federal Republic of Germany, France, Britain and Japan, continued to dominate the IMF structure.

Over the years, as member countries faced growing balance of payments difficulties, the IMF created additional facilities to extend credit to them. The IMF's monthly publication, *International Financial Statistics*, outlines the current status of these facilities. At the beginning of 1984, they included the following.

The *compensatory financing facility*, established in 1963, assists members, especially those producing primary commodities, to finance balance of payments deficits due to temporary factors outside their control. The IMF extended this facility in 1981 to help members finance excess cereal imports.

The *buffer stock financing facility*, established in 1969, helps members finance balance of payments costs related to their financial contributions to approved international buffer stocks for primary products.

The *extended facility*, created in 1974, makes resources available for longer periods and larger amounts than under the credit tranche policies (up to 140 per cent of the quota for up to three years) for members experiencing balance of payments difficulties due to structural imbalances.

The *oil facilities*, set up in 1975-76, provide funds for members confronting difficulties due to the rise of oil prices.

The *supplementary financing facility*, created in 1979, assists members facing large and prolonged payments difficulties. The IMF extended these further in 1981 to provide additional finance under standby and extended arrangements determined by guidelines adopted from time to time. In 1983, the guidelines specified access to IMF resources of up to 150 per cent of a country's quota under a one-year arrangement, and 450 per cent under a three-year arrangement.

To finance these expanding credits, the IMF borrowed funds under the General Agreements to Borrow (GAB) established in 1962. These, too, have been extended over the years. They permit the IMF to borrow from the ten largest capitalist industrial countries (the Group of Ten), Switzerland, oil-exporting countries, and others with strong external positions.

Table 14.2 shows the position of the African oil and non-oil exporting countries compared to all countries (total) of 31 October 1983.

Table 14.2
All Purchases by African Countries from the International Monetary Fund, 1947-84[a]

Country	*1947-79*	*1980*	*1981*	*1982*	*1983*	*1984*	*Total 1947-84*	*As per cent of total*
Benin	...	1.19	...	...	1.8	...	3.8	0.03
Burkina Faso	0.8	...	...	...	...	...	0.8	...
Burundi	36.3	...	...	...	...	...	36.3	0.29
Cameroon	40.8	...	...	...	13.0	7	60.8	0.48
Central African Republic	13.0	5.9	17.0	2.4	5.7	6.5	83.4	0.66
Chad	15.3	...	7.1	...	3.3	3.2	21.8	0.17
Congo	18.5	...	...	...	3.3	2.5	24.2	0.19
Djibouti	...	...	...	...	...	0.6	0.6	...
Equatorial Guinea	2.8	9.5	7.2	1.3	1.4	...	22.1	0.17
Ethiopia	43.9	...	66.1	23	...	4.2	137.7	1.1
Gabon	17.5	...	...	...	...	7	24.6	0.19
Gambia	12.3	1.5	9	16.9	0.9	2.5	43.3	0.34
Ghana	204.9	...	...	8.5	275	213.6	702	5.61
Guinea	32.8	...	0.6	15.9	4.7	...	54	0.43
Guinea Bissau	1.9	...	2.4	...	4	1.9	6.5	0.05
Ivory Coast	58.3	12.2	328.7	115.4	167.8	41.4	722.8	5.79
Kenya	212.9	60	30	150.4	132.6	46.2	631.8	5.06
Lesotho	0.6	...	...	2	...	...	2.6	0.02
Liberia	65.6	18.4	47.5	64.4	62	35.5	293.4	2.35
Madagascar	28.8	39.2	39	57.7	15.2	41.4	221.3	1.77
Malawi	35.9	24.4	30	14.7	34.2	37.8	177	1.42
Mali	35.4	19.4	...	25.4	17.6	24	107.9	0.86
Mauritania	20.7	19.4	10.3	18.8	2.1	...	21.2	0.17
Mauritius	54	35	68	28	31.6	24.8	24.13	1.93
Morocco	291.1	184.5	192.8	433.3	134.8	180.0	1416.4	11.33
Niger	...	...	...	...	30.8	14.4	45.2	0.36
Nigeria	19.5	...	...	308.7	77.4	...	405.6	3.24
Rwanda	14.1	...	...	...	...	...	14.1	0.11
Sao Tome & Principe	...	...	...	...	...	0.9	0.9	0.01
Senegal	65.9	43.3	57.7	53.2	37	31.5	288.6	2.31
Seychelles	...	...	...	...	0.7	...	0.7	...
Sierra Leone	50	9.5	33.7	5.1	23.6	19.0	140.6	1.12
Somalia	23.7	6	25.9	37[b]	47.4	...	140.1	1.12
South Africa	980.1	...	...	902.2[b]	...	...	1882.3	15.06
Sudan	367.1	142.8	165.6	71.8	193.0	45.5	985.8	7.89
Swaziland	1.9	...	...	4.3	10.0	...	16.2	0.12
Tanzania	138.6	40	15.9	1.7	6.1	...	202.3	1.62
Togo	7.5	16.6	7.3	...	21.9	18.0	71.2	0.56
Tunisia	78.2	...	...	...	...	...	78.2	0.62
Uganda	66.3	37.5	122.5	85	112.7	21.0	444.9	3.56
Zaire	284.8	78.4	194.6	131.6	130.3	158.0	1977.6	15.82
Zambia	439	50	359.3	415	188.4	147.5	1225.7	9.81
Zimbabwe	...	32.5	37.5	...	153.6	89.9	313.4	2.51
AFRICA total	*3780.5*	*874.1*	*1875.9*	*2620.7*	*1940.6*	*1225.9*	*124.96*	*100.00*
African purchases (as % of all members' purchases)	7.5%	23.3%	26.5%	29.8%[b]	13.7%	15.1%	13.4%	

[a] The principal way the fund makes its resources available to members to meet balance of payments difficulties is by selling them the currencies of other members or SDRs (Special Drawing Rights) in exchange for their own currencies. A member country to which the fund sells currencies or SDRs is said to make "purchases" or "drawings" from the Fund. Once a member country has spent its quota of its own currency in the Fund, it must then obtain credit from the Fund to purchase additional currencies of other countries. Since the Fund's resources are of a revolving character to finance temporary balance of payments deficits, members must subsequently repurchase their currencies from the Fund with the currencies of other members or SDRs. The Fund reports monthly on each member country's purchases.
[b] In 1982, the IMF permitted South Africa to purchase an equivalent of SDR 902.2 million, equal to 34 per cent of all currencies allocated to Africa, and raising the African share of world wide purchases from the IMF.

Source: *International Monetary Fund, International Financial Statistics,* December, 1984.

IMF "Conditionality"

Despite the continual expansion of its credit facilities, the IMF only finances a relatively small portion of the growing balance of payments needs of Third World countries. (For all African purchases from the IMF, see Table 14.2. Note that "purchases" are financed by IMF credit for all currencies purchased over the member states' quota in the Fund.) In 1983, it disbursed approximately $11 billion, but this vast sum provided only 16 per cent of the funds that member nations required to finance their balance of payments deficits. Nevertheless, the IMF played an increasingly important role because, as a condition of its assistance, it could require member nations to adopt measures which it deemed necessary in order to persuade transnational commercial banks that they could safely and profitably lend the much larger amounts needed.

In the face of deteriorating terms of trade and worsening export markets, African countries, like others in the Third World, drew more and more heavily on commercial banks through the Eurocurrency market to finance their overseas debts (see Table 11.3 on p. 200). The IMF played a growing role in Africa, as elsewhere, by requiring these governments to accept conditions before granting them loans. When a country suffered persistent balance of payments deficits, the IMF sent a team to investigate and advise the government on appropriate measures to overcome their difficulties. African and other governments had to accept this advice as a condition for further IMF assistance. Unless the IMF agreed to assist a particular country, the commercial banks also would generally withhold further loans.

Emphasizing that balance of payments deficits often occur when countries experience inflation, IMF teams typically recommended an essentially monetarist package of "austerity" measures designed to reduce inflationary pressures, holding down export prices to increase the volume of exports. The package typically incorporated some or all of the following recommendations:

a. The government should reduce its budget deficit. IMF spokespersons maintained that they did not insist on layoffs of government workers and reduced spending on health, welfare and education. Nevertheless, most governments, seeking to conform with IMF advice, faced little alternative but to adopt such measures.
b. Government should freeze wages to end (assumed) cost-push inflationary pressures.
c. Government should restructure taxes, reducing those on local and foreign private investors to attract more capital; and raise more broadly based taxes on lower-income groups to increase revenues and reduce government budget deficits.
d. The central banks should raise interest rates to reduce commercial bank lending, thus reducing those inflationary pressures caused by an expanded money supply.
e. The government should reduce foreign-exchange controls and import licensing to permit increased competition from imported goods, thus promoting efficiency and reduced local prices.

f. In general, government should reduce its interference in the economy. The IMF argued that state enterprises often become a financial burden; the private sector operates more efficiently and achieves lower costs. Competition among private firms, they maintained, would ultimately lead to reduced prices. For example, the IMF advisers recommended that the Ghana government sell its state enterprises to the private sector—which it did after the 1966 coup. They persuaded the Zambian government to end further government acquisition of private companies. They convinced Sudan that it should permit foreign banks to re-enter the arena of commercial banking which had earlier been nationalized. They pressed Tanzania to cut back on its state sector.

g. If these measures appear inadequate, IMF teams urge the government to devalue the national currency. In line with mainstream orthodoxy, they argue that this will reduce export prices, thus stimulating export sales; and raise import prices, thus reducing imports.

Once a government has agreed to some or all of these recommendations, the IMF team makes quarterly checks on their implementation. If a government fails to carry out the agreed measures, the IMF refuses further assistance until it complies.

The IMF team typically makes its proposals and its evaluation of government compliance in secret. The public usually sees only the end result: cuts in government spending and personnel; the changed tax structure; rising interest rates; reduced foreign-exchange controls; the sale of state enterprises; devaluation of the currency. The IMF maintains that the government must make the choice and take the responsibility, and generally prefers the advisory team to make its comments in confidence.

Critics of the IMF

Critics object to the IMF "conditionality" policies both from a mainstream, particularly the more liberal Keynesian, and from a Marxist viewpoint. They note that quantitative analyses by IMF experts of IMF adjustment programmes introduced during 1971-80 show that reduced balance of payments deficits accompanied changes in fiscal deficits in only 40 per cent of cases. They assert that even those cases claimed by the IMF as success stories failed when evaluated from the point of view of the welfare of the majority of the people. They argue that, given the objective conditions of the typical Third World economy, the IMF proposals inevitably undermine the living standards of the population:

a. Government measures to lay off workers aggravate already widespread unemployment, with ongoing negative multiplier effects.

b. Government cutbacks in health, education and welfare directly reduce already low living standards.

c. Wage freezes do not stop inflation, typically caused by factors other than wage increases; but as inflationary pressures persist they do reduce the real incomes of working people while increasing profits.

d. Restructuring of taxes along the regressive lines proposed by IMF teams tends to throw an increased burden on the lower-income groups, further reducing their living standards.

e. Raising the interest rate does little to hinder inflationary pressures, but thwarts small emergent businesses seeking loans for working capital, thus strengthening larger firms' oligopolistic position; and increases the cost to government of financing its domestic debt.

f. Reduced foreign-exchange controls and import licensing enables high-income groups to buy more luxury and semi-luxury items, reducing the availability of foreign exchange to purchase machinery and equipment to build factories providing jobs and producing necessities for lower-income groups; to the extent that imports compete with local industries, they tend to squeeze marginal local firms out of business, thus further aggravating unemployment, and tending to eliminate what little domestic industry already exists.

g. Curtailment of state participation in productive activities hinders efforts to direct local investable surpluses into plans to build a more self-reliant, balanced and integrated economy capable of providing increasingly productive employment opportunities and raising living standards.

h. Finally, devaluation tends to throw the burden of the crisis on low-income wage earners and the peasantry (see pp. 197-9). That is not to say a government should never devalue its currency, but that it should do so only in the context of carefully formulated plans, backed by adequate state control of key institutions, to build a more self-reliant, balanced national economy.

Critics of IMF policies do not argue that African governments confronting persistent balance of payments deficits have always made wise decisions in respect of the above issues; in many instances they have not. For example, they point out that African governments have frequently expanded the state bureaucracy and welfare provisions too rapidly, given the existing national product. They have often failed to take the steps necessary to restructure the national economy and invest in increased productivity to enable it to finance improved social consumption. But, the critics say, the IMF package makes that essential reconstruction less likely. In the long run, IMF conditions render the economy more, rather than less, dependent on transnational corporations and the uncertain world market; and throw the burden of the resulting economic crises onto low-income populations. As a result, governments adopting IMF proposals have tended to lose legitimacy with their populations. Their efforts to impose the unpopular IMF recommendations have not infrequently led them to adopt increasingly repressive measures, aggravating political as well as economic instability.

In 1980, representatives of African and other Third World governments met at Arusha, Tanzania, to call for a new international monetary system with two primary objectives: to achieve monetary stability with acceptable levels of employment and sustainable growth; and to support global development, especially for Third World countries.

The Arusha Initiative[2] called for a United Nations conference to discuss the main attributes of a new system based on: 1) democratic management and control, reflecting the interests of the majority of the peoples of the world; 2) universal participation by all countries which engage in international trade; 3) creation of an international currency dominated neither by one country nor by speculative movements; 4) a degree of automaticity in transfers of resources through reserve asset creation by the international community.

This would require creation of a new central international monetary authority. In the interim, the Arusha Initiative urged immediate transitional measures within the framework of the IMF:

a. The IMF should finance deficits arising as the natural consequence of serious, disciplined efforts at structural change, leaving sovereign states to choose their own social and economic models and development paths. The Arusha document characterized the IMF's quarterly performance tests, based on narrowly defined monetary variables, as "highly inappropriate to the conditions of a Third World country".
b. The IMF should more flexibly and automatically grant higher credit tranches to Third World countries for deficits attributable to factors for which they are in no way responsible, such as international inflation, weak and fluctuating export prices, low demand for their exports, deteriorating terms of trade and high interest rates.
c. The SDRs should become the principal reserve asset in international payments, reducing the role of (developed country) national currencies in international settlements.
d. A mechanism of appeal and international arbitration, independent of the IMF, should be set up to deal with disputes between the Fund and member countries applying for the use of Fund resources.
e. To finance Third World development deficits calls for massive transfers of resources beyond the capacity of the IMF. Industrialized countries, east and west, should accept the principle of redistributive taxation to mobilize the necessary funds (e.g. through an international tax on oil consumption in industrialized countries or a transfer of revenues from taxes levied by developed countries on items like tobacco[3] to the countries that exported them).

The Debt Crisis of the Early 1980s

By 1983, as international trade stagnated, increasing numbers of Third World countries hovered on the brink of defaulting on their mounting debts. As Table 14.2 shows (see p. 241) many countries in Africa had drawn heavily on the IMF over the years. Together, from 1980 to 1984, they almost tripled their entire previous drawings from the IMF. By the end of 1983, Third World countries held two-thirds of the total IMF credit. The African states' share of total drawings remained relatively small, but still provided the IMF with significant leverage to influence their policies. It is worth noting that South Africa's government had, by the end of 1983, obtained far more IMF assistance that any other African state except Zaire, having received about a sixth of total IMF credit to Africa.

Brazil's government, which had borrowed about US$5.2 billion from the IMF—about 7.9 per cent of the IMF's total reserves—declared a unilateral moratorium on the repayment of the principal on its international debt. The IMF hastily convened a meeting of transnational commercial bank representatives to obtain their help in providing Brazil and other big borrowers, including Mexico and Argentina, with the funds necessary to pay at least the interest on their debts. The IMF itself agreed to provide Brazil with resources totalling the equivalent of SDR4.9 billion. Under an extended arrangement in support of an agreed economic programme, Brazil could draw SDR4.2 billion—425 per cent of its quota—over the next three years. The remainder, the equivalent of Brazil's first credit tranche plus a drawing under the compensatory financing facility, was made available immediately, to cover the 8 per cent decline in Brazil's export earnings in 1982. Strikes and demonstrations throughout Brazil implied that the agreed economic programme imposed a heavy burden on the population.

The IMF worked closely with the major transnational banks to reach similar agreements with Mexico and Argentina. In 1984 and 1985, the Latin American nations met together to search for possible collective alternatives to accepting the IMF's conditions, but they failed to achieve the essential unity. Several African countries—like Zambia and Sudan—also accepted increasingly stringent IMF conditions in order to obtain its assistance in rescheduling the repayments on their foreign debts.

The major capitalist governments also agreed to help the IMF to play a greater role in staving off the apparent danger of a financial contraction comparable to the Great Depression of the 1930s. The finance ministers of the Group of Ten agreed at an emergency meeting in Paris to increase the General Arrangements to Borrow from SDR6.4 billion (roughly equivalent to US$7 billion) to SDR17 billion (US$19 billion) to prevent the IMF from running out of funds for assisting countries in trouble. The ministers also proposed to expand the IMF's general resources from SDR61 to SDR90 billion by raising the members' quotas. They also debated whether to expand the Special Drawing Rights, but could not agree. The US government opposed creation of new SDRs, arguing that this would boost the world money supply and fuel a new burst of inflation. As inflationary pressures appeared to recede in the face of world-wide recession, some US officials indicated they might alter their position. The proposed rescue operation, increasing the members' quotas, however, faced the opposition of the US Congress, which refused to provide additional funds to the IMF while reducing domestic social spending.

Optimists pointed to other factors which might reduce the pressures on developing countries. The central banks of the major capitalist countries began to reduce interest rates as inflationary pressures seemed less. In addition, in the early 1980s the value of the dollar declined, implying a reduction in debts denominated in the dollar; but in 1984 and 1985, the dollar's value soared to historically unprecedented heights.

Persistent stagnation of international trade, aggravated by the continued fluctuation of currency values, further weakened the position of many developing countries, including those in Africa. The transnational banks had become reluctant to make new loans without IMF support. Loans arranged by the IMF to bail out nations in difficulty could do little more than provide a breathing space in the hope that the world economy would revive.

Summary

The developed capitalist countries established the IMF after World War II to provide a flexible international medium of exchange. They sought to overcome the difficulties imposed by the more rigid gold standard of the past and re-establish the conditions viewed by mainstream economists as necessary to enable free international trade to flourish. Essentially, the IMF consists of a pool of funds on which member nations may draw to overcome temporary balance of payments deficits. IMF members vote on IMF policy, their votes being weighted according to their quota of the funds in the pool. The major capitalist countries control a majority of the votes.

As the international monetary crisis deepened, the IMF devised Special Drawing Rights to enable member nations to draw more funds to offset payments deficits. After the United States' devaluation of the dollar, the developed capitalist countries abandoned gold linked to the US dollar as the basis of the international medium of exchange. Unable to agree on an effective alternative, they allowed their currencies' exchange value to fluctuate.

Worsening terms of trade and increased balance of payments deficits made African and other Third World countries more reliant on foreign borrowing, both from the IMF and from transnational commercial banks. The IMF conditions for extending further loans, formulated along monetarist lines, however, aroused widespread objections. Third World countries, meeting in Arusha in Tanzania, favoured restructuring the IMF itself. Latin American nations called for, but failed to establish, the unity needed to achieve collective action to change IMF policy.

The IMF mobilized the transnational commercial banks and developed capitalist governments to provide additional funds to prevent the default of Third World debtor nations. Transnational banks expressed reluctance to make further loans for development purposes without still greater IMF support. The US government, pursuing monetarist principles, opposed IMF financial capacity and urged stricter IMF conditions for IMF assistance to Third World member states.

Notes

1. Otto Eckstein, "The Currency Roller Coaster", *Newsweek*, 31 Jan. 1983, p. 40.

2. South-North Conference on the International Monetary System and the New International Order, Arusha, Tanzania, 30 June-3 July 1980.

3. About $9 out of every $10 of total value of tobacco, the major export of Zimbabwe, is realized outside Zimbabwe by the transnational corporations that process and sell it and the foreign governments that impose high taxes on it. In a real sense, Third World farmers producing tobacco subsidize revenues to developed countries that buy it.

Exercises and Research

1. Analyse the main reasons for the changes in the features of the international medium of exchange up to World War II.
2. Explain how the IMF functions.
3. What theoretical principles underlay the initial establishment of the IMF and what consequences would their implementation have for development of the typical African economy?
4. Why and how did the 1971 devaluation of the US dollar affect the international monetary system?
5. In what sense and to what extent do SDRs represent a compromise in efforts to re-establish a more flexible, stable international medium of exchange?
6. What is the nature and purpose of the IMF's conditionality as it affects Third World countries? In the light of your knowledge of Third World countries' economies, evaluate a) the criticisms of the IMF conditions; b) the nature of the increased role of the IMF in the 1980s; c) the proposals for a new international monetary system.
7. Examine Table 14.2. What major changes can you discover in the pattern of IMF assistance in the last six years? How would you explain them?
8. Find out whether your country's government is a member of the IMF. If so, a) what is its quota and what percentage of the votes governing IMF decisions does it have? b) to what extent has it drawn on the IMF to offset balance of payments deficits? c) has an IMF team visited your country? If so what recommendations has it made? Has it proposed conditions for your government's further drawing on its funds? If it has, how would you evaluate these conditions?
9. Study the most recent *International Financial Statistics* (published monthly by the IMF) in your library. What changes have taken place in the Fund position of developing countries since 1983? How would you explain them?

Recommended Reading

(For annotations, see bibliography at the end of the book.)

Akinlan, *The Law of International Economic Institutions*
Alibar (ed.), *The Political Economics of Monetary Reform*

Allen and Kenen, *Asset Markets, Exchange Rates and Economic Integration*
Chachaoliades, *International Monetary Theory and Policy*
Cohen, *Organizing the World's Money*
Dean, *Plan Implementation in Nigeria*
DeVries, *The International Monetary Fund, 1966-1971*
Elliott, *Constraints on the Economic Development of Zambia*
Hanson and Marzouk, *Development and Economic Policy in the UAR*
Heller, *International Monetary Economics*
Henning, Pigott and Scott, *International Financial Management*
Hirsch, Doyle and Morse, *Alternatives to Monetary Disorder*
Hooker, *The Fund and China in the International Monetary System*
Hudson, *Money and Exchange Dealing in International Banking*
IBRD country reports
IMF, *International Capital Markets*
—— Surveys of African Economies
Issawi, *Egypt in Review*
Killick (ed.), *Adjustment and Financing in the Developing World*
Kindleberger and Lafargue, *Financial Crises*
Lees and Eng, *International Financial Markets*
Leipziger, *The International Monetary System and Developing Nations*
Lozoya and Bhattacharya, *The Financial Issues of the New International Economic Order*
Marcus, *Investment and Development Possibilities in Tropical Africa*
Martin and Smith, *Trade and Payments Adjustment*
Mikesell, *Foreign Exchange in the Postwar World*
Payer, *The Debt Trap*
Nsekela (ed.), *Southern Africa*
Seidman, *An Economics Textbook for Africa*
Swiderowski, *Exchange and Trade Controls*
Weisweiller, *Introduction to Foreign Exchange*

Periodicals

The Economist Intelligence Unit, *Quarterly Economic Reviews*
IMF Annual Reports
—— *International Financial Statistics*
IMF Survey
IMF and World Bank, *Finance & Development*

Chapter 15: Longer-Term International Finance

The Bretton Woods Conference participants expected the IMF to provide financial assistance to member governments to enable them to overcome balance of payments deficits and achieve international monetary stability. At the same time, they envisaged the need for an international lending agency to provide longer-term credit for reconstruction of economies ravaged by World War II and to help finance development. They therefore created the International Bank for Reconstruction and Development (IBRD), more popularly known as the World Bank. In addition, shortly after they attained independence, African states joined together to form their own African Development Bank (ADB), hoping to achieve greater self-reliance in the realm of finance.

This chapter describes the role of the IMF's "twin", the World Bank, and its affiliates, the International Development Association (IDA) and the International Finance Corporation (IFC). It also discusses briefly the ADB and its affiliated Fund.

The World Bank: The IMF's "Twin"

Structure and Functions

As in the IMF, each member nation's voting power in the World Bank is determined by its contribution to the bank's capital stock. By the early 1980s, five countries, with almost half the stock of the World Bank, cast almost half the votes governing its decisions (see Table 15.1). The relatively large holdings of the Federal Republic of Germany and Japan reflected their rapid post-war growth. African states combined, on the other hand, represent only a fraction of the remainder. As in the case of the IMF, no single African state, except South Africa, holds as much as 1 per cent of the stock.

The 20 executive directors of the World Bank operate in the Bank headquarters in Washington, DC, in the United States. The five largest stockholders appoint five of them. The rest are elected by region. The directors meet weekly to make policies. They must approve all loans. As the decade of the 1980s opened, A.W. Clausen, former head of the Bank of America, at the time the world's largest private commercial bank, became president of the World Bank.

Table 15.1
Major Shareholders of the World Bank, per cent of voting power (30 June 1983)

Country	*% of vote*
United States	19.20
United Kingdom	6.15
Germany, Federal Republic	5.97
Japan	5.94
France	5.03
China	4.09
India	4.01
Italy	3.22
Canada	3.47
Netherlands	2.65
Australia	2.24
Belgium	2.19
Top five countries	42.29
Top 12 countries	64.16

Source: World Bank, Annual Report, 1984.

Table 15.2
Source of Total World Bank Funds as of 1983-4

Source	*US$ billions*	*% of total*
1. Authorized capital, according to members' quotas, only 10% paid in, the remaining 90% constituting a guarantee for World Bank borrowing from commercial banks	51.0	80.7
2. Funds borrowed from commercial banks	9.7	15.4
3. Loan repayments	2.5	3.9
4. Sales of part of its loans to other investors, mainly commercial banks	0.001	0.001
Total	*63.201*	*100.00*

Source: Calculated from World Bank, Annual Report, 1984.

In addition to member nations' contributions, the World Bank borrows funds from the commercial banks to lend to member governments. From its birth in 1947 to 1977, the World Bank obtained funds from the sources shown in Table 15.2.

The World Bank's charter forbids it to compete with private enterprise including transnational commercial banks. The Bank's managers initially held that it should lend primarily to projects involving production for the world market, to ensure repayment. As African states began to attain independence in the 1960s, the Bank loaned them increasing amounts, primarily to build the infrastructure required by transnational corporations to extract raw materials. Once a private mining company decided to invest, the Bank frequently loaned funds to the relevant African government as part of the package. The government used the loans to finance the railways, ports, electricity generation plants and other infrastructure, while the mining firm financed the development of the mine they serviced.

For example, the World Bank loaned funds to the Federation of Rhodesia and Nyasaland to finance the Kariba hydroelectric power project, designed to produce electricity for the big mines owned by Anglo-American and American metal Climax in the Northern Rhodesian (now Zambian) Copperbelt, as well as the smaller mines and commercial farms of Southern Rhodesia (now Zimbabwe).[1] The World Bank agreed to help the Nkrumah government to finance the Volta Dam to provide electric power in Ghana only after the government had contracted with the Kaiser Aluminium Company to build an alumina smelter as the primary consumer of the project's electricity output.[2]

The Bank refused to finance projects proposed by African states if its experts did not consider them technically necessary. For example, the Bank, as well as the British and United States governments, rejected the Tanzanian and Zambian governments' request for funds to build the Tanzanian railroad to reduce Zambian dependence on South Africa and white-ruled Rhodesia. The Bank's authorities argued that Zambia already had adequate rail links through South Africa. Zambia and Tanzania finally contracted with the People's Republic of China to build the railway.

The World Bank also refused to finance construction of a tarmac road or railway from Botswana directly to Zambia to enable Botswana to ship copper, mined in Selebi-Phikwe, to Zambia's smelters. The Bank asserted that Botswana did not need the direct route to Zambia, as it already had links to South Africa and beyond where adequate smelting capacity existed. Ultimately, the Botswana Mining Company, a consortium of Anglo-American, American Metal Climax (AMAX), and the Botswana government, shipped the copper through South Africa to an AMAX smelter in Louisiana, USA, and thence to the West German buyer.

By the late 1960s, the World Bank had begun to finance more agricultural projects, including some involving small peasants. It tended to emphasize export agriculture, arguing that this ensured projects would earn the foreign exchange to finance loan repayments. For example, it financed small peasant tobacco farming in Malawi, and, through the Tanzania government bank for rural finance, helped fund ujamaa village export agricultural production. By the end of the 1970s, however, African states which had emphasized agricultural production for export confronted the necessity of importing food for their growing urban populations. The World Bank began to place more emphasis on financing staple food crops.

Like the IMF, the World Bank staff began to supervise the implementation of its lending programmes more strictly. By the late 1970s, the Bank began to make project loans in the light of their assessment of a country's total needs, capabilities and policies. The Bank sent teams to study a five-year programme of opportunities in a country requesting a loan, and reviewed that programme annually. Increasingly, it tended to condition its loans on a government's acceptance of its recommendations for overall programmes.

IDA: The World Bank's "Soft Loan Window"

By the 1970s, the World Bank had recognized that Third World countries required long-term loans at low interest rates. It established a "soft loan" affiliate, the International Development Association (IDA). The IDA made loans according to somewhat different criteria from those of the World Bank. Recipients had to be poor countries, with per capita annual incomes of less than US$520 in 1975 dollars, and with balance of payments difficulties making it unlikely that they could repay conventional loans. At the same time, they had to enjoy sufficient stability, as assessed by Bank experts, to ensure that they could repay long-term, low-interest loans. They should exhibit a genuine commitment to development, as defined by the Bank.

From its inception in 1964 to 1977, IDA obtained far less funds than the World Bank, primarily from the sources given in Table 15.3.

Table 15.3
Source of IDA Funds*

	Total from 1964 to 1977	
	US$ bill	*% of total*
1. Transfers from World Bank earnings	1.1	10.2
2. Capital subscribed in convertible currency by member countries	1.0	9.2
3. Contributions from richer IDA members	8.7	80.6
Total	*10.8*	*100.0*

*Twenty-six countries agreed to increase this amount by US$7.6 billion more by 1980; and in 1982 agreed to increase it by a further US$7 billion for 1983-4, despite the fact that ths US had reneged on its earlier pledge. Six of the countries declared, however, that the borrowers must use funds to buy goods from their respective countries.

From 1947 to 1984, the World Bank and the International Development Association, together loaned to African countries a total of US$50 billion, about 13 per cent of their total loans to all Third World countries. Table 15.4 shows the nine African countries which received the biggest loans during that 30-year period:

Table 15.4
The Ten African Countries which Received the Biggest Share of Combined World Bank and IDA Loans, 1947-1984

Country	*Amount Received (US$ millions)*	*Percentage of world total*
Egypt	3,468.2	2.6
Nigeria	2,609.2	1.9
Morocco	2,561.1	1.9
Kenya	1,864.2	1.4
Algeria	1,619.0	1.2
Tunisia	1,421.4	1.1
Ivory Coast	1,346.5	1.0
Tanzania	1,106.5	0.9
Sudan	1,038.9	0.8
Zambia	809.6	0.6
Sub-total	*17,844.2*	*13.4*

Source: World Bank, Annual Report, 1984.

Table 15.5
Combined World Bank and International Development Association loans, percentage distribution by sector, in Africa, 1947-1977

Sector	*World Bank (% of total)*	*International Development Association (% of total)*
Agriculture	18	32
Development Finance Corps.[a]	10	3
Education	3	6
Electric power	22	8
Industry	9	8
"Non-project"[b]	5	18
Population planning	0.3	1
Technical assistance	0.1	0.7
Telecommunications	2	4
Tourism	0.5	0.6
Transportation	25	20
Urban Development	1	1
Water and Sewage	3	3
Total[c]	100.0 = US$33 billion	100.00 = US$11 billion

[a] For loans to private and joint state private projects.
[b] Loans for general purposes, not projects, not otherwise listed.
[c] May not equal 100.0% due to rounding.

Both institutions loaned far more for economic infrastructural projects than for social projects. But the IDA loaned about 30 per cent of its funds, compared to the World Bank's 8 per cent, for social, as opposed to economic infrastructure.

After 1977, World Bank and IDA loans to sub-Saharan Africa grew rapidly, reflecting the growing economic crisis on the region. The two multilateral lending institutions' share of the region's total external debt did not grow, however, for African public and private sectors borrowed even more heavily from commercial sources.

Table 15.6
The Growth of World Bank and IDA Loans to Sub-Saharan Africa, 1970-1982 (in U.S. $ millions)

Source of loans	*1970*	*1975*	*1980*	*1982*
		(US $ millions)		
World Bank	590	1261	2549	3327
IDA	226	880	2573	3728
Total public and private debt	5419	14104	40643	48063
World Bank and IDA debt as % of total debt	15.1%	15.1%	12.6%	14.7%

Source: The World Bank, *Toward Sustained Development in Sub-Saharan Africa—A Joint Program of Action* (Washington D.C.: International Bank for Reconstruction and Development, 1984).

By the end of the 1970s, the IDA was making about 10 per cent of all World Bank loans, about a quarter of them to African countries. IDA loans mainly financed social infrastructure—schools, hospitals, water supplies—in accordance with the Bank's newly formulated "basic needs" doctrine. Lack of funds, however, limited the IDA's lending capacity. In the early 1980s, the US, caught up in its own stagflation, fell behind on its pledged contributions. By 1985, as part of its overall efforts to restrict all expenditures, except those for its growing military establishment, the US further reduced its contributions to the IDA.

The International Finance Corporation (IFC)

In the 1960s, the World Bank set up another affiliate, the IFC, to finance industrial projects in collaboration with private enterprise at commercial rates of interest. Since African countries remained relatively underindustrialized, they received only a tiny percentage of IFC loans.

After independence, Zimbabwe received the largest loan the IFC had made to date for the Hwange thermal plant (see pp. 207). The IFC agreed to lend US$200 million—equal to about half the foreign exchange required for the project and about a fifth of all IFC loans made to 119 countries in 1982. The IFC stipulated that all purchases for the plant must be open to international bid. As a result, a local Zimbabwean manufacturer, which would have used locally produced steel and employed local labour to make the three boilers required for the project, lost the bid to a British firm. Under the previous regime's import-substitution policy, the local manufacturer would automatically have received the contract. The IFC rule ignored the possible multiplier effects on Zimbabwean employment and incomes, as well as the foreign-exchange savings, of utilizing national production capacity and raw materials. Ironically, a South African affiliate of the British firm actually manufactured the boilers.

New World Bank Policies in the 1980s?

In 1981, the World Bank issued a report, *Accelerated Development in SubSaharan Africa,*[3] in response to a request made in 1979 by the African governors of the Bank for a review of the causes and possible cures of what they considered their economies' dim prospects. The report clearly implied that the Bank should only support governmental programmes which adopted its proposed *Agenda for Action*, and should persuade bilateral donors to do likewise. Subsequent comments by the World Bank president, Clausen, indicated his agreement that African states desiring further Bank assistance should restructure their economies along the lines recommended.

The report's proposed *Agenda* centred on several clusters of proposed actions generally recommended by more conservative mainstream economists.

First, African governments should expand their activities less rapidly, even in traditional public-sector areas, except to provide economic infrastructure to serve the private sector. Universal free access to basic services should, where possible, give way to user charges: for example, fees should be paid for health facilities and schooling. Private entrepreneurs should replace parastatal activity, especially in directly productive spheres of activity.

Second, African governments should seek not increased self-sufficiency but greater participation in international trade to provide market stimulation and price incentives to achieve greater efficiency. They should encourage increased exports of agricultural products to raise peasant earnings and foreign exchange; and of industrial commodities to diversify their exports. Governments should remove trade restrictions including import and foreign-exchange controls, which hinder increased integration into the world market on the basis of comparative advantage.

Third, African governments should train more middle- and high-level personnel and encourage more applied research. They should publish more financial reports and statistical data to facilitate monitoring of performance and preparation of new policies.

Fourth, governments should set priorities and articulate policies and programmes in a consistent manner, co-ordinating implementation and review.

Finally, donor countries should double concessional financial flows, linking them to the implementation of overall policies of structural reform of the kind outlined, rather than to particular projects.

Critics[4] viewed these proposals as part of the trend towards increasing pressure on African countries to conform with conditions along the lines of those already imposed by the IMF. Essentially, they rejected them on similar grounds.

First, rather than cut back on functions already at dangerously low levels from both economic and social points of view, most African states should raise more taxes and utilize their revenues more efficiently. Parastatals provided governments with the only available instruments for restructuring the national economy so as to achieve more balanced and integrated development.

Second, the report confuses African countries' need to expand exports to earn more foreign exchange with an emphasis on free trade comparative advantage arguments long shown to be unrealistic. Given the uncertainty of world markets and the impossibility of achieving balanced national agricultural and industrial growth in competition with increased transnational corporate imports, implementation of its recommendations would condemn African countries to perpetual specialization in raw-material exports and poverty.

Third, proposals that governments should increase training, research and data collection while obviously justifiable, seem to run counter to the argument that government should reduce spending on education.

Fourth, everyone agrees that governments should formulate and monitor priorities, but the report simply assumes, without proof—and in the face of considerable evidence to the contrary—that decreased government participation in the economy will facilitate attainment of these goals.

Finally, while all African governments would welcome increased concessional finance, donors seem unlikely to provide it. To tie future donor assistance to the report's *Agenda for Action*, given African experience to date, would render aid likely to undermine, rather than contribute to self-reliant development and higher living standards.

The African Development Bank (ADB)

Towards Self-Reliant Continental Financing

In 1967, after the independent African states established the Organization of African Unity, they sought to buttress their aspirations for self-reliant development by establishing the ADB. For the first decade, ADB sought to provide funds for African development uninfluenced by outside decision makers and so operated without non-African participation.

African states participated in the ADB by voting in accordance with their subscription to its capital, determined by their GDP. Nigeria, with 13.73 per cent of capital, exercised the largest vote. In contrast, the tiny state of Djibouti controlled only 0.35 per cent.

The ADB administration operates from its headquarters in the Ivory Coast. The board of governors, representing all the states, meets once a year to make policy. The board of directors, consisting of nine members elected by groups of states voting in accordance with their capital subscription, meets more frequently as required.

For the first decade, the ADB had few funds at its disposal. Although member states agreed to subscriptions totalling US$2.1 billion, they actually

Table 15.7
Summary of African Development Bank Group Activities (1973-1982) in millions of US$[a]

A) Funds loaned	*1973*	*1978*	*1982*	*Total, 1973-82*
Total number of group loans	16	75	77	613
Average group loan authorized	2.68	5.64	9.9	3872.42
Average amount disbursed	1.26	1.89	3.63	1294.85
Number of ADB loans each year	16	36	33	336
Average ADB loan authorized	2.68	5.71	12.09	2061.79
Average ADB loan disbursed	1.26	2.57	4.43	802.9
Number of ADF loans[b]		31	42	255
Average ADF loan authorized		6	8.52	1717.66
Average ADF loan disbursed		1.41	2.96	455.09
Number of Nigerian Trust Fund loans each year[c]		8	2	22
Average Nigerian Trust Fund loan authorized		3.96	4.3	99.86
Average Nigerian Trust Fund loan disbursed		0.67	4.68	36.86

B) Resources and Finance, 1982:	*US$ millions*
ADB:	
Authorized capital	5791.33
Subscribed capital	4264.14
Borrowing (gross)	1232.02
Outstanding debt	407.40
Reserves	136.75
Gross income	71.28
Net income	6.53
ADF:	
Subscriptions	1789.75
Other resources	87.31
NTF:	
Sources (gross)	202.17

[a] Conversion rates of UA for US$, 1967-1982:

1967-71	1UA = 1.00000 US$	1979	1UA = 1.31733 US$
1972	1UA = 1.08571 US$	1980	1UA = 1.27541 US$
1973-76	1UA = 1.20635 US$	1981	1UA = 1.16396 US$
1977	1UA = 1.21475 US$	1982	1UA = 1.10311 US$
1978	1UA = 1.30279 US$		

[b] Started functioning in 1974.
[c] Started functioning in 1976.

Source: African Development Bank, *Annual Report, 1982.*

paid in only US$340 million. The ADB borrowed US$880 million from other sources at varying rates of interest: Canada, Sweden and Australia loaned a tiny fraction, less than 2 per cent of the total, at 0 to 0.75 per cent interest;

Japan loaned about the same amount at 7.75 per cent interest. The ADB borrowed over half its funds on the Eurocurrency market at 15 to 19 per cent interest rates (it did not report all the rates it paid, presumably because they fluctuated with LIBOR). It issued bonds with a 7.75 to 8.75 per cent fixed rate of interest to obtain another third of its funds. It borrowed the remainder of the funds at 6.6 to 8.9 per cent fixed rates of interest.

Since the ADB had to charge its borrowers rates of interest sufficient to cover the rates it had to pay for these funds, soft loans could only account for a small fraction of the total volume of credit it made available.

The ADB, like the World Bank, made most of its loans for economic infrastructure. However, it loaned a significantly higher and growing proportion (a quarter of the total in 1981) to industrial development banks. Presumably, this reflected the African states' determination to participate directly in productive activities in the context of their efforts to restructure their economies.

The ADB loaned relatively small amounts, an average of 10 million Units of Account (UA-see note to Table 15.7) per country. In 1981, it loaned UA277 million for 35 projects in 24 African states. It usually lends in co-operation with other funding agencies, helping the African state to obtain the other funds, so as not to take the entire risk itself. The average project in which the ADB invested in 1981 cost UA18.82 million.

Table 15.8
African Development Bank Loans, per cent distribution by sector, 1978, 1980 and 1981.

Sector	*1978(%)*	*1980(%)*	*1982(%)*
Agriculture	13.8	10.27	25.5
Transport	25.7	23.76	16.9
Public Utilities	39.5	24.93	30.6
Industrial and Development Banks	20.6	37.6	21.1
Education and Health	0.3	3.44	5.8
Total	*100.0% = UA157 millions*	*100.0% = UA233 millions*	*100.0% = UA361 millions*

* For the annual value of the Unit of Account (UA) see Table 15.7.

Source: African Development Bank *Annual Report*, 1982.

Some examples of its 1981 loans illustrate the ADB's lending pattern. See Table 15.8 for distribution of loans by sector, and Table 15.9 for regional distribution. It loaned Botswana UA7.2 million for 16 years, with a five-year grace period, to help cover the UA23.93 million cost of arable land development. The African Development Fund (ADF) and the International Fund for African Development (IFAD) co-financed the project. The ADB loan financed

Table 15.9
Regional Distribution of ADB Loans, 1978-82 (in Millions of UA)

Country	*1978*	%	*1979*	%	*1980*	%	*1981*	%	*1982*	%
Central Africa	43.90	27.80	42.20	20.30	48.20	20.71	45.50	16.40	108.09	29.88
Angola	—		—		—		—		—	
Burundi	—		—		10.00		6.40		24.00	
Cameroon	—		5.95		15.40		—		33.33	
CAR	—		—		—		10.00		4.17	
Chad	—		—		—		—		—	
Congo	10.00		14.30		10.00		—		26.59	
Equat. Guinea	6.60		0.50		—		—		—	
Gabon	10.00		10.00		5.30		9.10		—	
Rwanda	3.30		—		—		—		—	
S.T. & Princ.	—		—		—		—		—	
Zaire	14.00		11.45		7.50		20.00		20.00	
East Africa	30.80	19.50	79.50	38.24	102.03	43.84	107.62	38.78	125.20	34.61
Botswana	0.65		8.00		10.00		17.20		25.00	
Comoros	—		—		—		10.00		—	
Djibouti	—		—		—		—		—	
Ethiopia	—		6.50		—		—		10.00	
Kenya	5.00		13.00		15.30		9.00		—	
Lesotho	—		8.00		8.73		—		—	
Madagascar	—		5.00		—		—		—	
Malawi	—		—		—		—		20.00	
Mauritius	1.60		8.00		—		10.00		3.00	
Mozambique	5.00		8.00		—		27.50		9.80	
Seychelles	3.75		—		—		—		1.10	
Somalia	—		—		—		—		—	
Swaziland	—		—		11.50		13.12		—	
Tanzania	—		15.00		14.50		5.00		—	
Uganda	5.00		—		30.00		7.80		15.00	
Zambia	9.80		8.00		12.00		8.00		10.00	
Zimbabwe	—		—		—		—		21.30	
Multinational	—		—		—		—		10.00	

Country	*1978*	*%*	*1979*	*%*	*1980*	*%*	*1981*	*%*	*1982*	*%*
North Africa	34.60	21.91	44.60	21.45	30.00	12.89	77.10	27.78	68.46	18.93
Algeria[a]	5.00		—		—		—		—	
Egypt	—		8.00		20.00		20.00		—	
Libya[b]	—		—		—		—		—	
Mauritania	5.00		5.00		—		—		14.86	
Morocco	15.00		15.60		—		30.00		10.00	
Sudan	4.60		—		—		7.10		—	
Tunisia	5.00		16.00		10.00		20.00		43.60	
West Africa	48.62	30.79	41.60	20.01	52.50	22.56	47.28	17.04	59.95	16.57
Benin	5.00		—		—		2.50		—	
Cape Verde	—		—		10.00		—		—	
Gambia	—		8.90		—		—		7.00	
Ghana	9.77		8.00		—		10.00		—	
Guinea	5.00		—		—		5.28		—	
Guinea Bissau	1.01		—		—		10.00		—	
Ivory Coast	8.40		8.00		8.00		—		10.00	
Liberia	4.20		6.20		—		13.00		17.40	
Mali	—		—		—		—		—	
Niger	—		4.35		7.00		—		8.00	
Nigeria[c]	—		—		—		—		—	
Senegal	—		6.15		24.00		—		—	
Sierra Leone	1.40		—		—		2.50		—	
Togo	2.00		—		3.50		—		—	
Upper Volta	—		—		—		4.00		—	
Multinational	11.84		—		—		—		17.55	
Total	*157.92*	*100.00*	*207.90*	*100.00*	*232.73*	*100.00*	*277.50*	*100.00*	*361.70*	*100.00*

[a]Algeria stopped borrowing in 1978.
[b]Libya has never borrowed from the Bank.
[c]Nigeria stopped borrowing in 1974.

Source: African Development Bank/Fund, *Annual Report, 1982.*

a third of the foreign-exchange cost, and a quarter of the local cost.

The ADB loaned Mozambique UA7.5 million for 20 years, with a five-year grace period, to finance part of a UA19.45 million Zambezi Valley rural development project. Co-financed by the ADB, this involved resettling 12,500 families in 50 villages and helping them grow cotton and foodstuffs. The ADB loan covered half the foreign-exchange cost and a fifth of the local expenditures.

In Swaziland, the ADB loaned the government UA5.3 million for 20 years, with a five-year grace period, to finance half the cost of a tarmac road through the lowveld sugar area to Mozambique. The Swedish International Development Association financed the other half of the cost. The ADB provided two-thirds of the required foreign exchange.

In Tanzania, the ADB provided UA5 million for 13 years with a three-year grace period to enable the Tanzania Investment Bank to finance the foreign-exchange requirements of small industries using local raw materials for the domestic and export markets.

Using funds obtained from several developed countries, the ADB provided some technical assistance, particularly for feasibility studies. By the end of 1981, it had spent UA29 million on 69 completed studies, 45 of which had led to projects partially financed by the ADB group.

Although it played a key role in financing particular projects like these, lack of funds rendered marginal its contribution to continental development. From 1967 to 1978, its loans totalled only US$1.38 billion, about 5 per cent of the outstanding public and private external debt of Sub-Saharan Africa.

The ADF and non-African Participation

By the early 1970s, a number of African states had begun to call for non-African state participation in the ADB in the hope of increasing its lending capacity. In 1974 the ADB, with the assistance of non-African countries, created the ADF. By 1981, the ADF had involved 23 non-African countries in providing finance for African projects. Several more countries, including India, Portugal and the Philippines, expressed interest in joining. The African Development Bank with 1.8 per cent of the ADF's capital, retained control over half the votes of its board of directors. The non-African states exercised the other half in accord with their capital subscription (see Table 15.10).

The ADF's primary sources of finance included subscriptions from participating states (FUA216 million in 1981) and net income from loans and investments (FUA25 million 1981). In 1981, the FUA (Fund Unit of Account, which differed slightly from the ADB's UA) was worth US$1.07.

The African Development Fund (ADF) expanded its loans rapidly to reach a total of FUA480 million in 1978, more than triple the African Development Bank's (ADB) loans that year, and FUA1,190 million, roughly four times total ADB credit, in 1981. The ADF loaned a smaller proportion of its funds than did the ADB to industrial and development banks, and much larger amounts to agriculture, education and health. (See Table 15.11 for distribution of ADF loans by country.)

In 1981, the ADF financed 36 projects in 26 states, primarily low-income

Table 15.10
The Capital Subscription and Votes of the African Development Bank and the Largest and Smallest Non-African States in the Board of Governors of the African Development Fund 1981

Subscriber	*Percentage of Capital Subscribed*	*Percentage of Total Vote*
African Development Bank	1.8	50.0
Biggest Non-African:		
Japan	15.2	6.89
United States	13.4	4.95
Smallest Non-African:		
Argentina	0.17	0.09
United Arab Emirates	0.7	0.42
Yugoslavia	1.0	0.56

countries. Three-quarters of the borrowing countries had per capita incomes of less than US$280 in 1976. The loans averaged FUA8.8 million. For example, Zambia received FUA8 million to finance the foreign-exchange cost of six sewage treatment units, costing a total of FUA14.42 million, in the mining town of Ndola. Botswana received an FUA8 million loan to cover the foreign-exchange cost and a third of the local costs of a secondary teacher training college. Malawi received an FUA8 million loan to cover the foreign-exchange component and two-thirds of the local costs of a rural health project.

The combined loans of the African Development Bank (ADB) and the African Development Fund (ADF) reached US$3.1 billion in 1981. But, due to the international economic crisis, African government's borrowing from other sources had grown as rapidly. The combined ADB-ADF contribution remained only about 5 per cent of total sub-Saharan African debt.

Non-African States Join the African Development Bank

In 1982, after several years of debate, the ADB governors agreed to invite non-African participation in the hopes of obtaining more funds. Over 20 foreign states had indicated an interest in joining. The African Development Bank's (ADB) governors formulated several principles in an effort to ensure continued African control: 1) the ADB's president would always be an African; 2) the the ADB would only make loans to African countries; 3) African states would retain two-thirds of the total vote, and all decisions would be made by a 50 per cent majority (thus, external participating states could not exercise a veto over proposed loans); 4) of the ADB's 18-member board, 12 must always be Africans; 5) where possible, the ADB's governors would only meet in Africa. On this basis, the governors arranged the participation of non-African states. The consequences of these arrangements, as they take place in the next few years, will require further analysis.

Table 15.11
African Development Fund Summary Statement of Approved Loans as at 31 December 1982 (Expressed in Units of Account)

Country	*Number of Loans*	*Amount Approved Less Cancellations UA*	*Unsigned Loans UA*	*Loans Signed UA*	*Amount Disbursed UA*	*Repayments UA*	*Outstanding Balance UA*
Benin	11	59,811,000	21,000,000	38,811,000	17,066,671	120,000	16,946,671
Botswana	5	24,550,000	—	24,550,000	7,501,417	46,260	7,455,157
Burundi	9	54,070,000	—	54,070,000	14,336,895	48,576	14,288,319
Cameroon	2	15,500,000	8,000,000	7,500,000	—	—	—
Cape Verde	5	20,350,000	—	20,350,000	1,332,697	—	1,332,697
Central African Republic	8	43,260,000	8,800,000	34,460,000	18,914,329	—	18,914,329
Chad	7	41,140,000	—	41,140,000	15,226,618	1,544,573	13,682,045
Comoros	7	44,300,000	17,750,000	26,550,000	5,364,021	—	5,364,021
Congo	1	8,000,000	—	8,000,000	920,604	—	920,604
Djibouti	1	2,600,000	—	2,600,000	157,346	—	157,346
Egypt	6	48,000,000	8,000,000	40,000,000	10,203,325	—	10,203,325
Ethiopia	12	97,200,000	23,000,000	74,200,000	26,933,767	—	26,933,767
Gambia	5	27,600,000	—	27,600,000	1,396,131	—	1,396,131
Ghana	1	8,000,000	—	8,000,000	3,844,614	—	3,844,614
Guinea	5	33,200,000	14,500,000	18,700,000	4,398,870	—	4,398,870
Guinea Bissau	6	33,000,000	8,000,000	25,000,000	10,583,832	861,136	9,722,696
Guinea Equitarial	1	7,600,000	—	7,600,000	76,883	—	76,883
Kenya	4	42,500,000	27,000,000	15,500,000	952,172	—	952,172
Lesotho	9	47,527,358	9,520,000	38,007,358	19,731,562	676,258	19,055,304
Liberia	1	9,000,000	—	9,000,000	—	—	—
Madagascar	6	44,470,000	—	44,470,000	12,159,694	—	12,159,694
Malawi	8	45,399,655	—	45,399,655	24,586,408	119,862	24,466,546
Mali	15	85,710,000	—	85,710,000	36,430,350	2,658,212	33,772,138
Mauritania	9	29,250,000	2,770,000	26,480,000	12,602,942	28,374	12,574,568

Country	*Number of Loans*	*Amount Approved Less Cancellations UA*	*Unsigned Loans UA*	*Loans Signed UA*	*Amount Disbursed UA*	*Repayments UA*	*Outstanding Balance UA*
Mauritius	1	3,700,000	—	3,700,000	2,722,230	—	2,722,230
Mozambique	9	63,700,000	—	63,700,000	12,321,777	23,599	12,298,218
Niger	6	34,342,000	10,207,000	24,135,000	9,355,392	1,995,066	7,360,326
Rwanda	13	64,820,000	—	64,820,000	19,784,724	263,962	19,520,762
Sao Tome and Principe	1	7,800,000	—	7,800,000	4,411,000	—	4,411,000
Senegal	5	25,200,000	13,030,000	12,170,000	6,114,772	—	6,114,772
Seychelles	2	10,500,000	—	10,500,000	2,490,059	—	2,490,059
Sierra Leone	6	32,550,000	—	32,550,000	6,557,263	—	6,557,263
Somalia	11	55,750,000	3,200,000	52,550,000	14,253,548	51,536	14,202,012
Sudan	7	43,621,719	—	43,621,719	6,272,241	—	6,272,241
Swaziland	2	8,305,662	—	8,305,662	3,310,651	234,556	3,076,095
Tanzania	11	63,135,000	21,535,000	41,600,000	22,776,784	—	22,776,784
Togo	8	47,950,000	16,500,000	31,450,000	19,912,103	88,268	19,823,835
Uganda	1	8,000,000	—	8,000,000	4,259,867	—	4,259,867
Upper Volta	9	51,400,000	10,000,000	41,400,000	24,350,043	1,533,102	22,816,941
Zaire	7	46,800,000	20,700,000	26,100,000	2,635,019	—	2,635,019
Zambia	6	41,600,000	—	41,600,000	2,262,616	—	2,262,616
Zimbabwe	3	16,000,000	8,000,000	8,000,000	—	—	—
Multinational	4	23,020,000	—	23,020,000	2,653,552	—	2,653,552
Total	*256*	*1,520,232,394*	*251,512,000*	*1,268,720,394*	*411,164,789*	*10,293,300*	*400,871,489*

Source: African Development Bank/Fund, *Annual Report, 1984.*

Summary

The World Bank, established at Bretton Woods at the same time as the IMF, lends long-term investment capital from funds provided by member nations and loans from transnational commercial banks. Its charter forbids it to compete with private enterprise. Its board of governors and directors vote in proportion to the funds subscribed by the member states, so, as in the IMF, the votes of the major capitalist states which provide most of the funds shape its policies. In Africa, it lends funds primarily to finance economic infrastructure to facilitate transnational corporate mining ventures and agricultural projects. In the 1960s, the World Bank opened its 'soft loan window', the IDA which provides about 10 per cent of its total loans and about a quarter of those it makes in Africa. The World Bank also established an affiliate, the IFC, to finance industrial projects at commercial rates of interest in collaboration with private enterprise.

In the early 1980s, the World Bank published an Agenda for Action which essentially recommended that African countries seeking funds should restructure their economies along the lines recommended by the IMF. Critics objected that aid given under those conditions would probably hinder self-reliant development and higher living standards.

In an effort to finance their own development after they gained independence, African countries joined together to create the ADB. The amount of funds the ADB alone could muster, however, contributed only marginally to the African nations' expanded borrowing. By the early 1980s, in the hopes of obtaining more funds, the African member states agreed to permit non-African nations to participate. They retained for themselves a voting majority in the bank's decision-making structures. Ongoing evaluation will be needed to determine the consequences of admitting non-African participants.

Notes

1. The Federation government constructed the plant on the Southern Rhodesian side of the Kariba, which gave the Smith regime control over it when Zambia proclaimed independence; as a result, the Zambian government had to finance construction of the Kafue Dam to ensure continued supplies of electricity while reducing dependence on the Smith regime.

2. The Ghana government financed the Tema port and township, as well as its share of the Volta project; combined, these constituted a major share of the heavy post-independence capital spending that contributed to the economic crisis the country confronted when world cocoa prices plummeted in the mid-1960s. The contract with Kaiser, which the Bank required the Ghana government to accept before it would agree to the loan, ensured that Kaiser could purchase Volta electricity at one of the lowest rates in the world, about a third of the price charged to Ghanaian consumers.

3. The main author, Elliott Berg, essentially adopted the conventional

mainstream view that African states must encourage foreign investment to expand exports; for a detailed critique, see *IDS Review,* Sussex, 1981.

4. For example *IDS Review*, Sussex, 1981.

Exercises and Research

1. Analyse the features of the World Bank in terms of their implications for the African countries: a) How is it run? b) What are the main sources of its funds? c) For what kinds of projects does the World Bank generally provide loans?
2. Compare the International Development Association (IDA) to the World Bank in terms of the features identified in Exercise 1.
3. What is the role of the International Finance Corporation (IFC)?
4. Evaluate the changes proposed for World Bank policies in the 1980s in terms of their implications for African economies.
5. Compare the African Development Bank (ADB) to the World Bank and its affiliates in terms of the features identified in Exercise 1. What do you think will be the consequences of increased non-African governments' participation in the African Development Bank? Give your reasons.
6. Find out whether your government is a member of the World Bank. If so:
   a) What percentage of the vote does your government exercise in determining policies of the World Bank?
   b) Has your government borrowed funds from the World Bank or its affiliates? If so, how much and on what terms? What kinds of projects has it used World Bank funds to finance?
   c) What percentage of total foreign loans has your government obtained from the World Bank?
   d) Has a World Bank team written a report on your country's economy? If possible, obtain a copy and evaluate it.
7. a) Obtain a copy of the latest ADB annual report. Has it made significant changes in its lending policies since non-members began to participate in providing funds? If so, what are their implications for African countries' development?
   b) Has your country obtained any loans from the ADB? If so, evaluate the projects financed and the terms on which the loans were obtained in comparison with loans obtained, if any, from the World Bank or its affiliates.

Recommended Reading

(For annotations, see bibliography at the end of the book.)

Ayer, *Banking on the Poor*
Bailey, *Africa's Industrial Future*
Brown and Cummings, *The Lagos Plan vs. the Berg Report*
Chibwe, *Arab Dollars for Africa*
Declaration of Tripoli
Fordwar, *The African Development Bank*
Gardiner and Picket, *The African Development Bank*
Hirsch, Doyle and Morse, *Alternatives to Monetary Disorder*
IBRD, *Accelerated Development in Sub-Saharan Africa: an Agenda for Action*
—— Country reports
Leipziger, *The International Monetary System and Developing Nations*
Nsekela (ed.), *Southern Africa*
Payer, *The World Bank*
Reuber, *et al.*, *Private Foreign Investment in Development*
Saksena, *Regional Development Banking*
Seidman, *An Economics Textbook for Africa*
Wood and Byrne, *International Business Finance*

Periodicals

The Economist Intelligence Unit, *Quarterly Economic Reviews*
ADB, *Annual Reports*
IBRD, *Annual Reports*
IMF World Bank, *Finance & Development*
Review of African Political Economy

Chapter 16: The Theory of Socialist Monetary Relations

Introduction: The Transition to Socialism

On attaining independence, many African governments proclaimed socialist goals, often claiming to support a special African form of socialism. In reality, however, particularly in the realms of money and finance, they frequently implemented measures informed by one or another variant of mainstream theory. The evidence suggests that they failed to restructure their inherited institutions. The crisis of the 1980s exposed their economies as vulnerable to international pressures, unable to satisfy even the basic needs of the majority of their populations.

Marxist theorists hold that only social ownership of the means of production can resolve the fundamental contradictions inherent in capitalism (see Chapter 2), contradictions which have inevitably culminated in general crisis. During the transition to socialism, they propose a very different role for monetary institutions and public finance from that recommended by mainstream economists. They base their arguments on their qualitatively different explanations of the historical development of capitalism.

Few textbooks written in English present either the debates concerning the role of monetary and financial institutions or evidence concerning the actual changes in their structures and mode of operation during the transition to socialism. This chapter outlines the evolution of Marxist theory as a guide for shaping monetary and financial institutions to help effect the transition. The following chapters briefly summarize some of the available evidence to show how socialist countries have altered banking and financial institutions in their efforts to build socialism.

No African state has yet successfully effected the transition to socialism. Socialist-orientated theorists argue about the reasons. Some claim that the low level of the productive forces inevitably inhibits efforts to build socialism; those interested in progress can initially do no more than attempt to identify and implement progressive institutional changes to modify state capitalism to foster increased productivity and small improvements in living standards. Only after the means of production develop further, imposing the necessity for social organization and increased social consciousness, will the workers and peasants be able to carry through a socialist transformation. Others maintain that more effective mobilization of an alliance between workers and peasants, accompanied by more appropriate changes in the inherited institutional structure, could take advantage of existing political and economic conditions to hasten the transition.

Whatever the reasons, no African state has as yet successfully effected the transition to socialism. Therefore, the remaining chapters of Part IV draw primarily on evidence from the more advanced socialist countries of Europe and Asia. This in no way implies that Africans can or should attempt to reproduce these experiences wholesale in their own countries. It serves only to indicate the possibilities and some of the difficulties encountered in reshaping monetary and financial institutions elsewhere.

Capitalist Socialization of the Means of Production

Marxists hold that an ongoing process of socialization of the privately owned means of production has characterized the maturation of capitalism from pre-monopoly through monopoly to a state monopoly stage. The evolving division of labour required to develop productive capacity could only take place in an increasingly socialized form: growing numbers of people work together, using more and more complex equipment, under increasingly co-ordinated management. This inevitably leads to the concentration of capital and the deepening of the social relationships of labour, creating closer linkages throughout the entire economy. It requires new forms of planned, centralized administration.

Under the conditions of private ownership characteristic of capitalism, this ongoing process of socializing the means of production has inevitably led to new contradictions which the capitalist state has had to resolve. In the stage of state monopoly capitalism the state has sought to reconcile these contradictions through intensified state regulation of the entire system. The ideology of private ownership and its predominance in all spheres, however, has restricted the capitalist state to intervening primarily through the financial system (control of the money supply through the banks; taxation and the budget; and price fixing). The debates between Keynesians and monetarists centre on the extent and kinds of measures the capitalist state should adopt in these areas. Marxists hold that in the long run, monopoly state capitalist regulation, whatever form it takes, inevitably aggravates the underlying contradictions which have culminated in the general crisis of the capitalist system.

The Transition to Social Ownership

Marxists conclude that only social ownership of the means of production can resolve the contradictions which inevitably arise from the private monopolistic ownership of increasingly socialized productive forces. Once it has taken power, the socialist political leadership must continually strengthen the participation of the workers and poor peasants, restructuring the entire state machinery to ensure that it represents their interests. The state must then employ the new institutions to shape a new mode of production, ensuring a growing accord between the social relations to the means of production and the production process itself. It must create the objective conditions in which production takes place, not to amass profit for a handful of private owners, but to meet the material and social needs of the working masses. Socialist governments, therefore, focus on implementing long-term plans to ensure production of the essential goods and services—the appropriate use values—to fulfil those basic needs. To achieve these goals, the government must restructure the whole set of inherited monetary and financial institutions to ensure the realization of closer and more direct relationships between the different kinds of physical use values.

The Initial Stage: State Capitalism

As an initial step in the transition to socialism the political leadership must establish a particular kind of state capitalism. The state, representing an alliance of workers and poor and middle-level peasants, must exert effective control over the economic "commanding heights"—banks, foreign and wholesale trade, and basic industries—leaving only the less significant sectors in private hands. In any particular country, the key question is whether over time the state perpetuates capitalist relations to the means of production; or, representing the workers and peasants, carries through the transition to fully socially owned means of production. This depends largely on the degree of commitment of the ruling party or coalition of parties to reshaping the inherited governing institutions and building a fully socialized political economy. This presupposes the effective restructuring of the party and state to ensure the representation and full participation of the closely allied working class and poor peasants.

No sub-Saharan African government has succeeded in progressing far beyond the initial stage of state capitalist intervention in the national economy.[1] True, the gross underdevelopment and distorted features of their externally dependent inherited economies have inevitably hindered the transition. Difficulties in building a firm alliance between the truncated proletariat and the scattered, impoverished peasants have hampered the consolidation of the political leadership required to create a truly socialist-orientated state. But far too often, the new administrative élite has wielded its enhanced state power to develop into a powerful bureaucratic bourgeoisie. Instead of restructuring the inherited institutions, it has accumulated wealth and privilege by buying large farms, accepting percentages on state contracts, and becoming well-paid directors of transnational corporate affiliates.

State acquisition of all or a majority of the shares of equity capital in firms controlling the "commanding heights", including the banks and financial institutions, does not in itself guarantee that a government will take the next steps towards socialism. Nationalized banks, for example, may simply provide relatively low-cost credit for national capitalists or transnational corporate managers to invest in the more profitable projects that perpetuate external dependence. Other state-owned financial institutions—insurance schemes, pension funds, housing programmes—may simply serve to mobilize domestically generated investable surpluses to finance import-substitution industries, high-rise office buildings and hotels, and the enlarged bureaucracy.

These only marginally alter the inherited growth pattern, still geared to the export of raw materials and the import of manufactured goods.

No Blueprints

To carry through the transition to socialism, the political leadership, consolidated around the unity of the workers and peasants, would have to restructure state-owned institutions to implement and monitor plans incorporating a long-term industrial strategy. That strategy should ensure a steady increase in productivity and rising living standards in every sector. Ultimately, it should lead to a more balanced, integrated and self-reliant economy.

That Marxists generally agree on the need to socialize the ownership of the means of production to resolve the contradictions inherent in capitalism does not, however, mean that they have a blueprint for building socialism. On the contrary, they engage in innumerable debates at every stage of the process and at every level of government about the best ways not only to implement particular plans but to build socialism itself.

The outcome of these debates varies from one socialist country to another. As more and more countries have embarked on "the" socialist path, it has become increasingly clear that not one, but a multitude of paths exist. This is not to suggest that historical materialist theory, based on its explanation of the inherent contradictions of capitalism, fails to offer common principles to guide the building of socialism. Most Marxists generally agree on those common principles. But in different countries and at different times, the political leadership has made the changes suggested by those principles in different ways. At least two factors help to explain these differences. Each country inherits different objective conditions, class forces and contradictory tendencies which its political leaders and planners must understand and take into consideration when formulating and adopting specific measures to establish socialism. Then the steps taken in any one country to resolve one set of problems may give rise to further contradictions, leading to further debates as to their causes and the best possible solutions.

Unfortunately, most countries that have embarked on building socialism do not publish their arguments in English and so English-speaking readers have relatively little opportunity to study the original debates, especially those relating to money and finance. Part 10 of this book aims primarily to clarify the issues debated by socialist economists seeking to reshape monetary and financial institutions so as to achieve socialism. In doing so, as noted in the Introduction, it has had to draw mainly on the experiences of countries where adequate information on these issues is published in English. Unfortunately, this has meant leaving out the experiences of less developed countries.

This chapter outlines Marxist theory on how financial institutions should be restructured to implement socialist plans. It first summarizes the theory of socialism as a transitional stage on the way to communism; it then sketches the initial debate over the role of money in that transition; and it finally outlines the monetary and financial principles required to effect the process of building socialism.

Socialism as a Transition

Communism as a Higher Stage

Marxists view socialism as a transitional phase before the higher stage of socio-economic development, communism. Only communism, Marx held, could eliminate the basic antagonisms inherent in previous class societies, enabling women, men and children to co-operate to realize their full potential as human beings. But Marx never discussed either socialism or communism in great detail. He concentrated his major research and writing on capital, seeking to reveal the nature and causes of the contradictions in capitalism that would lead the masses to strive to build some form of socialism and ultimately communism. In a sense, he proposed socialism and the ultimate form of communism essentially as ideals capable of eliminating the fundamental contradictions arising out of capitalist exploitation. Inevitably, the process of building these new societies in the real world encounter contradictions which must be analysed and resolved by the historical materialist method.

"From Each according to his or her Ability, to Each according to Work Done"

In his *Critique of the Gotha Programme*, Marx sketched out some ideas relating to the socialist transition. No government could simply eliminate overnight the inequality and contradictions inherited from capitalism. The transition would inevitably take time, even decades, for three reasons.

First, the inherited productive forces could not produce enough commodities to provide everybody in the country with all the goods he or she might like to have. Socialist political economies, even after the elimination of exploitation of man by man in the form of the private extraction of surplus value, would have to devise some form of rationing scarce goods.

Secondly, the inherited form of technology developed under capitalism—involving fragmented, monotonous tasks for the great majority of workers—inevitably led to alienation. Capitalist managers, seeking to maximize efficiency and profit, made no effort to involve the workers' creativity in the process. Over time, new technologies as well as institutional reform would need to increase worker participation in the productive process, gradually eliminating the gap between mental and manual labour.

Third, capitalist ideology would not disappear overnight, despite the increasingly socialized ownership of the means of production. The conditions of capitalism had taught men and women, over centuries, to strive for personal gain. Re-education to transform people into socialist citizens, willing to share on the basis of need, would take time. During that transition period, incentives—payments according to work done—remained an important stimulus to increase productivity to reach the levels of output required to pay everyone according to need.

These arguments buttress the attempt, common in socialist countries, to distribute income on the principle *from each according to his or her ability; to each according to work done*. Over time, the socialist economy's productive forces will improve, creating conditions for distributing more and more goods and services on the basis of need. Diagram 16.1 illustrates how, as rising planned investment (A) leads to increases in GDP, the society can provide more and more social services (B) to all according to their needs: more educational opportunities, more health services and more cultural and recreational facilities.

Figure 16.1
The planned Growth and Distribution of Production

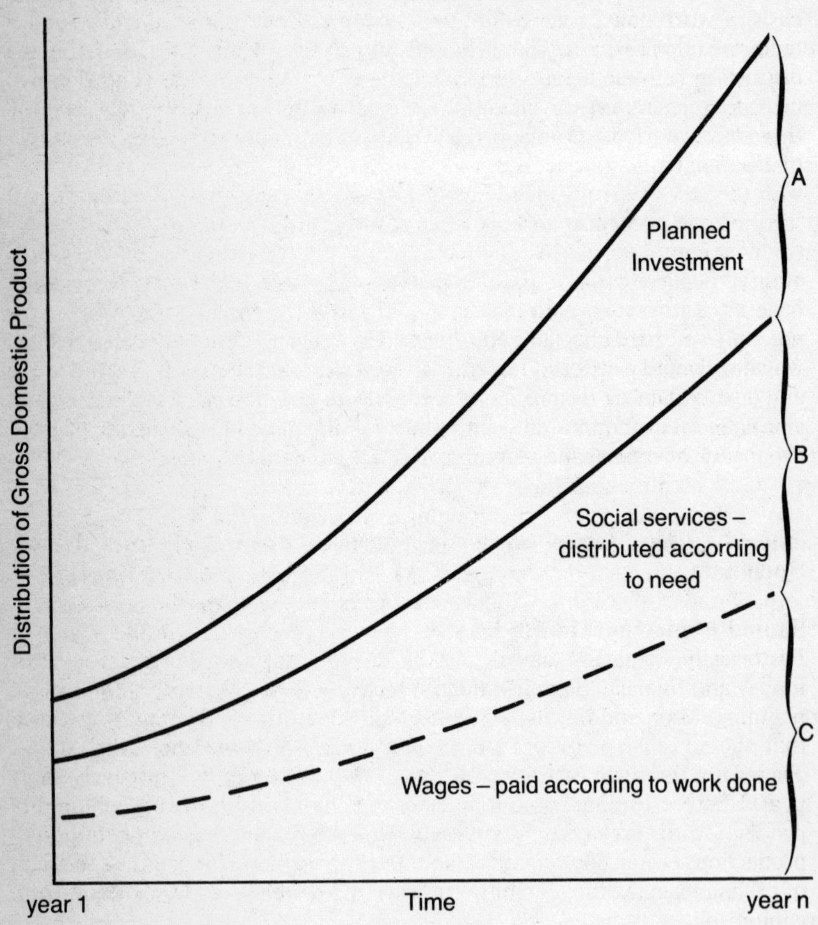

"From Each according to Ability; to Each according to Need"

At the same time, people will gradually learn new ways of sharing, of evaluating their own roles, not solely in terms of personal gain, but in terms of satisfaction with increased collective welfare from which all will benefit. The status of women will improve as growing employment opportunities draw them as equals into the increasingly socialized labour force. The improved productive force will gradually remove from the family sector much of the household drudgery imposed on women by the past social division of labour. Over time, the production of more goods and services provided on the basis of need, will reduce the significance of differential wages (C), paid on the basis of work done. Science and technology will increase productive forces, replacing unpleasant unskilled work by automation, gradually eliminating the distinction between mental and manual labour. New forms of education will help new generations of men and women to discover the personal benefits they may gain from co-operative activity. They will realize the advantages of ensuring that everyone receives a share of the growing output in accordance with the new principle underlying the more advanced stage of communism: "From each according to ability; to each according to need."

Under communism, then, human relationships will turn, not on a person's ability to make money, to obtain exchange value, to maximize personal benefits. Rather, the rapid growth of planned productive capacity will foster, not only improved social welfare, but also expanded human relationships which will enable every child, woman and man to realize her or his full value and dignity. During the prolonged transition to and through socialism, money and financial institutions must also change in order to contribute to the planned expansion of productive capacity essential to realize these goals.

The Ongoing Debate over the Changing Role of Money Under Socialism

Should Money be Abolished?

Historically, socialists tended initially to underestimate the importance of money and financial planning and the necessity of its coherence with physical planning. Marx and Engels, writing in the 19th century, had initially assumed that the socialist revolution would mature in developed capitalist states. Therefore, the socialist transition process would last only a relatively short period before leading to communism and the abolition of all commodity production for exchange. Many early theorists argued that non-commodity production, production for use without the intervention of money as a medium of exchange, constituted an important feature differentiating socialism from capitalism.

Lenin exposed the way monopoly capital, by the end of the 19th century, had fostered uneven development. This made it possible, and even necessary, to build socialism first in relatively more backward countries. At the same time, it inevitably prolonged the process of transition to socialism on a world scale.

Nevertheless, some Marxist theorists urged the abolition of exchange value and money at the beginning of the transition to socialism. During the so-called "war communism" period (1918-21) in the Soviet Union, they sought to justify theoretically the attempt to distribute products directly without the use of money, an effort arising in part from the hard conditions and gross shortages caused by the civil war. By the end of the first year, however, this system had clearly failed to function efficiently. During the New Economic Policy, a planned retreat which included the restoration of capitalist relations in limited sectors, the monetary system and banks were restored as a primary lever of state direction of the overall economy. As socialist productive relations evolved, most Marxists accepted the continued use of money under conditions of commodity production of a special type.

However, Marxist theorists continued to debate what particular features of money and financial institutions were necessary to promote socialist commodity production. Over the years, the discussions centred on two crucial issues: first, to what extent and how should the national plan and budget (as compared to decentralized decisions of workers in enterprises) govern the accumulation and reinvestment of capital? Second, what role should profits, prices and taxes play in the transition to and within socialism? For some years, the destruction caused by World War II and the negative impact of the Stalinist personality cult hindered necessary scientific research into the relevant questions. In the post-war era, the relative underdevelopment of the socialist countries in eastern Europe and Asia introduced new elements into the debate.

The Modified Role of Money and Financial Institutions

Despite disagreements on specific aspects socialist theorists today generally agree on the necessity of some form of monetary and financial relationships during the socialist transition. First, socialist production requires a high degree of division of labour in which specialized industrial branches produce and therefore must exchange specialized goods. This creates the necessary conditions, though not a sufficient theoretical reason, for continued use of money as a medium of exchange. If a socialist economy operated like a single large factory, it could produce goods and simply distribute them without the use of money. Where socialization of the means of production has proceeded only to a limited extent, however, the existence of different types of enterprises as separate units requires money to facilitate exchange. State-owned factories, though owned by the entire population through the state, still exist as relatively independent units. They and other types of nationally owned enterprises must exchange goods with each other, as well as with co-operatively owned agricultural enterprises and privately owned handicraft enterprises. Furthermore, employees of state enterprises receive wages, while self- and cooperative-employed individuals also receive cash incomes. These money incomes to households also constitute a demand for finished consumer goods. The planned use of money is essential to facilitate the continuing expansion of trade which, in turn, promotes the continuing specialization and the growth of productivity.

Secondly, the use of money enables the socialist state to introduce an incentive system within the national plan to ensure that all enterprise employees realize that they, together with society as a whole, have a common collective interest in increasing their productivity. National economic planning must take into consideration the twofold character of socialist enterprises: the employees of particular enterprises must retain responsibility for and gain from the expanded output of their own products; at the same time, all the nation's inhabitants will benefit from overall increases in productivity. The planners must find ways to relate the workers' wages, bonuses and living conditions to their contribution to planned increases in the national product. The workers and the economy as a whole have not yet increased productivity sufficiently to provide goods to all according to need. The planners must devise some means of ensuring payments to individuals and groups of workers in every enterprise which reflect their increased productivity. The planned use of money facilitates payment according to the actual work they have performed.

In other words, the characteristics of socialist production and exchange necessitate creation of a valid method of calculating the value of activities within and between enterprises, between them and government authorities, and between them and the population as workers and consumers. Socialist planning of economic relations requires the exchange of products according to an agreed principle of equivalence, a standard to measure the relative value of goods based on the socially necessary labour required to produce them. An enterprise which produces at a cost below this level contributes to the essential surplus which the economy must invest in new machinery and equipment to improve the level of productivity. The planned use of money provides the necessary medium of exchange.

Under socialism, the persistence of quasi-commodity production for exchange makes monetary and financial relationships important features of the socialist production process. Planned development of the economy requires attention to these relationships. First and foremost, the state must ensure that the financial system functions to facilitate planned socialist development in a manner very different from the way it operates under capitalism. A socialist financial system must function differently from that under capitalism in several respects:

Firstly, the financial system, itself, cannot dominate the economy. The planned character of the economy must remain its dominant feature. The financial system must ensure that the total money supply (the amount of money and its velocity of circulation) and the sum of prices of all commodities correspond with the total overall value of the goods produced.

Secondly, under socialism, commodity production must not separate producers into competing economic units; rather financial plans must provide an instrument for co-ordinating their physical activities and increasing productivity.

Thirdly, the general planned character of socialist production, the entire system of management planning and stimulation of the economy, must take into account the objective categories of value identified by the labour theory of value. That is, socialist financial planning must take into account the relative amounts of the socially necessary labour time required to produce commodities. It must subordinate and utilize these categories to achieve the overall goals of planned development. Failure to recognize objective value categories hampers their positive use to advance planned socialist productivity.

In short, socialist financial and physical planning is essential for the attainment of socialist goals.

The Five Key Tasks of Socialist Financial Planning

During the transition to socialism, the state must develop appropriate financial institutions, including the state budget, to mobilize locally generated surpluses to finance the planned physical reconstruction of the economy.

The preconditions for effective financial planning include: first, the expropriation of the monopoly banks and creation of a socialist banking system; second, monetary reforms; third, extension of the volume and effective range of the national budget; fourth, coherence between government finance and the financial activities of the socialist economy, including enterprises and co-operatives; and, fifth, utilization of the financial system to support national plans and control, checking the reality of the plans and the efficiency of operation on every level.

In this context, financial planning must help to achieve five specific tasks:

1) Consciously create a socialist sector, promoting newly founded socialist property, and assisting working-class representatives to occupy the economic as well as the political commanding heights of the national economy;
2) Introduce national economic planning to reshape the entire economic and social structure in a socialist direction;
3) Pave the way for co-operatively owned development of small and medium-sized industrial enterprises, farms and wholesale and retail traders;
4) Impose constraints on the increase of capitalist ownership, avoiding the danger that simple commodity production may give rise to a new capitalist class;
5) Reshape the entire system of public administration to enable it to cope with the first four tasks; that is, plan the economy; recruit new staff from the working class imbued with a working-class ideology; and build new institutions ensuring worker participation at every level.

Summary

Marxist theorists maintain that monopoly state capitalism tends to rely heavily on financial intervention in its vain attempt to regulate and eliminate the contradictions which arise out of private monopolistic ownership of increasingly socialized means of production. Only a socialist transition can lay the foundation for finally eliminating the contradictory features that have engulfed the interlinked capitalist industrialized and Third World economies in a general crisis.

But Marxists vigorously debate how to effect the transition to and through socialism. Their arguments extend to changes required in the arena of monetary and financial relationships. They agree that money and financial institutions must play a vital, albeit continually changing, role in helping to carry through the transition. As a precondition, the state, representing the workers, peasants and supportive nationalist elements, must take over and restructure the entire financial system. At all times, planners must then ensure that the financial system is such as to facilitate plans designed to increase productivity. It must facilitate the development of socialist ownership of the means of production, planned management and methods of stimulating increased worker productivity. In short, it must play a key role in the transformation of the economy from one of scarcity, characterized by distribution according to work done, to one of plenty, with distribution according to need.

Notes

1. In southern Africa, the Mozambican and Angolan governments have taken over large parts of the modern-sector economy, but South African destabilization measures have effectively thwarted their efforts to take the next steps towards the full transition to socialism.

Recommended Reading

(For annotations, see bibliography at the end of the book.)

Abalkin, *Socialism Today*
Anchishkin, *The Theory of Growth of a Socialist Economy*
Barnett, *China's Economy in Global Perspective*
Bettelheim, *The Transition to Socialist Economy*
Donnithorne, *China's Economic System*
Lardy, *Economic Growth and Distribution in China*
Laski, *The Rate of Growth and the Rate of Interest*
Lenin, *State and Revolution*
Ma Hong, *New Strategy for China's Economy*
Marx, *Critique of the Gotha Programme*
Nove, *The Soviet Economic System*
Ola and Onimode, *Economic Development of Nigeria*
Richman, *Industrial Society in Communist China*
Turgeon, *The Contrasting Economies*
Xu Dixin *et al.*, *China's Search for Economic Growth*
Xue Muqiao, *China's Socialist Economy*
Zwass, *Money, Banking and the Creation of Credit*

Periodicals
Beijing Review
Development and Peace
Far Eastern Review
Public Enterprise

Chapter 17: Planning and the National Budget

The Changing Role of Public Finance

Disappearance of Separation between Public and Productive Sector Finance

As a socialist-orientated society increasingly socializes the ownership of the means of production, the separation between public finance and productive activities—characteristic of capitalist economies, including those in Africa—disappears. Increasingly, the socialist state employs the national budget as its central economic instrument for the overall planning process.

During the transition to socialism, Marxist theory holds that the political leadership must restructure state machinery until it is qualitatively different from that of state capitalism. On behalf of the working people, the state gradually takes over ownership of all the major means of production, starting with the commanding heights: the banks and financial institutions, foreign and internal wholesale trade, and basic industries. Thus, more or less rapidly, it eliminates the underlying source of the basic contradictions, exploitation and gross inequalities inherent in capitalist economies. Over time it creates the objective conditions essential to implement the co-ordinated physical and financial plans required to realize the high levels of productivity which large-scale modern technology makes possible in industry, agriculture and distribution. In the process, the socialist state eliminates the distinction between public and private finance, and develops the national budget as its key instrument for implementing economic plans.

The Persistence of Private Elements

The transition takes time. Elements of the private-sector economy persist, sometimes for decades, influencing government's ability to implement its plans. This may reflect various factors, including the nature of existing productive forces and the level of education of the population. The persisting private elements may include privately owned handicraft workshops, small retail establishments, and various professions. In Poland, private farmers, employing hired labour, still cultivate a major share of the nation's arable land.

The nature and extent of the elements of private ownership which persist during the transition in any particular country necessarily affect the comprehensiveness and effectiveness of co-ordinated national development plans. In general, however, the socialist state reshapes the national budget as its primary means of co-ordinating physical and financial plans.

The Socialist Economic Mechanism

In most socialist countries, the state employs the national budget as the key economic instrument through which it integrates financial relations into the whole system of management, planning and incentives. Within this system, financial relations assume a relatively independent form, not simply subordinated to physical relations. Thus, financial relations must help the whole system to control, regulate and direct physical relations and production.

Since financial relations remain relatively independent from physical relations, planners must devote special attention to them. Socialist states employ the national budget to control and direct all sectors of the economy in accordance with the nation's financial and physical plans. Thus the national budget plays a very different role from under capitalism, where it simply covers government's own revenues and expenditures relating to administration, infrastructure and defence.

This chapter first summarizes the nature of the socialist physical and financial planning mechanisms; and, second, describes the key role of the national budget as an instrument for co-ordinating the nation's physical and financial plans.

Financial and Physical Planning

Comprehensive planning in socialist countries incorporates three major features.

Balanced Physical and Financial Planning

The national economic plan covers all aspects of the economy and defines its links to the social spheres (health, education, foreign policy, etc.). Implementation of the tasks identified in the plan requires more than planned physical inputs (labour, materials, etc.) and outputs (goods produced). It requires the accumulation and investment of investable surpluses—capital—to ensure the realization of the plans while avoiding inflation.

As Figure 17.1 suggests, financial planning must balance the demand for funds to finance the physical resources needed to increase production of goods with the supply of financial resources resulting in the distribution of income required to achieve consistently rising productivity and consumption while at the same time setting aside the funds necessary for further planned investment.

Popular Participation in the Planning Process

All levels of government, the various branches of industry represented by ministries, state corporations and co-operatives participate in the elaboration and implementation of the physical and financial plans. Preparation at all

Figure 17.1
Balanced Physical and Financial Planning

Physical plans re: allocation of resources (demand for funds)	*Financial plans re: allocation of financial resources (supply of funds)*
Labour force → Construction →	Wages and other forms of income to households
Equipment → Materials →	Investment in construction, equipment, materials

these levels requires an attempt to identify and, as fully as possible to meet the various group interests in order to stimulate their active participation in the realization of the chosen targets. The plan must incorporate appropriate incentives, in terms of distribution of financial funds, bonuses, wage increases, etc., to stimulate that realization. At the same time, the plan must emphasize the connection between overall financial relations and increased physical production; that is, it must not merely specify the amount of inputs required and the outputs produced, but also relate the planned prices and credits directly to increased productivity.

Unlike physical planning, financial planning provides the preconditions for calculating efficiency. The relative efficiency of many complex economic activities cannot be compared in physical terms. Expressed in monetary terms, however, they may be measured and compared to determine which provides the most efficient physical production path. As long as price levels reflect the real costs to society, financial plans, expressed in money terms, can help assure the effectiveness of the system of incentives at every level, while maintaining the overall coherence essential for co-ordinated planning activities. Expression of physical plan targets in financial terms facilitates monitoring the quantity and even the quality of output.

Financial planning brings into line the interests of different levels of government and producers: if workers in an enterprise, using the planned inputs, produce more than the planned target, they will receive additional funds to improve their working and living conditions, either directly in the form of higher wages or indirectly through improved social services.

The national planners must ensure that the overall system of income distribution corresponds to the overall financial targets: the overall financial demand created in the course of distributing income to stimulate production must correspond to the funds created in the physical production process. Also, the plan must relate to the structure of output, the particular commodities, to the demand created by the final distribution of income.

Step-by-Step Elaboration of the Plan

The process of elaborating the national economic plan, involving movement from general objectives to detailed plans for all levels of socio-economic development, constitutes a long process with feedback at each stage. The process starts when the central planning board, given available statistics, formulates a draft central plan based on consideration of possible alternative development paths.

The planners may express these first calculations on the allocation of physical resources in financial terms. They could never express the many complex physical quantities—machinery, trucks, houses, clothing, etc.—in comparable physical terms. Figure 17.2 shows the first rough allocation of national income. The planners may design the increase of Y_{ti} to Y_{to} expressed in fixed prices of the base year, to reflect the planned increased physical outputs.

Figure 17.2
Basic Distribution of National Income (Y)

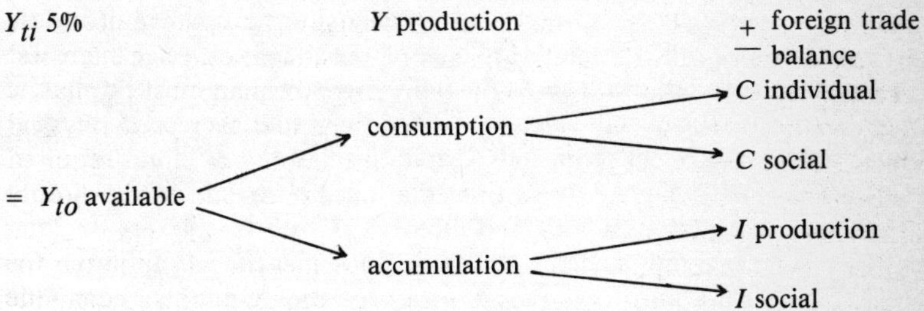

The planners then make detailed calculations as to the output of every enterprise, government agency and collective farm at the relevant plan level. In all cases, they assume as a precondition that prices will remain unchanged. This permits consideration of how the increased output will affect distribution. If workers in an enterprise increase their output, they may all enjoy increased incomes in the form of wages, bonuses and/or social welfare expenditures.

The planners may change the distribution of income by altering the physical and financial plans. They use the price system and the national budget as their primary instruments for changing the distribution pattern. In a fairly small socialist country, with a population of about 15 million, planners typically formulate about 500 essential balances on a state level. These relate the supply and demand for basic commodities. Then the draft plan is circulated to all levels of government and enterprise, as shown in Figure 17.3. The workers at each level and in each enterprise discuss the best way to achieve national objectives. At the same time, they could exercise local initiative, taking advantage of new technological innovations to increase productivity. If they do, the national output and hence national incomes will rise. Simultaneously, they will receive increased income at the enterprise level.

The National Budget

A Balanced Budget

As it moves along the road to socialism, the state typically must make greater and greater use of the national budget to implement its financial plans. Figure 17.4 illustrates the relationship of the national budget to the overall socialist economy. Given the total national income, the national budget encompasses far more aspects of the economy than under capitalism, for it must finance not only administration and expanding social services, but also the basic investments required to implement the nation's physical plans. A socialist state typically seeks to balance its budget. It does not borrow from the banking system for current expenditures, for it seeks to avoid inflationary pressures.

Expenditures

On the expenditure side, the government, through the national budget, determines the allocation of the major financial surpluses generated by the economy in three primary categories. First, as in a capitalist economy, the national budget finances public administration and national defence. Second, the national budget makes allocations for social consumption, providing the crucial link between the productive sectors and the social sphere. The greater the surpluses transferred to the state, the more funds the national budget may allocate to improve social consumption. Under socialism, this second category of expenditures is broader than under capitalism. It also assumes many of the functions of the financial institutions that, under capitalism, mushroom in the private sector alongside of and interlinked with the private banking system, such as building societies and insurance companies. Through the budget, socialist governments replace building societies to provide part of the investment funds required to expand urban housing stock to meet the housing needs of the entire urban population. Most socialist countries subsidize urban housing to keep rents down to about a tenth of the workers' income. Workers in industrial enterprises and peasants in agricultural collectives may also set aside part of their retained surplus funds to build additional housing for themselves.

During the initial transition phase, as quickly as personnel constraints permit, the state assumes control of insurance and pension schemes, integrating them into a national social security programme. Initially, especially where private insurance schemes have accumulated vast sums of money in the past, the introduction of a government programme may provide access to additional investment funds. More important, the socialist government consolidates and restructures the inherited schemes to reduce the cost of employee contributions for low-income workers and to provide uniform and equitable benefits to all. As productivity and the national income increase, the government may use the national budget to expand these benefits to provide more adequate health, accident and retirement insurance, if necessary subsidizing them. Typically, the trade unions and government co-operate in managing the state social security scheme. They aim to provide increased social security for the entire population as rapidly as increasing productivity and the growing national

Figure 17.3
Socialist Planning Structure and Process

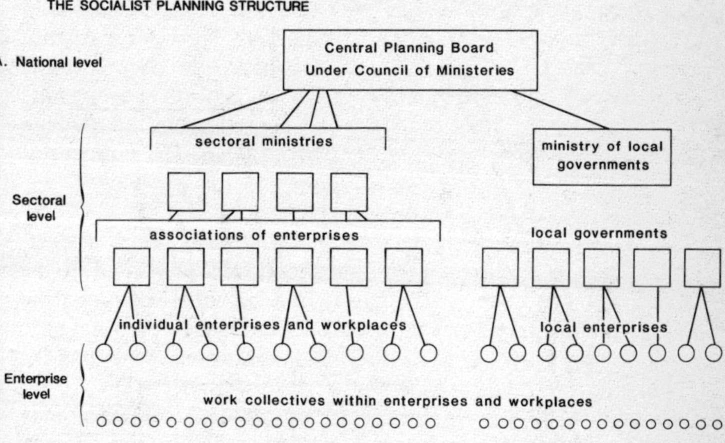

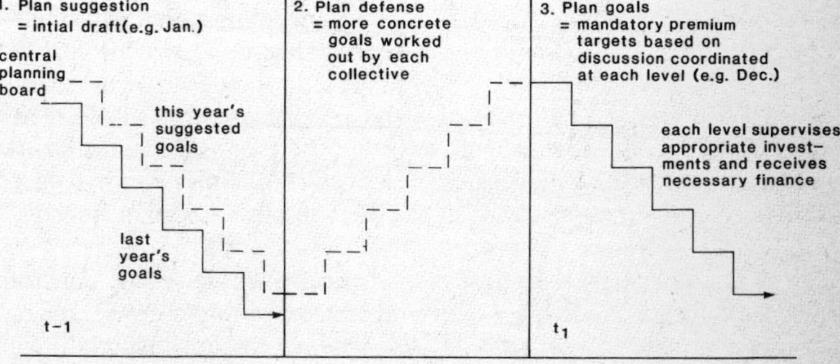

Figure 17.4
Schematic Presentation of Money Flows in a Socialist Economy

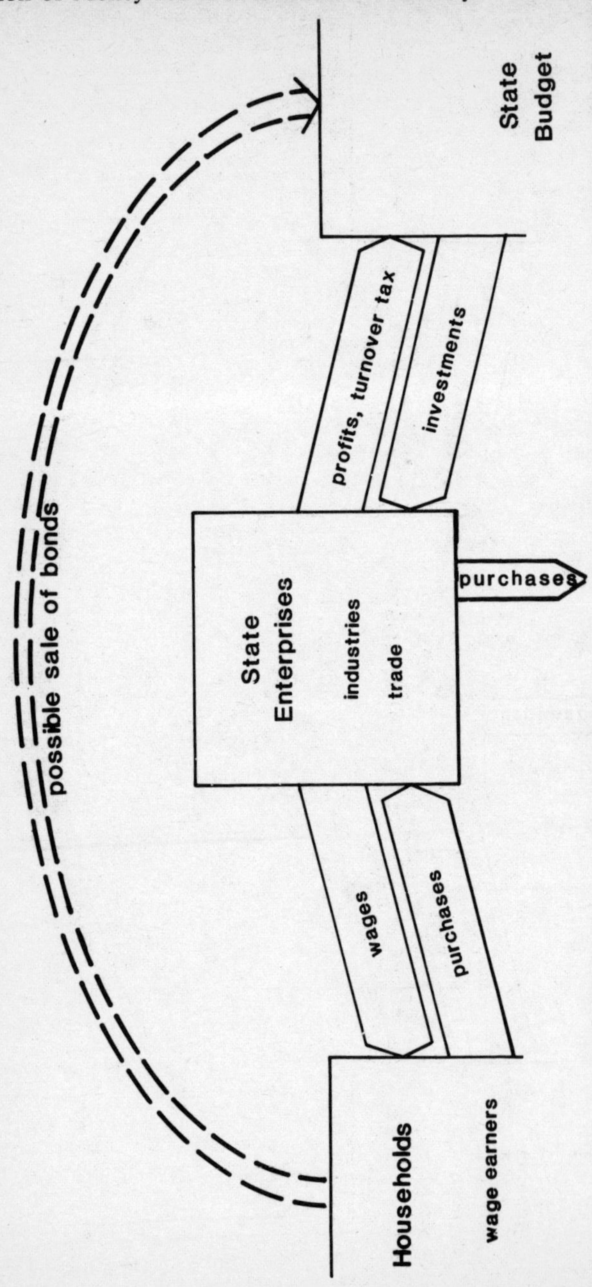

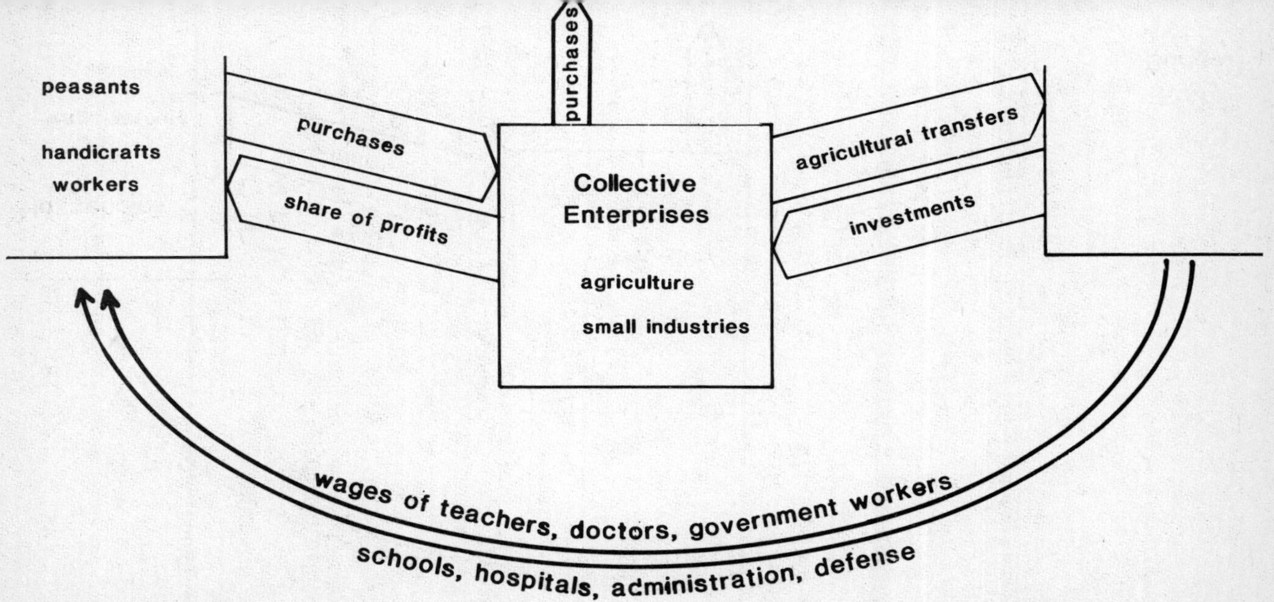
purchases
peasants
handicrafts
workers
purchases
share of profits
Collective Enterprises
agriculture
small industries
agricultural transfers
investments
wages of teachers, doctors, government workers
schools, hospitals, administration, defense

income permit.

In some socialist countries, the state also provides subsidies out of the national budget to keep the prices of consumer necessities low in order to raise the living standards of lower-income groups. For example, in the German Democratic Republic, such subsidies have become an increasingly significant budget item as the state has sought to keep prices of consumer necessities at the 1957 level. Other socialist governments have permitted prices of necessities to rise to cover costs, simultaneously permitting wages of lower-income groups to increase commensurately.

Table 17.1A
Expenditures through the National Budget in the Soviet Union, 1940, 1956, 1973

Expenditures	*1940*	*1956*	*1973*
Total expenditures (billions of roubles)	17.4	101.6	184.0
Of which (percentage distribution)	%	%	%
National economy	33.3	44.0	49.6
Social and cultural	23.6	37.5	36.6
Defence	32.7	12.5	9.7
Administration	4.0	1.3	1.0
Other	6.3	4.3	3.0
Total	*100.0*	*100.0*	*100.0*

Source: *The Soviet Economic System*, p. 237.

Table 17.1B
Distribution of National Government Expenditures in China, 1950, 1965, 1979

Expenditures	*1950*	*1965*	*1979*
Total expenditures (billions of yuan)	6.808	46.633	127.394
Of which (percentage distribution)	%	%	%
Economic	26.5	54.5	59.8
Social, cultural & educational	11.1	13.4	13.7
Defence	41.1	18.6	17.4
Administration & management	19.3	5.6	4.9
Debt payment	—	1.3	—
Other	2.9	6.4	4.0
Total	*100.0*	*100. 0*	*100.0*

Source: World Bank Country Studies[1] IBRD, *China: Socialist Economic Development, Vol. I. The Economy, Statistical System and Basic Data* (Washington, D.C., 1981)

The third category of socialist national budget expenditures allocates investment funds for new capital goods: machinery and equipment, factory buildings and urban housing. This category most significantly differentiates the socialist national budget from that of the typical capitalist country, where, except for occasional subsidies, even parastatals make capital investments outside the budget. Under socialism state allocations through the national budget influences the rapidity with which the economy introduces new scientific methods and technologies to accelerate the growth of productivity and the national income.

Table 17.1A and B indicates the relative order of magnitude of expenditures which the Soviet Union and China made through their national budgets on these three categories after World War II. The two economies differed significantly, both in terms of development and methods of economic management. Nevertheless, both invested a growing share of their national budgets on economic development. That after the 1950s China spent a higher proportion of investment than did the Soviet Union may reflect the lower initial level of its productive forces. The Soviet Union's expenditure of a higher share on social and cultural activities may represent the other side of the same picture. A country with a higher level of productive capacity, in which each investment is more efficient, may be able to devote a greater share of its national budget to social consumption.

During the Cultural Revolution, the Chinese government published little statistical data. Apparently, however, the Ministry of Finance continued to finance capital investment by grants provided through the budget. By the 1980s, more information had become available. Mounting domestic criticism of investment grants through the budget argued that they laid an undue emphasis on heavy industry and inefficient use of capital, since enterprises did not have to repay them. Reforms, therefore, shifted greater responsibility for short and intermediate investments funds to the banking system (see Chapter 18).

Budget Income[1]

On the income side, nationally owned economic enterprises provide the main source of income for the typical socialist state's national budget. The three primary channels through which income flows into the national budget include the following.

Normal Rate of Profit: The state planners stipulate as a minimum level of efficiency that each state enterprise should produce a normal rate of profit of 6 to 10 per cent of its investment in fixed assets and working capital. The enterprise must transfer this fixed minimum percentage directly to the national budget for redistribution to investment or social consumption. If the workers in an enterprise achieve better utilization of assets, they may retain and use the additional funds either to improve their own living and working conditions, or to invest in further increases in production in order to augment their own future incomes.

On the surface, these transfers appear similar to profit taxes imposed by a capitalist state. However, they constitute a considerably higher proportion of enterprises' profits since the socialist state participates directly in investment in productive sectors. Socialist planners consciously set the normal rate high enough to acquire enough surplus for investment to develop new industries in order to spread productivity to all sectors and regions of the economy and to achieve more equitable distribution of income through increased social consumption.

The amount of profit transferred to the national budget varies from industry to industry and enterprise to enterprise, reflecting the fact that different enterprises operate under differing objective conditions. For example, in mining, different mines operate under differing geological conditions. These determine their potential output and the profits each can expect to produce at given price levels. In manufacturing, some enterprises have more advanced machinery and equipment than others. Planners must take these objective conditions into account in determining the amount of funds each enterprise must transfer to the national budget. In cases of enterprises essential to national well-being, where equipment is obsolete or the scarcity of essential inputs raises costs, the state may provide planned subsidies, rather than require the transfer of profits to the national budget.

Turnover Taxes: The planners may set the final selling prices of certain products well above their production costs and the average profit rate to achieve a more appropriate pattern of national distribution. The state may then collect the difference, called a turnover tax. For example, the planners may set higher-than-cost prices for items considered luxuries, dangerous to health like cigarettes or alcohol, or in short supply like automobiles. The state transfers the added returns to the national budget. In a limited sense, these levies are comparable to excise taxes imposed in capitalist countries, but in socialist countries the planners consciously design them as an important feature of the overall national pattern of distribution.

Collective Farm Taxes: Like other state enterprises, state farms transfer a predetermined minimum amount of profits to the national budget. Collective farms, owned by the peasants who work them, however, may transfer a share of their incomes to the national budget through a form of tax. This tax may differ from region to region and farm to farm because production conditions—and consequently harvests differ. The tax which different collectives must transfer to the state, therefore, varies to enable the peasants, depending on their collective efforts, to achieve relatively comparable living standards.

Other Sources: Other sources of income to the national budget include social insurance contributions from employees and enterprises; income from various administrative activities, like licences for automobilie driving, fines for driving badly, and so forth; and taxes on the incomes of privately paid people.

Taxes on individual incomes are typically graduated with income. During the transition to socialism, income taxes play an important role in reducing the gap between high and low incomes. Once the state has socialized all the means of production and plans income distribution, however, income taxes become far less significant than under capitalism. In some countries, they may be dropped altogether.

Several socialist states run lotteries which provide a small additional source of income.

Socialist states sometimes sell bonds to the public, which they promise to repay with a low interest rate. This serves to mobilize private savings for social ends. However, these bonds typically provide only a small percentage of total revenues.

Offsetting Foreign Trade Fluctuations: Depending on its significance for the national economy, foreign trade may influence the size of the national income and hence the national budget of individual socialist governments. Most trade with other socialist countries takes place at planned fixed prices for given amounts. So planners can, with a degree of certainty, determine its expected impact on the budget. Both the amounts and prices of goods traded with capitalist countries fluctuate, however, introducing significant unknowns into the planning process. If the terms of the trade deteriorate below levels anticipated by the national planners, the state must pay the enterprises out of the national budget to finance the losses. Of course, if the external terms of trade become more favourable than planned, the national budget receives the surpluses.

Taxation during the Transition to Socialism

The state may utilize taxation as a flexible instrument to facilitate the transition process, contributing to the structuring of incentives to attain national objectives. It may initially use taxes to reduce income differences arising from the past and persisting private ownership of some of the means of production. Graduated income taxes can reduce the high returns to individuals in the form of profits or super-high salaries, especially if the recipient would otherwise use them for speculative purposes or private consumption. Carefully designed tax incentives may reduce the tax if the recipient invests the funds received according to plan. The state may also use tax incentives to encourage individuals to participate in socialized forms of ownership; for example, during the early transition phase, several socialist states imposed higher taxes on private farmers than on those who joined co-operatives. Over time, as the socialization process advances, the significance of taxes as a separate form of government revenue declines as state enterprises transfer a major share of their profits directly to the national budget.

The Soviet and Chinese Budgets

Unfortunately, relatively little information appears in English on the sources of incomes of socialist governments. Table 17.2A and B indicates, in terms of general order of magnitude, the changing sources of revenues in the Soviet Union and China in the post-World War II period. The economies of the Soviet Union and China differ significantly, both in their levels of development and

Table 17.2A
The Soviet Budget Statement[a] (Percentage Distribution of Sources of Funds)

Sources of Revenue	*1940 (Pre-World War II)*	*1965*	*1973*
Total Revenue (billions of roubles)	18.0	102.3	187.8
Of which (% distribution)	%	%	%
Turnover taxes	58.8	37.8	31.5
Payments out of profit	12.2	30.2	31.9
Taxes on co-operatives	1.6	1.5	0.8
Mass bond sales	5.0	0.2	0.2
Direct taxes	5.0	7.5	8.4
Social insurance	5.0	7.6	4.9

[a] The state budget includes expenditures of local authorities and 16 republics, although each has its own budget, so the items are included only under general headings.

Source: Nove, *The Soviet Economic System*, p. 230.

Table 17.2B
State Budget Revenues, 1950, 1965, 1979

Sources of Revenue	*1950*	*1965*	*1979*
Total Revenue (in millions of yuan)	6.519	47.332	110.327
Of which (% distribution)	%	%	%
Enterprise profits	13.3	55.8	44.7
Tax revenue	75.1	43.1	48.7
Turnover Taxes[a]	36.2	34.9	42.8
Taxes on salt	4.1	1.5	0.9
Custom duties	5.6	1.2	2.4
Taxes on agriculture	29.3	5.4	2.7
Foreign borrowing	4.6	—	3.3
Other revenues	6.9	0.9	3.3

[a] The World Bank study calls these "taxes on industry and commerce".

Source: Calculated from World Bank Country Studies/IBRD, *China: Socialist Economic Development, Vol. I: The Economy, Statistical System and Basic Data* Washington, D.C., World Bank, (1980), Table 4.1.

methods of economic management. Their national planners aggregate data in somewhat different ways. The more developed an economy, the more highly educated the population in general—and management in particular—the more sophisticated the revenue system its planners may adopt. Table 17.2 suggests that both countries obtained increasing shares of their revenues from profits of state enterprises and from industrial and commercial enterprises, although after the reforms in the 1970s this share declined again in China.

Turnover taxes in both countries constitute a predetermined difference between the wholesale prices and the final selling prices of industrial and commercial enterprises. They are easier to administer than the collection of a given proportion of enterprise profits, since they are levied as a flat tax on goods sold. They affect relative prices. The state may impose low taxes on machinery, raw materials and intermediate goods to stimulate their production and use. Likewise, it may raise taxes on luxury and semi-luxury items to discourage their consumption (see Chapter 19 on pricing). In the Soviet Union in the post-World War II era such taxes provided a declining share of revenue, while direct profit provided an increasing share.

In the initial transition period, most socialist countries imposed an agricultural tax as a percentage of the "standard" or "normal" yield of an acre of land; if the farmers increased output above that norm, their retained income would be greater. This aimed to stimulate farmers to improve production levels. In China, agricultural taxes increased both absolutely and relatively until 1954 just before collectivization took place; then it declined relatively as a percentage of total revenue although in absolute terms, it remained stable at about 2.9 billion yuan.

In the post-war era, direct taxes on individual incomes in the more developed Soviet economy had already declined to less than 10 per cent of total revenue.[2] In China, they apparently provided an even smaller proportion of total revenues.

The Soviet Union levied a low graduated tax on incomes of employees working in state enterprises, increasing from 5.9 per cent to 13 per cent at higher levels. Artists and writers typically paid taxes equal to 13 per cent of the incomes they earned abroad. The state taxed incomes from private activities—e.g. of medical practitioners, craftspersons and teachers—starting at about 18 per cent for lower incomes of 100 roubles a month (that is, about three times what state employees would pay). The tax rose to a rate of 81 per cent per rouble earned over 7,000 roubles. To offset the loss of some 25 million people killed during World War II, the Soviet government sought to encourage large families by reducing taxes levied on married couples with children.

Summary

As the transition to socialism proceeds, the separation between public finance and investment in the productive sectors—typical in capitalist countries, including those in Africa—disappears. Because the transition takes time, however, elements of private ownership of the means of production persist.

Socialist countries have developed centralized economic mechanisms to integrate finance into their national systems of management, planning and incentives.

Comprehensive socialist planning requires balanced physical and financial planning. The political leadership seeks to ensure popular participation at every level of government and enterprise in the formulation and implementation of the plans. Initially, most socialist states centralized the accumulation and reinvestment of surpluses through the national plan to achieve more balanced, integrated national development. Over time, as worker education advanced and the production structure became more and more complex, most socialist states decentralized decision-making, relying more on finance mechanisms to provide control and stimulate innovation and increased productivity.

A socialist state generally uses the national budget as its primary instrument for implementing its financial plans in order to control, regulate and direct the planned changes in physical relationships and increased production. The socialist state budget allocates funds for more than the administration, defence and social and economic infrastructure typically financed by capitalist budgets. The socialist budget subsumes the functions of the many financial institutions that operate separately in capitalist economies, including the provision of insurance, pensions and housing. The budget may provide subsidies to raise living standards through reduced rents and lower prices of consumer necessities. Most important, the budget allocates investable surpluses to planned investment in new capital goods in order to spread productivity throughout the more balanced integrated economy.

On the income side, socialized enterprises pay a normal minimum rate of profit directly to the national budget. As socialization proceeds, this provides an increasing share of the total budget revenue. The normal rate of profit may vary among industries and enterprises, depending on their objective conditions of production. Any surplus profit the workers produce, over and above that normal rate, they may retain to finance their own bonuses, increased social services and improved housing. The planners may set prices for certain luxury items or goods in short supply above cost, and transfer the additional surplus to the budget. Collective farms typically pay taxes into the budget. These may differ from farm to farm because of differing conditions of production. Other sources of budget revenue include various fees and income taxes. As socialization proceeds, income taxes decline as a source of revenue. The state may use incentives to facilitate the transition process.

In short, the socialist state seeks to use the national budget as its primary instrument for co-ordinating financial and physical plans to implement the transition to social ownership, increased productivity and rising living standards.

Notes

1. Different socialist states utilize different techniques and different terminology for collection of revenues through the state budget.

2. No one in private productive activities could employ other workers in order to obtain surplus value; hence income differentials were not as great as in private-enterprise economies.

Exercises and Research

1. Why does the separation between public finance and finance of productive activities disappear as the transition from capitalism to socialism takes place? a) What role are private elements likely to play during the transition to socialism? b) What is the primary aim of the socialist economic mechanism?
2. What three main features do most comprehensive socialist plans incorporate, and why?
3. At what stage in their development have most socialist states found it possible and necessary to decentralize decision-making concerning investments?
4. What role does the national budget play in financial planning in most socialist states? a) How do the expenditures covered by the national budget under socialism differ from those in the government budget under capitalism? b) Compare and contrast the sources of revenue included in the national budget under socialism with those of a typical capitalist government. Explain the reasons for the differences.
5. In what main ways would a government be likely to restructure taxes during the transition to socialism?
6. Compare your government's approach to financial planning with that of a typical socialist country:
   a) Contrast your country's government budget with that of a typical socialist country, both in terms of the types of expenditures covered and the sources of income.
   b) Examine your country's National Accounts and tax data relating to distribution of income. Estimate the amount of income the state would have available if it made institutional changes along socialist lines.
   c) What approach to taxes would you recommend for your country if it sought to implement a transition to socialism?

Recommended Reading

(For annotations, see bibliography at the end of the book.)

Abalkin, *Socialism Today*
Anishkin, *The Theory of Growth of a Socialist Economy*
Donnithorne, *China's Economic System*
Gurley, *China's Economy and the Maoist Strategy*
Hooker (ed.), *The Fund and China*
Ma Hong, *New Strategy for China's Economy*
Nove, *The Soviet Economic System*
Richman, *Industrial Society in Communist China*
Turgeon, *The Contrasting Economies*
Xu Dixin *et al.*, *China's Search for Economic Growth*
Xue Muqiao, *China's Socialist Economy*

Periodicals

Beijing Review
Development and Peace
Far Eastern Economic Review
The Hungarian Journal
Public Enterprise

Chapter 18: The Banks under Socialism

Marxist theorists generally agree that under socialism, the state must use the banking system as an important instrument for economic control. It provides an additional steering mechanism for ensuring fulfilment of national plans. Therefore, as one of the first steps in the transition to socialism, the state should exert control over and restructure the inherited banking system. It must expropriate the monopoly-operated commercial banks. In many less developed countries, as in Africa, these are foreign-owned. Simultaneously, the state should block all bank and credit balances of smaller capitalist banks and capitalist enterprises in other sectors. This limits the private sector's ability to hinder further steps towards socialist development.

The state must fundamentally restructure the central bank. As under capitalism, the central bank acts as the bank for the government, issues currency and handles all foreign-exchange transactions. Under socialism, the central bank must also impose direct controls to ensure that the entire banking system conforms with and contributes to fulfilment of the national plans. It reorganizes the banking system to help collect locally generated investable surpluses and direct them to critical sectors of the economy. In close conformity with national plans, the banking system must ensure efficient use of all funds at all levels. It provides a means of monitoring the activities of managements of nationalized enterprises, stimulating and advising them on how best to achieve and exceed plan targets.

This chapter first summarizes the evidence as to how socialist governments have developed the banking system to control the money supply and provide an additional steering mechanism to ensure fulfilment of national plans. Second, it outlines the principles socialist banks have evolved for providing bank credit to foster attainment of planned goals.

Socialist Control of the Money Supply

As in a capitalist monetary system, a socialist economy uses two kinds of money: coins and notes, issued by the central, or state, bank; and transfers of funds through bank deposits, including those created by the issuance of credit. Only actual consumers—workers, who receive wages, and peasants who receive shares of their collective farms' incomes for consumption needs—may make payments with actual coins and notes. All government authorities, industrial and distributive enterprises and collective farms must make their purchases and sales through the banks. This enables the socialized banking system to monitor and control the extent to which the various levels of production and administration actually conform to their planned expenditures and incomes.

To ensure monetary stability, the banking system must control the allocation of credit according to the national financial plan. Unlike the capitalist system, socialist governments generally do not borrow from the banks or sell treasury bills, as this would be inflationary. The banks may only extend loans to productive enterprises on the basis of planned investment requirements. This ensures material backing for the expansion of the money supply through new credit in the form of production and distribution of commodities. In other words the banking system seeks to ensure the stability of the currency through the planned expansion of the money supply, including credit, in relation to the actual production and sale of goods.

The Evolving Structure of Socialist Banking Systems

Just as no blueprint exists for the overall transition to socialism, so socialist governments have experimented with the appropriate way to restructure the inherited banking system to ensure that it performs as an effective steering mechanism. As part of its early effort to eliminate the use of money under the difficult conditions of war communism, the Soviet government first nationalized the private commercial banks and then abolished the state bank. But in 1921, at the outset of the New Economic Policy, when it allowed private farmers and even some private industrial and trade enterprises to operate, the government re-established the state bank as an essential control device. Lenin visualized the state bank, with branches in every rural district and every factory to provide country-wide accounting for the production and distribution of goods, as the "skeleton of the socialist economy". In the early 1930s, after collectivization of agriculture and the establishment of socialist ownership of the means of production throughout the economy, the Soviet government restructured the banking system on the basic principles later adopted by most other socialist countries.

As their economies developed, the various socialist countries continued to experiment, evolving different relationships between the banks and other nationalized enterprises according to their own theoretical perceptions and to their own historically shaped circumstances. In the 1970s, as part of their attempts to decentralize their economies and increase enterprise management responsibilities to be more appropriate to their increasingly complex and integrated socialist economies, several governments further modified their banking systems.

The limited space here available permits only a brief outline of the more significant changes made by the socialist governments in their banking systems both to reflect and facilitate the socialist transition process.

Monitoring the Private Sector

Whatever the particular form adopted in any one country, a socialist banking system, like any other, must always service foreign trade, domestic industry and trade, agriculture, and the general public. During the early phase of the transition to socialism, the authorities typically required not only state and collective enterprises, but also all private owners of any enterprise to deposit their funds in the state banks. In that phase, the state banks carried out three primary tasks with respect to private enterprise:

First, they sought to control private-sector activities, limiting their further development, monitoring their use of funds, and implementing measures relating to credit and interest rates as these affected their growth. Second, the banks sought to direct the development of the capitalist sector in the context of the planned economy. Since that sector's prime aims differed from those of the national economy, the state bank had to develop appropriate credit and interest policies to make it conform with, rather than undermine, the planned development of the national economy. Third, the bank, by holding the funds of the private sector, acquired access to the investable surpluses that that sector generated; and could redirect them to provide credit to finance the growth of the socialized sectors.

As the transition to socialism advanced, private enterprise played a diminishing role in the economy. By the 1970s, some two decades after the eastern European countries began the transition to socialism, private enterprise operated only in limited areas of the retail trade, handicrafts and some professions. The significance of the banks' operations in servicing the private sector inevitably declined. Other branches, in contrast, had expanded and evolved to meet the needs of the growing socialized sectors.

Specialization of Socialist Banks

As the socialist economies developed, the banking system became more specialized to meet their increasingly complex financial requirements. Well-qualified cadres were employed to deal with the particular financial requirements of each sector of the national economy.

Foreign Trade Banks: From the outset, the state banks always financed foreign trade. This constituted an important aspect of the socialist state's takeover of all foreign trade to ensure that it contributed to national economic development. The state exercised a protective function, reducing the impact on the nation's of transnational corporate behaviour and fluctuations in the capitalist world market. In so far as a socialist state trades with capitalist countries, it cannot entirely eliminate those influences.

The state bank typically establishes a foreign-trade branch which, in co-operation with the foreign-trade ministry, acts as a banker for all enterprises engaged in foreign trade. The foreign-trade bank plays a more important role in smaller socialist countries like Hungary or the German Democratic Republic where foreign trade absorbs more than a third of national output.

To illustrate the role of the state bank in financing foreign trade, suppose a potash enterprise wishes to sell potash abroad. It sells it to the relevant state-owned foreign-trade enterprise for local currency at the price set by the planners for the domestic market. The foreign-trade enterprise sells it to the foreign buyer for foreign currency, which it then deposits in the state foreign-trade bank. The foreign-trade bank, in turn, repays the foreign-trade enterprise an equivalent amount in local currency. The difference—surplus or deficit—between the price of the domestic product and the foreign sales price provides a measure of the efficiency of the potash producer, indicating whether or not the state has subsidized the foreign sale. At the same time, the intervention of the foreign-trade enterprise and the foreign-trade bank protects the domestic firm from international fluctuations in the price of potash.

The state foreign-trade bank, by providing the necessary finance, facilitates transactions like that of potash in the foreign market. At the same time, it insulates the local firms against world price changes. It also monitors all other foreign-trade transactions to ensure they contribute to fulfilment of the national plans.

Agricultural Banks: Socialist state banks typically established special sections or branches to provide credit for the agricultural sector. These evolved to facilitate collectivization of agriculture and to foster increased agricultural productivity.

In the early phases of the transition to socialism, the state banks usually provided credits for small peasants participating in land reform programmes. At the same time, the authorities required larger-scale capitalist farmers to keep their deposits in the state bank. This enabled the banking system to shift unemployed reserve funds from the bigger farms to smaller ones, and eventually to co-operatives.

Socialist agricultural credit programmes varied significantly from country to country, partly on account of differences in each country's circumstances, including its size and level of the development, and partly on account of political decisions resulting from those differences. In all socialist countries, it took years to implement land reform: to break up large estates; to help small peasants and former landless workers to increase their productivity; and eventually, to build some form of collective production system.

A brief review of the agricultural credit policies adopted in the initial transition phase in the German Democratic Republic (GDR) and the People's Republic of China illustrates two significantly different approaches.

During the first stage of land reform until 1960 in the relatively developed German Democratic Republic, capitalist farmers could still hold 20 to 100 hectares and employ workers. However, the government required the large capitalist farms to deposit their funds in the co-operative bank. These provided funds to grant credit to small peasants, many of them formerly landless, who, following the break-up of farms of over 100 hectares, had received 6 to 10 hectares. The state bank did not provide long-term credit for investment to the remaining larger capitalist farmers. Instead, it initially loaned funds to enable the small peasants to purchase new equipment and buildings. The state bank charged the peasants no interest and, in many cases, did not require the beneficiaries of the initial reform to repay the credits in full. Beginning in 1952, the small peasants began to organize into co-operatives to acquire more advanced machinery and equipment that none, alone, could purchase and utilize efficiently. The state bank provided growing amounts of credit to co-operatives to buy the new machines. It no longer gave credits to small peasants unless they joined the co-operatives. This provided an important incentive to form co-operative farms.

In the much larger and far less developed economy of the People's Republic of China, the government set up several different agricultural banks in the first 16 years of its transition to socialism (1949 to 1965), as it attempted to deal with the initial difficulties of financing impoverished peasants, and then with the changing situation as the agricultural sector became increasingly collectivized.

In 1951, the Agricultural Co-operation Bank, a subsidiary of the People's State Bank, assumed responsibility for all banking activity in the rural areas, including state investment in agriculture. In 1955, as collectivization of agriculture accelerated, the Agricultural Bank, also operating under the People's Bank, replaced it. This bank managed funds allocated from the national budget for investment in agriculture. It provided both long- and short-term credits to co-operatives, state farms and individual peasants. It particularly aimed to assist peasants form producer co-operatives. In 1957, the People's Bank itself apparently took over the functions of financing agricultural development. In 1963, after the Great Leap Forward, the state established another Agricultural Bank to channel and co-ordinate funds from various ministries to the communes in the rural areas in order to ensure the unified control and direction of credit.

Throughout the transition period, the Chinese government also stimulated the creation of rural credit co-operatives to encourage peasant self-help in financing their own development. The credit co-operatives drew funds from bank loans and rural savings deposits. The bulk of their funds came from short-term deposits made by the peasants themselves. The credit co-operatives made most of these loans on an annual basis. By 1955, 130,000 credit co-operatives had come into existence. They, too, helped finance the building of producer co-operatives. In 1958, they became credit departments of the emerging communes, and simultaneously, acted as local offices of the People's Bank.

In China, as in many parts of Africa, some elements apparently sought to manipulate the credit co-operatives to their own advantage. In the early 1960s, the Communist Party organ, *The Red Flag*, called for the expulsion of "landlords, rich peasants, counter-revolutionaries and bad types who have infiltrated credit cooperatives".[1] Asserting that agricultural credit could play a critical role in achieving a socialist transition in the countryside, the party called for poor and lower-middle peasants to fill leading positions in the credit co-operatives. It stressed that all credit workers should pay special attention to poor and lower-middle peasants who formed production teams. They should reject ability to repay as the sole criterion for loans.

Bank for Industry and Commerce: Socialist state banks typically established socialized branches to service socialized industry and trade. These branches evolved over the years as both sectors grew in scope and complexity. At first, the state branch banks usually handled only short-term credit and clearing operations. They provided credit primarily to finance the mechanization of production or expansion of output of consumer goods which enabled an enterprise to repay the loan from its earnings within a year.

The state initially typically established separate investment banks to finance capital projects in each sector. These aimed to discourage unplanned investment policies, funding only those investments designated in national plans.

Over time, the socialist countries began to reduce the institutionalized separation between investment banks and state banks providing short-term credits for industry and trade. The growing complexity of their increasingly industrialized economies required greater flexibility. At the same time, the improved competence of enterprise managements and bank personnel permitted more decentralized decision-making. Nevertheless, all industries and trading enterprises typically must keep their funds in the appropriate state bank branch. This enables the bank to monitor all their purchases and sales. Thus the state bank can determine the extent to which any particular enterprise may have under- or overfulfilled its target. The bank may extend credit to an enterprise for additional investments, as well as for working credit, in accordance with the plan. Bank personnel receive extensive specialized training to enable them to advise enterprise managements in particular branches of industry or trade concerning their special financial problems.

Savings Banks: The state banking system generally includes some form of savings bank, which holds savings deposited by individual members of the general population. The bank pays individual depositors a low rate of interest, typically around 3 per cent, to encourage savings. It also provides credit to individuals, for example to people who want to build their own family houses. In the German Democratic Republic, where the birth rate dropped as women entered the labour force, and labour shortages became a major concern, the savings bank specifically provided credits to young married couples to encourage them to have more children. The bank advanced this credit without interest, subsidizing it from the national budget.

Basic Principles of Socialist Banks

Part of the Overall Plan Implementation Mechanism

In general, despite variations according to the needs of particular countries, socialist banking systems have functioned according to similar basic principles as an important feature of the overall plan implementation mechanism. In every case, the state banking system constitutes a major instrument of state control over the economy. Private commercial banks, competing for customers, find no place under socialism. Socialist banks seek neither high profits nor uncommonly large volumes of credit. Indeed, in a socialist economy, either would reflect failures rather than successes. The socialist state seeks to tailor bank functions to fulfil economic needs, defining the range of lending and credit activities. Divergence from the norm may constitute an infringement of socialist law.

A centralized planning system requires that the centralized banking system function as an integral part of the administrative apparatus. It cannot pursue separate goals. The state bank constitutes the centre of the banking system, both serving and protecting state interests. It plans and steers money and credit flows. Branches make loans, clear accounts, and manage cash circulation. The state bank refinances credits granted by its associated branches and banks their money deposits.

Bank Finance for Socialist Enterprises

The Enterprises' "Own Funds": When a socialist enterprise commences production in any sector of industry, agriculture or trade, it typically receives from the national budget an endowment, a funding capital. The amounts received are determined according to certain norms. These constitute the enterprise's "own funds". Management uses its "own funds" to finance its fixed and working assets.

Bank Credit: Once it is operational, the enterprise may seek credit from the bank to finance inventories which may exceed the initial norm, assets affected by seasonal fluctuations, and other gaps in funds that cannot be planned beforehand. Over time, socialist states have broadened the scope of bank credits, permitting them to finance heavy industry not subject to seasonal fluctuations, and a specified percentage of current output. In some countries, banks also provide enterprises with credit to finance unplanned stocks and temporary drains on an enterprise's own funds caused by miscalculations.

Several factors may influence the amount of credit a state bank provides. Enterprise managers, seeking to increase their output in the hope of overfulfilling targets may request additional credit. The bank, on the other hand, as part of its supervisory role, aims to avoid inflation by limiting the expansion of credit to the amount required to meet targets. It may withhold credit from enterprises in order to reduce demand for material resources and prevent hoarding of scarce inputs.

The Bank's Clearing Functions: In socialist countries, all enterprises' financial transactions typically go through the state banking system. Banks provide the only source of credit. No enterprise may lend funds, provide bills of exchange, or discount credit for other enterprises. This enables the state banks to monitor all payments and credit transactions. A supply enterprise, selling goods to a buyer in another city, must present its claim in the form of a document submitted to the bank which then collects the amount owed by transferring it from the buyer's to the seller's account. The bank may pay the supplier's claim from the buyer's clearing account if it contains sufficient funds; or it may grant an earmarked payments credit; or it may wait until the buyer has enough money in its own account to redeem the claim. These constitute various forms of what is called "bank collection".

A buying enterprise uses money orders to pay for goods only if the supplier is in the same locality. Enterprises may generally use cheques only to pay transport firms. As Table 18.1 shows, bank collections, at least in the Soviet Union, have become the predominant form of settlement procedure.

Table 18.1
Settlement Transactions in the Soviet Union

	1971 %	*1974 %*
Bank Collection	60.1	63.8
Money Orders	28.1	27.5
Cheques	8.6	5.4
Letters of Credit	3.2	3.3
	100.0	100.0

Source: *Den'gi i Kredit*, 9/1975, p. 34, cited in Zwass, *Money, Banking and Credit*.

Table 18.2
Structure of Working Funds of Enterprises in Soviet Union and Poland

	Poland %	*Soviet Union* %
Working Funds	100.0	100.0
Own Funds and Similar	22.3	28.0
Bank Credits	39.6	45.0
Creditors	21.9	20.4
Others	16.2	6.6

Source: *Narodnoe khoziastvo SSR 1974, Information Bulletin*, Narodowy Bank Polski, 1975, p. 19, cited in Zwass, *Money, Banking and Credit*.

Although enterprises generally may not utilize commercial credit unless the bank is willing to accept the buyer's application for payments credit, the buyer may simply owe the money to the supplier until it can pay. Obligations to such creditors, as Table 18.2 shows, may account for a considerable amount—as much as a fifth—of an enterprise's working funds.

In the early phase of socialist banking, the banks generally drew a strict line of demarcation between credits and the enterprises' own funds, and between capital and working funds. The state, not the enterprises, controlled the allocation of most profits, most of which enterprises transferred to the state budget for investment in projects defined by the state planners. As part of the overall 1970s reform aimed at greater decentralization, when enterprises received more powers to control their own investment decisions, the authorities tended to relax this line of demarcation.

Banks' Resources and Credit

Sources of Bank Funds: Socialist bank resources typically consist of: 1) the funds deposited by the nationalized sectors and co-operatives, including those of central institutions (the state budget, insurance organizations, etc.), industrial enterprises and foreign-trade enterprises; 2) monies deposited by private individuals in cash and savings deposits.

Table 18.3 indicates the sources of bank funds in Hungary and Poland in the mid-1970s, a pattern similar to those of other European socialist countries. The item "banks" includes foreign credits.[2] For Poland, the item "banks" also included savings bank deposits. The proportion of enterprises' own funds and money deposits in Hungary exceeded that in Poland, while the percentage of state funds in Hungary was smaller. This apparently reflected Hungary's efforts to increase the enterprises' own funds and decrease budget subsidies as part of its overall decentralization programme.

Table 18.3
Structure of Bank Resources in Poland and Hungary at the End of 1974

	Poland (Million zlotys)	*%*	*Hungary (Million forints)*	*%*
Own Funds	27,712	2.6	16,807[a]	6.1[a]
Reserve Funds, Deposits, etc.	—	—	696	0.2
Banks	401,152[b]	37.4[b]	95,538	34.7
Enterprises				
Time Deposits	161,111	15.0	50,742	18.5
Sight Deposits	162,484	15.1	49,120	17.9
Budget Funds	196,062	18.3	13,993	5.1
Bank Notes and Coins	117,151	10.9	34,609	12.6
Other	7,082	0.7	13,468	4.9
Total	*1,072,754*	*100.0*	*274,973*	*100.0*

[a] Hungarian banks' own funds were made up of founding capital: 300,000 shares worth of 20 forints each—6 billion forints—and profits of 10,807 million forints.
[b] Poland's banks included savings banks, holding 269 billion zlotys, or 25% of Poland's total bank resources.

Source: *Information Bulletin*, Nardowy Bank Polski, 1975, p. 35; *Handelsblatt*, 29-30 August 1975, p. 10, cited in Zwass, *Money, Banking and Credit*.

Relationship between Bank Resources and Credit: The assets and liabilities of socialist banks must balance, like those of capitalist countries. Nevertheless, the relationship between socialist banks' resources and credits differs significantly from those of capitalist banks. Socialist bankers generally view both lending and raising funds as creative, growth-promoting activities, rooted firmly in economic processes which influence one another. In a planned socialist economy, no capital or money markets exist. Most Marxists economists hold that socialist banks should accumulate monetary resources as a precondition for lending funds. Banks plan and grant credits, not on the basis of accumulated funds with anonymous buying power, but on the basis of the need for money to finance planned current production and sales. Not only should planners determine in advance the volume of credits the banks will make available to the economy, but also the extent to which money deposits must cover them. In other words, the banks should function primarily, not to create credit to maximize profits, but to mobilize and direct savings for investment in enterprises or sectors according to plan.

Local branch banks do not attempt to match the credits they grant with their own resources. A branch bank in an undeveloped rural area, for example, could not, out of the limited deposits of its clients, provide the credits necessary to expand agricultural and industrial activity. It must acquire funds deposited in branches in more developed regions. The central banking authorities must take responsibility for maintaining the balance between resources and credit on a national level, contributing over time to planned balanced and integrated national development.

Planned Credit Expansion: The state bank must steer the total monetary circulation in both its cash and non-cash forms according to an overall plan. It uses credit as its primary instrument for expanding the money supply and skims off excess funds through repayment. Local branch banks typically only determine the credit needs of the local district. The state bank compiles credit applications from the different sectors of the economy as the basis for its overall credit plan. This enables it to determine how much money the economy needs for current production (short-term credits) and investment projects financed by bank credits (long-term credits) rather than budget subsidies. The planning periods vary from country to country, ranging from quarter-year and one-year plans for short-term credits to five-year plans.

Table 18.4 lists the items included in the credit plan of the Soviet State Bank, essentially similar to that of other European socialist states.

Measures of Bank Performance: Socialist banks have evolved various techniques for granting credit in accordance with their overall credit plans to supervise and foster efficient enterprise performance and help eliminate flaws. They have had more difficulty in devising direct parameters for measuring their own performance. Since the bank's profits may result from higher rates of interest charged for overdue credits, banks cannot show efficiency by maximizing interest as their share of profits. Above-average monetary resources, a large volume of money in circulation, inordinately high

Table 18.4
The Soviet State Bank's Credit Plan

Credit resources	*Use of resources*
Bank funds	Short-term credits (itemized)
Monetary funds of the state budget	Credit for stocks, broken down by branch of the economy
Money deposits of enterprises and organizations involved in production	Long-term credits (state of debt at end of planning period)
Money for capital investment projects	Price difference (refers mainly to foreign trade)
Money for credit institutions (Investment Bank and Foreign Trade Bank)	Deductions from bank earnings
Savings of population	Cash holdings of State Bank and other assets
Profits of State Bank	
Other resources	

Source: Zwass, *Money, Banking and Credit.*

savings deposits and cash assets of enterprises or state budget reserves—any of these would tend to indicate inefficiency. Excess private savings of individuals and enterprises might reflect their inability to purchase needed items because of failures of supplier enterprises to achieve targeted outputs. State budget reserves might accumulate, not only from the overfulfilment of budget income, but also from delays in implementing major capital investment programmes. Authorities, therefore, have traditionally used minimization of overdue credits and obligations between enterprises as the primary criterion for judging state banks' efficiency.

Bank Monitoring of Enterprise Finance

Early Direct Controls: In the early stages of socialist development, socialist banks conducted careful direct supervision of the economic activities of enterprises associated with them. Trained bank personnel analysed enterprise reports, cleared procedures for payments to suppliers, and supervised the use of funds allocated through the state budget. When deviations from targets occurred, bank personnel notified party authorities or superior bodies.

Modified Techniques of Control: By the 1970s, after enterprise management skills improved, most state banks found it possible to relax these direct supervisory activities for most enterprises. The relationship between a bank and a particular enterprise may differ, however, depending on the enterprise's performance. The bank may relax controls for prospering enterprises, but strengthen them for those that perform poorly. The former typically could obtain very short-term credit, for 20 days or so to cover supplier claims or pay salaries and wages, without even presenting supporting documents. In contrast, the bank might require a poorly performing enterprise that could not make its payments to bank or suppliers on time to pay higher interest rates, or it might simply refuse to give it further loans. In an especially serious case, where the enterprise could not present adequate proof of improvement, the authorities might declare it insolvent and require a restoration programme.

The 1970s reforms tended to emphasize the requirement that poorly performing firms pay higher interest rates, rather than total withdrawal of credit. Bank authorities no longer tended to declare enterprises insolvent. Instead, they intervened directly to help overcome the difficulties identified. Thus the reforms aimed to facilitate, rather than hinder, the enterprise's efforts to solve its own problems. When an enterprise deviated from the planned balance between growth in productivity and expanded wage payments, the banks might stop bonus payments to its administration.

Interest Rate Policies

Initially, socialist banks assumed that interest rates should simply cover bank costs. Therefore they tended to charge relatively low rates—1 to 2 per cent a year, or 3 per cent for overdue credits.[3]

In their effort to diminish the banks' supervisory and administrative functions in later years, some socialist governments began to lay more emphasis on the manipulation of interest rates to encourage enterprises to choose more intelligently between the use of their own funds and bank credits. Socialist banks worked out various kinds of graduated systems for different credit purposes. They raised the rates charged for unplanned and overdue credit. Some attempted to adjust interest rates to meet the needs of the overall economy, not just those of individual enterprises or the bank.

The Soviet banks, for example, continued to charge 1, 2 and 3 per cent, respectively, for clearing credits, planned stocks and capital investments. But they raised the rate for non-seasonal commodity stockpiles to 6 per cent and for overdue credits to 8 per cent. The Polish banks raised the rate by 2 to 4 per cent a year if an enterprise departed from a planned expenditure. The Rumanian authorities set a graduated rate for planned credits, ranging from 0.5 per cent (for example, for factory kitchens to cook workers' meals) to 5 per cent (for industrial machinery and equipment). They imposed a higher 4 to 7 per cent rate for loans to overcome payment difficulties caused by economic problems, and up to 12 per cent for overdue credits. The Hungarian National Bank tended to use bank credits to bridge short-term payments difficulties in production and turnover. If an enterprise delayed payment beyond 90 days, the bank raised the interest rate by 1 per cent for each succeeding 90 days to a ceiling of 10 per cent.

Summary

Socialist states typically use the banking system as an important additional steering mechanism to ensure fulfilment of national development plans. Therefore, as an early step in the transition to socialism, the state must take over and restructure the inherited banking system. All government authorities, industrial enterprises and collective farms must make their purchases and sales through the state banking system, thus providing a built-in mechanism to monitor their performance according to national plan objectives. At the same time, the state banking system must extend credit in accordance with financial plans closely linked to physical plans to maintain essential monetary stability.

Over the years socialist banking systems have evolved to meet the changing needs of their restructured and increasingly complex national economies. Specialized branches with well-trained experts deal with the different sectors of the national economy: foreign trade, agriculture, industry and commerce.

Socialist banking systems today function in accordance with an essentially similar set of basic principles. Socialist enterprises receive their initial capital investment from the national budget in accordance with planned objectives. They may request bank credit for working capital, seasonal needs, and a few unplanned contingencies. In recent years, the banks have also helped to finance enterprises' longer-term investment needs if they comply with planned targets.

The state banking system as a whole seeks to balance its overall financial resources, reflecting the nation's accumulation of funds generated through concrete productive activities, and the expansion of credit to further augment the national output. Plan authorities typically evaluate the banking system's performance primarily in terms of its ability to minimize overdue credits and obligations between enterprises, indicating its success in helping enterprises to attain plan targets. Over the years, as enterprise management capacity has improved and the economy has become increasingly complex, the state banks have tended to shift from direct controls of enterprise activities to indirect techniques, including greater manipulation of interest rates.

Notes

1. 12 December 1963, cited in Donnithorne, *China's Economic System*, p. 411.

2. In the 1970s, when the possibility of East-West détente seemed especially hopeful, a number of socialist countries borrowed from capitalist countries in order to buy advanced machinery and technology to accelerate their industrial growth. When the economic crisis of the late 1970s and 1980s engulfed the capitalist economies, sharply reducing their demand for imports, including those from socialist countries, the latter—particularly Poland and Romania—encountered severe difficulties in repaying their debts to the capitalist commercial banks.

3. They were the first to extend loans at these low rates to Third World countries. The World Bank set up the IDA following criticisms of the higher rates it had been charging.

Exercises and Research

1. Why do most Marxists suggest that the first steps in the transition to socialism should include nationalization of the banking system? a) Why is state control of the banking system considered necessary to control the money supply? b) How have socialist states developed the state banking system as a steering mechanism for economic development?
2. Why and how have socialist states developed specialized banks as part of the state banking system? Contrast the specialized roles of foreign-trade banks, agricultural banks, and banks for industry and commerce with those of commercial banks in capitalist economies.
3. Explain why and how socialist banking principles differ from those of a capitalist system. a) Why do state banks monopolize control over all credit available to enterprises? b) What relationship exists between the socialist banking system's resources and credit expansion? What are the implications of this relationship for development of neglected areas? c) What is the relationship between socialist bank credit and the national financial plan? d) How do socialist banks measure their performance?
4. Evaluate the reasons for and the implications of the modifications introduced in the 1970s in the relationship between the state banking system and enterprises? Compare the socialist banks' interest-rate policies with those of capitalist banks.
5. Contrast the policies of the central and commercial banks in your country with those of the typical socialist state. What do you think is the significance of the differences for the pattern of credit allocation and economic development in your country? Draw on data relating to bank assets and credit in your country to support your conclusions.

Recommended Reading

(For annotations, see bibliography at the end of the book).

Abalkin, *Socialism Today*
Anchishkin, *The Theory of Growth in a Socialist Economy*
Donnithorne, *China's Economic System*
Hooker (ed), *The Fund and China*
Laski, *The Rate of Growth and the Rate of Interest*
Ma Hong, *New Strategy for China's Economy*
Nove, *The Soviet Economic System*
Richman, *Industrial Society in Communist China*
Xu Dixin *et al., China's Search for Economic Growth*
Xue Muqiao, *China's Socialist Economy*
Zwass, *Money, Banking and Credit*

Periodicals

Beijing Review, especially Special Features Series No. 3, 1982
Development and Peace
Far Eastern Economic Review
The Hungarian Journal
Monthly Review
Public Enterprise

Chapter 19: Economic Efficiency and the Socialist Pricing System

The Necessity of Price Stability

Planned socialist economies require price stability, not in the sense that prices never change, but in the sense that those price changes which do take place are controlled. This is for two reasons. First, as under capitalism, inflationary price increases would reduce real buying power and distort income distribution. Secondly, socialist planning at both the national and the enterprise level requires price stability. At the national level, prices determine the amount of funds transferred to the national budget and the funds that may be allocated through the budget to national investment and social consumption. If prices fluctuated, national planners could not formulate the necessary long-term plans, usually covering five-year periods, for the expanding production and incomes of the many separate enterprises and the entire nation.

The price system in a socialist economy has three primary functions:

1) It provides a means of measuring value, a rough approximation of the socially necessary labour time required to produce particular use values. This is essential for physical planning.
2) It provides an instrument to stimulate workers, productive enterprises and social agencies to fulfil planned social and economic tasks.
3) As national productivity increases, the appropriate development of prices helps to establish a socialist pattern of income distribution.

Socialist Economic Accounting

At the enterprise level, efficient planning and production require socialist economic accounting. Socialist economic accounting, in turn, depends on the validity of the system of calculating prices.

The Theory of Socialist Economic Accounting

Under socialism, economic accounting comprises the system of shaping planned economic relationships between enterprises and individuals. As socialist commodity production became increasingly complex, socialist theory emphasized that workers and managers in each enterprise should assume greater responsibility for planning and implementing their activities to achieve centralized plan targets. Each enterprise is an economic unit, gaining and distributing income. It enters into contracts to buy and sell products and to dispose of fixed assets and circulating funds. It must also assume responsibility for maintaining, enlarging and investing funds to increase its productivity. Within each enterprise, wages must be paid to employees according to the work they do to give them a material interest in improving their entire range of activities. This constitutes the material basis for stimulating improved participation in management, planning and socialist competition to increase the quantity and quality of the enterprise's output.

Theoretically, an enterprise utilizes economic accounting to: 1) dispose of its own funds, as separate from those of other enterprises, in accordance with the principle of equivalence; 2) ensure that all its employees have an independent economic interest in their conditions and the results of their productivity; 3) buy and sell products as commodities.

To facilitate attainment of these goals, economic accounting measures the enterprises' expenditures and their outcomes, comparing them to social requirements as laid down in the plans. Economic accounting also contributes to the equitable distribution of income, while stimulating employees to increase productivity. All these measurements and comparisons are made in terms of money prices. Hence, their validity depends on long-term price stability.

The System of Socialist Economic Accounting

Figure 19.1 shows the core of the system of economic accounting. It reveals the relationship between gross and net profits and prime costs and purchases.

The Profits of Enterprise: The prime costs of an enterprise determine the relationship between physical and financial planning at the enterprise level. Essentially, economic accounting translates the physical inputs of raw materials and labour, determined according to relevant norms and standards, into price terms. Any surplus income the enterprise obtains, over and beyond these prime costs, constitutes its gross profit. This profit of the socialist enterprise is that part of social value, expressed in terms of money, which nearly accords with the surplus value resulting from the material production process. Under socialism, thus surplus is not—as under capitalism—expropriated by a few private owners of the enterprise. Rather, it belongs to the state, representing the entire population.

The system of economic accounting separates the enterprise's profit into two components. One, the centralized net income belonging to the state, the enterprise transfers to the national budget for the state to utilize for social purposes (see Chapter 17). The second component belongs to the workers of the enterprise. Within the framework of national regulations, they may decide on whether to allocate it to increased production, to cash bonuses, or to improve social services for themselves and their families.

The planners attempt to structure prices so that when the enterprise maximizes its profits, including the share received by the workers, it maximizes benefits to society. Net profit provides an important source of accumulation

Figure 19.1
Socialist Financial Planning at the Enterprise Level

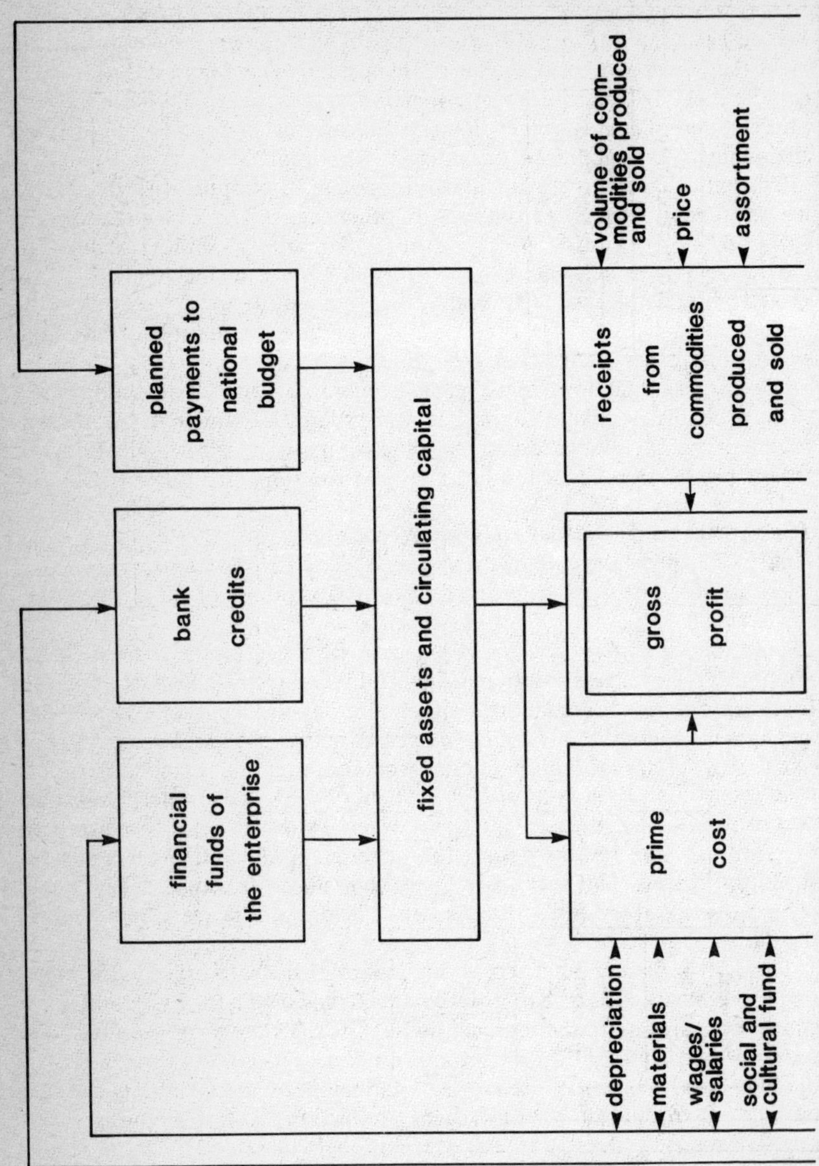

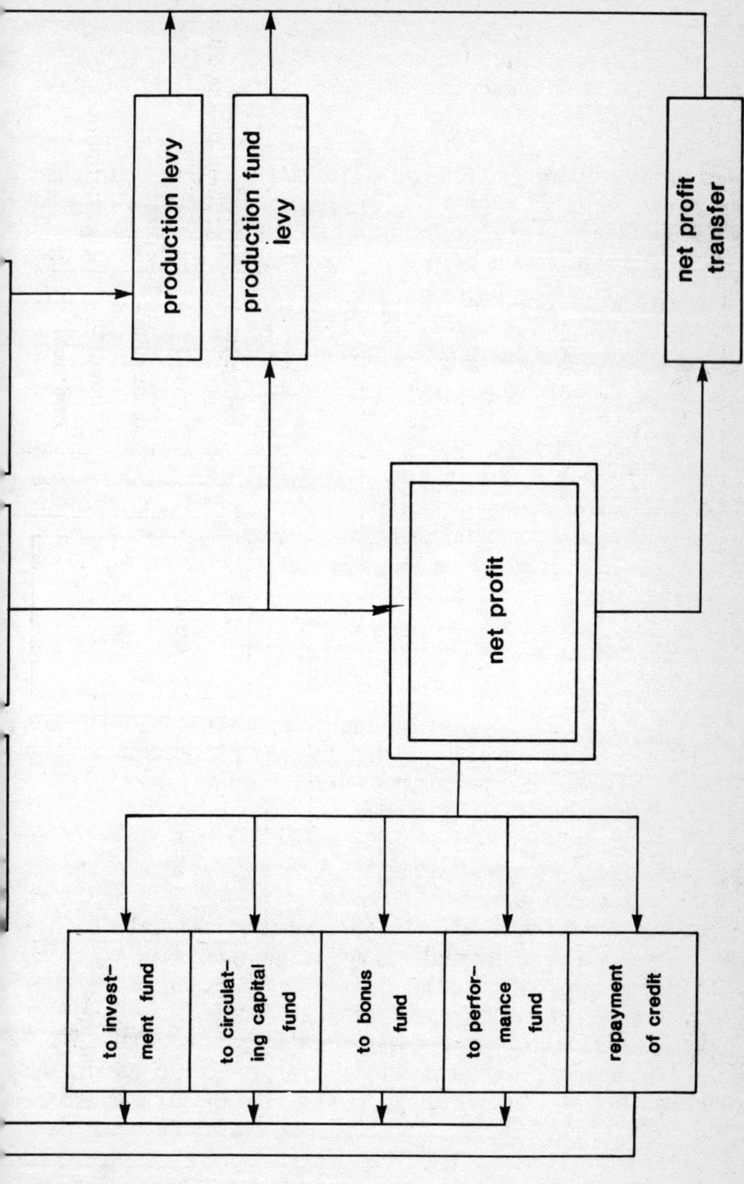
production levy
production fund levy
net profit transfer
net profit
to invest-ment fund
to circulat-ing capital fund
to bonus fund
to perfor-mance fund
repayment of credit

and social consumption for the enterprise, as well as a yardstick of its economic efficiency. At the same time, net profit provides a form of stimulation through the creation of special funds for the use of the enterprise (see the left side of the chart). It gives the workers the necessary material incentives to increase output. In the long run, as the workers' consciousness rises, and the development of technology increases productivity while reducing the separation between mental and manual labour, the importance of these material incentives should diminish.

Social Considerations Relating to Enterprise Profits: Under socialism, unlike capitalism, profit cannot act as an exclusive yardstick, especially for social efficiency. Socialist planners must consider the social implications of four sets of factors which may affect the profits of an enterprise:

(1) Changes in price may influence the volume of profit without necessarily reflecting changes in the economic behaviour of the enterprise.

(2) Profit only partially reflects expenditure for use values produced, for the enterprise cannot change prices continuously in response to changed demand.

(3) Profit does not express the degree to which production actually meets demand; for example, if an industrial enterprise sells its output to a wholesaler, its profits may only reflect the increase in the stocks of the wholesale enterprise, not necessarily an increase in final consumption necessary to contribute to increased production or higher living standards.

(4) The social conditions of production, like workers' safety and education and environmental protection, may increase prime costs and reduce profits.

National economic accounting, then, not only acts as a stimulator but also provides a means of taking into consideration the social implications of these four sets of factors when setting the prices which determine the size and use of the net profit available to an enterprise.

The Allocation of Net Enterprise Profits: An enterprise may allocate the net profit it retains to several funds:

The *investment fund* provides the depreciation funds which may be invested to replace machinery and equipment as they become run down.

The *performance fund* may be used in three ways: 1) to encourage employees to achieve higher output by increasing their net income if they fulfil or overfulfil the plan; 2) to finance improved living and working conditions for the workers; 3) to finance activities to rationalize production, to make small improvements at low cost that may bring greater net income to the enterprise and its employees in the future.

The *bonus fund* may be used to encourage higher output by giving special bonuses to individuals or groups for outstanding performance; or by providing yearly bonuses—as much as a month's salary to all employees. If the enterprise achieves a higher-than-planned net profit by reducing the costs of production or producing more output than planned, it enlarges the bonus fund.

The *social fund* contributes to improved working conditions, especially for late shift workers and working mothers; housing; sports and cultural activities; youth organizations; and health and social services.

The Impact of Price Changes on Profits: Every change in prices affects the pattern of funds and subsidies formulated in the national plans. It almost inevitably affects enterprises' ability to improve their employees' conditions. For this reason, socialist planners continually seek to improve the price system, to overcome the contradictory tendencies that persist during the socialist transition.

Maintaining Price Stability

Socialist countries' efforts to establish and maintain price stability tend to fall into two separate phases: the initial transition to social ownership; and the phase of socialism itself. The measures introduced by the Chinese government, while determined by particular historical circumstances, illustrate typical policies to control inflation during the initial transition stage. The experiences of the eastern European countries indicates different approaches adopted in the socialist phase.

The Chinese Experience

As in many countries prior to the transition to socialism, rampant inflation disrupted the Chinese economy under the nationalist government. Runaway inflation had rendered the national currency essentially worthless. The pre-communist government had raised its budget deficits from 20 per cent of expenditures in the 1930s to 70 per cent in the 1940s, primarily to finance its military expansion. For the most part, it had borrowed from the banks. The resulting increase in the money supply accelerated inflation: from 1935 to 1938, prices rose by 60 per cent; in the next year, 1939 to 1940, they doubled; the following year, they rose two and a half times; from 1941 to 1945, they tripled annually. With increased trade following the defeat of Japan at the end of World War II, the inflation rate temporarily slowed. But when the government resumed the civil war in a renewed attempt to defeat the communists, inflationary pressures again multiplied, pushing prices up at the unbelievable rate of 7.5 million times between 1946 and 1949.

Chronic inflation sharply distorted income distribution. Employees' wages failed to keep pace with rising prices. Profiteers made millions. They misallocated resources, hoarding goods or spending their incomes on luxury items, while the majority of the population barely survived. By the final stages, workers had to convert their money wages to goods immediately, before they became worthless. People took time off from their jobs to carry bundles of paper money to buy groceries. Finally, they resorted to barter. Government-issued currency cost more to print than their value in exchange. By the time the communists took power in 1949, the Chinese economy lay in ruins.

Consumer goods were extremely scarce. The entire transport system had collapsed.

Imposing Price Stability: The new government immediately imposed price control and rationed necessities. It took a year to stabilize prices, a year during which the people rebuilt rudimentary transport networks and started up old industries. By 1950, prices had actually declined. A number of smaller businesses went bankrupt in the still largely private enterprise economy. With the outbreak of the Korean War (1950-53), inflationary pressures resumed; but, after an initial 20 per cent price rise, by 1952, despite the war, the government had restored price stability.

How did the Chinese communist government achieve price stability? As a first step, it expanded the state bank, the People's Bank of China.[1] The new government discriminated between the private banks, immediately taking over the biggest banks and eliminating foreign banks. The Communist Party organ, *Red Flag*, asserted, "capitalism supplies the essential prerequisites for the foundation of socialism, and the big banks are one of these prerequisites." Therefore, "the big capitalist banks are not abolished or simply discarded, but are grabbed as ready-made organs to serve socialism."[2]

The government initially permitted medium and small banks to continue to operate. A number went bankrupt in 1950, however, as a result of the anti-inflationary measures. Eventually, the government socialized the rest of the banks. First the People's Bank acquired shares in them to establish joint state-private ownership. Sometimes the former managers remained, continuing to receive fixed salaries. Gradually, the People's Bank exerted full control over their activities.

Currency Reform: The People's Bank immediately issued a new uniform currency. Previously, several currencies had circulated throughout the country: the virtually worthless nationalist money, issued by the previous government; the currency issued by the communists in the liberated areas, which remained relatively stable; and foreign currencies. By 1949, the People's Bank had replaced these with a new, unified currency, the *jen-min-pi.*[3]

A Balanced Budget: The Chinese communist government introduced measures to restore industry and agriculture to their pre-war levels so as to augment production and distribution of goods and alleviate shortages. Simultaneously, it imposed a balanced budget, restored confidence in the currency, and controlled the supply of money and credit through the People's Bank.

To balance the budget, the government cut expenditures. In particular, it reduced the previous government's swollen and corrupt bureaucracy. Simultaneously, it reorganized the tax system to increase taxes on the higher-income groups, particularly in the developed urban centres. It centralized fiscal management by transferring local government functions to the central government. It unified the local and central government into a single national budget. Most important of all, it created conditions ensuring growing employment of the previously underemployed resources, especially human resources.

Credit Control: As in most other socialist countries, the People's Bank became the only source of credit. Initially, it did not even grant credit to individuals. They could obtain loans from private sources, and the state imposed limits on the interest charges they had to pay. The People's Bank encouraged peasants in the rural areas to establish credit co-operatives based primarily on their own savings deposits (see Chapter 18).

When the Korean War started, the government financed its increased military expenditure by non-inflationary means. It broadened the tax base and improved the administrative efficiency of collection. It covered the remaining deficit, about a tenth of the budget, by selling bonds to the public and by citizens' contributions.[4] The People's Bank followed a tight, deflationary credit policy. It curbed speculation and refused credit for any projects that might involve hoarding as a basis for black-market operations.

To ensure continuing confidence in the currency, the government guaranteed the purchasing power of wages, salaries, bank deposits and bond issues by expressing their value in terms of baskets of commodities. These varied from region to region, but generally included food staples, cotton cloth, coal and vegetable oils. The authorities quoted the value of each unit once a week or every ten days. In other words, a person who deposited 10 jen-min-pi in the bank would know that he could buy the equivalent amount of goods stated on the day of the deposit, no matter what happened to the future value of the jen-min-pi; the bank guaranteed it. In the long run, the guarantee depended on the government's ability to ensure adequate production and maintain people's confidence in the currency.

Controlling Inflationary Pressures under Socialism

Inflationary Factors: Even after socialism is established, inflationary pressures may still persist. Critics point out that socialist countries invest heavily in basic industries with long-time horizons for completion. This inevitably expands demand more rapidly than production of consumer goods.

Critics also claim that collective agricultural production has lagged, causing socialist countries which had earlier exported foodstuffs and raw materials to import them. Mainstream critics go further and object to socialists' efforts to administer prices, arguing that price fluctuations in the "free market" would ensure better allocation of resources.

Socialist planners hold, however, that, in the long run, they must ensure adequate investment in basic industries to spur increasingly efficient productivity throughout the economy. They point out that the rates of growth in socialist countries have generally outstripped those of capitalist countries.

Socialist theorists maintain that growing populations and higher incomes accompanying increased productivity have raised the domestic demand for agricultural produce formerly exported. To increase agricultural productivity, industry must produce more agricultural machinery, equipment and fertilizers. At the same time, only by collectivizing their productive activities will peasants be able to afford to purchase and efficiently utilize the new machinery and equipment.

In Poland, where agriculture remained predominantly (three-quarters) in the private sector, levels of agricultural efficiency remained relatively low. Polish planners sought to offset this deficiency by investing even more heavily than other socialist states in heavy industry, borrowing heavily from foreign capitalist commercial banks to finance imported machinery and equipment. The economic crises in Europe hindered the export of Polish goods required to earn the funds needed to repay these foreign debts. The western banks put pressure on the Polish government to reduce its expenditure on food subsidies. In the late 1970s, the Polish government raised the prices of agricultural produce, leading to widespread protests.

Socialist theorists admit that several factors may contribute to disequilibrium between demand and supply in a planned socialist economy. First, enterprises may seek to accumulate excessive inventories to avoid the effects of shortages. This increases the demand for products without contributing to increased supplies of final consumer items. Second, although planners seek to establish overall limits on wages and peasant incomes to contain their demand within the national productive capability, enterprises and collectives pay bonuses as monetary incentives. These may increase demand more rapidly than planned. Third, as industry expands, it requires greater supplies of raw materials. Prime costs tend to rise as mineral deposits are depleted and less fertile soils are cultivated to grow needed agricultural crops. Fourth, as socialist countries expand their trade with capitalist countries, the rising import prices may introduce inflationary pressures into their economies. Just as deteriorating terms of trade aggravate inflationary pressures in African countries so rising import prices require socialist states to export more of their own resources to acquire planned imports of machinery and equipment. In 1973 alone, the rising prices of goods imported from capitalist countries reduced the purchasing power of Czechoslovakia's exports by 29 per cent.

Limiting General Price Increases: Socialist planners generally reject the capitalist method of achieving a balance between the supply and demand for goods, namely, permitting prices of scarce commodities to rise. This, they maintain, leads to inequitable distribution of goods, enabling only those with higher incomes to purchase necessities in short supply. Instead, they seek to plan the simultaneous growth of production and demand. To overcome unequal distribution of necessities in short supply, especially in the early stages of the transition process, they would prefer to ration necessities. In the longer run, they seek to overcome shortages through planned industrial development to raise productivity in all sectors.

Despite inflationary pressures, socialist governments have generally succeeded in imposing and maintaining overall price stability. They have usually contained inflationary pressures by maintaining a strict incomes policy, keeping wage increases in line with rising productivity, and restricting money expansion through credit to the actual production of goods and services. Most European socialist states have kept the general level of price increases policy, keeping wage increases in line with rising productivity, and restricting money expansion through credit to the actual production of goods and services. Most European socialist states have kept the general level of price increases below the relatively low rates registered in the Federal Republic of Germany, and well below the higher rates of inflation in Italy and Britain. In the decentralized economy of Yugoslavia, however, inflation rates rose in the mid-1970s to about 23 per cent. As Poland and Hungary opted for more market influence and decentralization, they, too, experienced rising prices. The 1982 Comecon handbook showed 1981 prices in Poland rose 19 per cent, and in Hungary 5 per cent.

Some Details of Socialist Price-Setting Techniques

Consumer Prices

Socialist planners typically distinguish between consumer prices and prices for industrial goods, using somewhat different administrative principles for determining each. Socialist economists do not always agree about the best kind of price sytem for consumer goods. In some countries, like the German Democratic Republic, the authorities establish three sets of consumer prices:

1) Strictly fixed prices for all goods and services related to the basic needs of the population, including foodstuffs and clothing; rents (usually about a tenth of the family income); public transport; and electricity for domestic use. The state finances these low fixed prices through subsidies.
2) Prices of higher-quality, more fashionable consumer goods must cover costs and normal profits. These change as production costs change; for example, if raw-material costs rise, they will probably go up.
3) The prices of the highest-quality imported luxury items, those using sophisticated technologies (like electronics equipment) or characterized by shortages (e.g. cars) must cover not only production costs and normal profits, but also additional surpluses which are transferred to the national budget. These additional surpluses help finance the subsidies required to keep prices for consumer necessities low. They also tend to fall more heavily on the higher-income groups who can afford the luxuries. Along with planned reductions of wage differentials and graduated income tax, this technique narrows the gap between the highest- and lowest-income groups.

Socialist planners in other countries reject this three-tiered system. They argue that, while low-priced consumer necessities advantage some, they also encourage waste; for example, they claim that very low bread prices may encourage peasants to feed bread to their pigs. Once socialist reconstruction has eliminated the inherited skewed income distribution and distorted resource allocation pattern, they argue, the government should set prices to cover costs and strive to increase productivity to raise living standards for all groups. This will also permit the consumers to determine through the market which goods to purchase.

Industrial Goods Prices

Socialist planners generally set the prices of industrial goods, that is, machinery, equipment and materials for production in all sectors of the economy, according to three main principles: a) they should cover costs and enable enterprises to gain a normal profit; b) they should stimulate the economically efficient use of energy, raw materials, imported goods and labour; c) they should stimulate the production of goods at the highest possible scientific and technical standards, terminating the production of obsolete products.

These principles, together with the inflationary pressures imported from the capitalist world market (like rising oil prices), tend to lead to rising prices for industrial goods. The material conditions for the domestic production of industrial goods in the European socialist countries have worsened as they have depleted available resources, especially for minerals and energy-based materials. The prices of investment goods, especially in construction activities, have tended to grow faster than the production of consumer goods. This reflects the lack of increasingly productive technical equipment and investments in uncompleted projects.

The calculation of industrial goods' prices usually takes into consideration the following factors:

Prime cost + profit	=	cost prices, not changed by subsidies and levies (related to the national budget)
Factory prices	=	price at which products are sold to wholesalers
Industrial delivery prices + wholesale margin	=	price at which products are sold to retailers
Wholesale price + retail margin	=	final price at retail level

Planners must analyse how each price change affects all others. As a socialist economy matures, this interconnectedness underscores the necessity of formulating complex input-output analyses which, over the five-year-plan periods, take into account changing prices.

Whatever price systems socialist economists adopt, they must consider the impact of three factors on the prices they set for particular commodities: a) the way the price of the particular components of production—labour, materials, machinery and equipment—influence the value of the commodities and, in the long run, help or hinder the desired increase in labour productivity; b) the way the planned use of different equipment and the declining availability of national resources may modify prices of some components; c) the way the scarcity of supply in relation to demand, the social importance of certain goods, or the desire to introduce special incentives to stimulate technological progress may cause variations in the price of other components.

Summary

Socialist economies must ensure price stability, not only to avoid the income distribution distortions that typically accompany inflation, but also to formulate and implement long-term plans. Socialist planners have developed the science of socialist economic accounting to achieve efficient planning and production between the national economy and enterprises; among enterprises; and between enterprises and their workers. Socialist economic accounting requires that planners structure prices to ensure that, when the enterprise maximizes its profit, it stimulates the workers to increase productivity, thus maximizing the benefits to society in terms of meeting its requirements.

Socialist measures to stabilize prices may be grouped into two phases, those introduced in the transition to socialism, and those employed under socialist conditions. As illustrated in China, rampant inflation often characterizes pre-socialist economies, whereas elsewhere, during the transition to socialism, the new government restored monetary stability by nationalizing the banks, introducing a thoroughgoing currency reform, and rigorously restricting credit to match increased output. Once socialism has been established, inflationary pressures may persist since scarcity still prevails. Socialist planners claim, nevertheless, that rigorous financial planning implemented through the national budget and the socialist banking system enables them to maintain relative price stability.

Socialist countries do not always agree on the appropriate approach to price formation, either for consumer goods or industrial commodities. Some planners use subsidies to hold down the prices of consumer necessities, while raising those of luxury and semi-luxury goods in short supply to produce an offsetting surplus. Others argue that once reconstruction has built a balanced, integrated economy, planners should let consumer goods' prices respond to market demand. As for industrial commodities, the prices set must cover costs and enable enterprises to gain a normal profit and stimulate efficient use of resources at the highest possible technical standard.

In short, socialist planners continue to debate the details of the price-fixing techniques designed to stimulate workers to increase output to meet social needs. This reflects the need for continuing efforts to reconcile the contradictory tendencies which inevitably persist during the socialist transition. Nevertheless, they generally hold that planned utilization of the national budget and the state banking system assures the relatively stable prices required to formulate and implement plans to augment productivity and raise the living standards of the entire population.

Notes

1. The People's Bank had been operating in the liberated areas since the 1930s, so its managers already had experience and some trained personnel.
2. 4 January 1964, cited in Donnithorne, *China's Economic System*, p. 403.

3. In the German Democratic Republic, under somewhat similar circumstances, the state bank issued the new currency at differing rates. It provided new currency for the old at a one-to-one ratio for workers and other small bank depositors. It provided the new currency at a rate of one new note for every two or more of the old to larger capitalist depositors. Thus it used the currency reform to begin to reduce the income distribution gap.

4. Unlike capitalist governments, it did not sell bonds to the banks which would have reintroduced inflationary pressures.

Exercises and Research

1. Explain why socialist planning requires price stability.
2. Analyse how economic accounting might contribute to increased productivity and increasingly equitable income distribution under socialism.
3. What is the concept of gross profit in a socialist economy?
   a) Contrast this concept to that of Gross Operating Profit in the national accounts of typical capitalist economies.
   b) Discuss the extent and significance of the allocation of profits to different sectors of the population under socialism as compared to capitalism.
   c) Explain why profit cannot be the exclusive yardstick for measuring social efficiency under socialism.
   d) How does a typical socialist enterprise allocate the profits it retains?
4. Analyse the way the new Chinese government established price stability after it took power, identifying the critical steps it took and explaining why those steps appeared necessary.
5. What do critics of socialism claim to be the cause of inflationary pressures under socialism? How do socialist governments typically seek to prevent inflationary increases in the general price level?
6. Contrast the consequences of rationing goods with permitting prices to rise as a means of allocating necessities in scare supply.
7. Discuss the advantages and disadvantages of different socialist methods for determining price levels.
8. If your country's government sought to establish socialism, what steps would you recommend that it undertake to ensure price stability? Discuss specific measures it would need to implement in regard to the particular financial institutions existing in your country. Give the reasons for your proposals.

Recommended Reading

(For annotations, see bibliography at the end of the book.)

Abalkin, *Socialism Today*
Anchishkin, *The Theory of Growth in a Socialist Economy*
Donnithorne, *China's Economic System*
Gurley, *China's Economy and the Maoist Strategy*
Hooker (ed.), *The Fund and China*
Ma Hong, *New Strategy for China's Economy*
Nove, *The Soviet Economic System*
Richman, *Industrial Society in Communist China*
Turgeon, *The Contrasting Economies*
Xu Dixin *et al.*, *China's Search for Economic Growth*
Xue Muqiao, *China's Socialist Economy*
Zwass, *Money, Banking and Credit*

Periodicals

Beijing Review
Development and Peace
Far Eastern Economic Review
The Hungarian Journal
Public Enterprise

Chapter 20: An Unfinished Conclusion

By the 1980s, financial crisis had engulfed most of the independent states of Africa. Many of the measures that their governments introduced worsened the impact of this crisis on the majority of their populations. For this reason, if for no other, scholars and practitioners need to re-examine their theoretical tools and policy prescriptions for dealing with the complex, interrelated issues of money, banking and public finance.

This text provides the framework for that kind of critical review. It proposes a problem-solving methodology to enable readers to analyse for themselves the underlying causes of the financial difficulties confronting African states; and the solutions offered by the major alternative theories available in the literature. Critical examination of those theories in the light of the growing amounts of evidence drawn from African experiences should facilitate assessment of which theory offers a more useful guide to needed institutional change.

Two major categories of theory purport to offer comprehensive explanations and solutions to the monetary and financial problems plaguing African states. The first, here dubbed "mainstream", constitutes the predominant set of theories not only in industrialized capitalist countries but also in African universities and government circles. The literature abounds with debates among mainstream theorists, especially between monetarists and Keynesians, on many of the critical issues here discussed. Nevertheless, they agree on the basic assumptions and principles underlying their arguments. Market forces under conditions typically assumed to be competitive tend to bring supply and demand to rest at an equilibrium price where all factors of production receive returns equal to their marginal products. This also holds true for financial markets, where interest rates serve as prices determining the supply of and demand for money. Governments should, therefore, limit their interventions in the economy primarily to indirect central bank measures; tax, budgetary expenditure and borrowing; and, where necessary, limited subsidies and autonomous public enterprise.

The second major category of theorists on monetary and financial issues is the Marxist category which provides qualitatively different explanations of the political and economic problems confronting Third World countries, and advocates socialism. Although many African states have explicitly opted for socialism, few have successfully formulated or implemented the institutional changes required to achieve it. Furthermore, Marxists are almost alone among the proponents of socialism in focusing attention specifically on the way money, banking and public finance relate to the essential transformation.

Like mainstream theorists, Marxists debate among themselves the details of their analysis. However, they generally adopt a methodology, historical materialism, which differs fundamentally from that underpinning mainstream theories. Most Marxists agree that the contradictions inherent in capitalism, revealed by the labour theory of value, inevitably culminate in crises like those plaguing African governments in the 1980s. They advocate that Third World governments, representing an alliance of workers, peasants and supportive nationalist elements, take over the nation's economic "commanding heights"—including banks and financial institutions—and restructure them to effect a gradual transition to socialism.

Given severe limits on space, this text has been unable to do more than outline the basic issues and theoretical debates, presenting a limited range of evidence to enable readers to make an initial evaluation of them. This text offers its readers no final conclusions. Rather, they should treat it as an introduction to a far more complex study. The text will have achieved its goal if it stimulates much-needed research and evaluation among African theoreticians, policy makers and students on how to reshape monetary and financial policies and institutions to make them contribute more effectively to increased productive employment opportunities and rising living standards for the great majority of the African peoples.

Annotated Bibliography

Books and Chapters of Books

This bibliography could not include all the works on so wide a field as money, banking and public finance relating to capitalist and socialist development in Africa, let alone the rest of the world. It attempts to bring together the main works relating to relevant topics in Africa, and some more general works dealing with the basic principles of both major categories of theory. It does not attempt to include the spate of recent articles on relevant topics, but suggests some periodicals which focus on these issues.

Abalkin, L.I., *Socialism Today: The Economic System of Socialism* (Moscow: Progress Publishers, 1980). A Soviet author discusses planning and the use of incentives in a socialist economy.

Abdi, A.I., *Commercial Banks and Economic Development: The Experiences of Eastern Africa*, (New York: Praeger, 1977). A mainstream analysis of mobilization of domestic savings via commercial banks and other financial institutions in the context of East African banking systems, 1950-73.

Ahmad, N., *Deficit Financing, Inflation and Capital Formation—the Ghanaian Experience, 1960-65*, (Munich: Weltforum-Verlag GmbH, 1970). Using mainstream theory as a guide, analyses statistics to assess the effect of government deficit financing of capital and current expenditures and consequent inflationary pressures in conditions called "investment without growth".

Ajay, S.I., and Oyo, O.O., *Money and Banking, Analysis and Policy in the Nigerian Context*, (London: George Allen & Unwin, 1981). Writing for Nigerian students of monetary economics, the authors use Nigerian illustrations to discuss the mainstream debates concerning money and banking.

Akinlan, S.A., *The Law of International Economic Institutions in Africa*, (Leyden: A.W. Suthoff, 1977). A description of the laws governing international institutions that affect African economies, including local, regional and continent-wide institutions.

Aliber, R.Z. (ed.), *The Political Economics of Monetary Reform*, (London: Macmillan, 1977). Papers from a series of conferences in the 1970s dealing with institutional and mainstream theoretical issues arising from the "most severe" shocks to international financial arrangements "since the Great Depression".

Allen, P.R., and Kenen, P.B., *Asset Markets, Exchange Rates and Economic Integration*, (London: Cambridge University Press, 1980). A mainstream treatise analysing the effectiveness of national monetary and fiscal policies and appraising the costs and benefits of economic unions, especially monetary unions.

Amin, S., *Accumulation on a World Scale*, (New York: Monthly Review Press, 1974) (2 vols). A Marxist critique of the inability of mainstream theories to explain underdevelopment, and discussion of how international capitalist accumulation fosters underdevelopment in the disarticulated economies of the Third World, particularly Africa.

—— *Imperialism and Unequal Development*, (New York: Monthly Review Press, 1977). Marxist analysis of the role of imperialism in causing unequal development in Third World countries.

Anchishkin, A., *The Theory of Growth in a Socialist Economy*, (Moscow: Progress Publishers, 1977). A member of the USSR Academy of Sciences uses models to provide an analytical description of principles of economic growth under socialism.

Anderson, J.O., *Studies in the Theory of Unequal Exchange between Nations*, (Finland: Abo Akademi, 1976). Utilizes the law of value to analyse unequal exchange between nations, including a critique of Emmanuel's thesis.

Angelini, A., Eng, M., and Lees, F.L., *International Lending, Risk and the Euromarkets*, (London: Macmillan Press, 1979). Written in consultation with private and international bankers in the context of the upsurge of transnational corporations, the Euromarket, and the "unprecedented growth of international commercial banks" culminating in new problems of stagnation, inflation and currency fluctuation.

Aromolaran, A., *West African Economics Today*, (Ibadan: Progresso Economic Research Centre, 1968). Mainstream discussion of West African economies, with chapters on money and banking, currency boards, central banks, commercial banks, the Lagos Stock Exchange, the Nigerian National Development Bank, foreign aid, and government public enterprise.

Arowolo, E.A., "The Taxation of Low Incomes in African Countries", *IMF Staff Papers, XV*, (July 1968).

Ayida, A.A. (ed.), *Reconstruction and Development in Nigeria*, (Ibadan: Oxford University Press, 1971). Includes chapters on trends in banking and monetary policy to 1968, balance of trade and payments, fiscal measures, prices, wages and costs.

Ayres, R.L., *Banking on the Poor—the World Bank and World Poverty*, (Cambridge, Mass.: MIT Press, 1984). A Fellow with the British Overseas Development Council traces the evolution of World Bank policy under McNamara, 1968-81.

Bailey, R., *Africa's Industrial Future*, (Colorado: Westview Press, 1977). A mainstream approach to industrialization, which includes a chapter on international finance through the World Bank, concluding that private foreign investment still has a role to play though perhaps through "new versions of the mixed economy".

Baldwin, R.E., *Economic Development and Export Growth—A Study of Northern Rhodesia, 1920-1960*, (Berkeley: University of California Press, 1966). A mainstream analysis of Zambia's dual economy, including a discussion of public-sector finance in the pre-independence era.

Baran, P., *The Political Economy of Growth*, (New York: Monthly Review Press, 1957). A Marxist analysis, based largely on evidence from Latin America, of how locally generated investable surpluses are misutilized in Third World countries.

Barber, W.J., *The Economy of British Central Africa—A Case Study of Economic*

Development in a Dualistic Society, (Stanford: Stanford University Press, 1961). A mainstream analysis of the penetration of the money economy and its impact in aggregate and by sector, including its effect on income distribution.

Barnett, A.D., *China's Economy in Global Perspective*, (Washington, DC: The Brookings Institute, 1981). A consultant to several US government agencies focuses on post-Mao trends which call for rapid increases in world trade, including import of capital, goods and technology, encouraging foreign investment and foreign borrowing. Includes discussion of state budget.

Belassa, B. (ed.), *Changing Patterns in Foreign Trade and Payments*, (New York: W.W. Norton and Co., 1978) (3rd edn). Mainstream theorists discuss trade liberalization and adjustment problems; oil, commodities and the New International Economic Order; foreign investment and transnational corporations; international economic interdependence and proposed market reforms as perceived in the mid 1960s.

Bettelheim, C., *The Transition to Socialist Economy*, (trans. B. Pearce) (Atlantic Highlands, NJ: Humanities Press, 1975). A French Marxist considers the problems of transition to socialism.

Bird, R.M., *Taxing Agricultural Land in Developing Countries*, Cambridge, Mass: Harvard University Press, 1974). A mainstream analysis of alternative systems of taxing agriculture in Africa.

Boddy, M., *The Building Societies*, (London: Macmillan Press, 1980). The history and role of building societies in the housing and financial markets of England, emphasizing that building societies have "become major financial institutions . . . integrated with the rest of the financial market".

Brenner, M.M., *The Politics of International Monetary Reform—The Exchange Crisis*, (Cambridge, Mass: Ballinger Publishing Co., 1976). A mainstream economist reviews the exchange crisis of 1973, the theories and practices of the major financial and trading nations, the introduction of floating exchange rates, and the ongoing debate of their consequences.

Brown, Robert, and Cummings, Robert, *The Lagos Plan vs. The Berg Report*. (Lawrenceville, Va: Brunswick Publishing Co., 1984). A comparison and critique of the World Bank report, written by Berg, in light of the Lagos Plan for Action proposals.

Butterworths' Taxation Statutes Service (Durban, South Africa: Butterworths). A branch of an international tax analysing service, it provides looseleaf reports on tax laws and administration in South Africa and the Federation of Rhodesia and Nyasaland.

Carlson, R.S., Remmers, H.L., Hekman, C.R., Eiteman, D.K. and Stonehill, A.I., *International Finance—Case Studies and Simulation*, (Reading, Mass: Addison-Wesley Publishing Co., 1980). Case studies used in teaching mainstream international finance in US universities to help future businessmen consider alternate approaches to dealing with foreign-exchange risks, working capital, international banking, government controls and taxes. One study focuses on the options facing transnational banks investments in Africa, given different national environments.

Chachaoliades, M., *International Monetary Theory and Policy*, (New York: McGraw Hill, 1978). A textbook providing the mainstream explanations for the consequences of flexible versus fixed exchange rates for employment, capital movements and balance of payments equilibria.

Channon, F., *British Banking Strategy and the International Challenge*, (London: Macmillan, 1977). A history of post-World War II private British financial institutions as they entered into competition with American, Japanese and

European banks in the international monetary markets, joining international consortia to strengthen their positions.

Chibwe, E.C., *Arab Dollars for Africa*, (London: Croom-Helm, 1976). A Commissioner of Taxes and Permanent Secretary to the Zambian Treasury reviews the role of Arab funds in financing African development, focusing on their potential contribution through development banks.

Cliffe, L. and Saul, J. *Socialism in Tanzania*, (East Africa Publishing House, 1973 2 vols). A series of chapters on Tanzania's efforts to implement a transition to socialism, including an excellent analysis on the banks following nationalization by John Loxley.

Cline, W.R., and associates, *World Inflation and the Developing Countries*, (Washington, DC: Brookings Institute, 1981). A discussion of recent data relating to causes of inflation, as suggested by mainstream theories, in developing countries.

Clower, R.W., Dalton, G., Harwitz, M., and Walters, A.A., *Growth without Development—An Economic Survey of Liberia*, (Northwest University Press, 1966). Includes chapters on planning and fiscal policy, foreign concessions and foreign aid, and concludes, within a mainstream framework, that policy prescriptions for development will fail if government authorities are not interested in development to meet people's needs.

Cohen, B.J., *Organizing the World's Money—The Political Economy of International Monetary Relations*, (New York: Basic Books, 1977). Mainstream examination of the difficulties inherent in improving the international monetary system, given politically sovereign states and formally independent national currencies.

—— *Banks and the Balance of Payments*, (Montclair: Allanheld, Osmon & Co., 1981). Mainstream analysis of the growing financial intermediations of private banks as they affect global balance of payments and the capitalist international monetary system, with evidence from specific countries.

Cohen, J.M. and Koehn, P.H., *Ethiopian Provincial and Municipal Government—Imperial Patterns and Post-revolutionary Changes*, (East Lansing: African Studies Center, Michigan State University, 1980). Focuses on an analysis of local government in Imperial Ethiopia, with case studies, including tax collection. A chapter on post-revolutionary changes considers implications for efforts to increase participation.

Cox-George, N.A., *Finance and Development in West Africa—The Sierra Leone Experience*, (London: Dennis Dobson, 1961). Discusses public finance in the world wars and the Great Depression years, tentatively suggesting that, not Furnival, but Hobson or Lenin provide a better explanatory theory of the role of commercial interests in shaping development.

Curran, W., *Banking and the Global System*. US investment banker describes the changing relationships between individual depositors, corporations and banks in the modern capitalist economic system.

Daniels, M.B., *Corporate Financial Statements*, (New York: Arno Press, 1980). Discusses some of the problems of preparing and comprehending corporate financial statements, including valuation of plant and treatment of reserves for company executives and shareholders.

Davies, R.W., *The Development of the Soviet Budgetary System*, (Cambridge: Cambridge University Press, 1958). A British economist examines the historical pre-World War II development of the Soviet financial system, attempting to distinguish those aspects shaped by its specific pre-revolutionary Russian heritage and the particular circumstances of Soviet development from those deriving from socialist planning theory and practices.

Davis, S.I., *The Management Functions in International Banking*, (London: Macmillan, 1979). Based on a questionnaire filled out by 40 senior bank officials and 30 senior corporate officers, discusses the bankers' perspective on the new issues affecting international banks since the "international banking crisis of confidence" of the 1970s.

Dean, E., *Plan Implementation in Nigeria: 1962-1966*, (Ibadan: Oxford University Press, 1972). Includes a chapter on financing the six-year plan, and concludes that the failure to obtain revenue goals was more serious than rising costs; also shortfall in foreign aid led to rapid increase in foreign borrowing, both conventional loans and suppliers' credits.

Declaration of Tripoli on the World Bank Report entitled "Accelerated Development in Sub-Saharan Africa: An Agenda for Action", *African Development*, Vol. VII, No. 3, 1982. A 1982 declaration of the planning ministers of African states called together by the Economic Commission for Africa, holding that the Report strategy is contrary to the Lagos Plan of Action and the political, economic and social aspirations of the African people.

DeKock, G., *A History of the South African Reserve Bank (1920-52)*, (Pretoria: J.L. Van Schaik Ltd, 1954). Initially written as a doctoral thesis at Harvard University, describes the history and role of the South African Reserve Bank built by the minority state as the foundation of its industrialized apartheid system.

Dell, S. and Lawrence, R., *The Balance of Payments Adjustment Process in Developing Countries*, (New York: Pergamon Press, 1980). Written in co-operation with the UNDP, UNCTAD and Third World country analysts, shows that developing countries have confronted "a burden of adjustment out of all proportion to the degree of their responsibility for the international disequilibrium that had prevailed in recent years"; and makes recommendations to help developing countries overcome these problems.

DeVries, M.G., *The International Monetary Fund, 1966-1971—The System Under Stress*, (2 vol). An IMF staff member describes the Fund's role and provides the background documents for the six years during which it created SDRs and expanded its activities, but prior to the breakdown of fixed exchange rates. Part of a full history of the Fund by the same author.

Dobb, M., *Welfare Economics and the Economics of Socialism—Towards a Commonsense Critique*, (Cambridge: Cambridge University Press, 1970). A British Marxist economist examines some possible implications of the marginalist approach, introduced by mainstream theorists, for socialist planning.

Donnithorne, A.G., *China's Economic System*, (New York: Praeger, 1967). A scholarly analysis by an English author of the development of Chinese financial institutions, with separate chapters on the fiscal system, banking, currency and credit, price policy, etc.

Drury, A.C., *Finance Houses—Their Development and Role in the Modern Financial Sector*, (London: Waterlow Publishers Ltd, 1982). Describes emergence of finance houses to provide commercial and industrial credit, including leasing facilities, as a source of corporate finance in Great Britain.

Due, J.F., *Taxation and Economic Development in Tropical Africa*, (Cambridge, Mass: MIT Press, 1963). A US economist reports on his 1962 study of tax structures in eight former British colonies in Africa, attempting to assess their impact on development in the different circumstances confronted by each government.

Duffy, G., and Giddy, J.H., *The International Money Market*, (Englewood Cliffs,

NJ: Prentice Hall, 1978). Draws on mainstream concepts to analyse Eurocurrency markets, including determination of interest rates and credit creation as affected by public policies.

Dyker, D.A., *The Process of Investment in the Soviet Union*, (Cambridge: Cambridge University Press, 1982). A British economist assesses the cycle of fixed capital investment in the Soviet Union in the context of mainstream welfare economics and decision theory, including case studies of investment projects as well as overall plan design.

Edwards, H., *Export Credit*, (London: Shaws Linton Publications, 1980). A handbook of information for exporters seeking credit in England, it contains useful details—almost a checklist—to facilitate the process of financing exports.

Eicher, C.K., and Liedholdm, C. (eds), *Growth and Development of the Nigerian Economy*, (East Lansing: Michigan State University Press, 1970). Includes chapters on fiscal role of marketing boards, government expenditures, 1950-62 contractor finance and suppliers credits.

Elliott, C. (ed), *Constraints on the Economic Development of Zambia*, (Nairobi: Oxford University Press, 1971). A mainstream analysis of issues including financial constraints, the fiscal system, and foreign exchange during the early years of Zambian independence.

Elyanov, A.Y., *Economic Growth and the Market in the Developing Countries*, (Moscow: Progress Publishers, 1977). A Marxist analysis of the rise of commodity forms in developing countries' economies, the structure of income distribution, the specific features of personal and production consumption, and its impact on the rate and proportions of reproduction. Utilizes extensive factual illustrative material, and suggests ways of resolving some contradictions of the newly free states' economic development.

Eshag, E., *Fiscal and Monetary Policies and Problems in Developing Countries*, (Cambridge: Cambridge University Press, 1983). A Keynesian view of institutional constraints on developing country governments' use of fiscal and monetary instruments and foreign capital to achieve adequate and appropriate investments without aggravating internal and external imbalances.

Ewusi, K. (ed.), *The New International Economic Order and UNCTAD IV*, (Accra: University of Ghana, 1975). Includes a critique of the international monetary system by J.H. Frimpong-Ansah, Chairman of Standard Bank of Ghana.

Falkena, H.B., *The South African State and Its Entrepreneurs*, (Johannesburg: Ad Donkor, 1980). From an explicitly "white" mainstream viewpoint, discusses the size and scope of state intervention in the economy, including the role of public enterprises, public sector as consumer, public sector as planner of socio-economic order and stabilizer of economic activity via fiscal policy.

Fitzgerald, E.V.K., *Public Sector Investment Planning for Developing Countries*, (London: Macmillan, 1978). Discusses factors to consider in financing public investments in a state capitalist developing country where government provides the bulk of capital formation, arguing, however, that the state of the art prevents social or environmental considerations.

Fordwar, K.D., *The African Development Bank*, (New York: Pergamon Press, 1981). A former president of the African Development Bank describes its development and the debates prior to the admission of non-African states as contributors to its funds and on its board of directors.

Frankel, S.H., *Capital Investment in Africa—Its Course and Effects*, (London: Oxford Press, 1983). A survey of the course of capital investment in colonial Africa up to the 1930s, accompanied by the mainstream interpretation common to that era.

Frowan, S.F. (ed.), *A Framework of International Banking*, (Surrey: Gailford Press, 1979). A series of papers by British bankers and academics seeking to explain the recent changes in international banking, including increased private-sector financing responsibilities for balance of payment adjustments without clearly defined lender-of-last-resort facilities.

Galbraith, J.K., *Money, Whence It Came, Where It Went*, (Boston: Houghton Mifflin, 1975). An American institutionalist economist describes the history of money and financial institutions, primarily in the US, concluding that reliance on monetary policy alone is likely to have perverse consequences. Governments must, therefore, rely on fiscal measures; wage and price controls in the context of an equitable incomes policy; and increased reliance on planning techniques.

Gardiner, R. and Picket, J., *The African Development Bank 1964-1984—an Experiment in Economic Cooperation and Development*, (Abidjan: ADB, 1984). Uncritically describes the functioning of the Bank over two decades.

Germidis, D., *International Subcontracting—A New Form of Investment*, (Paris: Development Centre of the OECD, 1980). Reviews several case studies of subcontracting as a potential means of financing development, providing a catalyst to foster the inflow of foreign funds.

Ghai, D. (ed.), *Economic Independence in Africa*, (Nairobi: East Africa Literature Review Bureau, 1973). Includes chapter by B. Van Arkadie on growth and problems of state sector in independent African states and various approaches for overcoming difficulties encountered; emphasizes the danger of bureaucratic élite control.

Green, M.R., *Risk and Insurance*, (Cincinnati, Ohio: Southwestern Publisher, 1977) (4th edn). A US textbook examines basic insurance and reinsurance concepts in a capitalist economy, with a chapter on international insurance.

Green, R.H., and Seidman, A., *Unity or Poverty? The Economics of Pan Africanism*, (London: Penguin Books, 1968). Examines impact of colonial balkanization on development possibilities in Africa, and suggests continental monetary and financial institutions as part of strategy for African unity.

Gurley, J.G., *China's Economy and the Maoist Strategy*, (New York: Monthly Review Press, 1976). A socialist economist analyses Maoist strategy and its influence on China's economic development. Includes a chapter on the financial system, comparing the role of financial institutions before and after the revolution; and one on markets, prices and profit motive; it concludes the Chinese model is not universally applicable.

Halm, G.N., *A Guide to International Monetary Reform*, (Lexington: D.C. Heath & Co., 1975). A mainstream introduction to, and critical commentary on, IMF's reform proposals, arguing for greater exchange-rate flexibility.

Hansen, B., and Marzouk, G.A., *Development and Economic Policy in the UAR (Egypt)*, (Amsterdam: North-Holland Publishing Co., 1965). From a mainstream perspective, discusses proclaimed socialist economic development of Nasser's Egypt, including chapters on trade and payments, savings investment and foreign deficit, public finance and fiscal policy. Calls for more statistical information.

Hartman, H., *Enterprise and Politics in South Africa*, (Princeton, NJ: Princeton University Press, 1962). Argues, from mainstream viewpoint, that business interests and the South African government are opposed; analyses relations between them and the effect of politics on capital flow.

Harvey, C. (ed.), *Papers on the Economy of Botswana*, (London: Heinemann,

1981). Includes chapters on taxation of income from cattle farming, aid management in Botswana, incomes policy and foreign investment.

Havrilesky, T.M., and Boorman, J.T., *Current Perspectives in Banking—Operations, Management and Regulation*, (Illinois: AHM Publishing Corp, 1980) (2nd edn). A book of readings analysing changes in US capitalist bank management and bank regulations, both within the US and internationally, as a result of the so-called "banking revolution" in the post-World War II era. Compiled for neoclassical money, banking and financial courses in US.

Hazlewood, A., and Henderson, P.D., *Nyasaland—The Economics of Federation*, (Oxford: Basil Blackwell, 1960). A mainstream analysis of the federation including chapters on redistribution of income between territories, public capital expenditures in Nyasaland, tariffs and their impact on labour migration.

Helleiner, G.K., *The IMF and Africa in the 1980s*, (Princeton, NJ: Department of Economics, Princeton University, 1983). Discusses IMF policies and their impact on African economies in the crisis of the 1980s.

Heller, H.R., *International Monetary Economics*, (Englewood Cliffs, NJ: Prentice-Hall, 1974). Mainstream analysis of how the international monetary system may adjust to disturbances, attempting to assess costs and benefits of alternative methods.

Henning, C.N., Pigott, W., and Scott, R.H., *International Financial Management*, (New York: McGraw Hill, 1978). A mainstream textbook analysis of international finance, foreign exchange and Eurocurrency markets following the breakdown of fixed exchange rates.

Henry, J.A., *The First Hundred Years of the Standard Bank*, (ed. H.A. Siepmann), (London: Oxford University Press, 1963). A historical description of Standard Bank operations throughout Africa written in close collaboration with Standard Bank officials.

Hewson, J.R. and Sakakibara, E., *The Eurocurrency Markets and Their Implications—A New View of International Monetary Problems and Monetary Reform*, (Levington, Mass: Lenington Books, 1975). Within the mainstream, examines implications of changing international monetary system in the early 1970s.

Heywood, J., *Foreign Exchange and the Corporate Treasurer*, (London: A. & C. Black, Ltd, 1978). A British banking expert in foreign-exchange dealings provides an introduction and reference sources for businessmen who must deal with fluctuating exchange rates.

Hicks, U.K., *Development Finance—Planning and Control*, (Oxford: Clarendon Press, 1965). An expert who helped former British colonies to develop financial techniques provides an overview of the financial problems and possibilities new African countries confronted in the mid-1960s.

Hirsch, F., Doyle, M.W. and Morse, E.L., *Alternatives to Monetary Disorder*, (New York: McGraw Hill, 1980s Project/Council on Foreign Relations, 1977). Discusses political and economic implications of alternative approaches to resolving disruption of international capitalist monetary system from a "Western liberal" point of view.

Hooker, A.W. (ed.), *The Fund and China in the International Monetary System. Papers presented at a colloquium held in Beijing, China, Oct 20-29, 1980* (Washington DC: IMF, 1983). Papers by IMF and Chinese experts on the international monetary system and the role of China in the world economy.

Houghton, D.H., *The South African Economy*, (Cape Town: Oxford University Press, 1976) (4th edn). A mainstream textbook by a South African author includes chapters on trade and payments, the role of the banks, financial institutions and the public sector.

Hudson, N.R.L., *Money and Exchange Dealing in International Banking*, (London: Macmillan Press, 1979). A British international banker describes the dealing practices and money markets of major countries and currencies to help businessmen deal with the problems arising from the internationalization of banking and the volatility of foreign-exchange markets in the 1970s.

Ilugbuh, T.O., *Nigeria's Experience in Domestic Financing of Development*, (Zaria: Institute of Administration, Ahmadu Bello University, 1967). Discusses rising Nigerian government expenditures after independence, and the need for increased domestic effort, given the lack of foreign aid; recommends new taxes on income, real estate and sales, plus elimination of subsidies introduced in the colonial era for civil servants and legislators.

Inness, D., Anglo-American and The Rise of Modern South Africa (New York: Monthly Review, 1984). A carefully researched description of the scope and nature of the Anglo-American Group holdings throughout the world.

International Bank for Reconstruction and Development (IBRD) (Baltimore: Johns Hopkins Press) has published a series of books on specific African countries which typically include chapters on the role of banks and public finance.

—— *Towards Sustained Development in Sub-Saharan Africa, A Joint Programme of Action*, (Washington DC: IBRD, 1984). The World Bank's prescription for overcoming the obstacles to African development in the mid-1960s.

—— *China: Socialist Economic Development*, (Washington DC: IBRD, 1981). World Bank analysis of development and the 1970s reforms in China.

International Monetary Fund (IMF), *International Capital Markets*, (occasional papers) (Washington DC). Reviews developments in international lending with data for individual countries.

—— *The Monetary Approach to the Balance of Payments*, (Washington DC: IMF, 1977). Research papers prepared over two years by IMF staff as a contribution to the early development of the monetary approach to balance of payments problems.

Issawi, C., *Egypt in Review—An Economic Analysis*, (London: Oxford University Press, 1963). Discusses state-capitalist development in Nasser's Egypt (''Arab Socialism''), and includes a chapter on foreign trade and payments, finance and public finance.

Jackson, E.F. (ed.), *Economic Development in Africa (1962)*, (Oxford: Basil Blackwell, 1965). Mainstream papers at a pre-independence conference in Malawi discuss taxation and tax capacity; choice of taxes, budgets, fiscal measures to promote investment, investment policy and money, incomes and foreign balances.

Jones, D., *Aid and Development in Southern Africa—British Aid to Botswana, Lesotho and Swaziland*, (London: Croom-Helm, 1977). A mainstream analysis of case studies to determine if aid helps or hinders developing countries.

Jucker-Fleetwood, E.E., *Money and Finance in Africa—The Experiences of Ghana, Morocco, Nigeria, the Rhodesias and Nyasaland, the Sudan and Tunisia from the Establishment of their Central Banks until 1962*, (London: George Allen & Unwin, 1965). A mainstream evaluation of the early post-World War II banking structures in relation to development in several African countries.

Kaldor, N., *The Scourge of Monetarism*, (Oxford: Oxford University Press, 1982). A strong condemnation, along Keynesian lines, of the impact of monetarist theory and practice in England.

Kane, J.A., *Development Banking*, (Lexington: D.C. Heath, 1975). Surveys development banks in Third World countries and their role in providing government-sponsored financial intermediaries to foster development.

Kellet, R., *The Merchant Banking Arena, with Case Studies*, (London: Macmillan, and New York: St Martin's Press, 1967). "Layman's" analysis of merchant banks' development and links with modern industry, viewed as a positive feature.

Killick, T. (ed.), *Adjustment and Financing in the Developing World*, (Washington DC: International Monetary Fund, 1982). Papers from a joint IMF-Overseas Development Institute seminar debating the causes and policy implications of accelerated inflation and payments imbalances in the 1970s and 1980s for the IMF and developed countries which dominate it.

Kindleberger, C.P., and Laffargue, J., *Financial Crises*, (Cambridge: Cambridge University Press, 1982). Papers presented at a 1979 conference provide a mainstream review of the history of financial crises, the current foreign debt problems of developing countries, financial instability, and international lenders of last resort.

Koneacki, Z.A. and J.M., *An Economic History of Tropical Africa*, (London: Frank Cass, 1977). Vol. 1 presents a historical analysis of pre-colonial trade and the impact of the slave trade, and a discussion of long-distance trade, media of exchange and standards of value. Vol. II includes a paper mainly from a mainstream perspective, discussing the colonial period, including the fiscal role of marketing boards in Nigeria; savings and investments by Africans; capital investment in sub-Saharan Africa; and foreign investment and technology diffusion.

Lardy, N.R., *Economic Growth and Distribution in China*, (Cambridge: Cambridge University Press, 1978). A US university professor attempts to explain the Chinese administrative system of allocating resources while achieving equity and distributive goals. Compares economic and financial planning of the 1950s with the more decentralized approach of 1960s.

Laski, K., *The Rate of Growth and the Rate of Interest in the Socialist Economy*, (Vienna: Springer Verlag, 1972). A Polish economist in the Austrian Institute for Research discusses the role of interest in socialist planning, noting similarities and differences in comparison with mainstream growth theory.

Lassen, R., *Currency Management*, (Cambridge: Woodhead-Faulkner, 1982). An executive of the British firm Thomas Cook discusses how private companies manage fluctuating currencies to minimize the effects of exchange-rate movements on their trading activities.

Lees, F.A., and Eng. M., *International Financial Markets*, (New York: Praeger Publishers, 1975). A mainstream text provides a historical and theoretical conceptual framework within which the financial markets of major nations influencing international trade flows are analysed;also the structure and scope of Eurodollar, Eurobond, and international markets for foreign exchange; and markets of developed capitalist and less developed countries.

Leipziger, D.M., *The International Monetary System and Developing Nations*, (Washington, DC: US Agency for International Development, 1976). Papers from a 1975 US State Department Conference on international monetary issues affecting developing nations including statements from the IMF, World Bank, UNCTAD, Organization of American States, US Federal Reserve Board, Treasury Department, US Senate Staff, US State Department and AID.

Lenin, V.I., *State and Revolution*. In Collected Works (Moscow: Foreign Languages Publishing House, 1960). A classic historical materialist analysis of the role of the state.

—— *Imperialism—The Highest Stage of Capitalism*. In Collected Works (Moscow: Foreign Languages Publishing House, 1960). Historical materialist analysis of finance capital and its impact on uneven development, creating the necessity of initially building socialism in one country.

Lewis, W.A., *Reflections on Nigeria's Economic Growth*, (Paris: Development Centre of OECD, 1966). A well-known mainstream theorist examines Nigeria's economic development in the post-war era, concludes fiscal achievement was an "outstanding feature"; and holds that limits on domestic saving thwarted targeted investment of 16% of GDP, leading to a crisis after past surpluses were exhausted and foreign aid failed to expand.

Leys, C., *Underdevelopment in Kenya. The Political Economy of Neo-colonialism, 1964-1971*, (Berkeley: University of California Press, 1974). Analyses the political economy of Kenya to show how international forces over several generations affected the land and the people. The growth of foreign capital, the interlinkage of foreign and African capital, and their effect in terms of neocolonizing the society are examined.

Lister, R. and E., *Annotated Bibliography of Corporate Finances*, (London: Macmillan, 1979). Given the extensive and growing literature concerning corporate finance in capitalist economies, it is impossible to sample it adequately. This annotated bibliography provides the reader with a full range of sources, organized by topic, available in English at the end of the 1970s.

Livy, B.L. (ed.), *Management and People in Banking*, (London: The Institute of Bankers, 1980). A compilation of readings by British bankers, businessmen and academics discussing issues of modern bank management in the context of the post-World War II "banking revolution", brought about by such factors as mergers, computerization, government regulations and international expansion.

Llewellyn, D.T., *International Financial Integration—the Limits of Sovereignty*, (London: Macmillan, 1980). A former IMF staff member examines operations and procedures of financial markets and banking operations to assess the impact of increased international capital flows on national efforts to use traditional techniques to control monetary policies.

Lombard, J.A. (ed.), *Economic Policy in South Africa*, (selected essays) (Cape Town: Citadel Press, 1973). South African government officials and university economists, adopting a mainstream approach, examine fiscal and monetary policy.

Lozoya, J., and Bhattacharya, A.K., *The Financial Issues of the New International Economic Order*, (New York: Pergamon Press, 1982) (2nd edn). A United Nations Institute for Training and Research volume of papers, primarily by Third World authors with various perspectives, examines the international monetary system, external debt, private bank finance, capital markets, petrodollars and collective self-reliance.

Ma Hong, *New Strategy for China's Economy*, (translated Yan Lin) (Beijing: New World Press, 1983). Explains reasons for reforms of late 1970s-early 1980s and describes new economic management techniques.

Marcus, E. and M.R., *Investment and Development Possibilities in Tropical Africa*, (New York: Bookman Associates, 1960). Mainstream explanation of reasons why foreign capital failed to invest much in Africa, finding obstacles largely in lack of skills and entrepreneurial attitudes and habits of work. Finance and role of development banks, foreign-exchange constraints, European banks and private investment are also covered.

Marris, P., and Somerset, A., *African Businessmen—A Study of Entrepreneurship and Development in Kenya*, (London: Routledge & Kegan Paul, 1971). Assuming private entrepreneurship is the key to development, the authors interviewed over 80 businessmen who received development bank (ICDC) loans to discover factors fostering enterprise. Most said access to capital was the biggest problem. Evaluates role of ICDC in providing loans, concludes government's main role should be to provide skills since private lenders doubt African businessmen's competence.

Martin, J.P., and Smith, A., *Trade and Payments Adjustment under Flexible Exchange Rates*, (London: Macmillan Press for the Trade Policy Research Center, 1979). Academics and western bank economists utilize mainstream concepts in an effort to analyse the consequences of flexible exchange rates and the role of SDRs as they affect international trade and welfare.

Marx, K., *Capital*, (London: Dent, Everyman's Library, 1957). A historical materialist analysis of the labour theory of value and the way money functions to conceal the extraction of surplus value by the capitalist class; includes some discussion of the role of the banks in the 19th century.

—— *Value, Price and Profit; Wage Labour and Capital*. In Selected Works (2 vols) (Moscow: Foreign Languages Publishing House, 1958). Two classics presenting the labour theory of value in relatively simplified form.

—— *Critique of the Gotha Programme*. In Selected Works (2 vols) (Moscow: Foreign Languages Publishing House, 1958). Briefly outlines Marx's vision of socialist distribution of income, including key passages on the abolition of commodity relations.

Mikesell, R.F., *Foreign Exchange in the Postwar World*, (New York: 20th Century Fund, 1954). Almost a classic among mainstream works on foreign exchange, aims to provide a theoretical and practical framework for understanding international currency problems, including the role of GATT, the IMF, and international reserve problems.

Mikesell, R.F., and Zinser, J.E., "The Nature of the Savings Function in the Developing Countries: A Survey of the Theoretical and Empirical Literature", *Journal of Economic Literature*, Vol. II, March 1973. Mainstream analysis of constraints on savings.

Morton, K., *Aid and Dependence, British Aid to Malawi*, (London: Croom Helm, 1975). A mainstream examination of the background of UK aid to Malawi after independence; an extended appendix examines the Commonwealth Development Corporation, budgetary assistance, development finance and their impact on Malawi's development.

Murray R., *Multinationals beyond the Market*, (New York: Wiley, 1981). An analysis of the evolution of transfer pricing mechanisms used by transnational firms.

Newlyn, W.T., *Money in an African Context—Studies in African Economies*, (Nairobi: Oxford University Press, 1967). Uses mainstream monetary theory to discuss the evolution of banks and monetary and fiscal policy in Tanzania, Kenya and Uganda.

Newlyn, W.T., and Rowan, D.C., *Money and Banking in British Colonial Africa*, (Oxford: Clarendon Press, 1954). From a mainstream perspective, describes the development of currency boards, the banking systems, and other financial institutions in the former British colonies in Africa.

Nkrumah, K., *Neo-Colonialism, the Last Stage of Imperialism*, (London): Heinemann, 1965). The former president of Ghana relates Lenin's theory of imperialism to post-independence Africa, including chapters on imperialist finance, the role of foreign investments in Africa, especially of the South African-based Anglo-American Group, and monetary zones and foreign banks.

Nnoli, O., *Path to Nigerian Development*, (Daker: Codesria, 1981). A socialist critiquc of Nigerian development and underdevelopment, arguing these results from imperialism and the role of local capital in collaboration with foreign capital via public enterprise, government shares in industry, etc.

Nove, A., *The Soviet Economic System*, (London: G. Allen & Unwin, 1977). A careful analysis of the Soviet economy, including its financial planning mechanisms.

Nsekela, A.J. (ed.), *Southern Africa—Towards Economic Liberation*, (London: Rex Collings, 1981). Includes a chapter on the SADCC, financial institutions and mechanism for economic co-ordination emphasizing its tentative, exploratory nature, and suggesting issues requiring further investigation.

Odenigwe, G.A. (ed.), *A New System of Local Government (Government by the Community in the East Central State of Nigeria)*, (Enugu: Divisional Administrative Department, East Central State Government, 1977). Part IV discusses finance of local administration, and how it developed in independent Nigeria. Ch. 10 discusses an alternative approach to administration for nationalist development.

Okigbo, P.N.C., *Nigerian Public Finance*, (Evanston: Northwestern University Press, 1965). A study of the historical evolution of Nigeria's federal fiscal structures prior to independence.

Ola, O., and Onimode, B., *Economic Development of Nigeria: The Socialist Alternative*, (Nigerian Academy of Arts, Science and Technology, 1975). Includes chapters by Nyerere, Babu, Senghor, Kanza, Potekhin, Palmberg and Jumba-Masagazi.

Onoh, J.K., *Strategic Approaches to Crucial Policies in Economic Development—A Macro Link Study in Capital Formation, Technology and Money*, (Rotterdam University Press, 1977). A Nigerian author, using mainstream tools, analyses capital formation and monetary policy in the African context, though argues the need to introduce behavioural sciences to understand the limits on their use.

Ord, H.W., and Livingstone, I., *An Introduction to West African Economics*, (London: Heinemann, 1969). A neoclassical analysis, including introductory discussions of money, currency boards, central banks, income, employment and price levels, inflation and the value of money; international trade and payments; and government and public enterprise, and taxation.

Organization for Economic Cooperation and Development (OECD), *Investing in Developing Countries*, (Paris: OECD, 1978) (4th edn). Surveys incentives for private foreign investors in developing countries as provided by the Development Assistance Committee of OECD.

—— *International Investment and Multinational Enterprises*, (Paris: OECD, 1981). Examines changing trends in direct private investment in the 1970s, including the shift to services rather than industrial or raw materials production.

Payer, C., *The Debt Trap and the IMF*, (New York: Monthly Review Press, 1975). A Marxist analysis of the role of the IMF in Third World Countries.

—— *The World Bank—A Critical Analysis*, (New York: Monthly Review Press, 1982). A Marxist analysis of the International Bank for Reconstruction and Development during the 1970s.

Platt, C.J., *Tax Systems of Africa, Asia and the Middle East—A Guide for Business and the Professions*, (Hants: Gower Publishing Corp. 1982).

Summarizes data on incomes and capital gains taxes in 35 developing countries, including 14 independent African states and South Africa, providing a brief background and the basic legislation as amended.

Price-Waterhouse & Co., *Corporate Taxes: a World-wide Summary, and Information Guide: Individual Taxes: a world-wide summary*, (New York: Price Waterhouse, 1983). Price-Waterhouse publish information on corporate and individual taxes in individual countries to assist business enterprises in deciding whether to invest there.

Public Enterprise in Nigeria, Proceedings of 1973 Annual Conference of the Nigerian Economic Society, (Ibadan: University of Ibadan, 1974). Includes chapters on pricing policy, investment and financial performance, and a case study of financial and commercial policies of the Nigerian Railway Corporation.

Report of a Working Party, *Who Controls Industry in Kenya*, (Nairobi: East African Publishing House, 1968). Chapters describing "men with the money" including private financial institutions, who runs them and their links to foreign capital; government finance, including government development corporations, their directors and role in the economy; and foreign finance, including UK, US, and other countries' aid and investments.

Reuber G.L. *et al.*, *Private Foreign Investment in Development*, (London: Oxford: Clarendon Press, 1973). Prepared under the auspices of the OECD, presents data and evaluates the extent and role of foreign manufacturing investment in less developed countries from an essentially mainstream perspective.

Richman, B.M., *Industrial Society in Communist China*, (New York: Random House, 1969). A Canadian management expert reports on his first-hand study of the administration of industry in the Chinese socio-economic environment through the 1960s. Includes a chapter on the economic constraints posed for the banking system, fiscal policy and the state budget.

Robinson, E.A.G. (ed.), *Economic Development for Africa South of the Sahara*, (London: Macmillan, 1965). Neoclassical analysis of post-war colonial economic development, includes two chapters on monetary and fiscal policy in relation to African development of historical interest.

Rodney, W., *How Europe Underdeveloped Africa*, (Dar es Salaam: Tanzania Publishing House, 1972). Marxist historical analysis of the impact of the slave trade and imperialism on Africa, including the extraction of surplus value.

Rogers, B., *White Wealth and Black Poverty, American Investments in Southern Africa*, (London: Greenwood Press, 1976). A study of the role of US investments in the context of racist rule in southern Africa.

Rosenstein-Rodan, P.N. (ed.), *Pricing and Fiscal Policies—A Study in Method*, (London: Simson Shand Ltd., 1964). Papers by several, mainly mainstream authors examining different aspects of the Indian state-capitalist government fiscal and pricing policies.

Roussakis, E.N., *International Lending by U.S. Commercial Banks—A case book*, (New York: Praeger, 1981.) A casebook for US students and bankers on the issues created by international capitalist bank expansion and lending in the 1970s, focusing on specific international bank-company relationships.

Sabine, B.E.V., *A History of Income Tax*, (London: George Allen & Unwin, 1966). Describes the evolution of the institution and administration of income tax in England from its inception until the 1960s, indicating the nature of the theoretical debates and objective conditions that contributed to its development.

Saksena, R.M., *Regional Development Banking*, (Bombay: Somaiya Publishers, 1972) A comparative analysis, in a mainstream theoretical framework, of the regional developments of western Europe, Latin America, Africa and Asia, concluding that the success of such banks in developing countries depends significantly on assistance from developed countries.

Sandbrook, R., *The Politics of Basic Needs—Urban Aspects of Assaulting Poverty in Africa*, (Toronto: University of Toronto Press, 1982). Examines extensive historical data on causes of poverty; Chapter 3 discusses the role of the state in the process of capitalist accumulation, concluding: "statist forms of national developmentalism or bureaucratic collectivism" appear more likely than either neocolonialism or socialism.

Sarant, P.C., *Zero-base Budgeting in the Public Sector—A Pragmatic Approach*, (Reading, Mass: Addison-Wesley Publishing Co., 1978). The director of Management Analysis Training of the US Civil Service Commission explains zero-base budgeting which requires review and justification of old, as well as new programmes, as used to increase US government efficiency.

Saylor, R.G., *The Economic System of Sierra Leone*, (Durham, NC: Duke University, 1967). From a neoclassical perspective, analyses state intervention in a "small West African state". Chapter 6 deals with development planning, money, banking and fiscal policy.

Schatz, S.P., *The Capital Shortage Illusion: Government Lending in Nigeria*, (Oxford: Clarendon Press, 1965). This book explores the reasons why small African businesses encounter difficulties even when credit is available.

Seidman, A., *Comparative Development Strategies in East Africa*, (Nairobi: East African Publishing House, 1970). Includes brief description of money, banking and public finance in Tanzania, Kenya and Uganda.

—— *Ghana's Development Experience, 1952-1966*, (Nairobi: East African Publishing House, 1978). Includes discussion of role of commercial banks and public finance in the context of Ghana under Nkrumah.

—— *An Economics Textbook for Africa*, (London: Methuen, 1980) (3rd edn). Presents elementary economic concepts from both capitalist and socialist theoretical perspectives, including trade and payments, international currencies, the World Bank and IMF, and public finance and commercial banks.

—— *Planning for Development in Sub-Saharan Africa*, (New York: Praeger, and Dar es Salaam: Tanzanian Publishing House, 1974). Discusses the theory and practice of planning for development in Sub-Saharan Africa, drawing especially on the experiences of former British colonies.

Seidman, A. and N., *US Multinationals in South Africa*. (Westport: Lawrence Hill, 1977). Detailed analysis of US firms' investments in South Africa, including role of US commercial banks and bank loans.

Seidman, A., and Makgetla, N., *Outposts of Monopoly Capital*, (Westport: Lawrence Hill, 1980). Examines role of transnational corporations in competitively investing in South Africa, and the implications for the changing international division of labour. Includes analyses of transnational corporate banks' key role in this process.

Shaffer, H.G. (ed.), *The Soviet Economy—A Collection of Western and Soviet Views*, (New York: Meredith Corp, 1969) (2nd edn). A collection of papers on western and Soviet views on various aspects of Soviet economic development, including the transition to communism, and economic planning, economic reforms and price determination.

Swiderowski, J., *Exchange and Trade Controls—Principles and Procedures of International Economic Transactions and Settlements*, (Essex: Gower Press, 1975). A former IMF official draws on evidence from IMF files to argue that, used selectivity with other measures to help achieve national goals, external controls are an acceptable means of implementing economic policy, but they may have undesirable side-effects.

Szentes, T., *The Political Economy of Underdevelopment*, (trans. I. Vegas) (Budapest: Akademiai Kiado, 1971). A Marxist critique of mainstream theories and an analysis of the causes of underdevelopment in Africa by a Hungarian economist.

Teriba, O., and Diejomaoh, V.P., (eds), *Money, Finance and Nigerian Economic Development: Essays in Honour of Obasanmi Olakanpo*, (Ibadan: Nigerian Economic Society, Ibadan University Press, 1976). Conference papers, largely from a mainstream perspective. Part I looks at Nigerian instruments of monetary control, money multiplier, credit policies of Nigerian commercial banks, the challenge of international monetary reform, and international monetary problems relating to Nigerian development. Part II discusses the economic structure and instability of public revenues based on Nigerian and Ghanaian experiences; the problems and possiblities of using import taxes in Nigeria; and the role of aid in Nigeria.

Teriba, O., and Kayode, M.O., (eds), *Industrial Development in Nigeria*, (Ibadan: Ibadan University Press, 1977). Includes chapters on public enterprise, industrial policy and tax incentives, government loans to African businessmen and industrial estates.

Terry, C., *The Desert Bankers—The Story of Standard Bank of South West Africa*, (Cape Town: W.J. Flesch & Partner, 1978). Historical description of Standard Bank's operations in Namibia, written from the bank's point of view.

Thirwall, A.P., *Financing Economic Development*, (London: Macmillan, 1976). Discusses the problem of financing development from a mainstream viewpoint. Argues that, to attain growth, a specific amount of capital as a percentage of Gross Domestic Product must be invested. If local savings cannot supply this amount, foreign funds must be obtained to fill the gap.

Thomas, D.B., *Capital Accumulation and Technology Transfer—A Comparative Analysis of Nigerian Manufacturing Industries*, (New York: Praeger, 1975). Using econometric tools and models drawn from mainstream theoretical framework, attempts to estimate the effect of capital accumulation and technology transfer on economic development in Nigeria.

Thomas, D.B., *et al.*, *Importing Technology into Africa—Foreign Investment and the Supply of Technological Innovations*, (New York: Praeger, 1976). A critical appraisal of the role of foreign investment and transnational corporations in transferring technology to African economies; concludes governments must insist on reorientation of transnationals to ensure due consideration of host countries' development goals, including complete transfer of technology and knowhow.

Truu, M.L. (ed.), *Public Policy and the South African Economy—Essays in Memory of Desmond Hobart Houghton*, (Cape Town: Oxford University Press, 1976). South African mainstream economists discuss various South African economic issues, including an econometric model of the South African monetary sector, monetary policy in South Africa, exchange rate policy and imported inflation.

Turgeon, L., *The Contrasting Economies: A Study of Modern Economic Systems*, (Boston: Allyn & Bacon, 1969). Includes a bibliography. A valuable comparative analysis of capitalist and socialist economies, drawing primarily on the United States and Soviet experience. Includes chapters on pricing, public finance and taxation, and banking as well as on consumption and investment decision making and wage policy.

United Nations (UN) Economic Commission for Africa, *Budget Planning and Management, Report of a Seminar*, (Addis Ababa, 3-13 October 1966). Seminar papers and discussion of budgetary systems in African countries, relationship of national budgets to plans, classifications of budgetary transactions, techniques of programme and performance budgeting and revenue programming, and accounting and control procedure.

US Department of Commerce, *Investment in the Federation of Rhodesia and Nyasaland, 1956*, (Washington DC: US Government Printing Office, 1956). A US government publication for US businessmen on the investment potentials in the Federation, including chapters on government policy on business and finance.

—— *Investment in Nigeria—Basic Information for United States Businessmen, 1957*, (Washington, DC: US Government Printing Office, 1957). US government publication on investment conditions for US businessmen in pre-independence Nigeria, includes chapters on "investment climate", colonial government's policy towards business, marketing boards, development corporations and Nigerian enterprise and foreign investors, public finance.

Uppal, J.S., and Salkever, L.R., (eds), *African Problems in Economic Development*, (London: Collier-Macmillan, 1972). Part V on Public Finance and Taxation includes a UNECA study presenting data showing African governments did not tax sufficiently to finance their expenditures; emphasizes the need to focus on revising tariffs to obtain more appropriate imports and increased revenues; and reduce expenditures on high expatriate officials' salaries via Africanization.

Van Biljon, F.J., *State Interference in South Africa*, (London: P.S. King & Son, 1939). Writing from a mainstream perspective before World War II, argues state action extended rapidly, reduced competition; includes sections on monetary policy and foreign trade policies.

Weisweiller, R., *Introduction to Foreign Exchange*, (Cambridge: Woodhead-Faulkner, Ltd, 1983). A systematic introduction to foreign exchange in a mainstream framework including attempts at monetary reform and fluctuating exchange rates.

Wellons, Philip, *Eurocurrency Loans*, (Paris: OECD, 1976). A lawyer discusses the nature and impact of Eurocurrency loans as a source of capital for Third World development.

Wetham, E.H., and Currie, J.I., *Readings in Applied Economics of Africa*, (Cambridge University Press, 1967). Vol. 2, Part V includes chapters on reform of East African taxation, commercial banking in East Africa, marketing boards in Nigeria, monetary effects of budgets in post-1966 Ghana, fiscal systems and growth of national income, and the cost of financing education.

Williams, G. (ed.), *Nigeria—Economy and Society*, (London: Rex Collings, 1976). A chapter by E.O. Akeredoluale argues that capital policies of Nigerian government have retarded indigenous entrepreneurs; there is a need for restricting foreign investments in Third World countries.

Wood, D., and Byrne, J., *International Business Finance*, (London: Macmillan, 1981). Examines the way transnational corporations may "increase their value through the international exploitation of their relative strengths" deliberately deemphasizing the distinction between trade and investment.

World Bank—*see* International Bank for Reconstruction and Development.

Xu Dixin, *et al.*, *China's Search for Economic Growth*, (Beijing: Foreign Language Press, 1983). Articles by Chinese scholars analysing past problems of Chinese economic policies and discussing proposed solutions. Includes articles on accumulation and financial institutions.

Xue Muqiao, *China's Socialist Economy*, (Beijing: Foreign Language Press, 1981). Discusses socialist principles in China, including incentives, role of money, law of value, planning and economic management.

Zwass, A., *Money, Banking and the Creation of Credit in the Soviet Union and Eastern Europe*, (trans. M.C. Vale) (White Plains, NY: M.E. Sharpe, 1979). A detailed descriptive analysis of the socialist countries' efforts to develop institutions appropriate to their increasingly complex planned economies.

Periodicals

A number of periodicals provide current information relevant to money, banking and public finance in Africa. Students are urged to consult these to up-date information provided in the text.

African Development, London, UK. Covers various aspects of African development, with frequent coverage of financial development issues.

Bank for International Settlements, Basle, annual reports. From central bank governors' perspective of the ten leading developed, capitalist countries. These reports summarize and evaluate the annual events relating to the international banking system.

Beijing Review, Beijing, China. Reports on current economic changes in China. See *China Today, Economic Readjustment and Reform*, Special Feature Series No. 3, 1982, for articles discussing post-Mao reforms, including one on the banks.

Development and Peace, Budapest, Hungary. A Marxist analysis of issues of peace and development, including occasional articles on financial issues.

The East African Journal of Economics, Nairobi, Kenya. Presents studies of East African economies, including some on monetary and financial topics.

The Economist Intelligence Unit, *Quarterly Economic Review* (of most African countries including South Africa, and annual supplements), London, *The Economist*. Includes discussions of currency, national accounts, public finance and foreign trade and payments.

Euromoney, (London). Current mainstream analyses of international financial issues and institutions.

Far Eastern Economic Review. Mainstream economists discuss economic developments in China and elsewhere in the Far East.

The Ghanaian Journal of Economics, University of Ghana. Presents economic articles mainly on Ghana, some relating to money, banking and finance.

The Hungarian Journal, (Budapest. Marxist analyses of development issues in Third World countries.

International Bank for Reconstruction and Development, *Annual Report*, Washington DC. Presents World Bank policies on major issues arising in the preceding year. Includes table and charts showing aggregate relevant data. World Development Report (Washington DC: annual). Reports on world development trends with a valuable statistical appendix providing data for individual countries.

International Monetary Fund, *Annual Report*, Washington DC, (annual). Describes

IMF activities for the year, providing summary aggregate data and discussing problems from IMF (mainstream) perspective.

—— *Government Finance Statistics Yearbook*, Washington DC, annual. Presents current data relating to individual IMF member countries' national expenditures, national revenues and public debt.

—— *International Financial Statistics*, Washington DC, monthly. Presents current foreign-exchange rates, balance of trade and payments, value and unit prices of major exports and the IMF position separately for each IMF member country.

IMF Survey, weekly. Reports on IMF issues and policies as developed to meet current problems.

International Monetary Fund and World Bank, *Finance & Development*, Washington DC quarterly. Contains mainstream theoretical analyses and evidence, generally supporting IMF-World Bank policies.

The Monthly Review, New York. A Marxist journal including articles dealing with development in the Third World.

Moody's Bank and Financial Manual, New York, Moody's Investor Service. Prepared primarily for potential investors, provides brief histories of US banks and financial institutions, their directors, their financial assets and their affiliates.

The Nigerian Journal of Economic and Social Studies, Ibadan University Press. Provides articles on many topics including a few on money, banking and public finance mainly in Nigeria.

Public Enterprise, Yugoslavia. Discusses issues of management of public enterprises from group socialist perspective, occasionally including financial issues.

Review of African Political Economy, London. Monthly socialist journal which includes Marxist analysis of current African economic development issues.

Standard Charter Review (formerly *Standard Bank Review*) published monthly by the Standard Chartered Bank, London. Contains reports on individual African countries in which it has branches from the perspective of one of the leading private British banks with interests in Africa.

United Nations, New York. *Statistical Yearbook*. A compendium of statistical tables providing economic and social data for all members countries of the UN.

Who Owns What in World Banking, (London). Provides a list of banks' national and international affiliations.

The Zimbabwean Journal of Economics, quarterly journal of the Zimbabwe Economic Society, Harare. Formerly the *Rhodesian Journal of Economics*. Articles focusing on Zimbabwe economic issues.

Government Documents from Individual African Countries

Although the particular titles vary from country to country, nevertheless most former British colonies have similar sets of documents. The French- and Portuguese-speaking countries, too, generally have documents along the same lines, though the titles may differ more.

Annual Economic Survey. Surveys general status of economy, and provides aggregate data on the particular sectors, including banking and finance. May include data on wages, prices and income distribution.

Annual Reports of private banks and financial institutions (either their companies abroad, their local affiliates, or both.

Annual Reports of government registrars of companies, banks, insurance companies, pension funds. May report on overall assets and liabilities on an aggregate basis and perhaps for individual companies. The registrar of companies' files may provide information on firms with investments in the economy, their overall investment and major shareholders, and members of the boards of directors.

Economic Plan Document. May contain overall analysis of the economy, and specific targets to be achieved by sector during the plan period, as well as overall approaches to financing their attainment.

Government Budget Estimates and the Minister of Finance or Treasury's budget speech. Usually provides overall estimates of government expenditures, sources of taxes and probably debt for the next year, as well as actual data for the previous year.

Report of Treasury or Ministry of Finance on taxes, especially income taxes. Often includes an analysis of income categories of companies and individuals who pay income tax.

Statistical Digest, (monthly, quarterly or annual). Typically contains statistical data on exports, imports, balance of payments, wages, prices, and income distribution, the banks and money supply, and government finance.

Index